DARK REIGN

AGENTS OF ATLAS

AGENTS OF ATLAS: DARK REIGN. Contains material originally published in magazine form as AGENTS OF ATLAS #1-5, SECRET INVASION: WHO DO YOU TRUST?, DARK REIGN: NEW NATION and GIANT-SIZE MARVEL ADVENTURES AVENGERS #1. First printing 2009. ISBN# 978-0-7851-3898-3. Published by MARVEL PUBLISHING, INC., a subsidiary of MARVEL ENTERTAINMENT, INC. OFFICE OF PUBLICATION: 417 5th Avenue, New York, NY 10016. Copyright © 2007, 2008 and 2009 Marvel Characters, Inc. All rights reserved. $24.99 per copy in the U.S. (GST #R127032852). Canadian Agreement #40668537. All characters featured in this issue and the distinctive names and likenesses thereof, and all related indicia are trademarks of Marvel Characters, Inc. No similarity between any of the names, characters, persons, and/or institutions in this magazine with those of any living or dead person or institution is intended, and any such similarity which may exist is purely coincidental. **Printed in the U.S.A.** ALAN FINE, EVP - Office Of The Chief Executive Marvel Entertainment, Inc. & CMO Marvel Characters B.V.; DAN BUCKLEY, President of Publishing - Print & Digital Media; JIM SOKOLOWSKI, Chief Operating Officer; DAVID GABRIEL, SVP of Publishing Sales & Circulation; DAVID BOGART, SVP of Business Affairs & Talent Management; MICHAEL PASCIULLO, VP Merchandising & Communications; JIM O'KEEFE, VP of Operations & Logistics; DAN CARR, Executive Director of Publishing Technology; JUSTIN F. GABRIE, Director of Publishing & Editorial Operations; SUSAN CRESPI, Editorial Operations Manager; ALEX MORALES, Publishing Operations Manager; STAN LEE, Chairman Emeritus. For information regarding advertising in Marvel Comics or on Marvel.com, please contact Mitch Dane, Advertising Director, at mdane@marvel.com. For Marvel subscription inquiries, please call 800-217-9158.

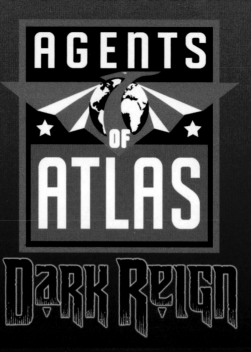

AGENTS OF ATLAS

Dark Reign

WRITER
Jeff Parker

ARTISTS
Carlo Pagulayan, Jason Paz & Jana Schirmer; Gabriel Hardman
& Elizabeth Dismang; and Clayton Henry & Jana Schirmer

LETTERER
Blambot's Nate Piekos

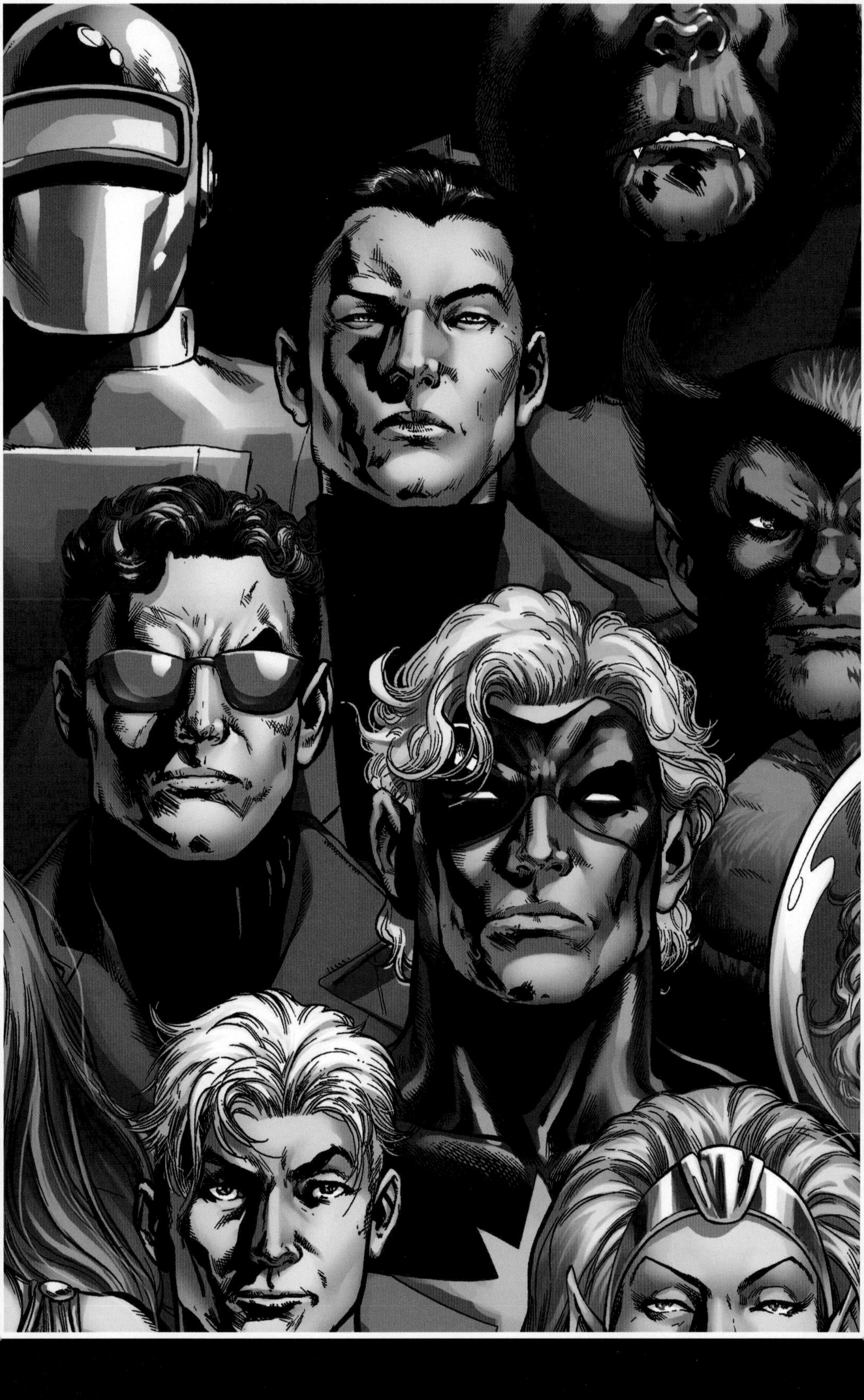

SECRET INVASION: WHO DO YOU TRUST? 2ND-PRINTING VARIANT
BY PHIL JIMENEZ, ANDY LANNING & CHRISTINA STRAIN

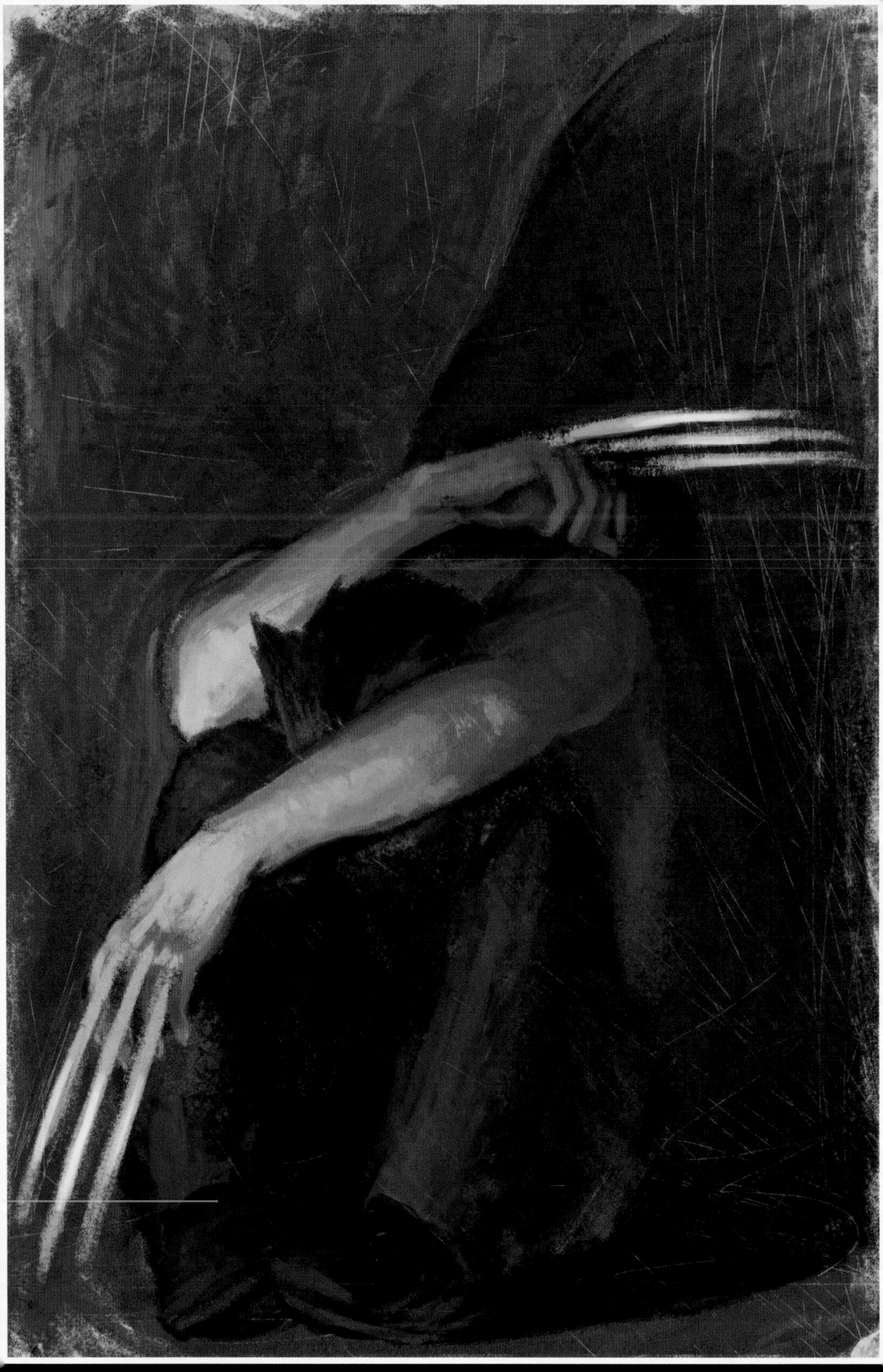

WOLVERINE ART APPRECIATION VARIANT BY GERALD PAREL

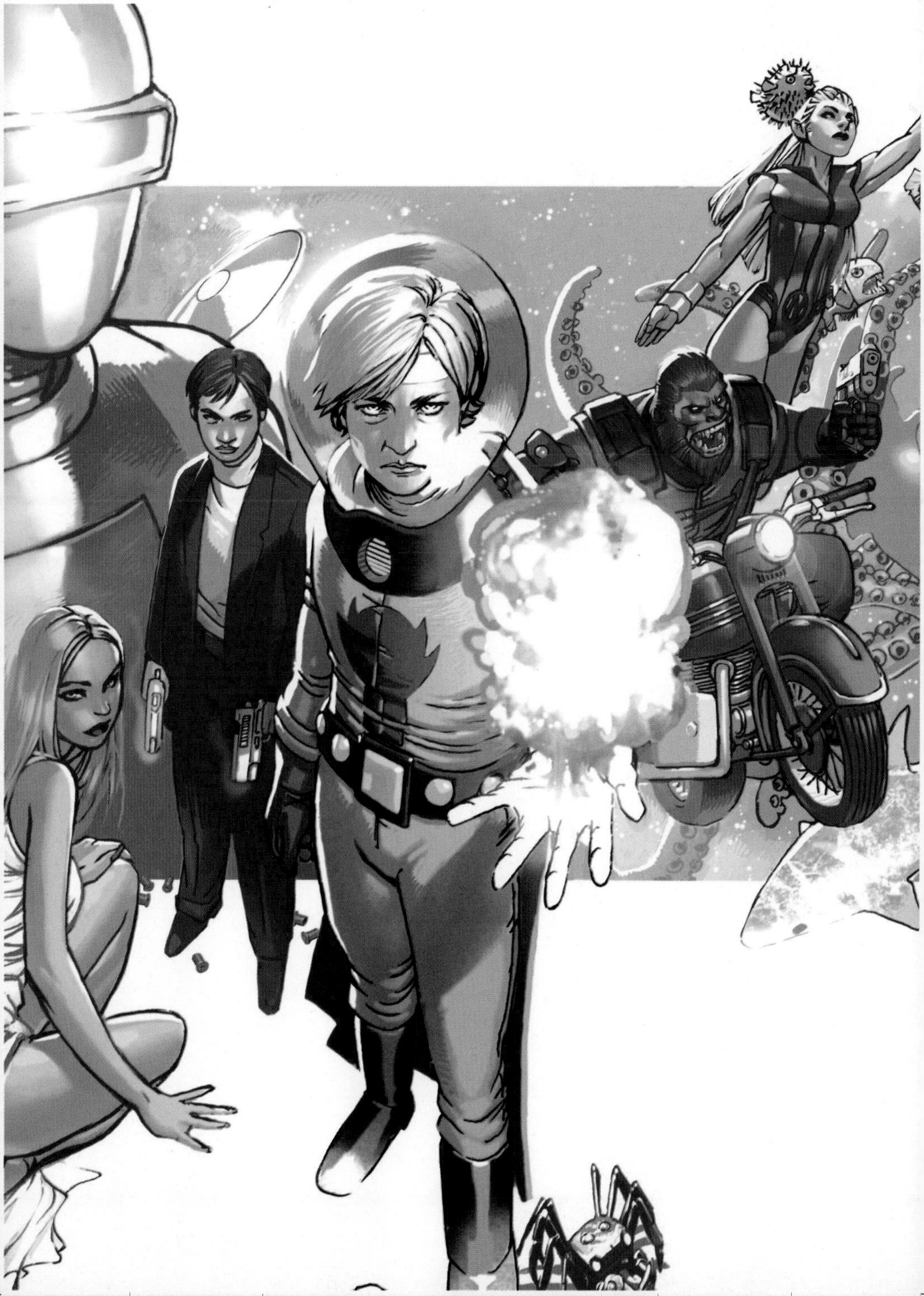

2ND-PRINT S BACHALO

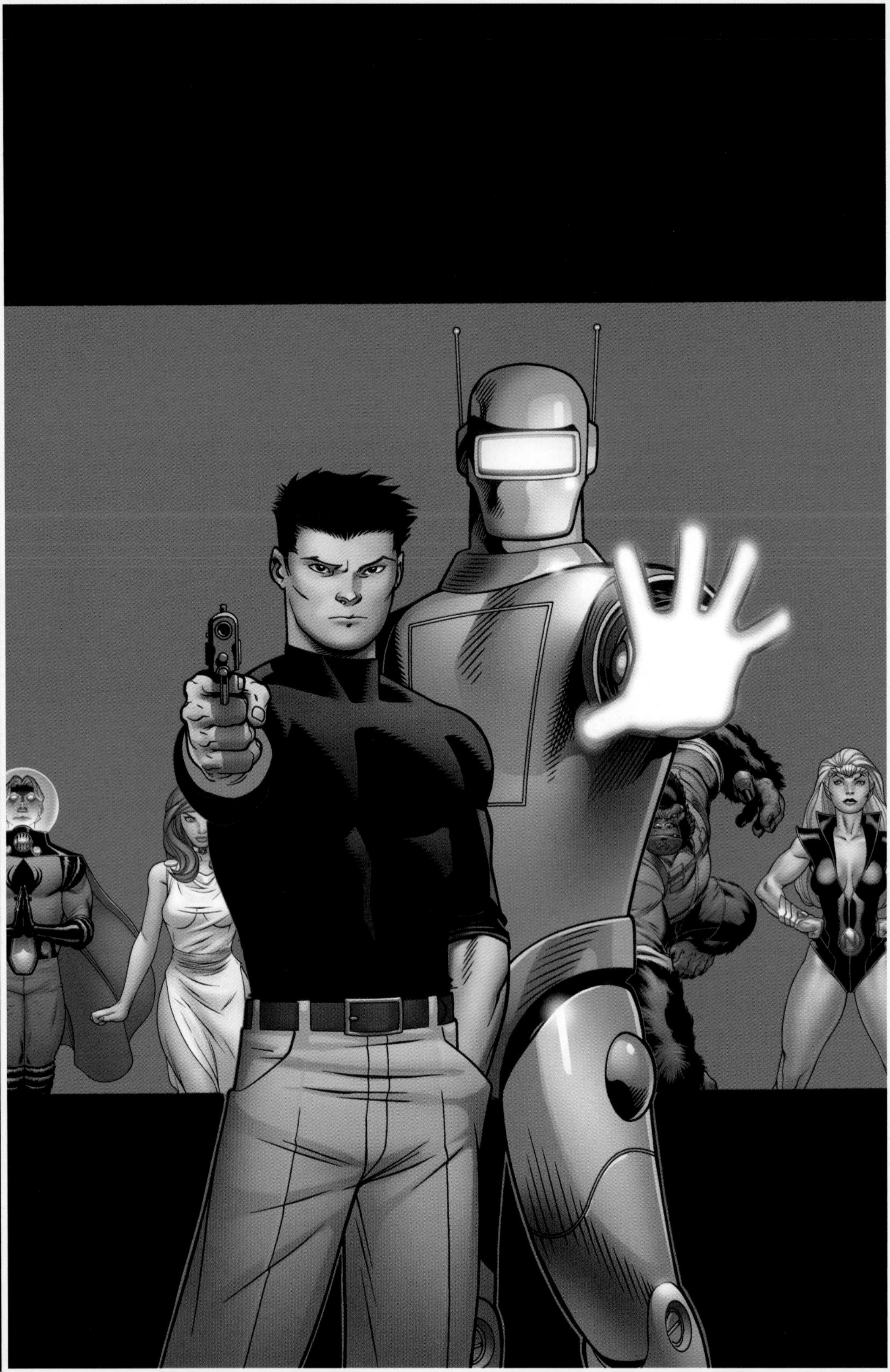

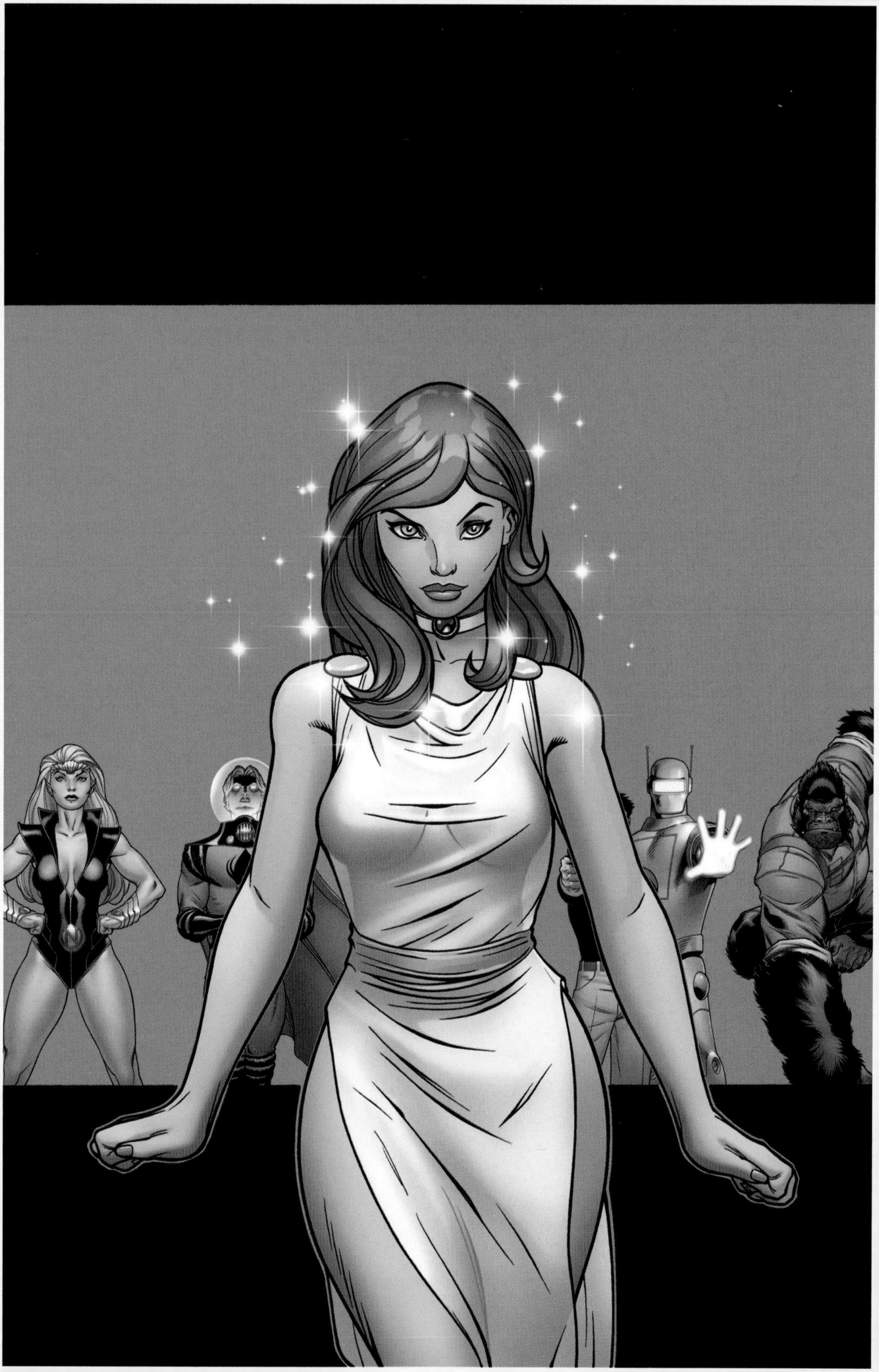

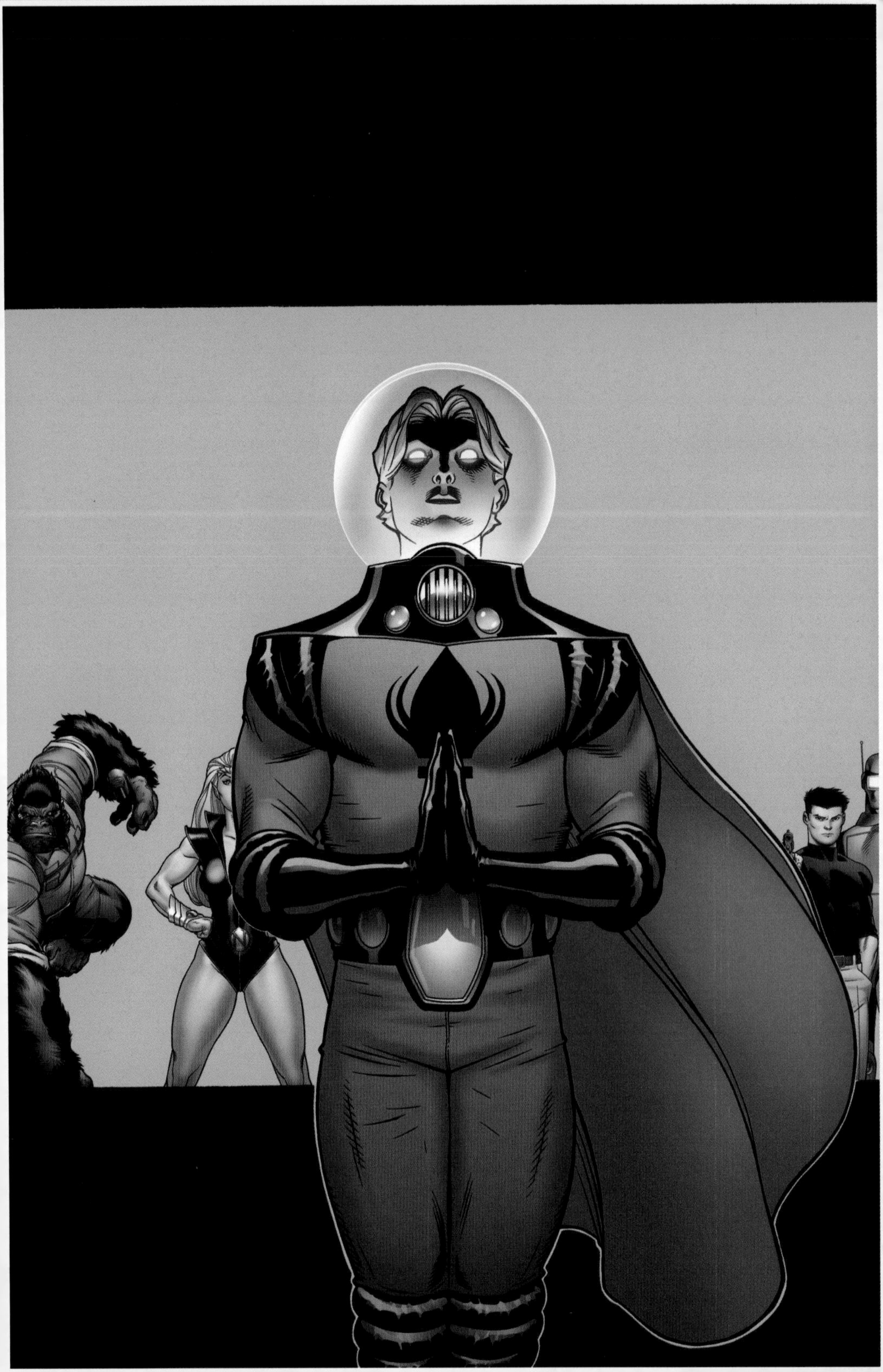

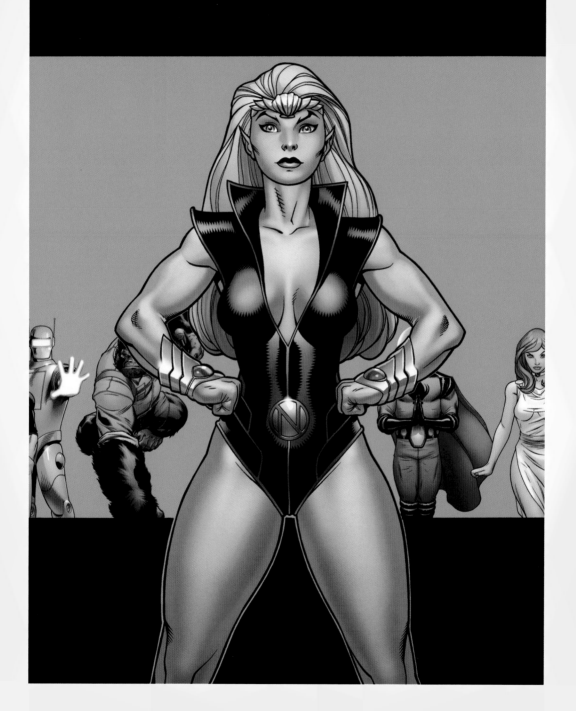

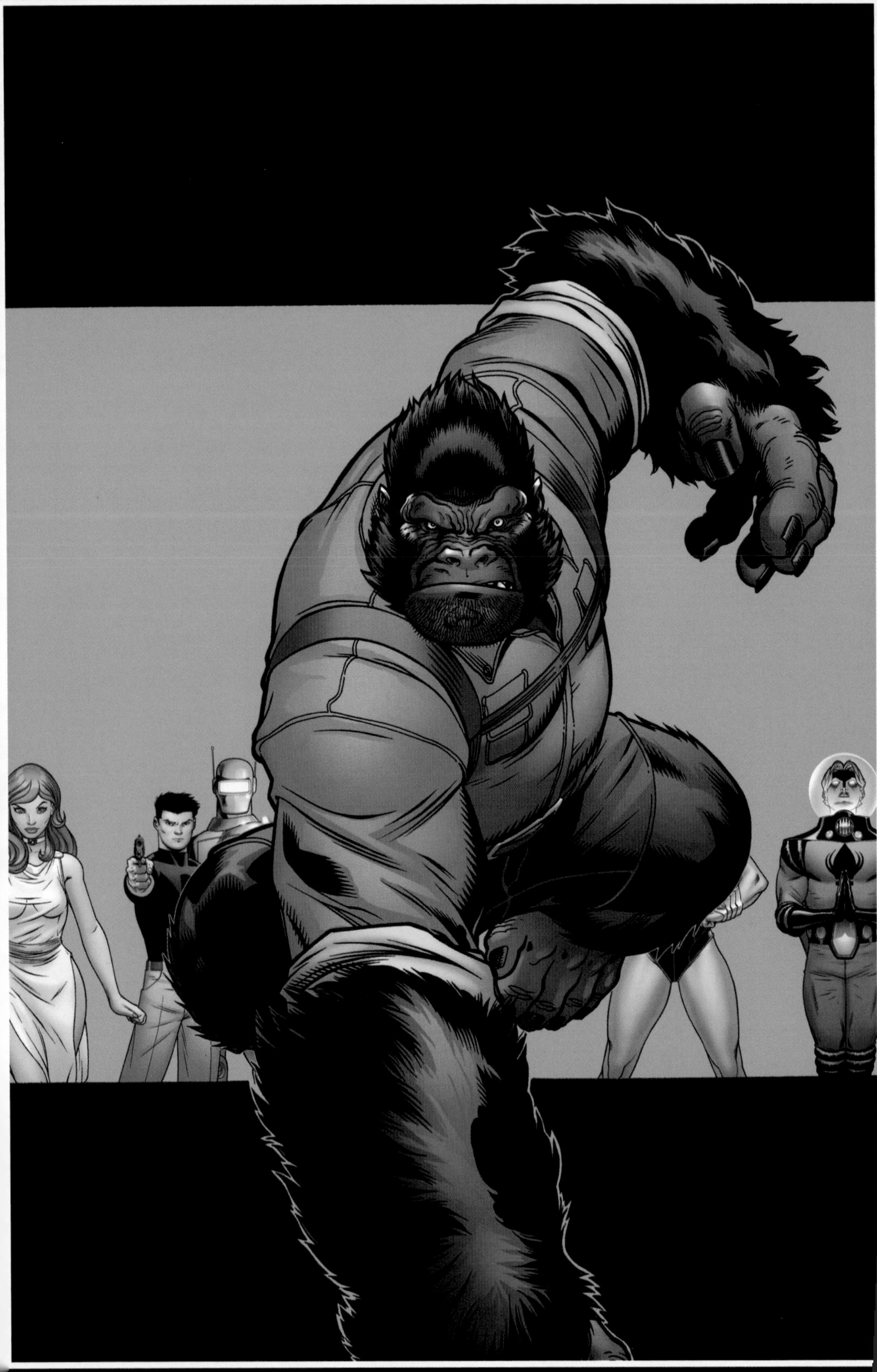

VARIANT COVERS BY ED MCGUINNESS, DEXTER VINES & JUSTIN PONSOR

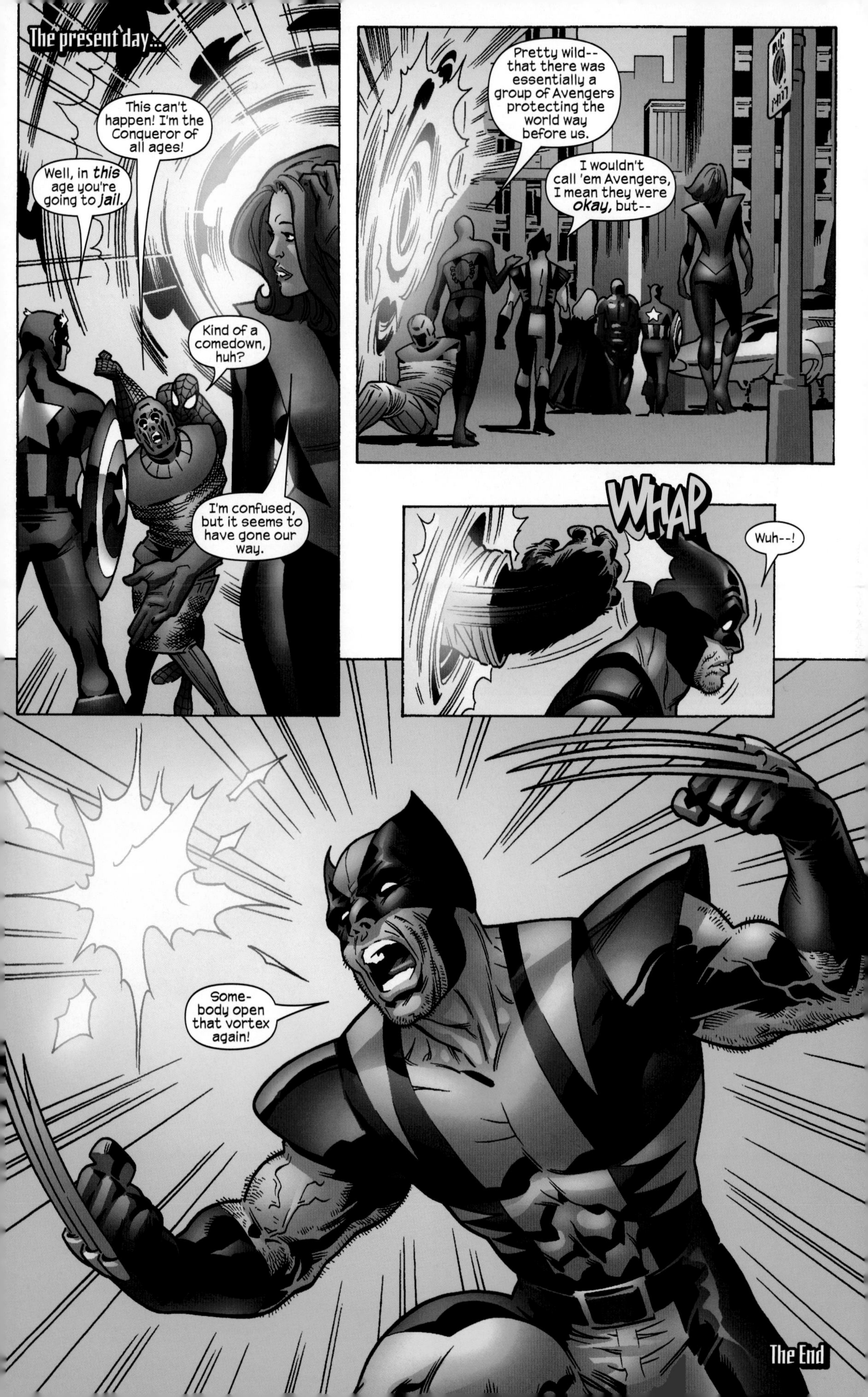
The present day...
This can't happen! I'm the Conqueror of all ages!
Well, in this age you're going to jail.
Kind of a comedown, huh?
I'm confused, but it seems to have gone our way.
Pretty wild-- that there was essentially a group of Avengers protecting the world way before us.
I wouldn't call 'em Avengers, I mean they were okay, but--
WHAP
Wuh--!
Some-body open that vortex again!
The End

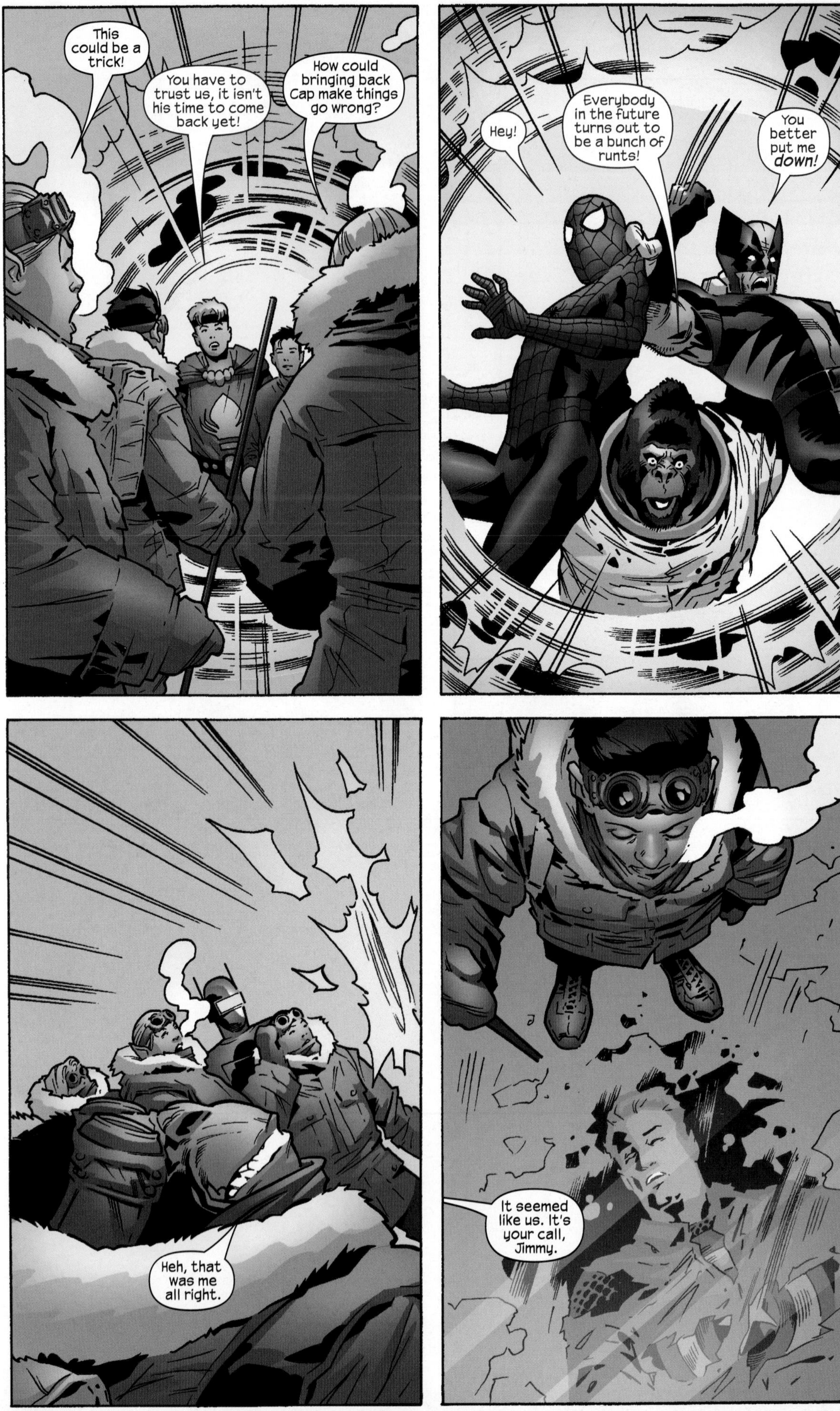
This could be a trick!
You have to trust us, it isn't his time to come back yet!
How could bringing back Cap make things go wrong?
Hey!
Everybody in the future turns out to be a bunch of runts!
You better put me down!
Heh, that was me all right.
It seemed like us. It's your call, Jimmy.

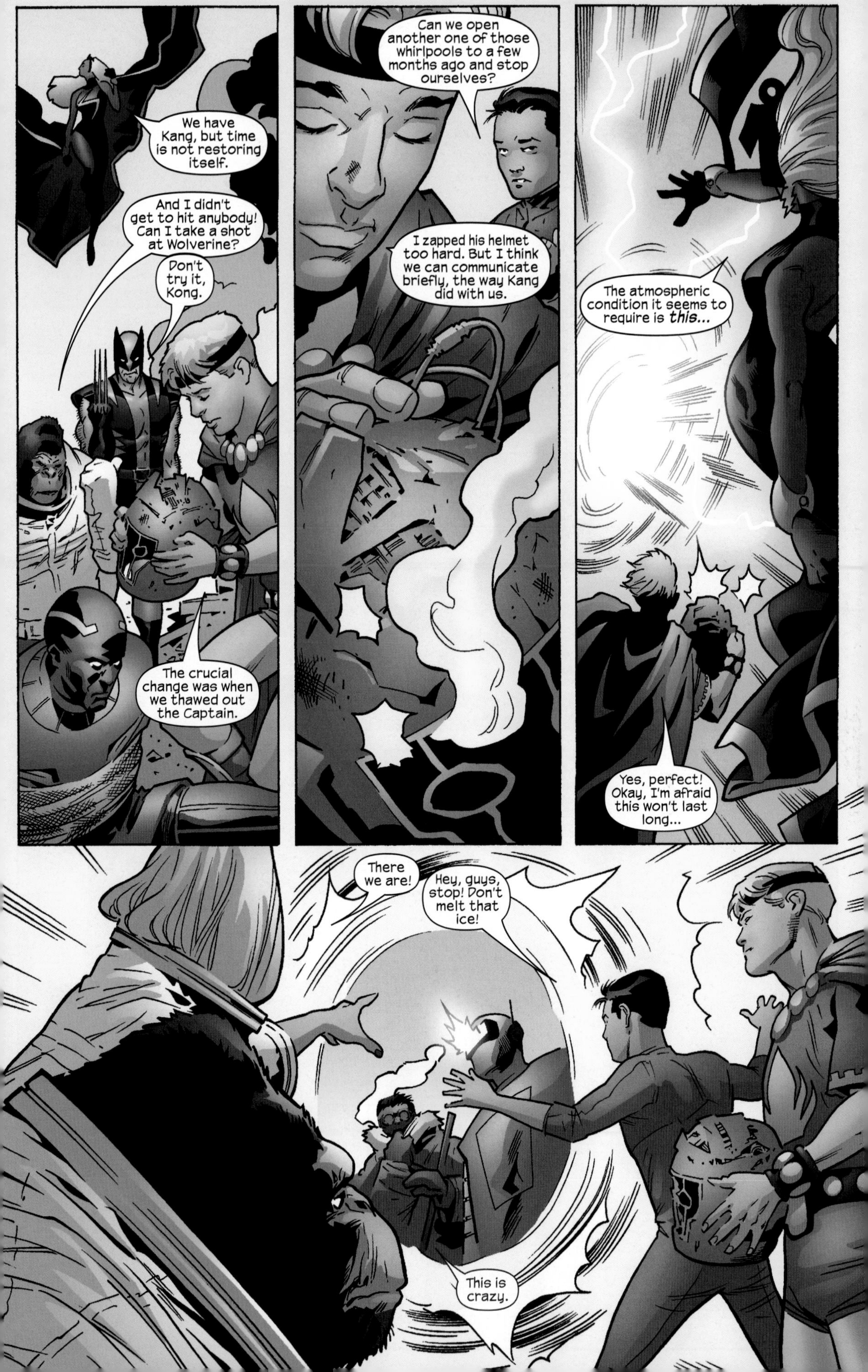

We have Kang, but time is not restoring itself.
And I didn't get to hit anybody! Can I take a shot at Wolverine?
Don't try it, Kong.
The crucial change was when we thawed out the Captain.
Can we open another one of those whirlpools to a few months ago and stop ourselves?
I zapped his helmet too hard. But I think we can communicate briefly, the way Kang did with us.
The atmospheric condition it seems to require is *this...*
Yes, perfect! Okay, I'm afraid this won't last long...
There we are!
Hey, guys, stop! Don't melt that ice!
This is crazy.

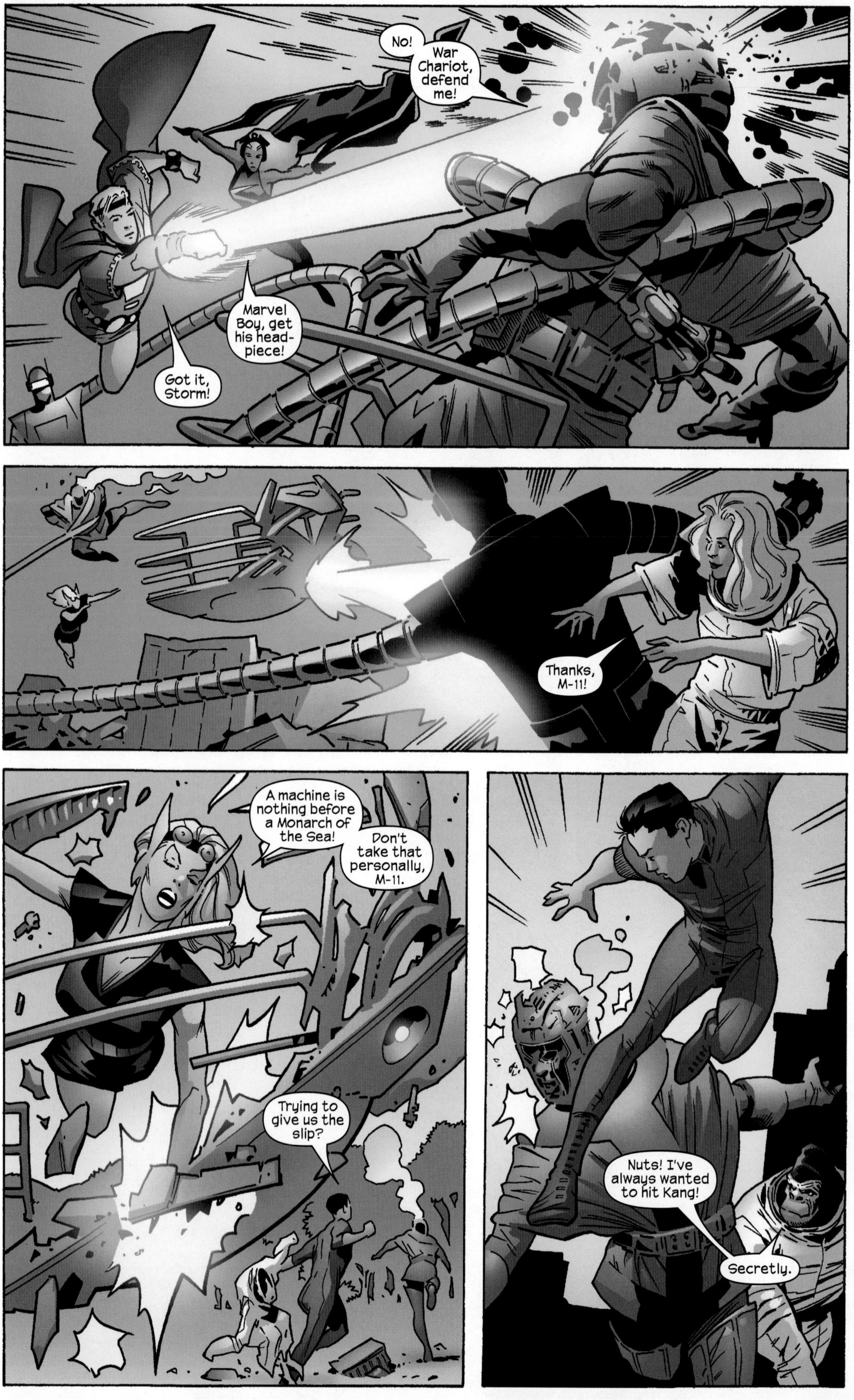
No!
War Chariot, defend me!
Marvel Boy, get his head-piece!
Got it, Storm!
Thanks, M-11!
A machine is nothing before a Monarch of the Sea!
Don't take that personally, M-11.
Trying to give us the slip?
Nuts! I've always wanted to hit Kang!
Secretly.

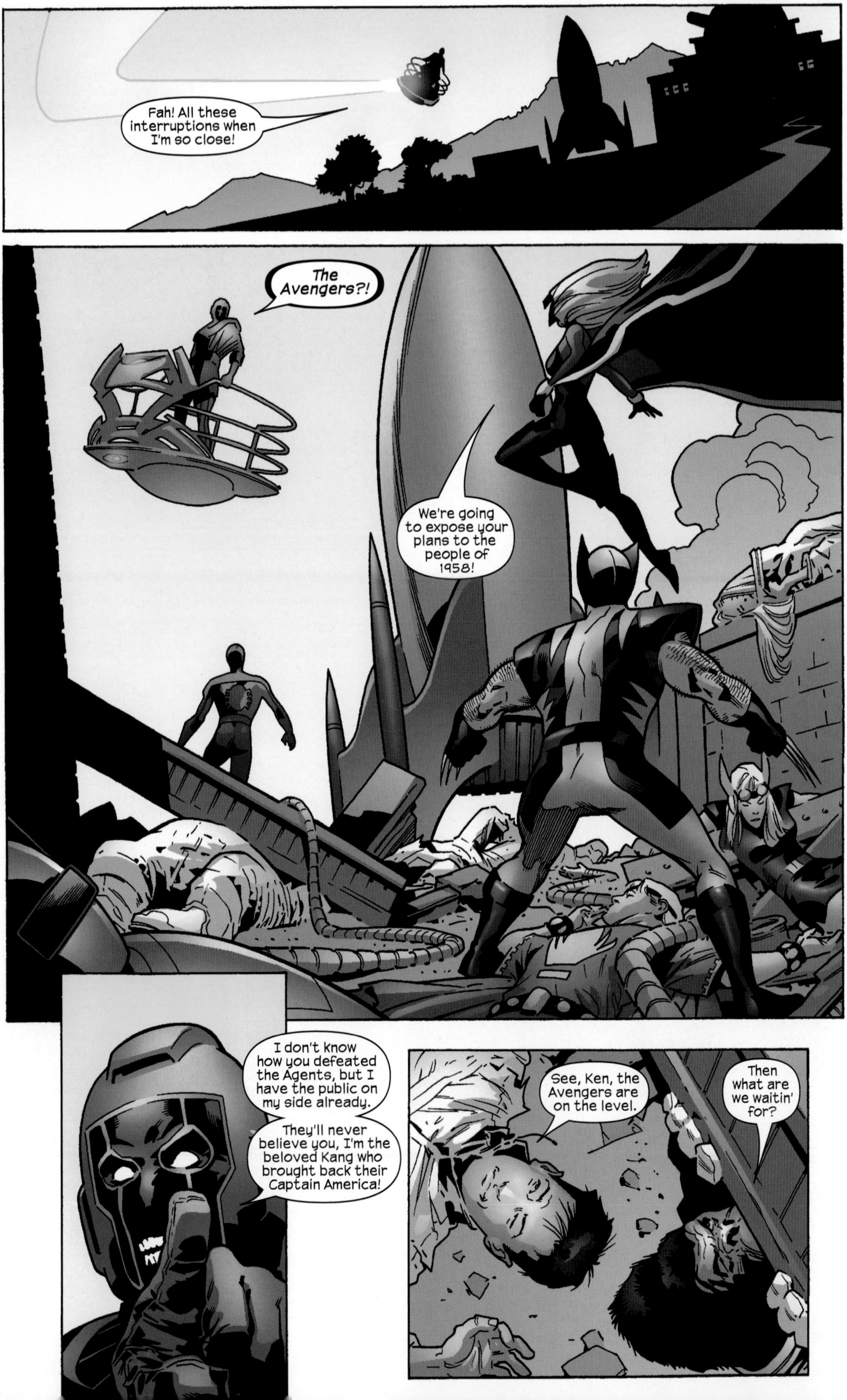
Fah! All these interruptions when I'm so close!
The Avengers?!
We're going to expose your plans to the people of 1958!
I don't know how you defeated the Agents, but I have the public on my side already.
They'll never believe you, I'm the beloved Kang who brought back their Captain America!
See, Ken, the Avengers are on the level.
Then what are we waitin' for?

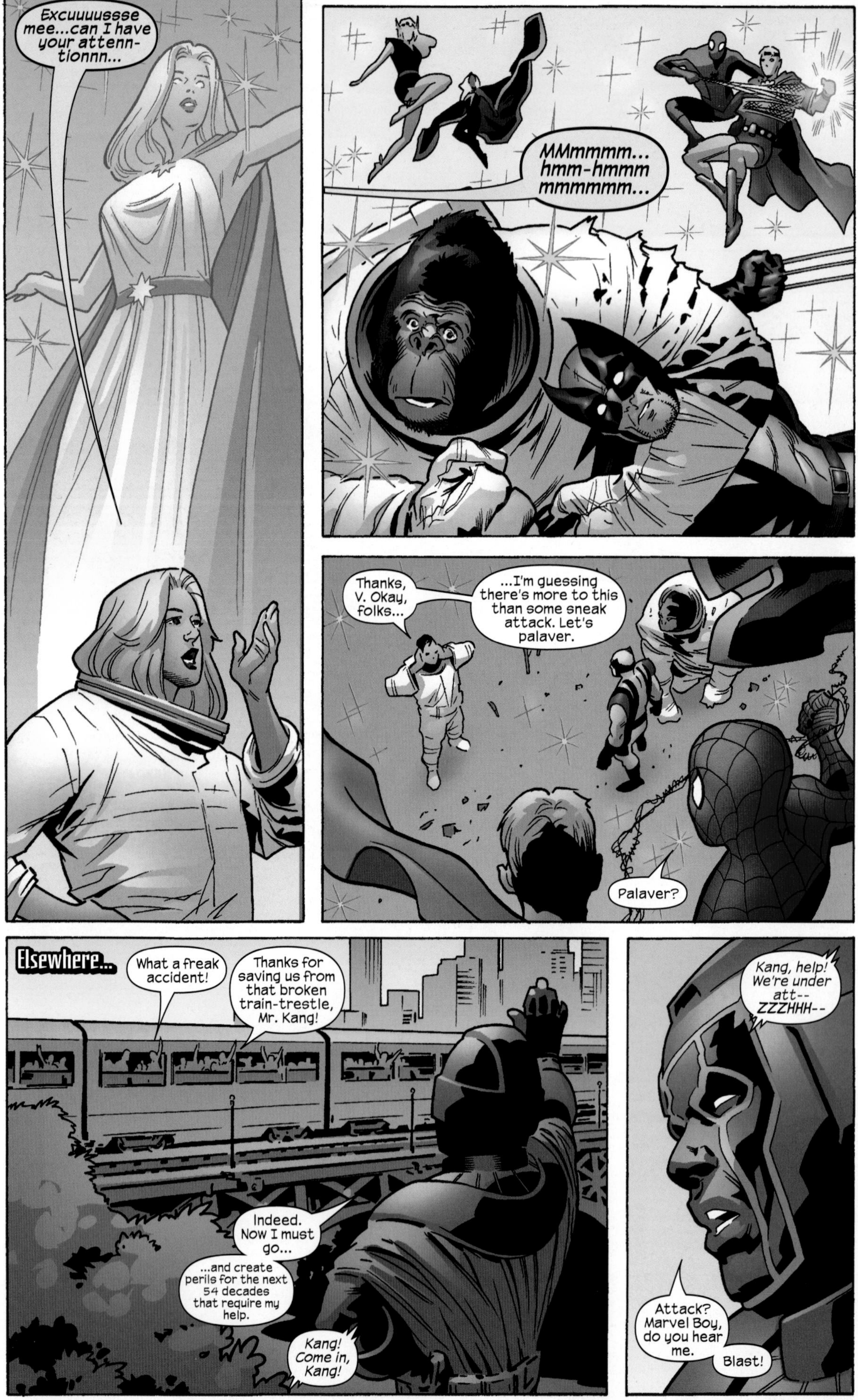
Excuuuussse mee...can I have your attenn-tionnn...
MMmmmm... hmm-hmmm mmmmmm...
Thanks, V. Okay, folks...
...I'm guessing there's more to this than some sneak attack. Let's palaver.
Palaver?
Elsewhere...
What a freak accident!
Thanks for saving us from that broken train-trestle, Mr. Kang!
Indeed. Now I must go...
...and create perils for the next 54 decades that require my help.
Kang! Come in, Kang!
Kang, help! We're under att-- ZZZHHH--
Attack? Marvel Boy, do you hear me.
Blast!

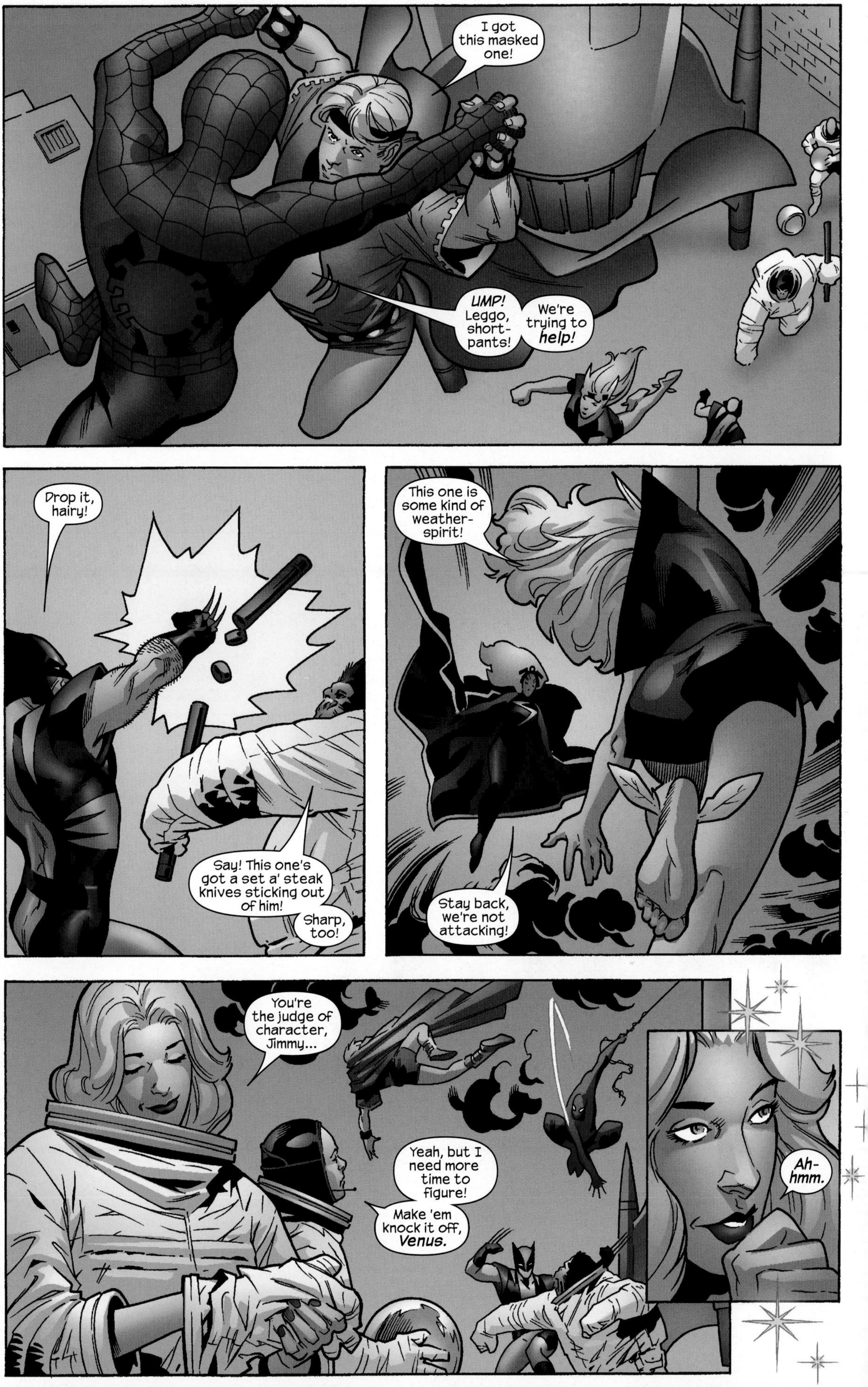

I got this masked one!
UMP! Leggo, short-pants!
We're trying to help!
Drop it, hairy!
Say! This one's got a set a' steak knives sticking out of him!
Sharp, too!
This one is some kind of weather-spirit!
Stay back, we're not attacking!
You're the judge of character, Jimmy...
Yeah, but I need more time to figure!
Make 'em knock it off, Venus.
Ah-hmm.

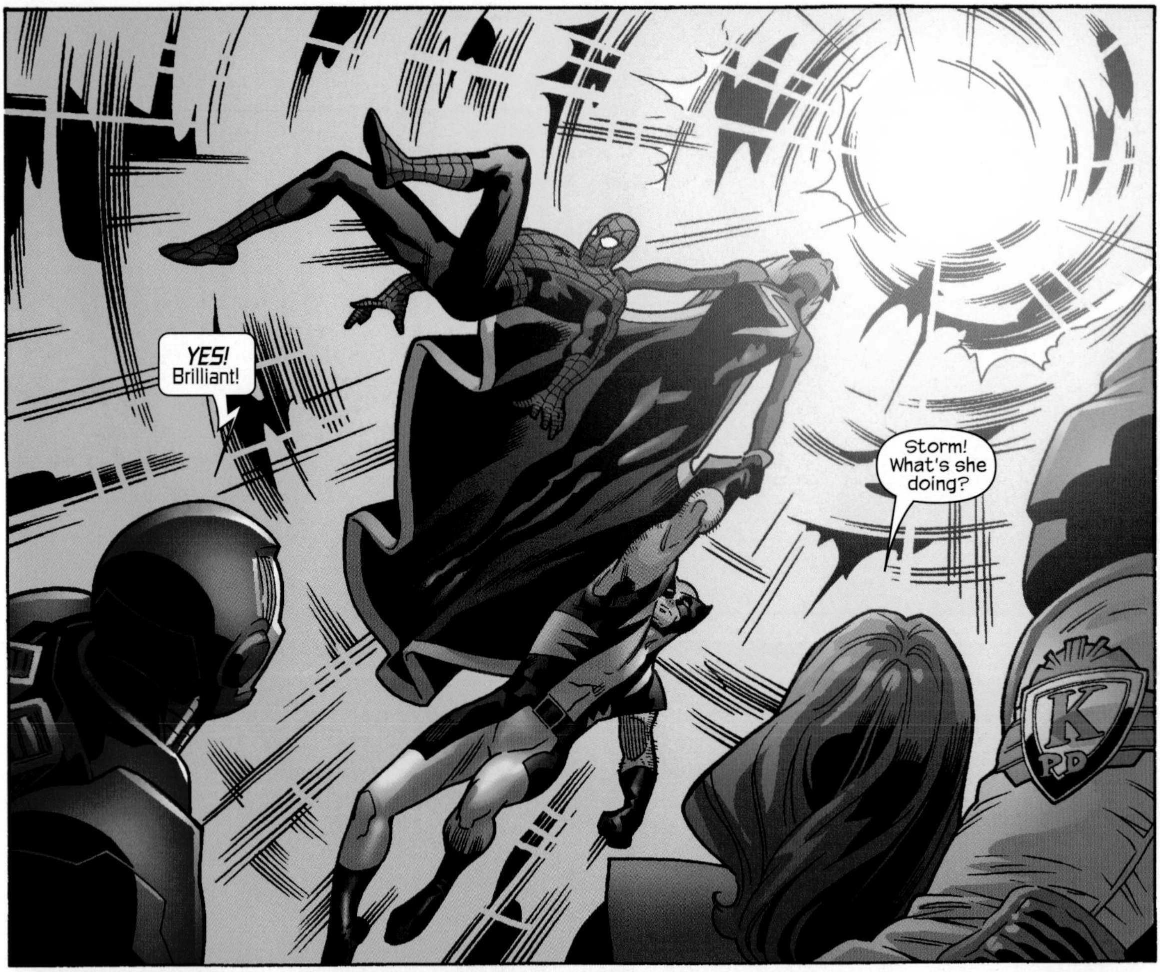
YES! Brilliant!
Storm! What's she doing?
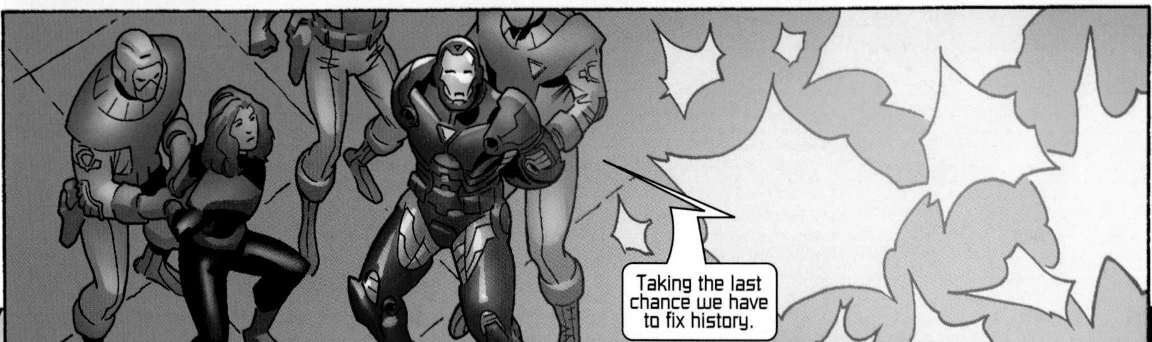
Taking the last chance we have to fix history.
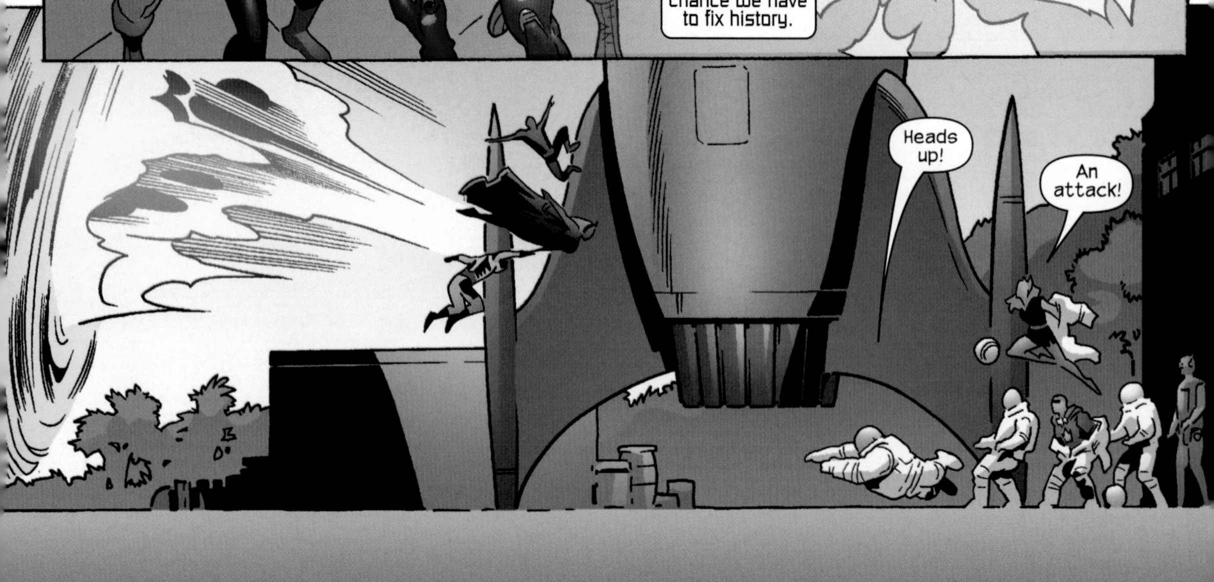
Heads up!
An attack!

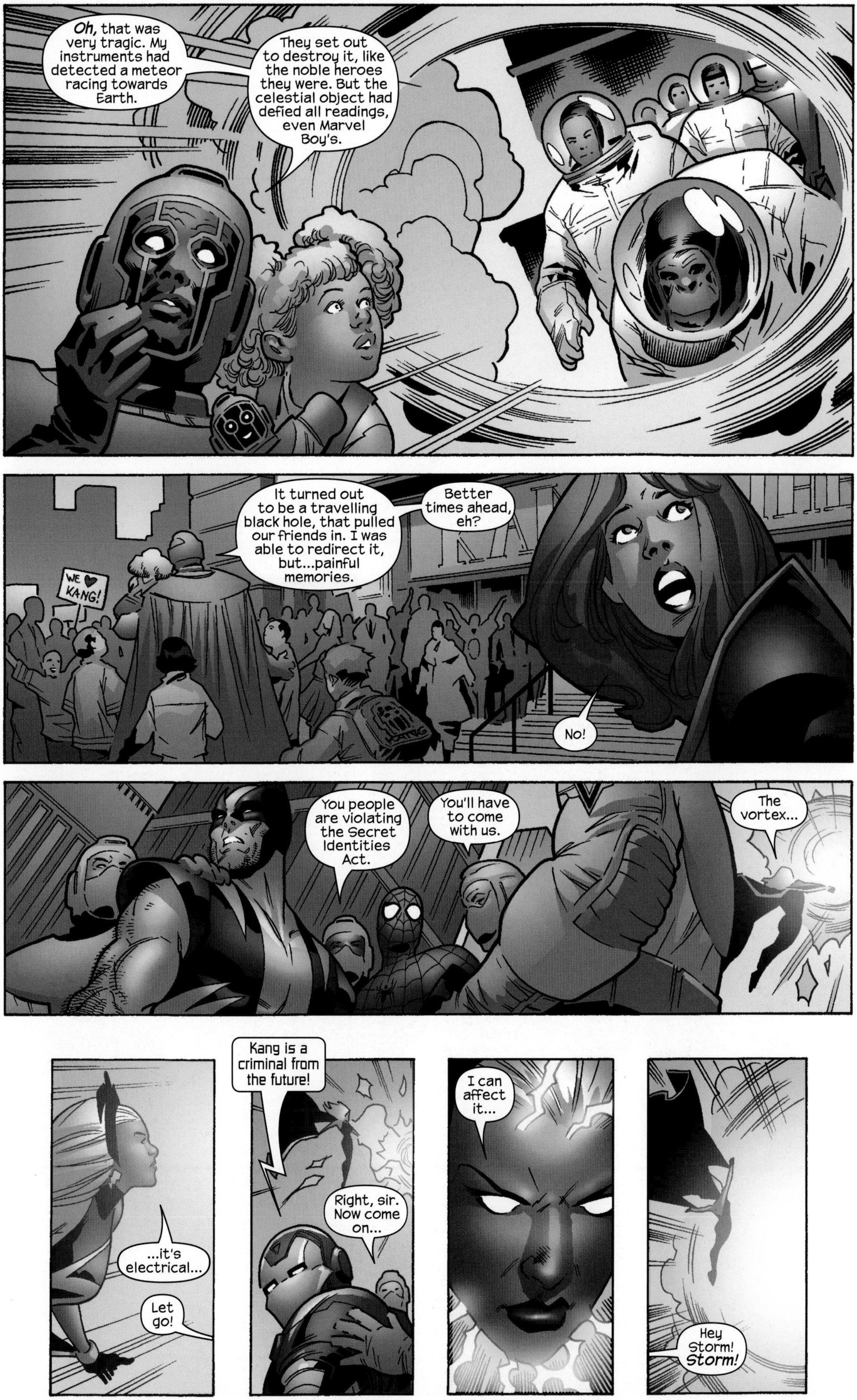
Oh, that was very tragic. My instruments had detected a meteor racing towards Earth.
They set out to destroy it, like the noble heroes they were. But the celestial object had defied all readings, even Marvel Boy's.
It turned out to be a travelling black hole, that pulled our friends in. I was able to redirect it, but...painful memories.
Better times ahead, eh?
WE ♥ KANG!
No!
You people are violating the Secret Identities Act.
You'll have to come with us.
The vortex...
...it's electrical...
Let go!
Kang is a criminal from the future!
Right, sir. Now come on...
I can affect it...
Hey Storm! Storm!

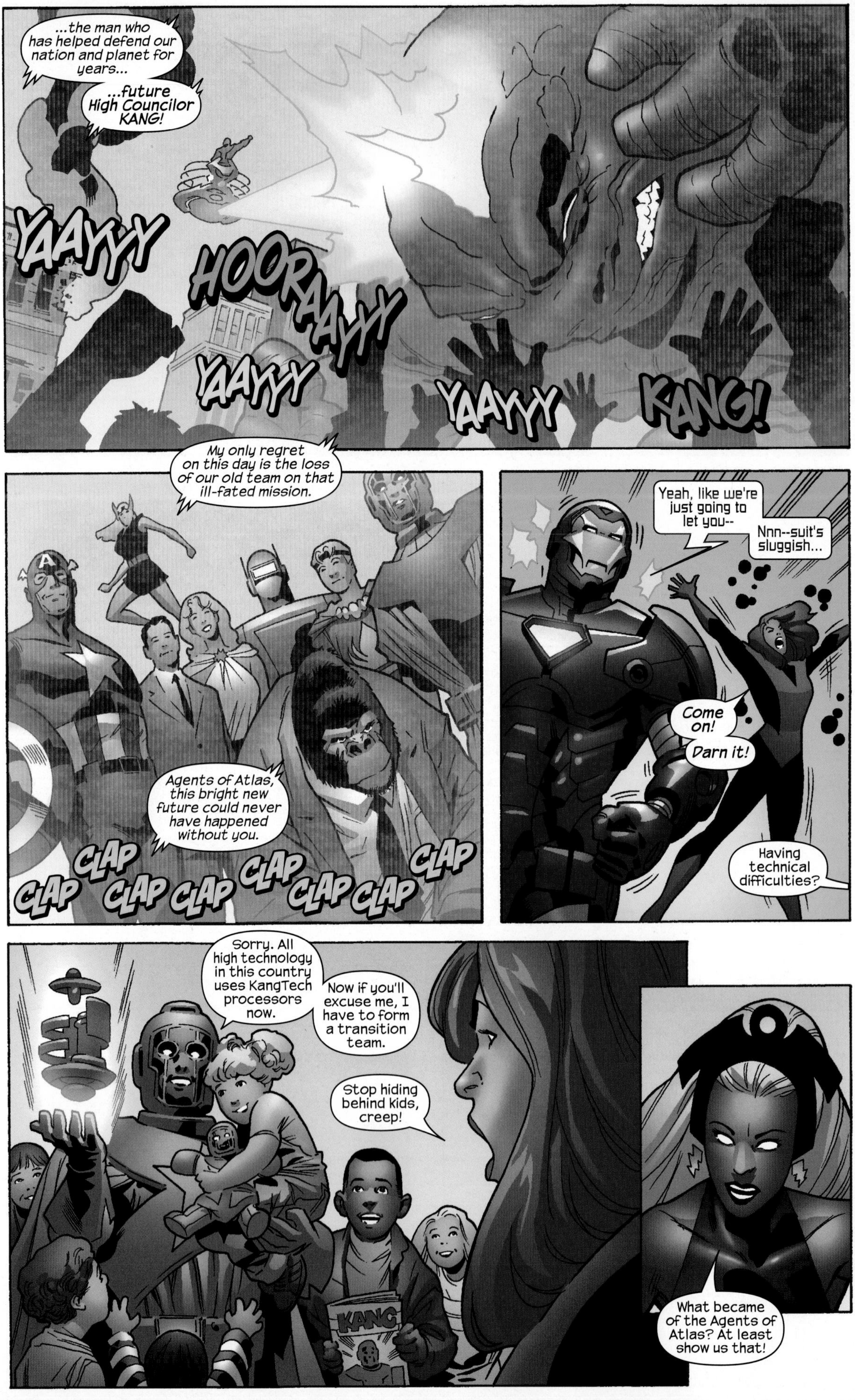
...the man who has helped defend our nation and planet for years...
...future High Councilor KANG!
YAAYYY
HOORAAYYY
YAAYYY
YAAYYY
KANG!
My only regret on this day is the loss of our old team on that ill-fated mission.
Agents of Atlas, this bright new future could never have happened without you.
CLAP CLAP CLAP CLAP CLAP CLAP CLAP CLAP
Yeah, like we're just going to let you--
Nnn--suit's sluggish...
Come on!
Darn it!
Having technical difficulties?
Sorry. All high technology in this country uses KangTech processors now.
Now if you'll excuse me, I have to form a transition team.
Stop hiding behind kids, creep!
KANG
What became of the Agents of Atlas? At least show us that!

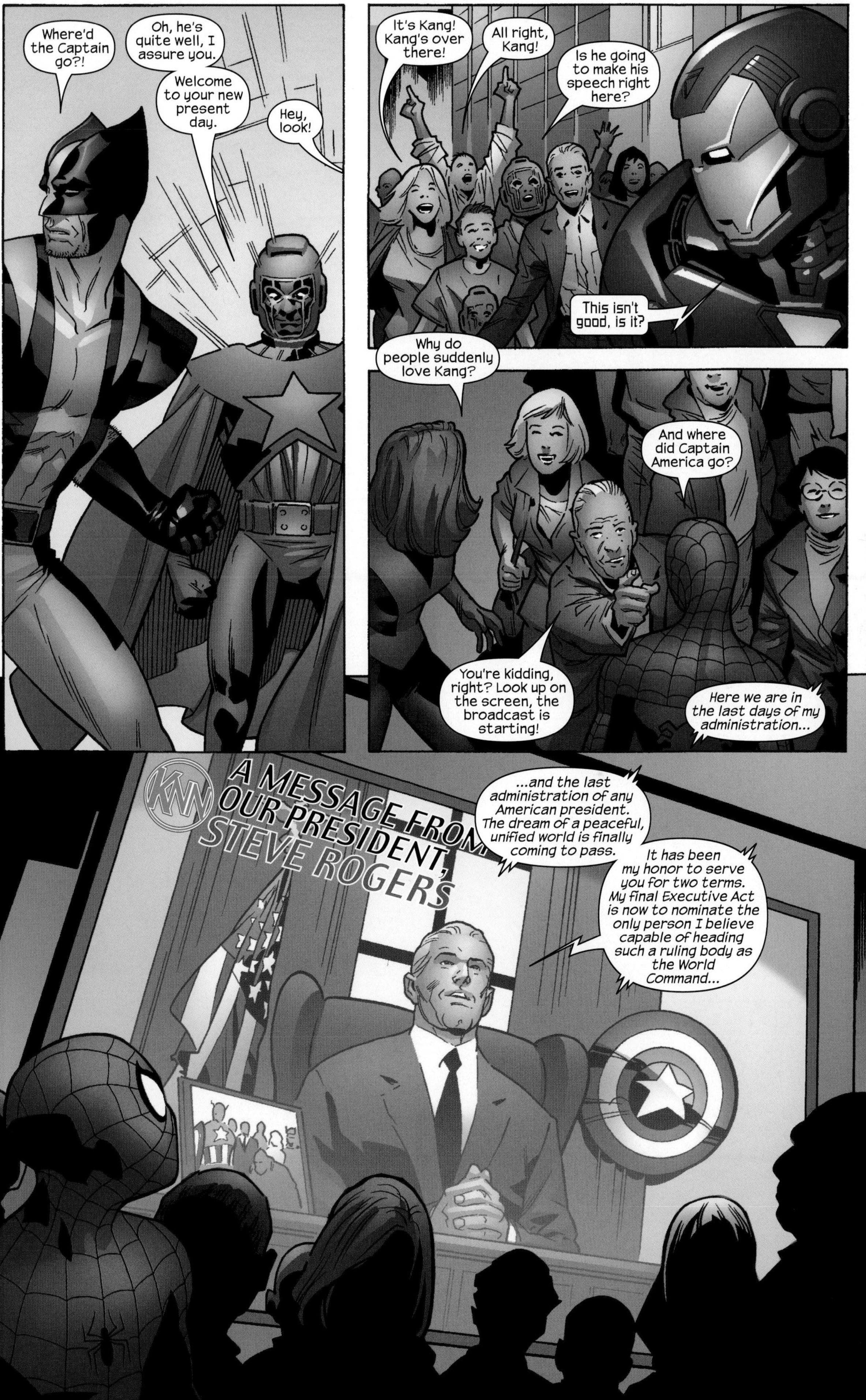
Where'd the Captain go?!
Oh, he's quite well, I assure you.
Welcome to your new present day.
Hey, look!
It's Kang! Kang's over there!
All right, Kang!
Is he going to make his speech right here?
This isn't good, is it?
Why do people suddenly love Kang?
And where did Captain America go?
You're kidding, right? Look up on the screen, the broadcast is starting!
Here we are in the last days of my administration...
KNN
A MESSAGE FROM OUR PRESIDENT, STEVE ROGERS
...and the last administration of any American president. The dream of a peaceful, unified world is finally coming to pass.
It has been my honor to serve you for two terms. My final Executive Act is now to nominate the only person I believe capable of heading such a ruling body as the World Command...

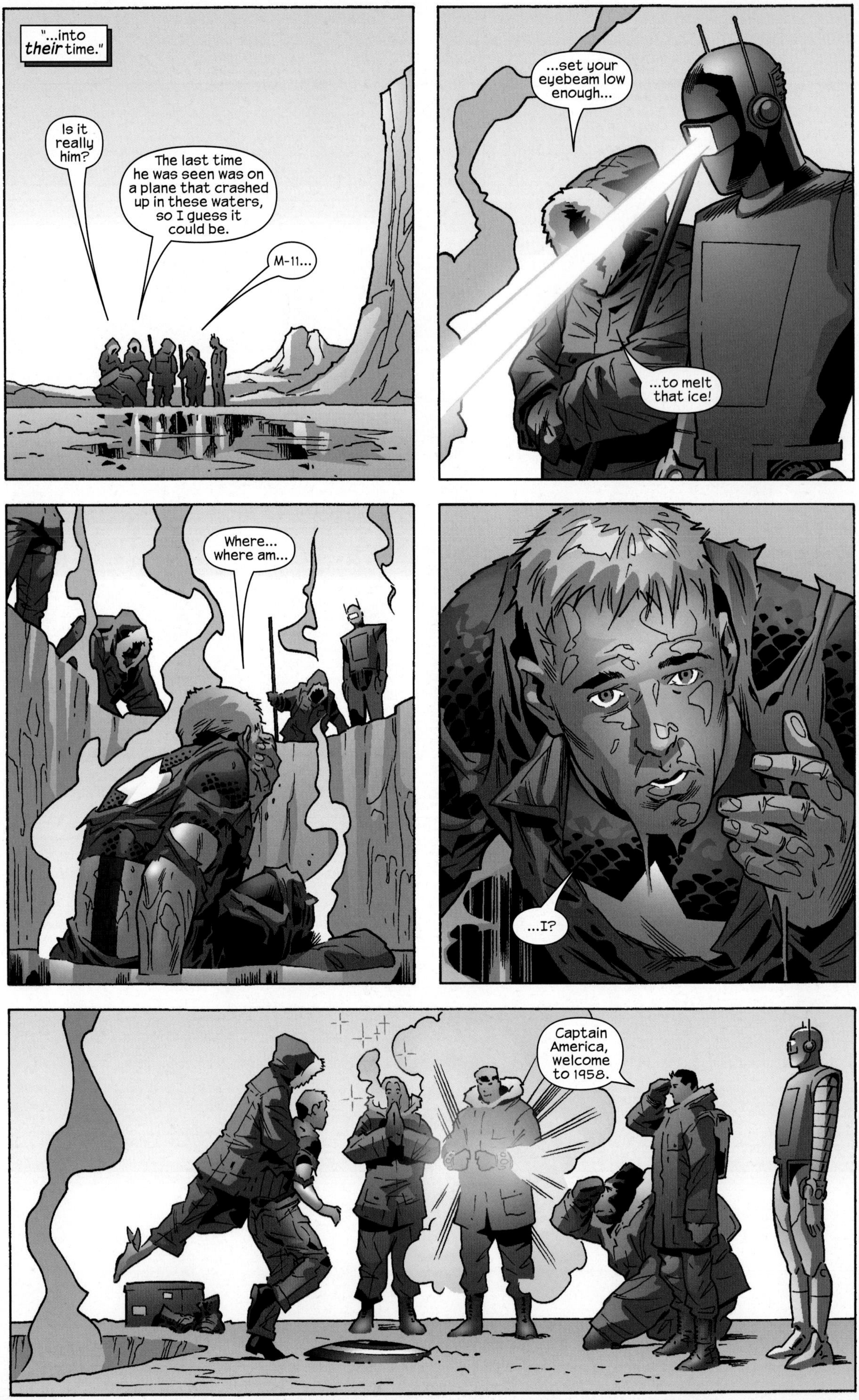
"...into *their* time."
Is it really him?
The last time he was seen was on a plane that crashed up in these waters, so I guess it could be.
M-11...
...set your eyebeam low enough...
...to melt that ice!
Where... where am...
...I?
Captain America, welcome to 1958.

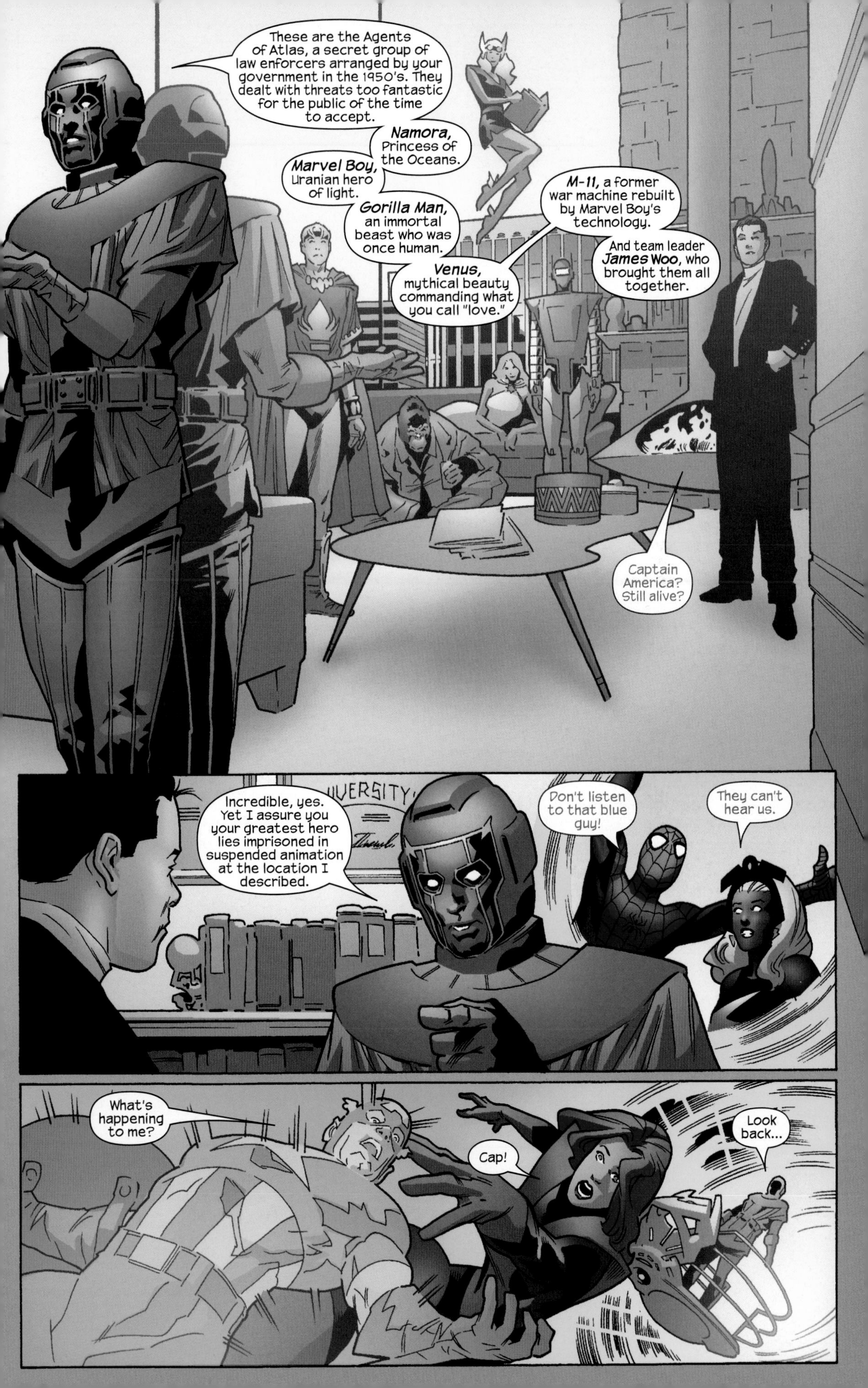
These are the Agents of Atlas, a secret group of law enforcers arranged by your government in the 1950's. They dealt with threats too fantastic for the public of the time to accept.
Namora, Princess of the Oceans.
Marvel Boy, Uranian hero of light.
Gorilla Man, an immortal beast who was once human.
Venus, mythical beauty commanding what you call "love."
M-11, a former war machine rebuilt by Marvel Boy's technology.
And team leader James Woo, who brought them all together.
Captain America? Still alive?
Incredible, yes. Yet I assure you your greatest hero lies imprisoned in suspended animation at the location I described.
Don't listen to that blue guy!
They can't hear us.
What's happening to me?
Cap!
Look back...

I believe Iron Man has equipment that may alert you all to Time/Space manipulations affecting you directly.

And I do.

So I needed to give you a chore while the Kang of 3066 sent a message for me.

Ah, what good timing.

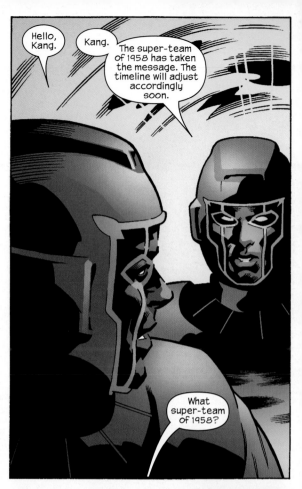

Hello, Kang.

Kang.

The super-team of 1958 has taken the message. The timeline will adjust accordingly soon.

What super-team of 1958?

Cap! You were around back then! Do you remember any other super heroes?

I was still frozen in the Arctic at that point, until the first roster of Avengers thawed me out.

Precisely. You've led this team to greatness, always interfering with my plans.

So I thought, what if you had been found sooner?

History flows in very specific ways and is actually quite difficult to alter.

Lasting changes can only be initiated by inhabitants of the time period, or time will soon correct itself.

For example, the timeline would only accept Captain America's return carried out by a super-team such as yourselves. My studies revealed such an earlier group.

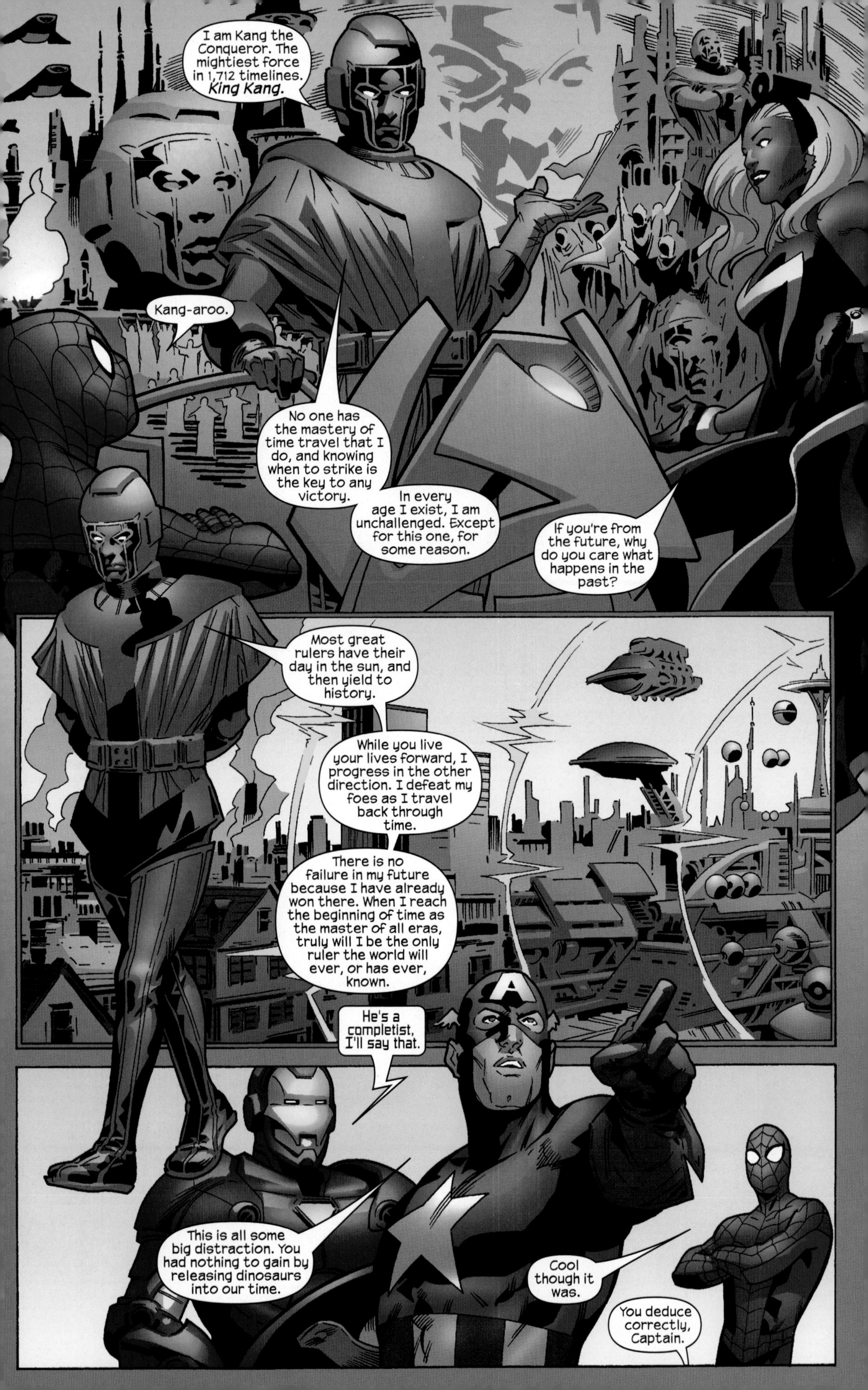
I am Kang the Conqueror. The mightiest force in 1,712 timelines. King Kang.
Kang-aroo.
No one has the mastery of time travel that I do, and knowing when to strike is the key to any victory.
In every age I exist, I am unchallenged. Except for this one, for some reason.
If you're from the future, why do you care what happens in the past?
Most great rulers have their day in the sun, and then yield to history.
While you live your lives forward, I progress in the other direction. I defeat my foes as I travel back through time.
There is no failure in my future because I have already won there. When I reach the beginning of time as the master of all eras, truly will I be the only ruler the world will ever, or has ever, known.
He's a completist, I'll say that.
This is all some big distraction. You had nothing to gain by releasing dinosaurs into our time.
Cool though it was.
You deduce correctly, Captain.

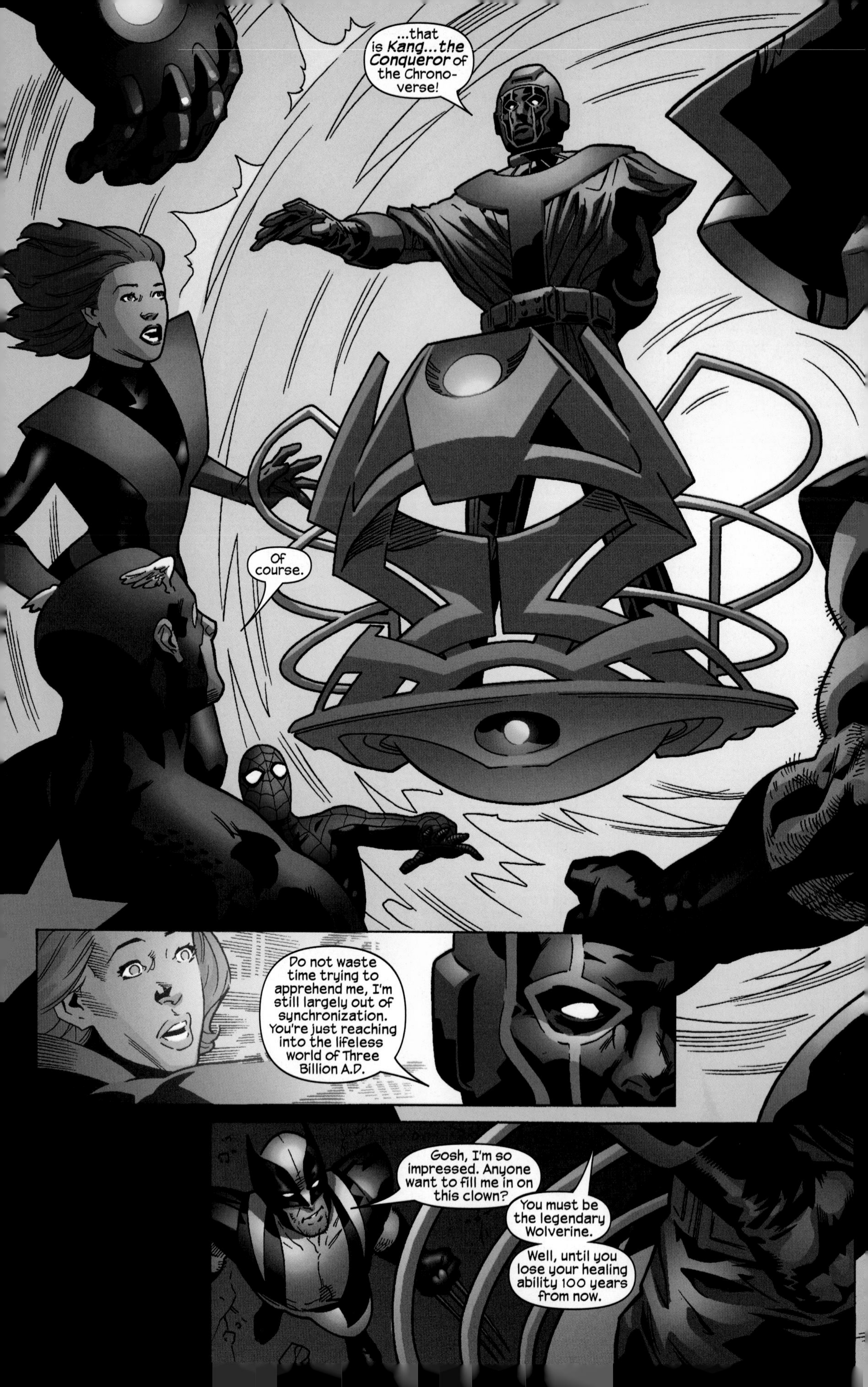
...that is Kang...the Conqueror of the Chrono-verse!
Of course.
Do not waste time trying to apprehend me, I'm still largely out of synchronization. You're just reaching into the lifeless world of Three Billion A.D.
Gosh, I'm so impressed. Anyone want to fill me in on this clown?
You must be the legendary Wolverine.
Well, until you lose your healing ability 100 years from now.

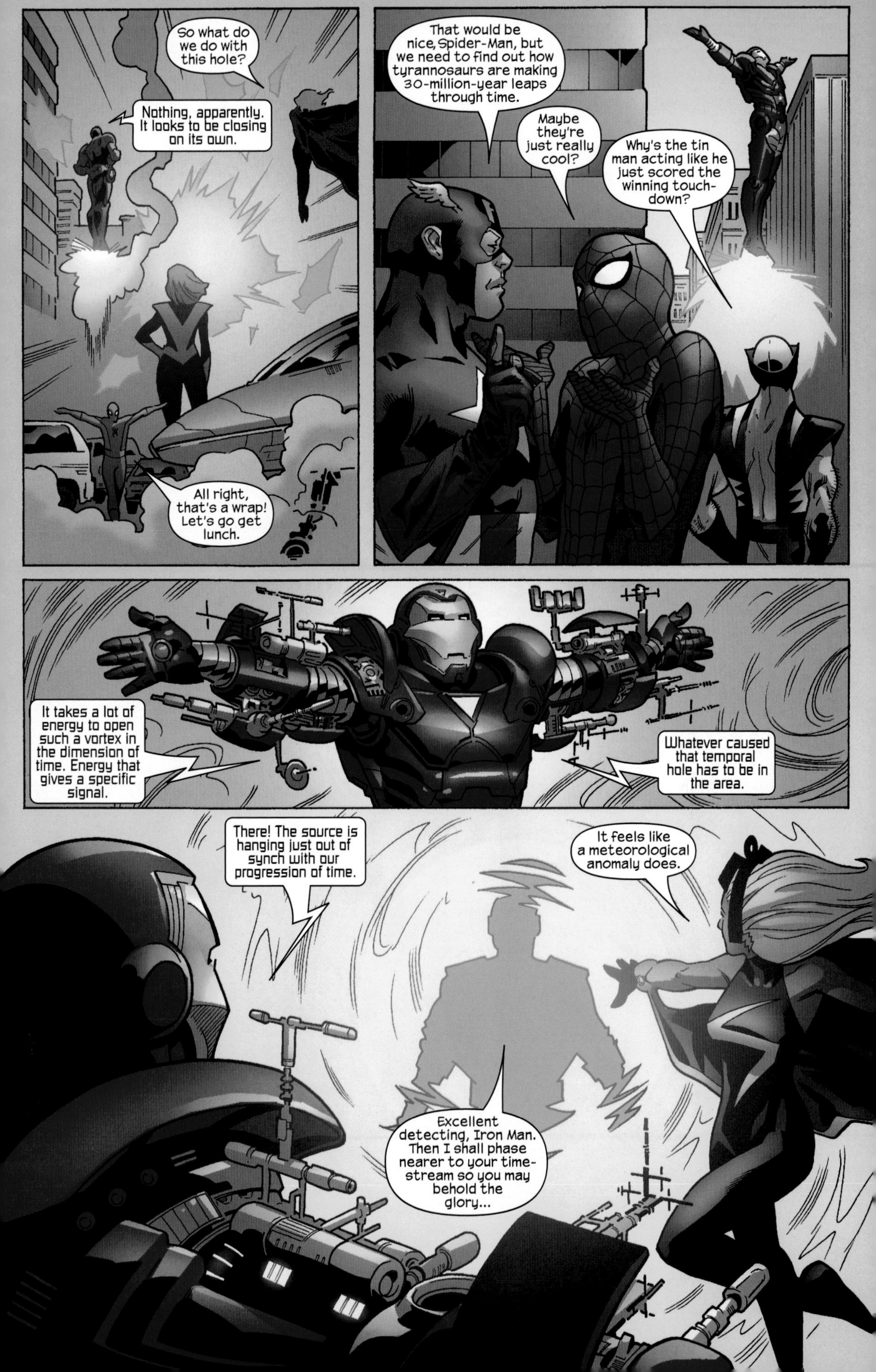

So what do we do with this hole?
Nothing, apparently. It looks to be closing on its own.
All right, that's a wrap! Let's go get lunch.
That would be nice, Spider-Man, but we need to find out how tyrannosaurs are making 30-million-year leaps through time.
Maybe they're just really cool?
Why's the tin man acting like he just scored the winning touch-down?
It takes a lot of energy to open such a vortex in the dimension of time. Energy that gives a specific signal.
Whatever caused that temporal hole has to be in the area.
There! The source is hanging just out of synch with our progression of time.
It feels like a meteorological anomaly does.
Excellent detecting, Iron Man. Then I shall phase nearer to your time-stream so you may behold the glory...

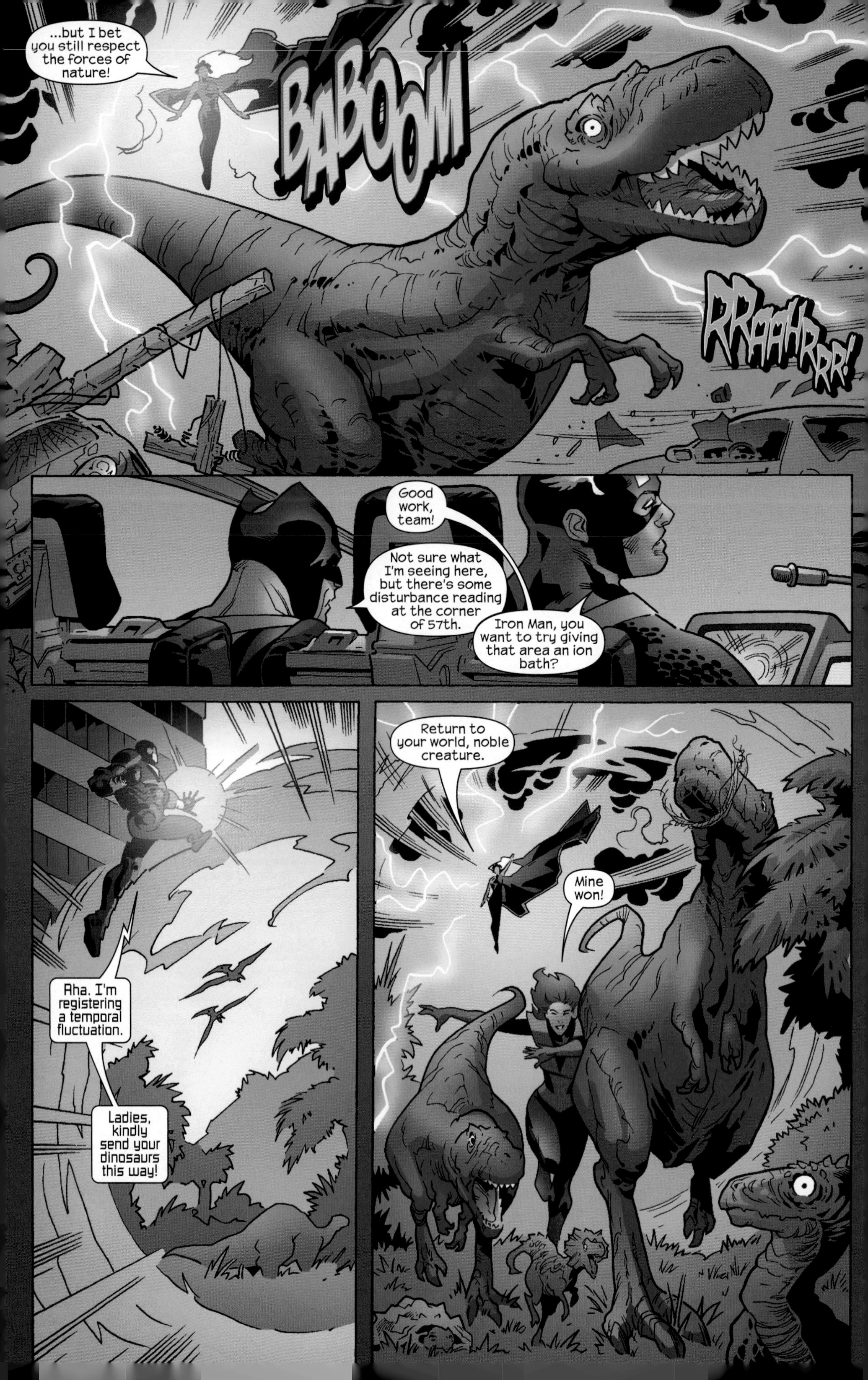
...but I bet you still respect the forces of nature!
BABOOM
RRAAHRRR!
Good work, team!
Not sure what I'm seeing here, but there's some disturbance reading at the corner of 57th.
Iron Man, you want to try giving that area an ion bath?
Aha. I'm registering a temporal fluctuation.
Ladies, kindly send your dinosaurs this way!
Return to your world, noble creature.
Mine won!

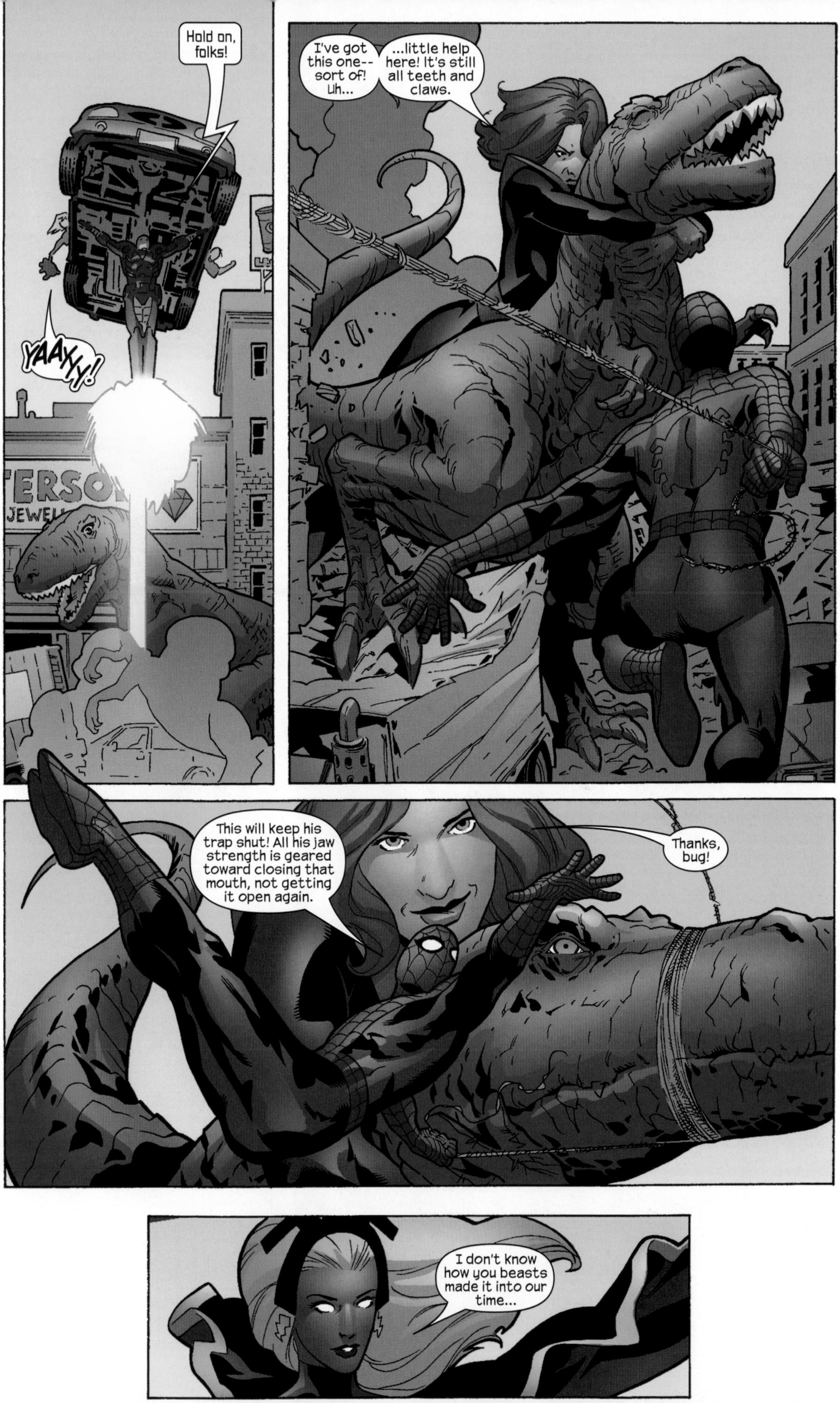
Hold on, folks!
YAAYYY!
TERSO
JEWEL
I've got this one-- sort of! Uh...
...little help here! It's still all teeth and claws.
This will keep his trap shut! All his jaw strength is geared toward closing that mouth, not getting it open again.
Thanks, bug!
I don't know how you beasts made it into our time...

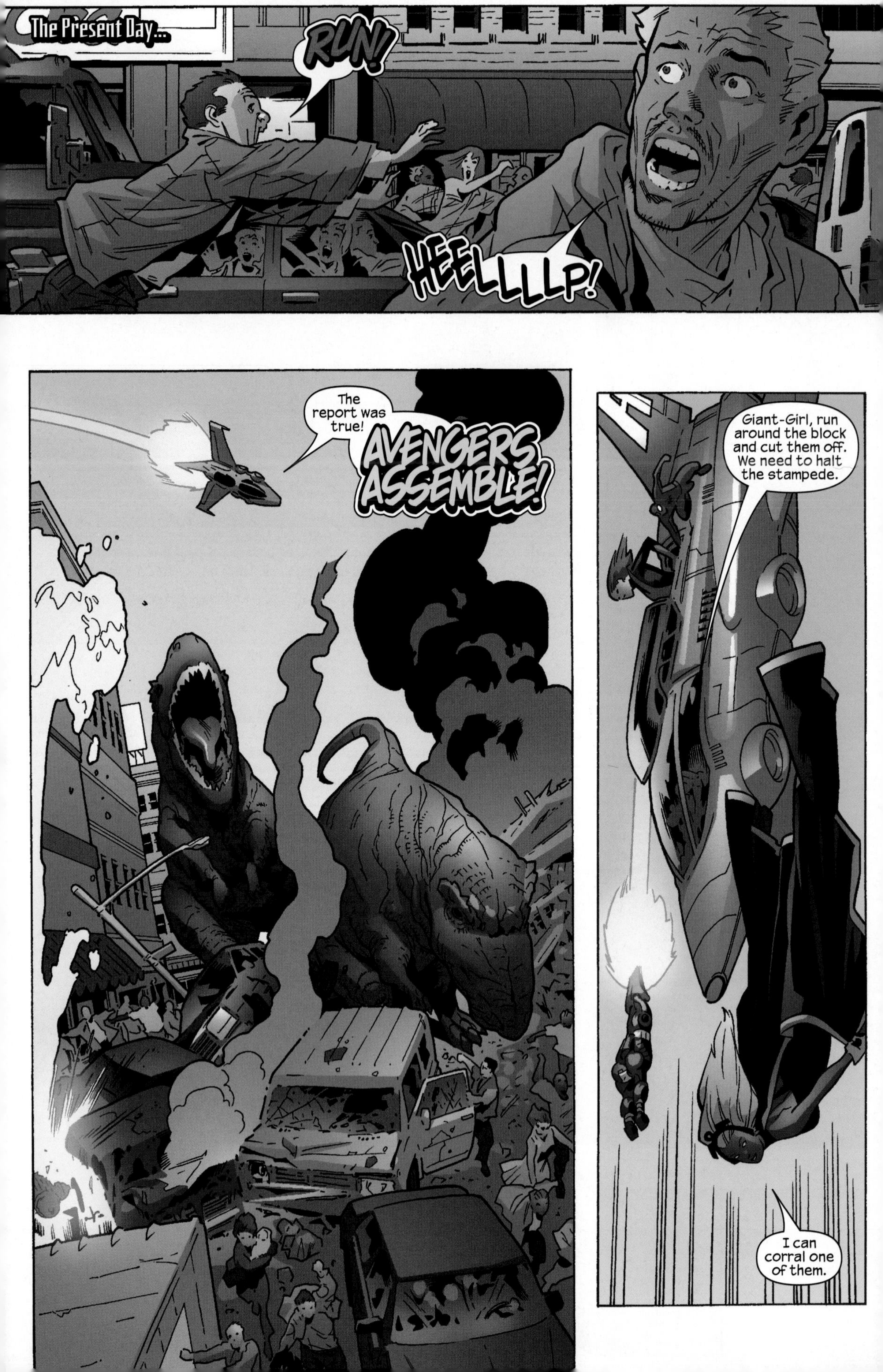
The Present Day...
RUN!
HEELLLLP!
The report was true!
AVENGERS ASSEMBLE!
Giant-Girl, run around the block and cut them off. We need to halt the stampede.
I can corral one of them.

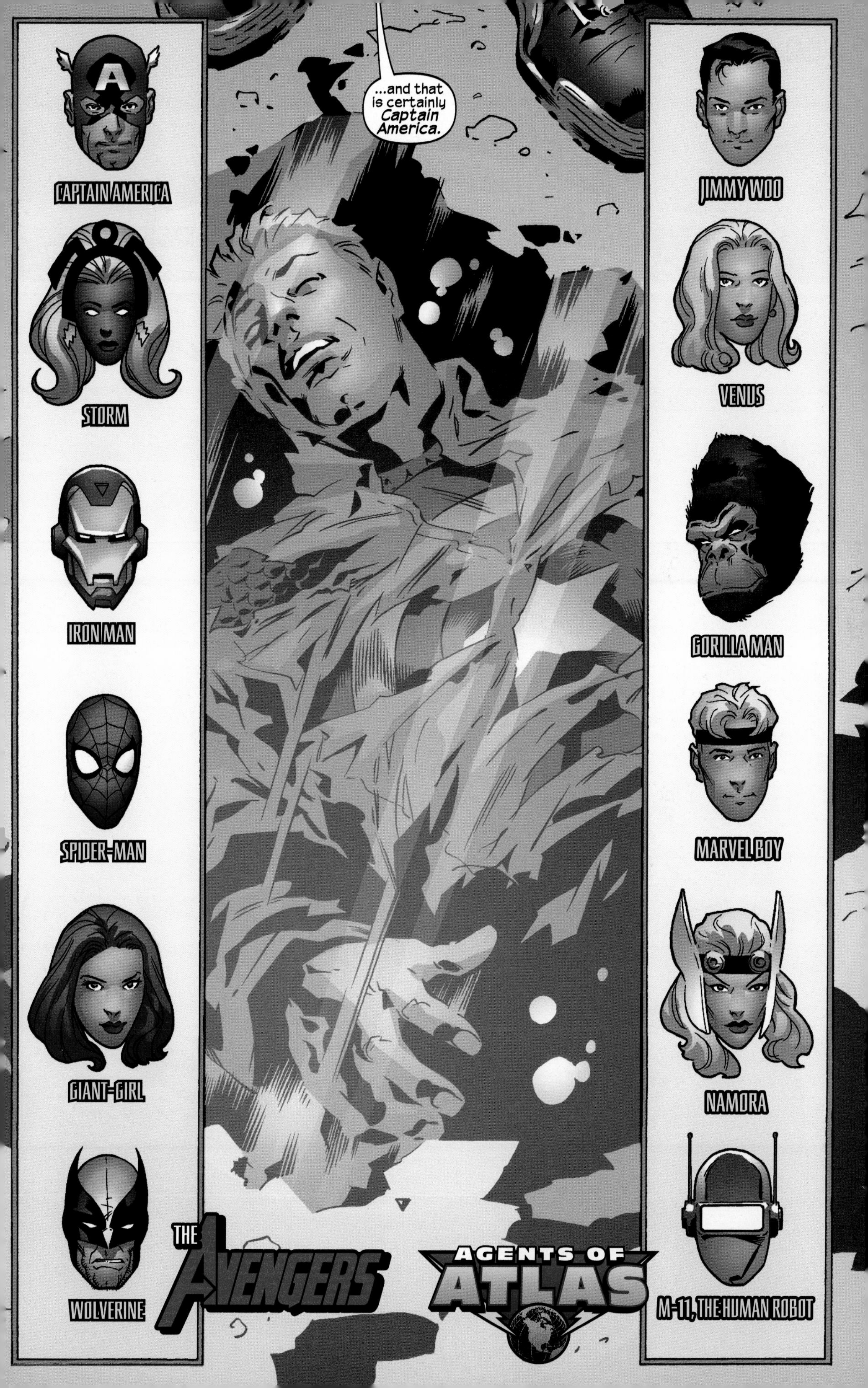
...and that is certainly Captain America.
CAPTAIN AMERICA
STORM
IRON MAN
SPIDER-MAN
GIANT-GIRL
WOLVERINE
THE AVENGERS
AGENTS OF ATLAS
JIMMY WOO
VENUS
GORILLA MAN
MARVEL BOY
NAMORA
M-11, THE HUMAN ROBOT

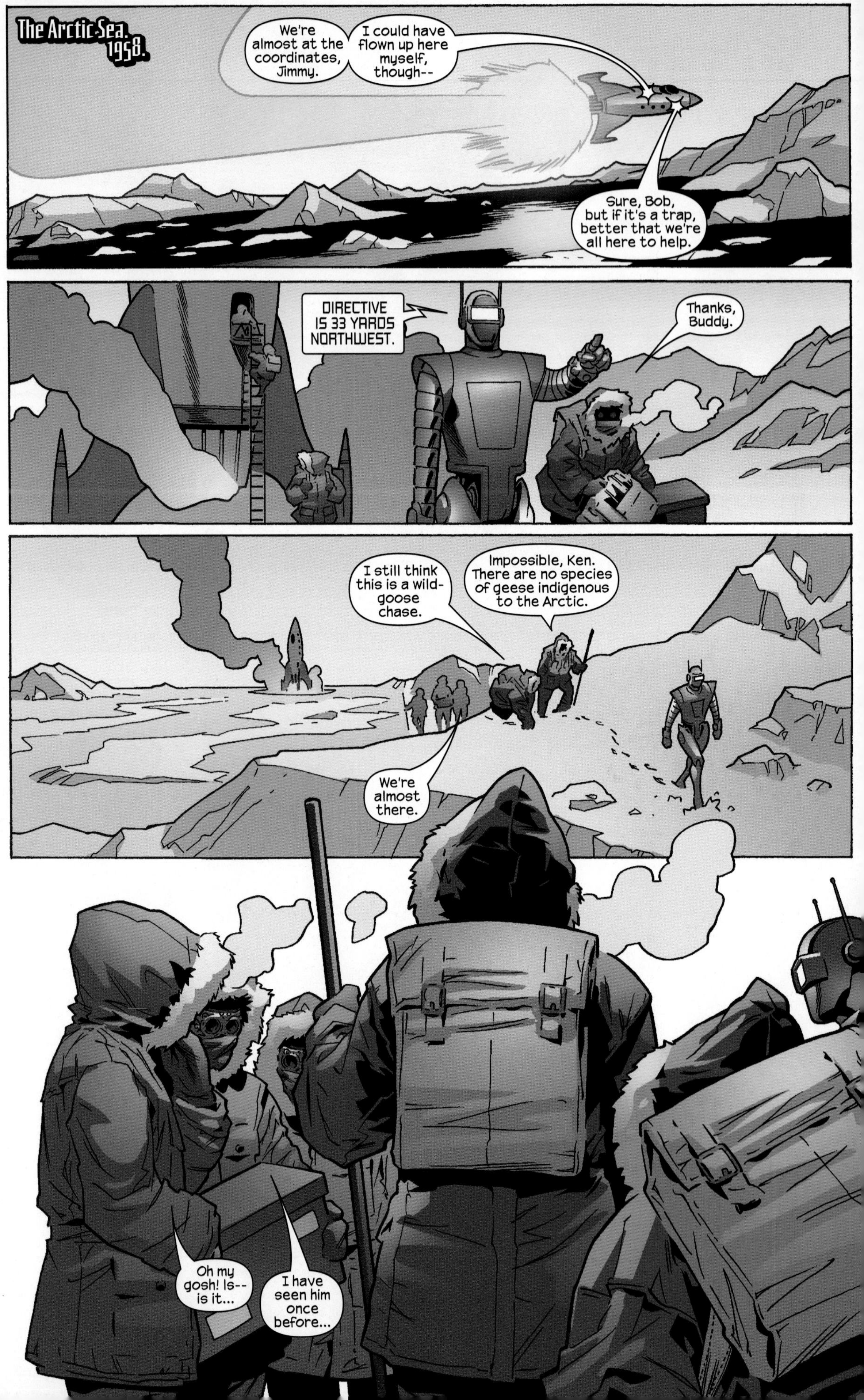
The Arctic Sea. 1958.
We're almost at the coordinates, Jimmy.
I could have flown up here myself, though--
Sure, Bob, but if it's a trap, better that we're all here to help.
DIRECTIVE IS 33 YARDS NORTHWEST.
Thanks, Buddy.
I still think this is a wild-goose chase.
Impossible, Ken. There are no species of geese indigenous to the Arctic.
We're almost there.
Oh my gosh! Is-- is it...
I have seen him once before...

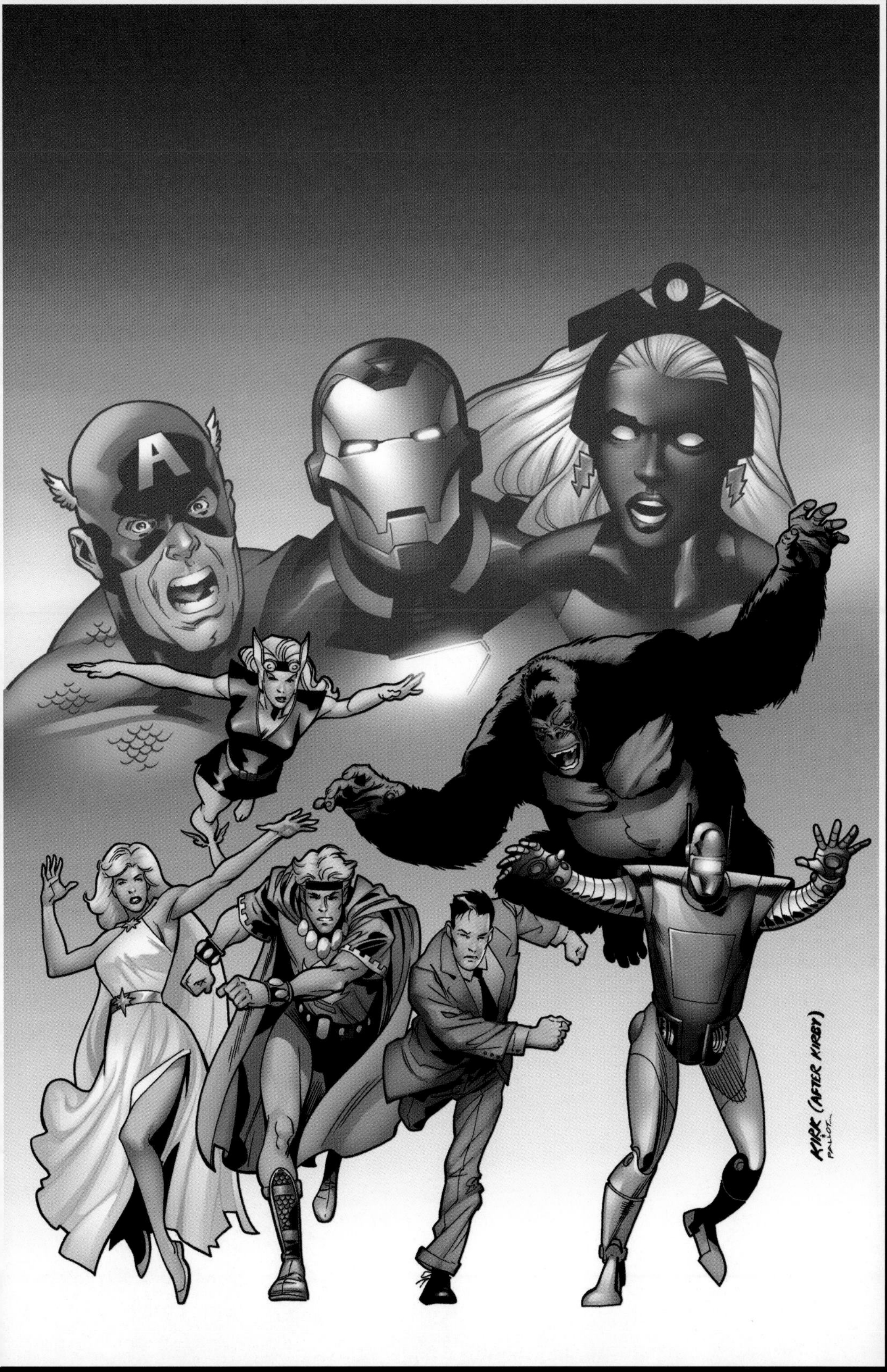
KIRK (AFTER KIRBY)
PALLOT

GIANT-SIZE MARVEL ADVENTURES THE AVENGERS

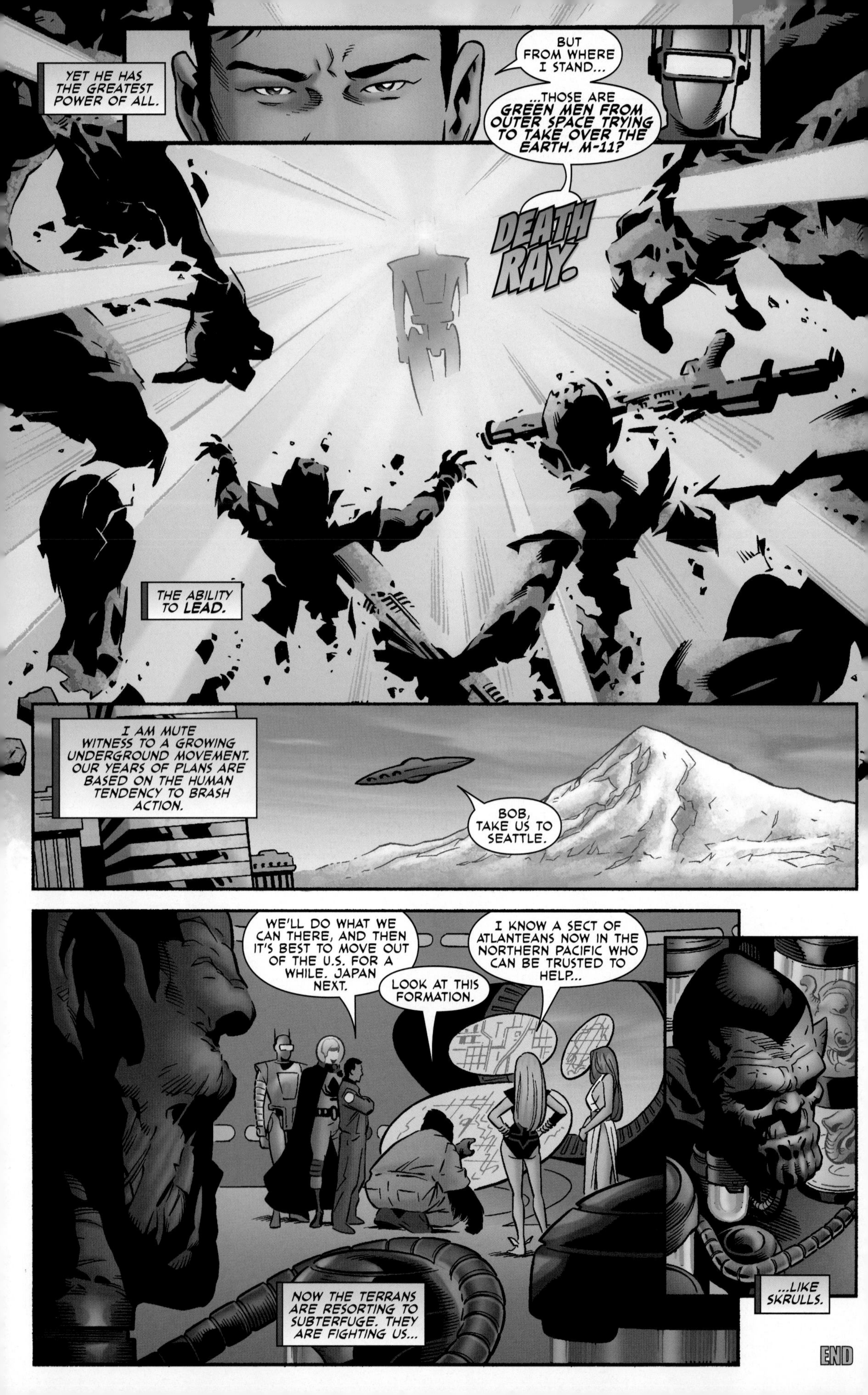
YET HE HAS THE GREATEST POWER OF ALL.
BUT FROM WHERE I STAND...
...THOSE ARE GREEN MEN FROM OUTER SPACE TRYING TO TAKE OVER THE EARTH. M-11?
DEATH RAY.
THE ABILITY TO LEAD.
I AM MUTE WITNESS TO A GROWING UNDERGROUND MOVEMENT. OUR YEARS OF PLANS ARE BASED ON THE HUMAN TENDENCY TO BRASH ACTION.
BOB, TAKE US TO SEATTLE.
WE'LL DO WHAT WE CAN THERE, AND THEN IT'S BEST TO MOVE OUT OF THE U.S. FOR A WHILE. JAPAN NEXT.
LOOK AT THIS FORMATION.
I KNOW A SECT OF ATLANTEANS NOW IN THE NORTHERN PACIFIC WHO CAN BE TRUSTED TO HELP...
NOW THE TERRANS ARE RESORTING TO SUBTERFUGE. THEY ARE FIGHTING US...
...LIKE SKRULLS.
END

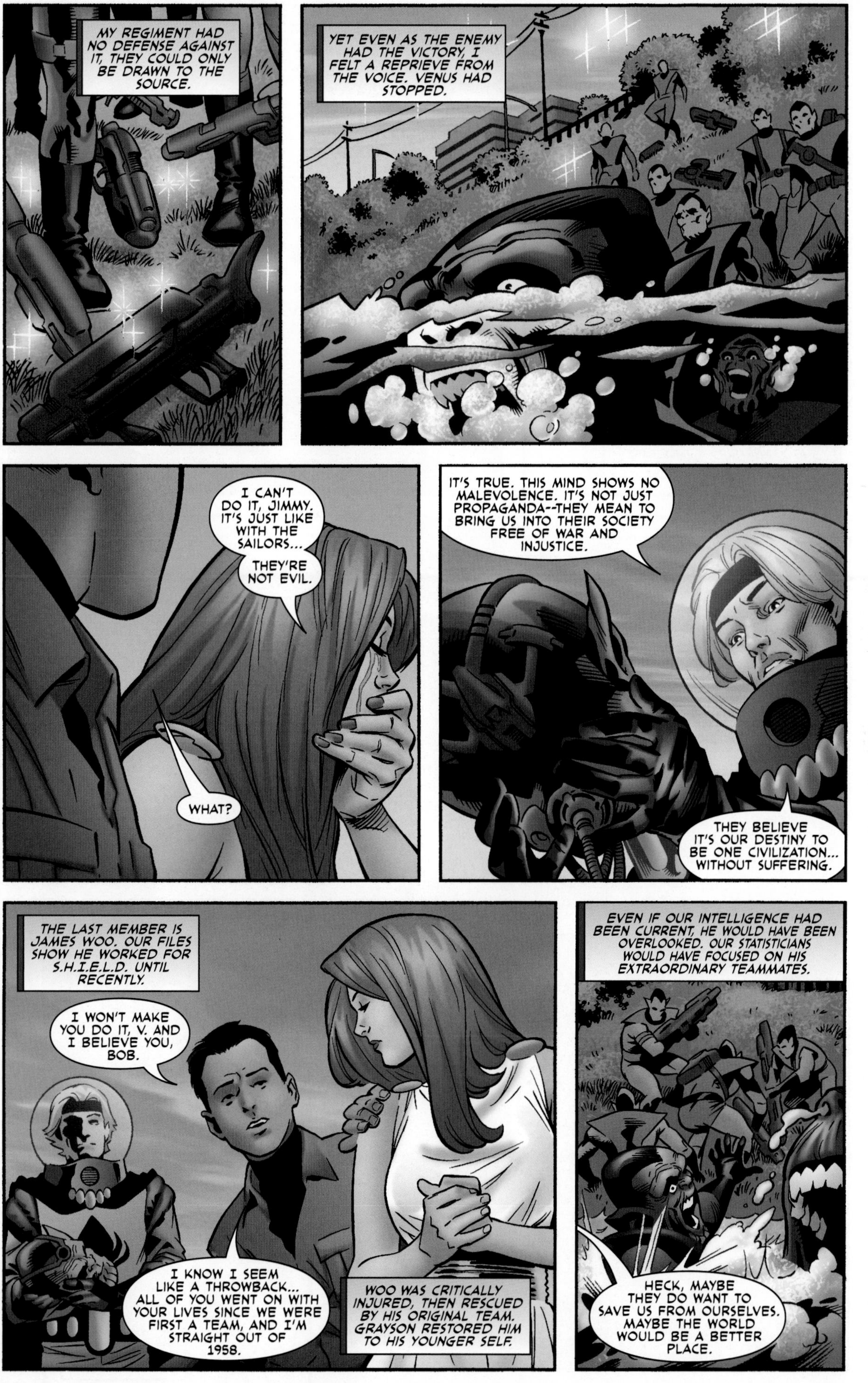
MY REGIMENT HAD NO DEFENSE AGAINST IT, THEY COULD ONLY BE DRAWN TO THE SOURCE.
YET EVEN AS THE ENEMY HAD THE VICTORY, I FELT A REPRIEVE FROM THE VOICE. VENUS HAD STOPPED.
I CAN'T DO IT, JIMMY. IT'S JUST LIKE WITH THE SAILORS...
THEY'RE NOT EVIL.
WHAT?
IT'S TRUE. THIS MIND SHOWS NO MALEVOLENCE. IT'S NOT JUST PROPAGANDA--THEY MEAN TO BRING US INTO THEIR SOCIETY FREE OF WAR AND INJUSTICE.
THEY BELIEVE IT'S OUR DESTINY TO BE ONE CIVILIZATION... WITHOUT SUFFERING.
THE LAST MEMBER IS JAMES WOO. OUR FILES SHOW HE WORKED FOR S.H.I.E.L.D. UNTIL RECENTLY.
I WON'T MAKE YOU DO IT, V. AND I BELIEVE YOU, BOB.
I KNOW I SEEM LIKE A THROWBACK... ALL OF YOU WENT ON WITH YOUR LIVES SINCE WE WERE FIRST A TEAM, AND I'M STRAIGHT OUT OF 1958.
WOO WAS CRITICALLY INJURED, THEN RESCUED BY HIS ORIGINAL TEAM. GRAYSON RESTORED HIM TO HIS YOUNGER SELF.
EVEN IF OUR INTELLIGENCE HAD BEEN CURRENT, HE WOULD HAVE BEEN OVERLOOKED. OUR STATISTICIANS WOULD HAVE FOCUSED ON HIS EXTRAORDINARY TEAMMATES.
HECK, MAYBE THEY DO WANT TO SAVE US FROM OURSELVES. MAYBE THE WORLD WOULD BE A BETTER PLACE.

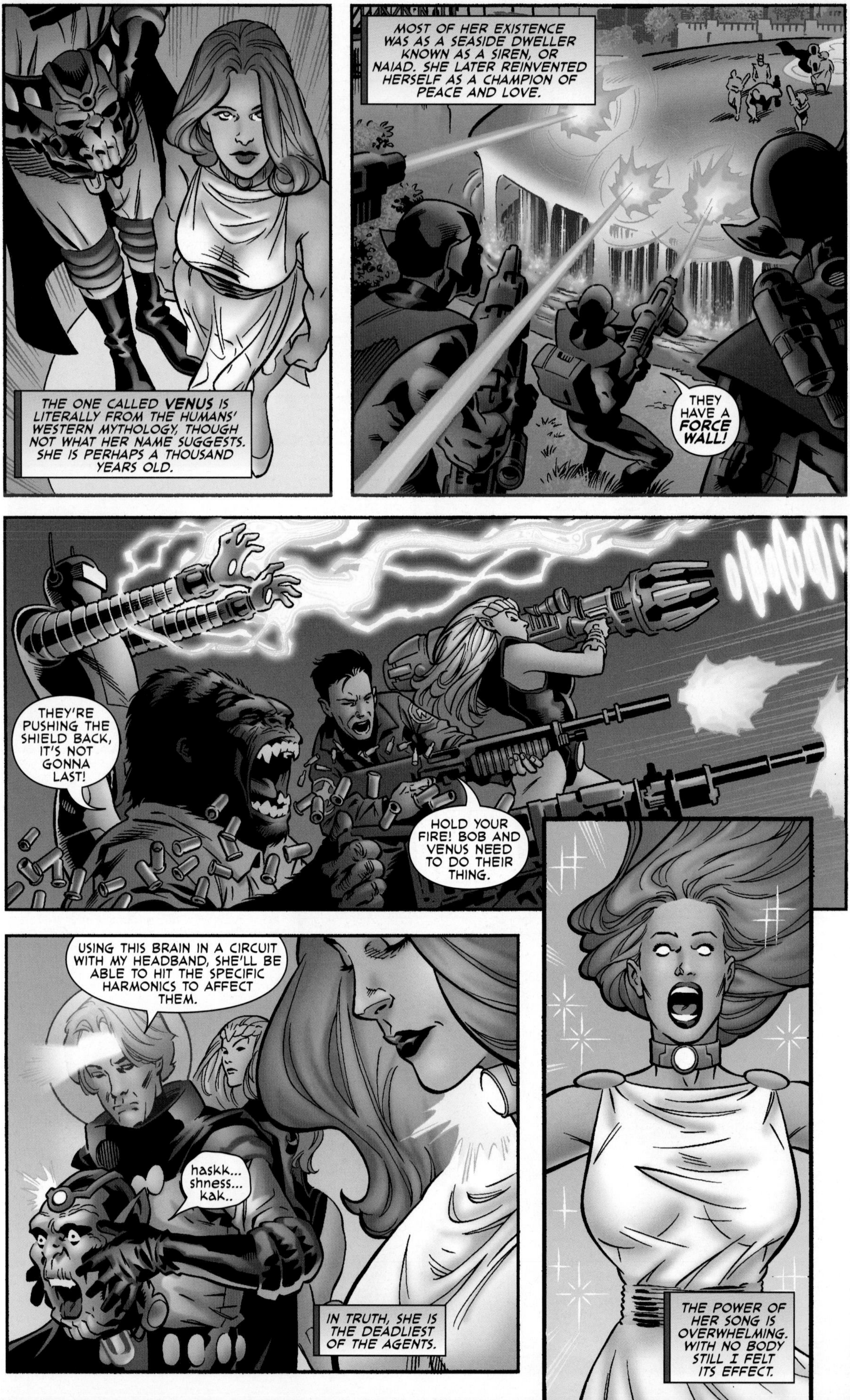
THE ONE CALLED VENUS IS LITERALLY FROM THE HUMANS' WESTERN MYTHOLOGY, THOUGH NOT WHAT HER NAME SUGGESTS. SHE IS PERHAPS A THOUSAND YEARS OLD.
MOST OF HER EXISTENCE WAS AS A SEASIDE DWELLER KNOWN AS A SIREN, OR NAIAD. SHE LATER REINVENTED HERSELF AS A CHAMPION OF PEACE AND LOVE.
THEY HAVE A FORCE WALL!
THEY'RE PUSHING THE SHIELD BACK, IT'S NOT GONNA LAST!
HOLD YOUR FIRE! BOB AND VENUS NEED TO DO THEIR THING.
USING THIS BRAIN IN A CIRCUIT WITH MY HEADBAND, SHE'LL BE ABLE TO HIT THE SPECIFIC HARMONICS TO AFFECT THEM.
haskk... shness... kak..
IN TRUTH, SHE IS THE DEADLIEST OF THE AGENTS.
THE POWER OF HER SONG IS OVERWHELMING. WITH NO BODY STILL I FELT ITS EFFECT.

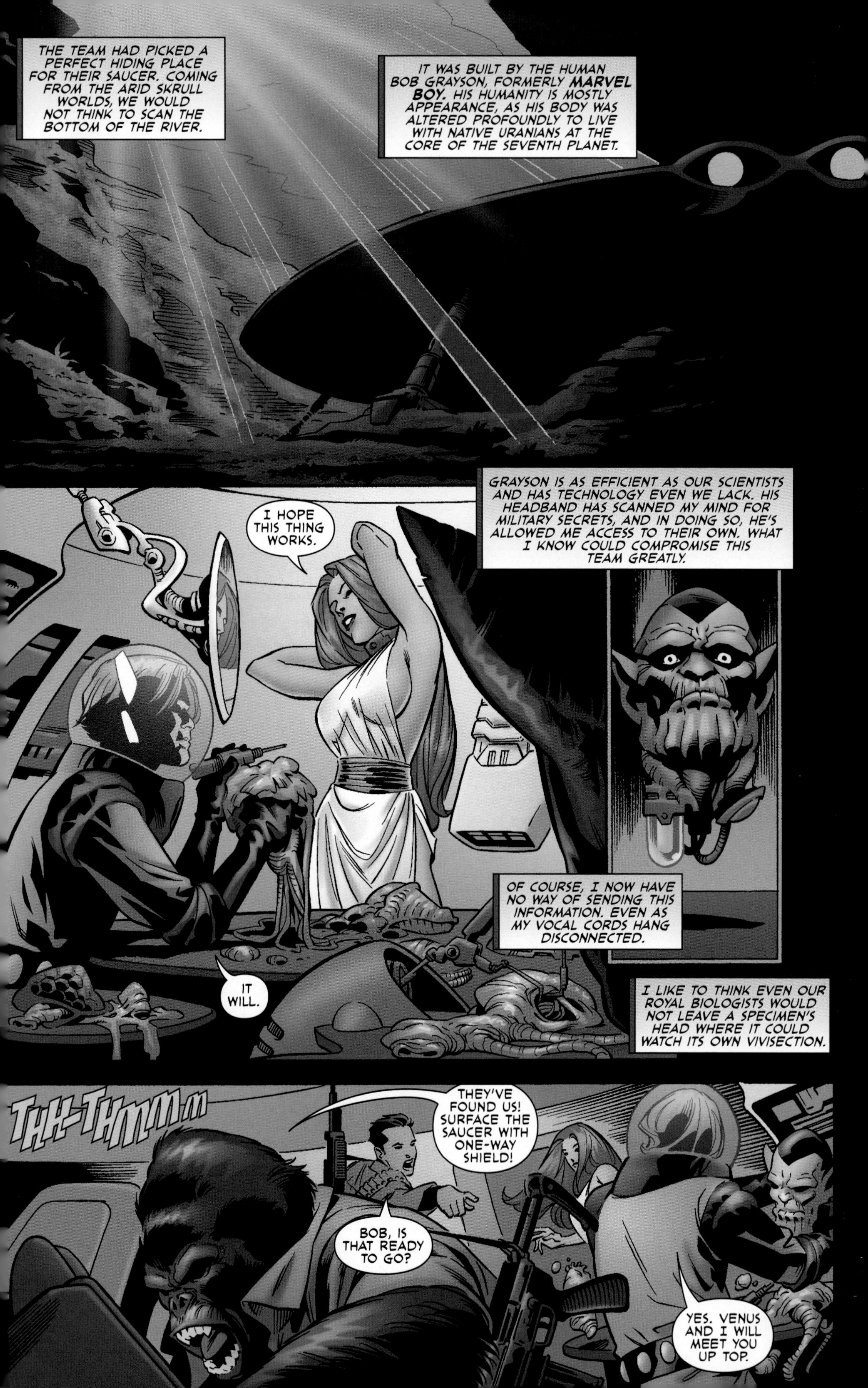
THE TEAM HAD PICKED A PERFECT HIDING PLACE FOR THEIR SAUCER. COMING FROM THE ARID SKRULL WORLDS, WE WOULD NOT THINK TO SCAN THE BOTTOM OF THE RIVER.
IT WAS BUILT BY THE HUMAN BOB GRAYSON, FORMERLY MARVEL BOY. HIS HUMANITY IS MOSTLY APPEARANCE, AS HIS BODY WAS ALTERED PROFOUNDLY TO LIVE WITH NATIVE URANIANS AT THE CORE OF THE SEVENTH PLANET.
I HOPE THIS THING WORKS.
GRAYSON IS AS EFFICIENT AS OUR SCIENTISTS AND HAS TECHNOLOGY EVEN WE LACK. HIS HEADBAND HAS SCANNED MY MIND FOR MILITARY SECRETS, AND IN DOING SO, HE'S ALLOWED ME ACCESS TO THEIR OWN. WHAT I KNOW COULD COMPROMISE THIS TEAM GREATLY.
OF COURSE, I NOW HAVE NO WAY OF SENDING THIS INFORMATION. EVEN AS MY VOCAL CORDS HANG DISCONNECTED.
IT WILL.
I LIKE TO THINK EVEN OUR ROYAL BIOLOGISTS WOULD NOT LEAVE A SPECIMEN'S HEAD WHERE IT COULD WATCH ITS OWN VIVISECTION.
THH-THMMM
THEY'VE FOUND US! SURFACE THE SAUCER WITH ONE-WAY SHIELD!
BOB, IS THAT READY TO GO?
YES. VENUS AND I WILL MEET YOU UP TOP.

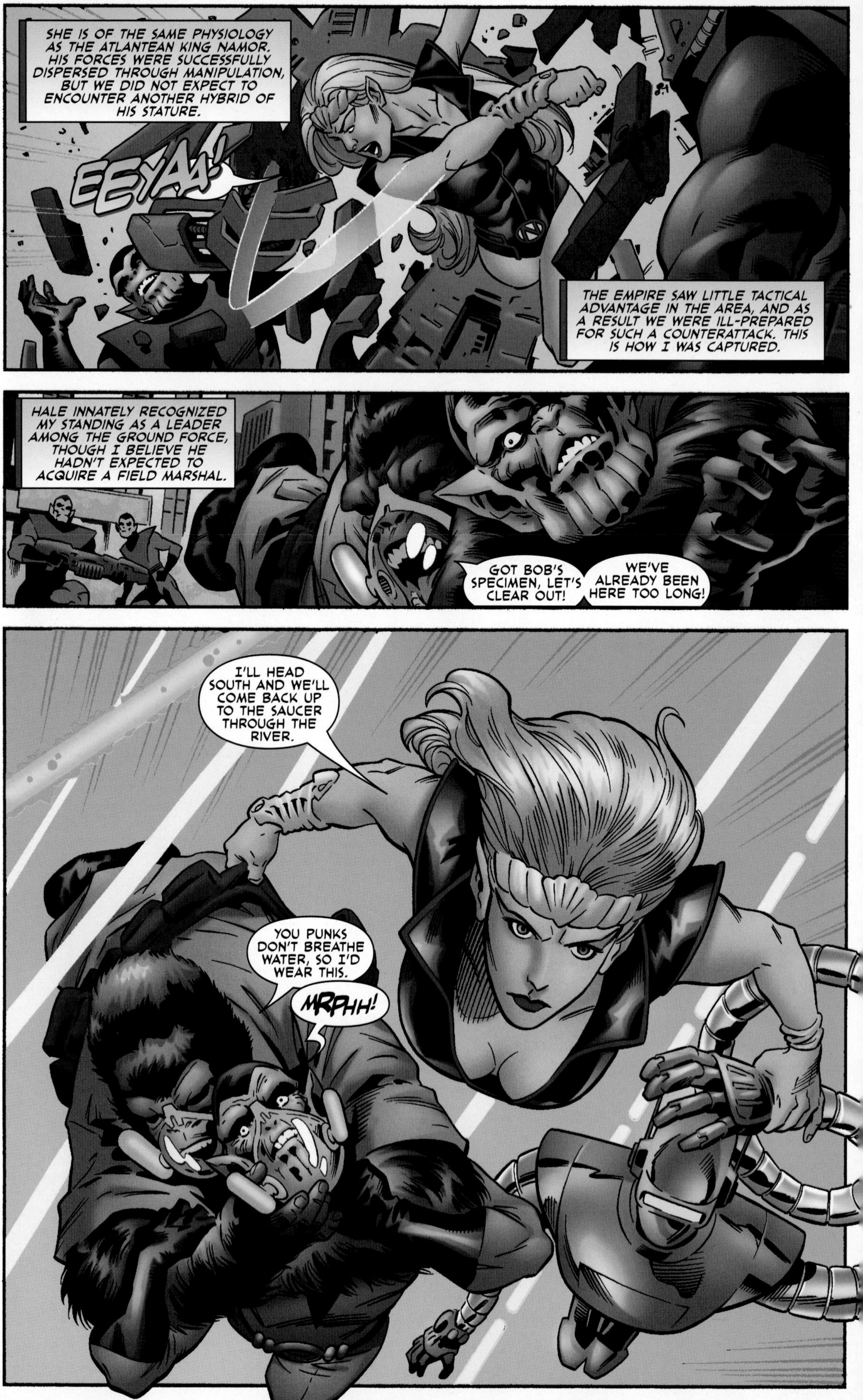
SHE IS OF THE SAME PHYSIOLOGY AS THE ATLANTEAN KING NAMOR. HIS FORCES WERE SUCCESSFULLY DISPERSED THROUGH MANIPULATION, BUT WE DID NOT EXPECT TO ENCOUNTER ANOTHER HYBRID OF HIS STATURE.
EEYAA!
THE EMPIRE SAW LITTLE TACTICAL ADVANTAGE IN THE AREA, AND AS A RESULT WE WERE ILL-PREPARED FOR SUCH A COUNTERATTACK. THIS IS HOW I WAS CAPTURED.
HALE INNATELY RECOGNIZED MY STANDING AS A LEADER AMONG THE GROUND FORCE, THOUGH I BELIEVE HE HADN'T EXPECTED TO ACQUIRE A FIELD MARSHAL.
GOT BOB'S SPECIMEN, LET'S CLEAR OUT!
WE'VE ALREADY BEEN HERE TOO LONG!
I'LL HEAD SOUTH AND WE'LL COME BACK UP TO THE SAUCER THROUGH THE RIVER.
YOU PUNKS DON'T BREATHE WATER, SO I'D WEAR THIS.
MRPHH!

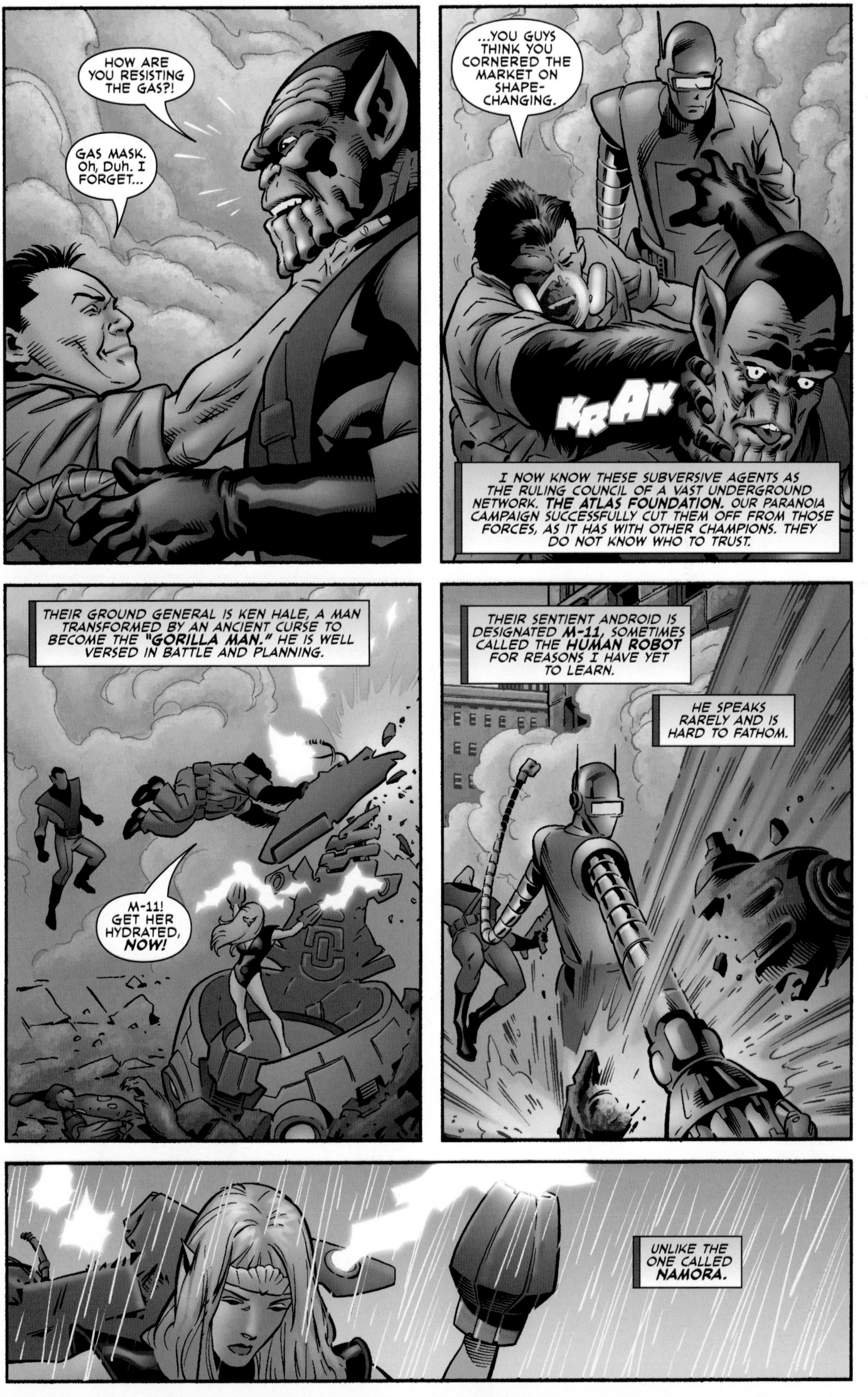
HOW ARE YOU RESISTING THE GAS?!
GAS MASK. Oh, Duh. I FORGET...
...YOU GUYS THINK YOU CORNERED THE MARKET ON SHAPE-CHANGING.
KRAK
I NOW KNOW THESE SUBVERSIVE AGENTS AS THE RULING COUNCIL OF A VAST UNDERGROUND NETWORK. THE ATLAS FOUNDATION. OUR PARANOIA CAMPAIGN SUCCESSFULLY CUT THEM OFF FROM THOSE FORCES, AS IT HAS WITH OTHER CHAMPIONS. THEY DO NOT KNOW WHO TO TRUST.
THEIR GROUND GENERAL IS KEN HALE, A MAN TRANSFORMED BY AN ANCIENT CURSE TO BECOME THE "GORILLA MAN." HE IS WELL VERSED IN BATTLE AND PLANNING.
M-11! GET HER HYDRATED, NOW!
THEIR SENTIENT ANDROID IS DESIGNATED M-11, SOMETIMES CALLED THE HUMAN ROBOT FOR REASONS I HAVE YET TO LEARN.
HE SPEAKS RARELY AND IS HARD TO FATHOM.
UNLIKE THE ONE CALLED NAMORA.

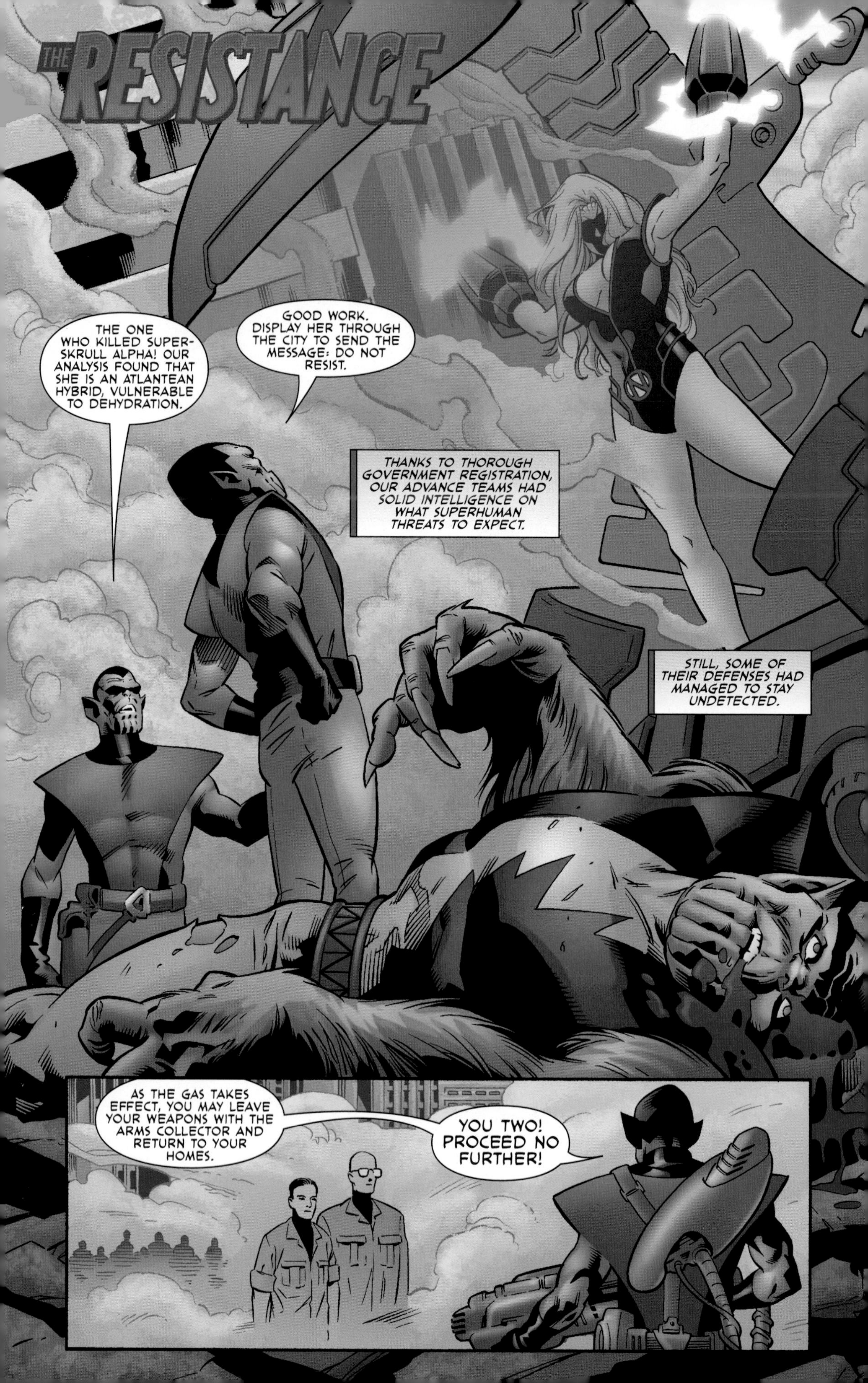
THE RESISTANCE
THE ONE WHO KILLED SUPER-SKRULL ALPHA! OUR ANALYSIS FOUND THAT SHE IS AN ATLANTEAN HYBRID, VULNERABLE TO DEHYDRATION.
GOOD WORK. DISPLAY HER THROUGH THE CITY TO SEND THE MESSAGE: DO NOT RESIST.
THANKS TO THOROUGH GOVERNMENT REGISTRATION, OUR ADVANCE TEAMS HAD SOLID INTELLIGENCE ON WHAT SUPERHUMAN THREATS TO EXPECT.
STILL, SOME OF THEIR DEFENSES HAD MANAGED TO STAY UNDETECTED.
AS THE GAS TAKES EFFECT, YOU MAY LEAVE YOUR WEAPONS WITH THE ARMS COLLECTOR AND RETURN TO YOUR HOMES.
YOU TWO! PROCEED NO FURTHER!

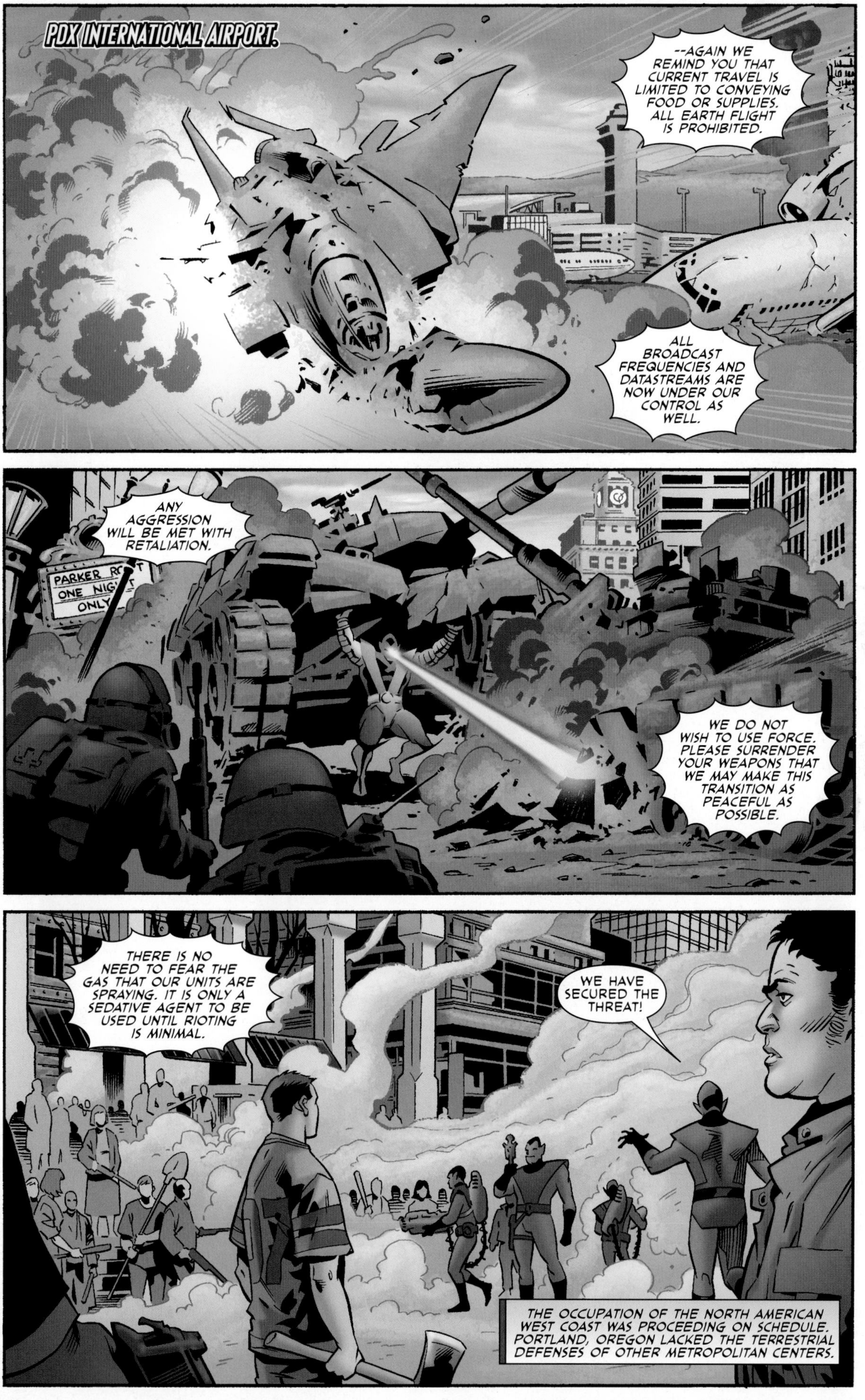
PDX INTERNATIONAL AIRPORT.
--AGAIN WE REMIND YOU THAT CURRENT TRAVEL IS LIMITED TO CONVEYING FOOD OR SUPPLIES. ALL EARTH FLIGHT IS PROHIBITED.
ALL BROADCAST FREQUENCIES AND DATASTREAMS ARE NOW UNDER OUR CONTROL AS WELL.
ANY AGGRESSION WILL BE MET WITH RETALIATION.
PARKER RO T
ONE NIG
ONLY
WE DO NOT WISH TO USE FORCE. PLEASE SURRENDER YOUR WEAPONS THAT WE MAY MAKE THIS TRANSITION AS PEACEFUL AS POSSIBLE.
THERE IS NO NEED TO FEAR THE GAS THAT OUR UNITS ARE SPRAYING. IT IS ONLY A SEDATIVE AGENT TO BE USED UNTIL RIOTING IS MINIMAL.
WE HAVE SECURED THE THREAT!
THE OCCUPATION OF THE NORTH AMERICAN WEST COAST WAS PROCEEDING ON SCHEDULE. PORTLAND, OREGON LACKED THE TERRESTRIAL DEFENSES OF OTHER METROPOLITAN CENTERS.

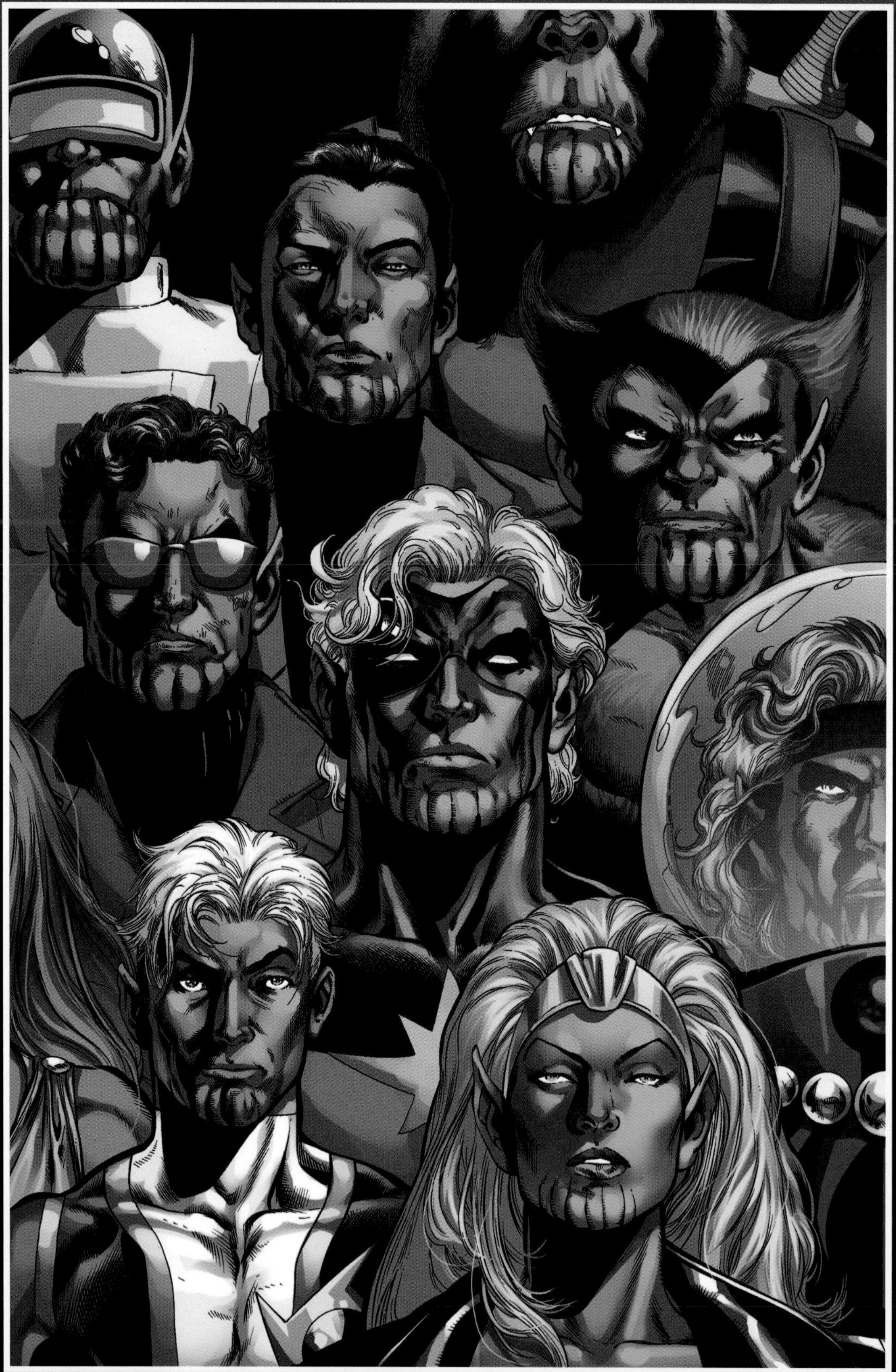

SECRET INVASION: WHO DO YOU TRUST?

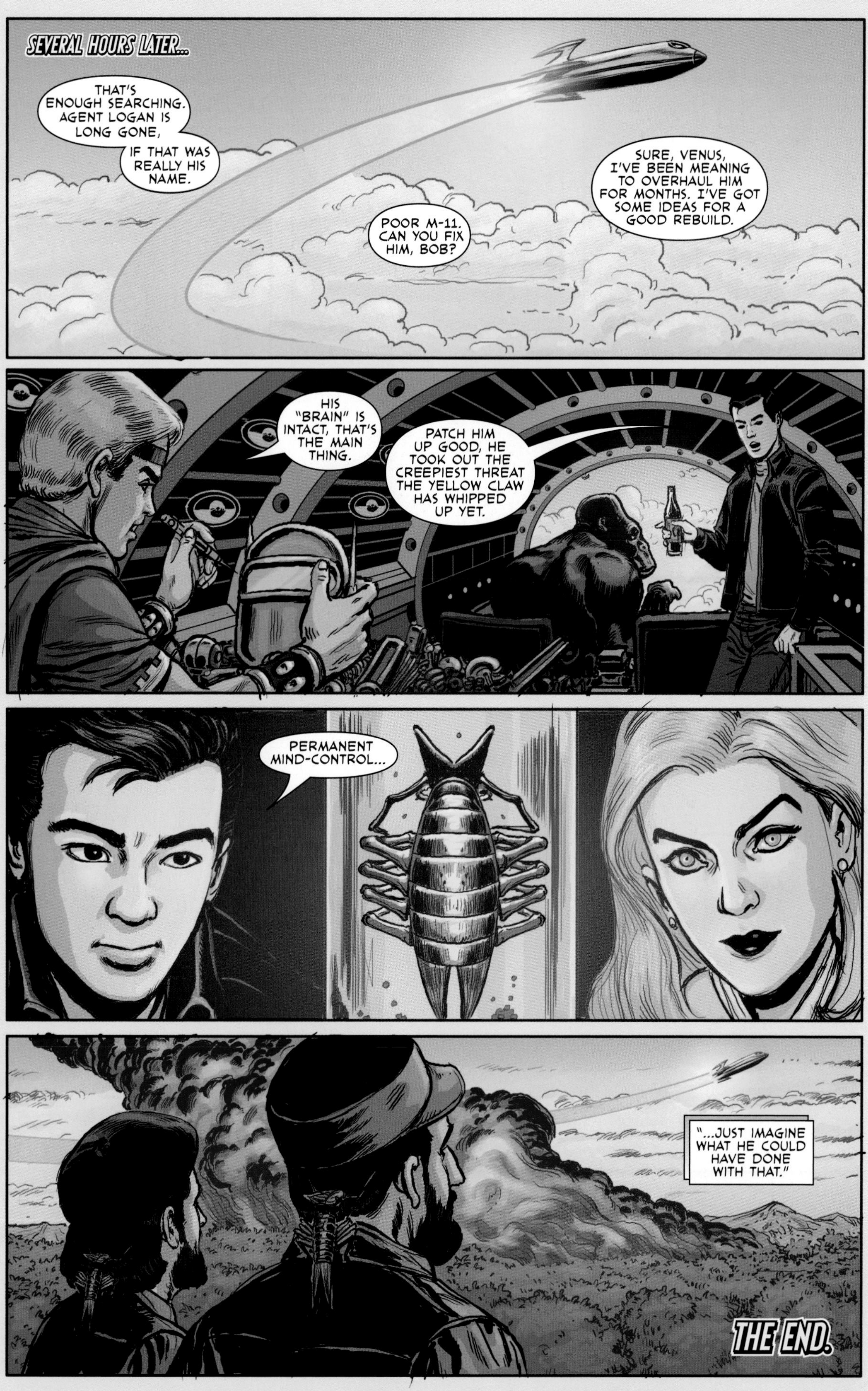
SEVERAL HOURS LATER...
THAT'S ENOUGH SEARCHING. AGENT LOGAN IS LONG GONE,
IF THAT WAS REALLY HIS NAME.
POOR M-11. CAN YOU FIX HIM, BOB?
SURE, VENUS, I'VE BEEN MEANING TO OVERHAUL HIM FOR MONTHS. I'VE GOT SOME IDEAS FOR A GOOD REBUILD.
HIS "BRAIN" IS INTACT, THAT'S THE MAIN THING.
PATCH HIM UP GOOD, HE TOOK OUT THE CREEPIEST THREAT THE YELLOW CLAW HAS WHIPPED UP YET.
PERMANENT MIND-CONTROL...
"...JUST IMAGINE WHAT HE COULD HAVE DONE WITH THAT."
THE END.

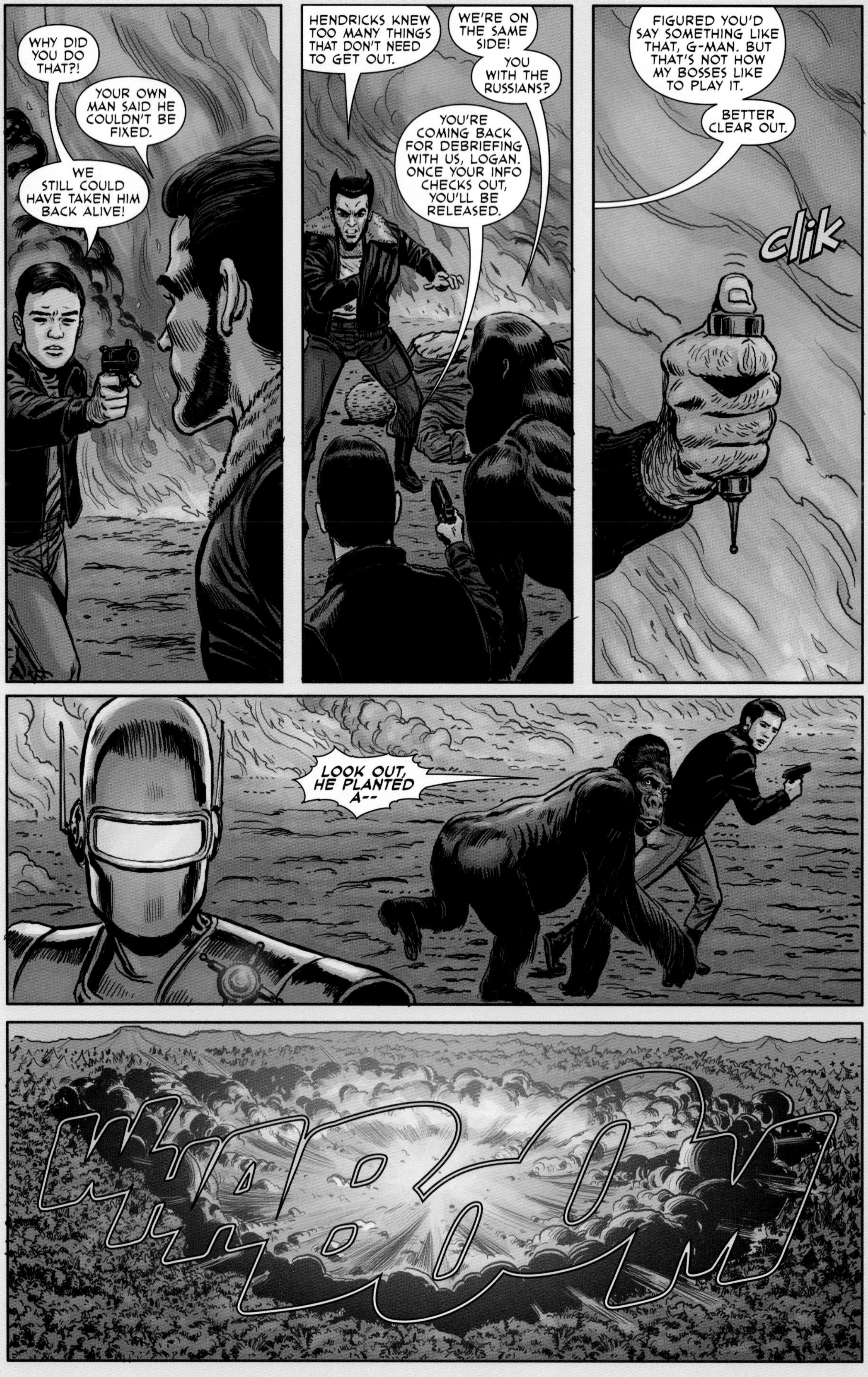
WHY DID YOU DO THAT?!
YOUR OWN MAN SAID HE COULDN'T BE FIXED.
WE STILL COULD HAVE TAKEN HIM BACK ALIVE!
HENDRICKS KNEW TOO MANY THINGS THAT DON'T NEED TO GET OUT.
WE'RE ON THE SAME SIDE!
YOU WITH THE RUSSIANS?
YOU'RE COMING BACK FOR DEBRIEFING WITH US, LOGAN. ONCE YOUR INFO CHECKS OUT, YOU'LL BE RELEASED.
FIGURED YOU'D SAY SOMETHING LIKE THAT, G-MAN. BUT THAT'S NOT HOW MY BOSSES LIKE TO PLAY IT.
BETTER CLEAR OUT.
clik
LOOK OUT, HE PLANTED A--
WHOOM

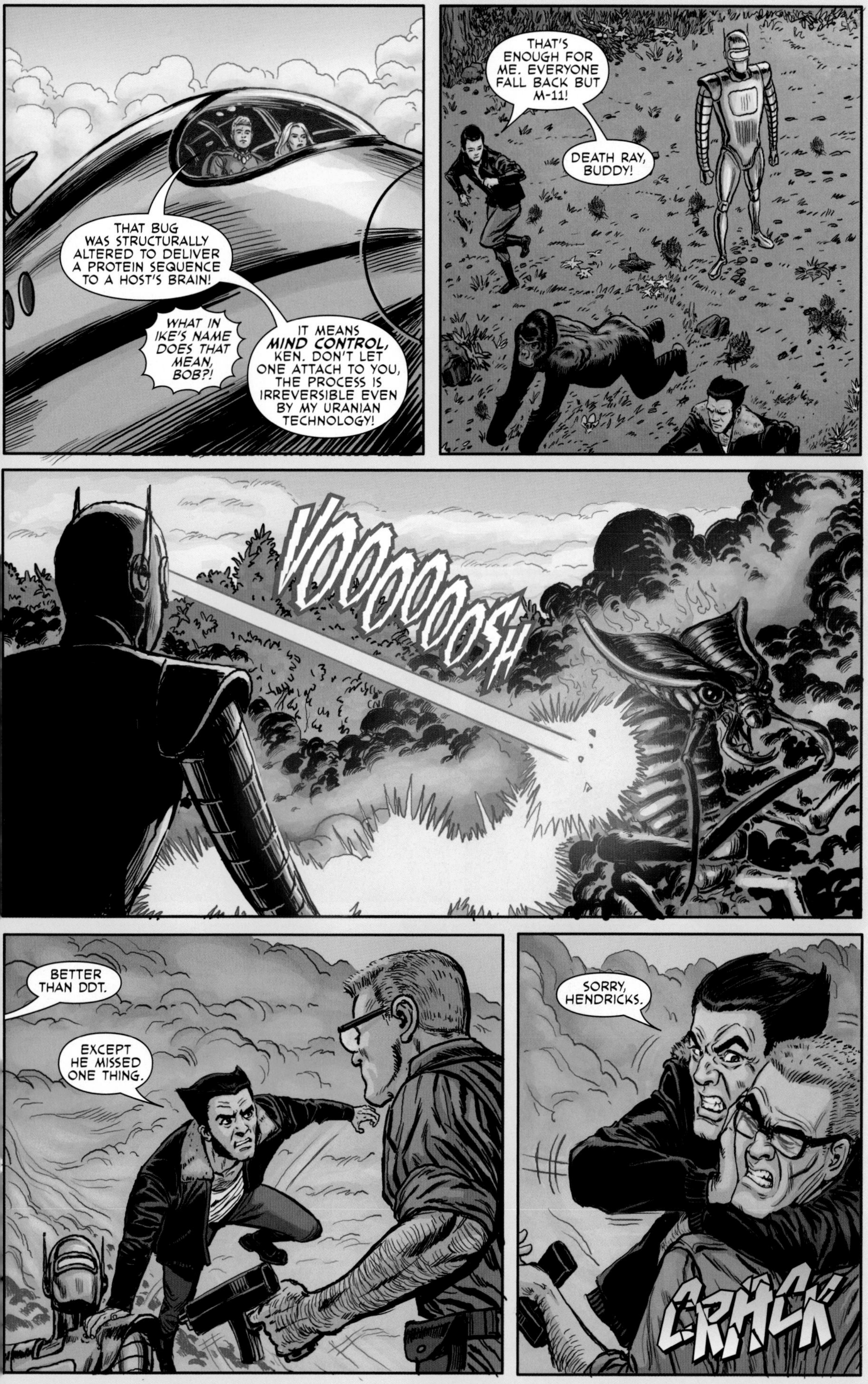
THAT BUG WAS STRUCTURALLY ALTERED TO DELIVER A PROTEIN SEQUENCE TO A HOST'S BRAIN!
WHAT IN IKE'S NAME DOES THAT MEAN, BOB?!
IT MEANS MIND CONTROL, KEN. DON'T LET ONE ATTACH TO YOU, THE PROCESS IS IRREVERSIBLE EVEN BY MY URANIAN TECHNOLOGY!
THAT'S ENOUGH FOR ME. EVERYONE FALL BACK BUT M-11!
DEATH RAY, BUDDY!
VOOOOOOSH
BETTER THAN DDT.
EXCEPT HE MISSED ONE THING.
SORRY, HENDRICKS.
CRACK

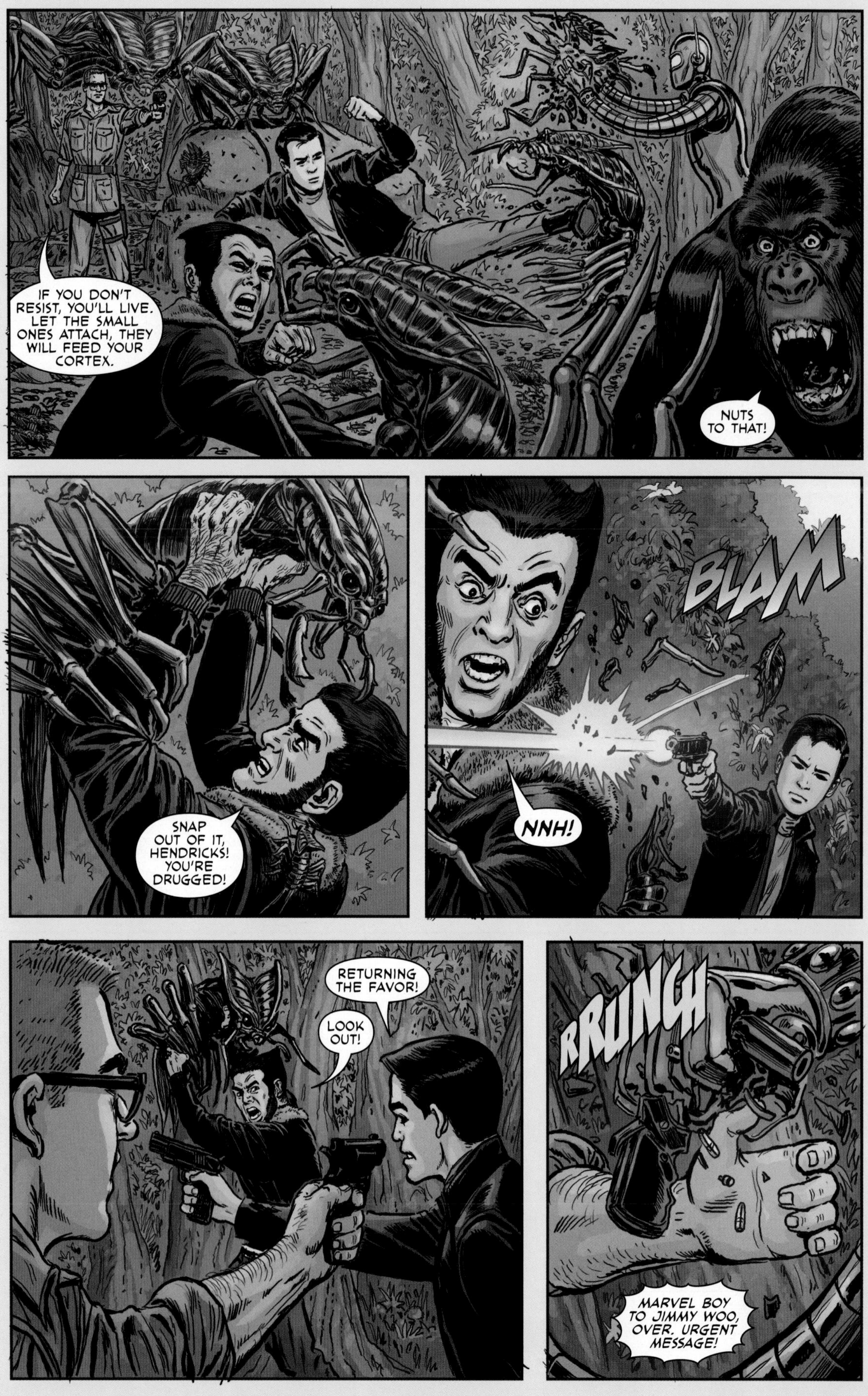
IF YOU DON'T RESIST, YOU'LL LIVE. LET THE SMALL ONES ATTACH, THEY WILL FEED YOUR CORTEX.
NUTS TO THAT!
SNAP OUT OF IT, HENDRICKS! YOU'RE DRUGGED!
BLAM
NNH!
RETURNING THE FAVOR!
LOOK OUT!
RRUNCH
MARVEL BOY TO JIMMY WOO, OVER. URGENT MESSAGE!

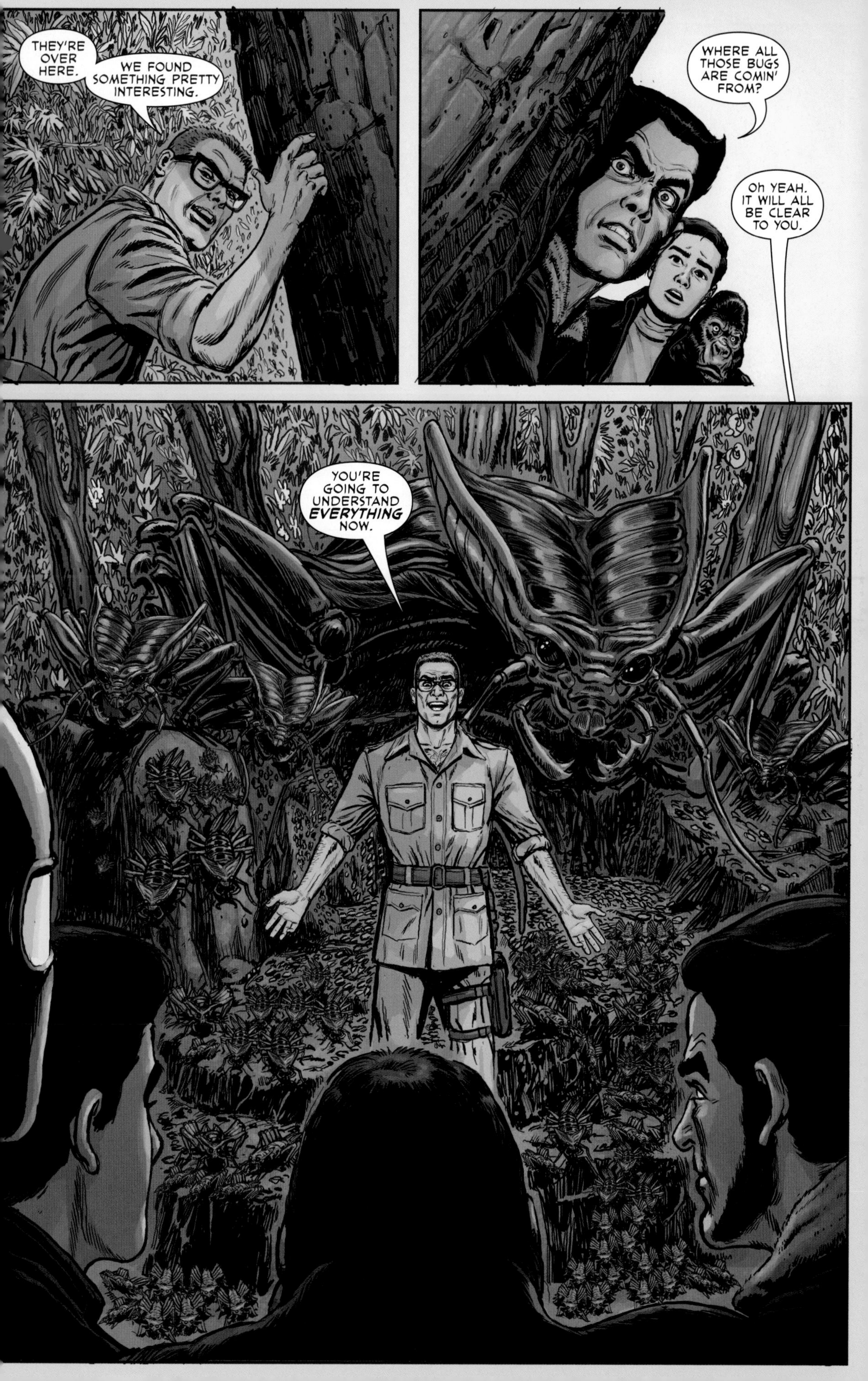
THEY'RE OVER HERE.
WE FOUND SOMETHING PRETTY INTERESTING.
WHERE ALL THOSE BUGS ARE COMIN' FROM?
Oh YEAH. IT WILL ALL BE CLEAR TO YOU.
YOU'RE GOING TO UNDERSTAND EVERYTHING NOW.

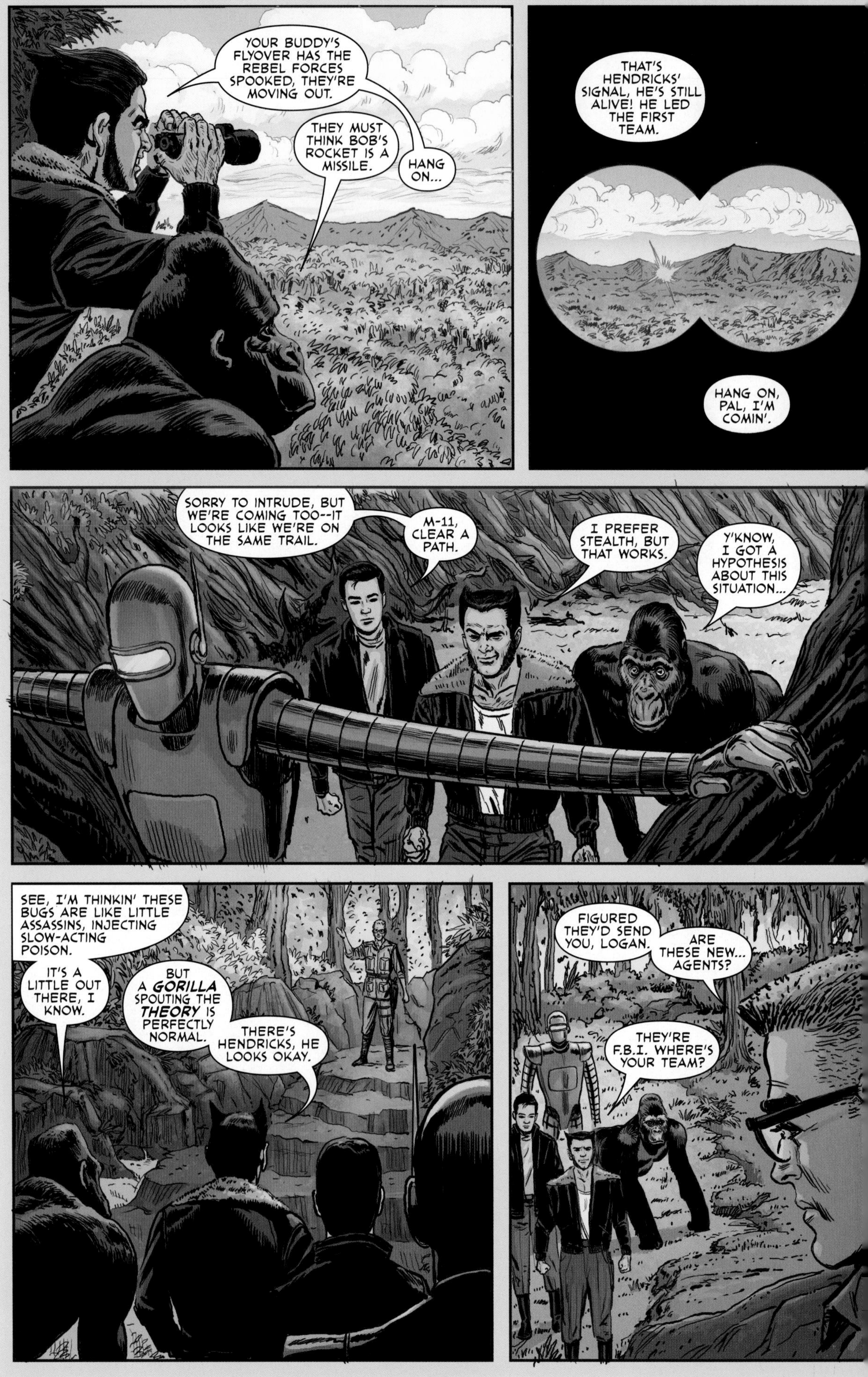
YOUR BUDDY'S FLYOVER HAS THE REBEL FORCES SPOOKED, THEY'RE MOVING OUT.
THEY MUST THINK BOB'S ROCKET IS A MISSILE.
HANG ON...
THAT'S HENDRICKS' SIGNAL, HE'S STILL ALIVE! HE LED THE FIRST TEAM.
HANG ON, PAL, I'M COMIN'.
SORRY TO INTRUDE, BUT WE'RE COMING TOO--IT LOOKS LIKE WE'RE ON THE SAME TRAIL.
M-11, CLEAR A PATH.
I PREFER STEALTH, BUT THAT WORKS.
Y'KNOW, I GOT A HYPOTHESIS ABOUT THIS SITUATION...
SEE, I'M THINKIN' THESE BUGS ARE LIKE LITTLE ASSASSINS, INJECTING SLOW-ACTING POISON.
IT'S A LITTLE OUT THERE, I KNOW.
BUT A **GORILLA** SPOUTING THE **THEORY** IS PERFECTLY NORMAL.
THERE'S HENDRICKS, HE LOOKS OKAY.
FIGURED THEY'D SEND YOU, LOGAN.
ARE THESE NEW... AGENTS?
THEY'RE F.B.I. WHERE'S YOUR TEAM?

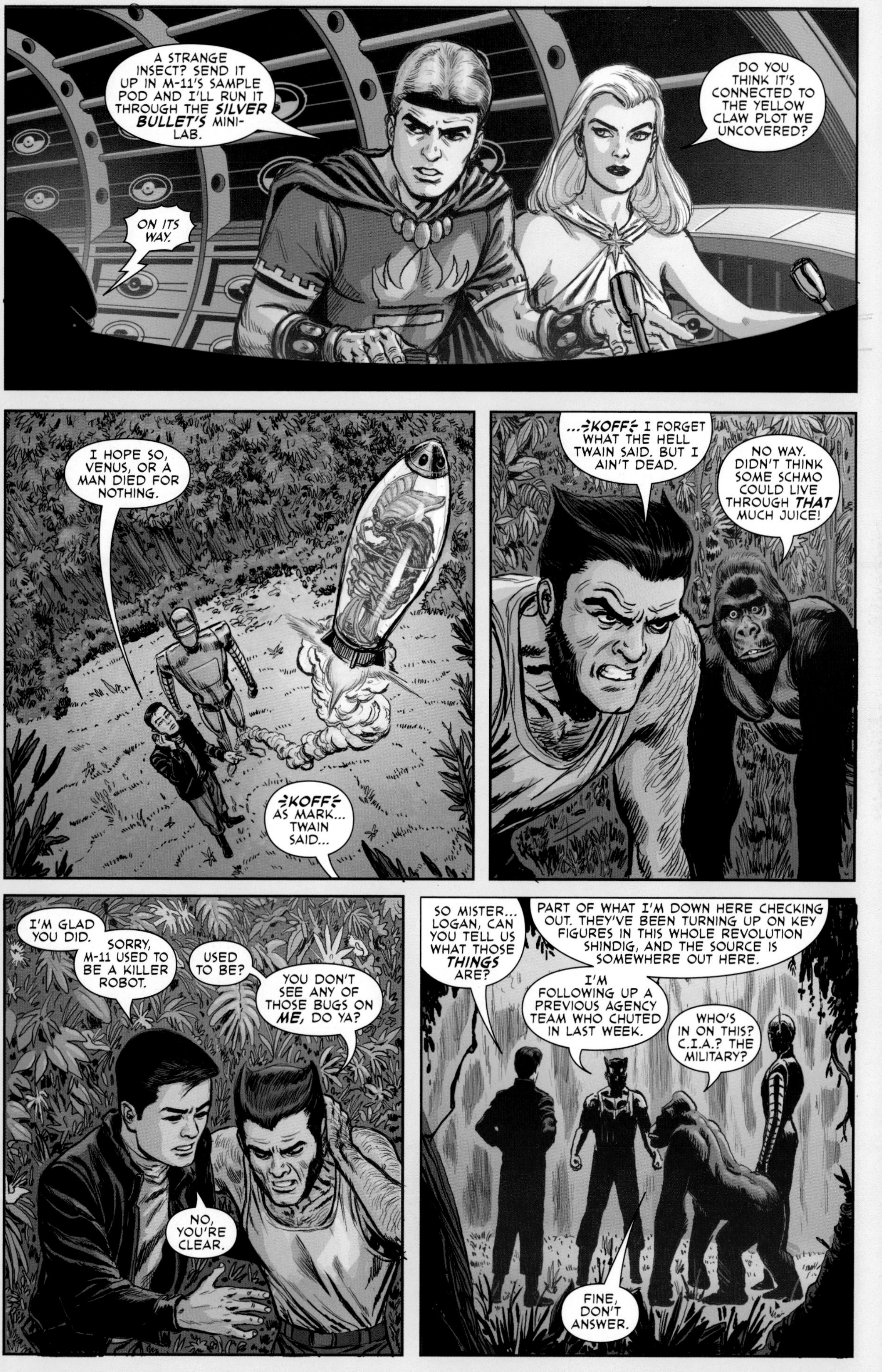
A STRANGE INSECT? SEND IT UP IN M-11'S SAMPLE POD AND I'LL RUN IT THROUGH THE SILVER BULLET'S MINI-LAB.
DO YOU THINK IT'S CONNECTED TO THE YELLOW CLAW PLOT WE UNCOVERED?
ON ITS WAY.
I HOPE SO, VENUS, OR A MAN DIED FOR NOTHING.
KOFF AS MARK... TWAIN SAID...
...KOFF I FORGET WHAT THE HELL TWAIN SAID. BUT I AIN'T DEAD.
NO WAY. DIDN'T THINK SOME SCHMO COULD LIVE THROUGH THAT MUCH JUICE!
I'M GLAD YOU DID.
SORRY, M-11 USED TO BE A KILLER ROBOT.
USED TO BE?
YOU DON'T SEE ANY OF THOSE BUGS ON ME, DO YA?
NO, YOU'RE CLEAR.
SO MISTER... LOGAN, CAN YOU TELL US WHAT THOSE THINGS ARE?
PART OF WHAT I'M DOWN HERE CHECKING OUT. THEY'VE BEEN TURNING UP ON KEY FIGURES IN THIS WHOLE REVOLUTION SHINDIG, AND THE SOURCE IS SOMEWHERE OUT HERE.
I'M FOLLOWING UP A PREVIOUS AGENCY TEAM WHO CHUTED IN LAST WEEK.
WHO'S IN ON THIS? C.I.A.? THE MILITARY?
FINE, DON'T ANSWER.

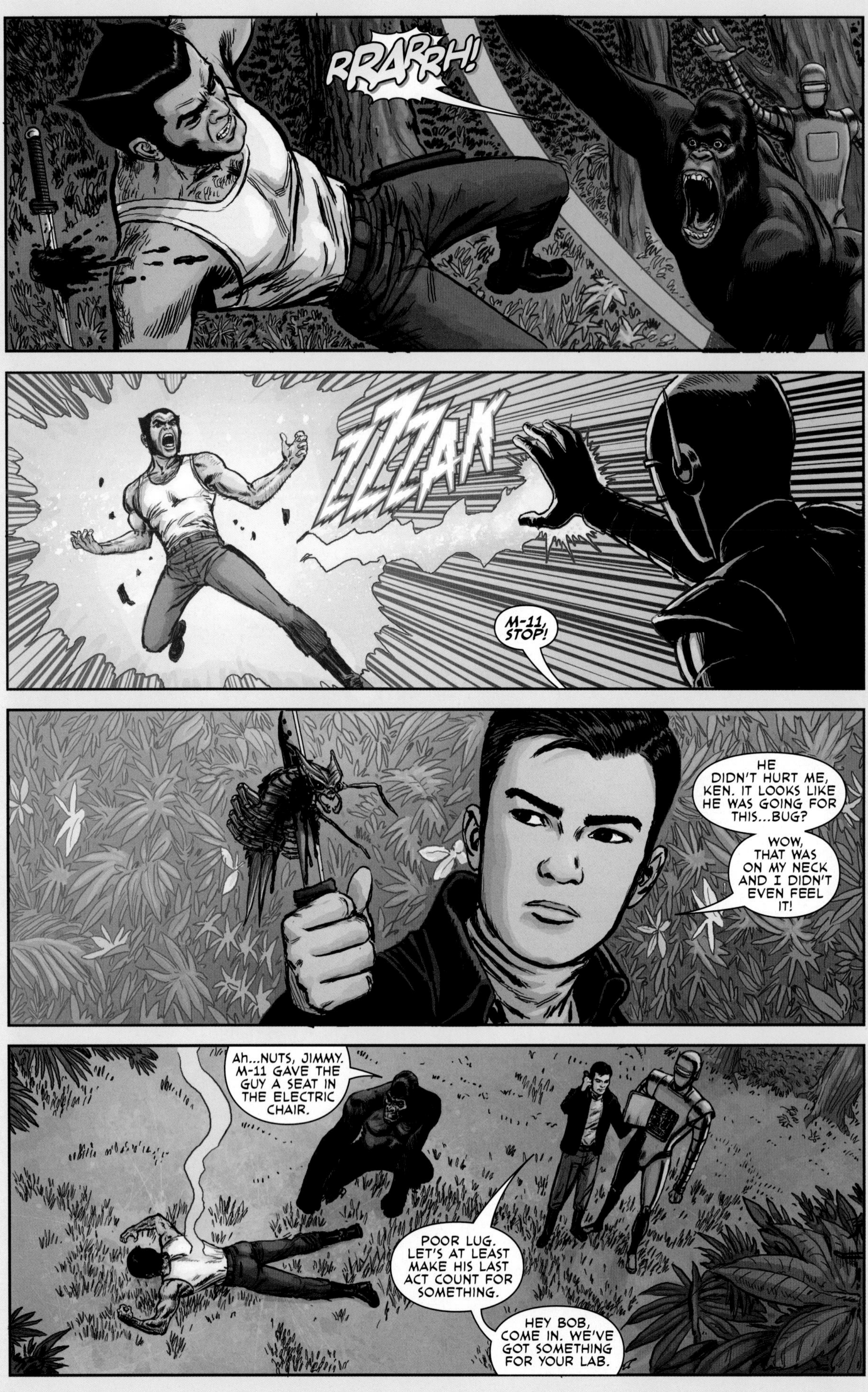
RRARRH!
ZZZZAK
M-11, STOP!
HE DIDN'T HURT ME, KEN. IT LOOKS LIKE HE WAS GOING FOR THIS...BUG?
WOW, THAT WAS ON MY NECK AND I DIDN'T EVEN FEEL IT!
Ah...NUTS, JIMMY. M-11 GAVE THE GUY A SEAT IN THE ELECTRIC CHAIR.
POOR LUG. LET'S AT LEAST MAKE HIS LAST ACT COUNT FOR SOMETHING.
HEY BOB, COME IN. WE'VE GOT SOMETHING FOR YOUR LAB.

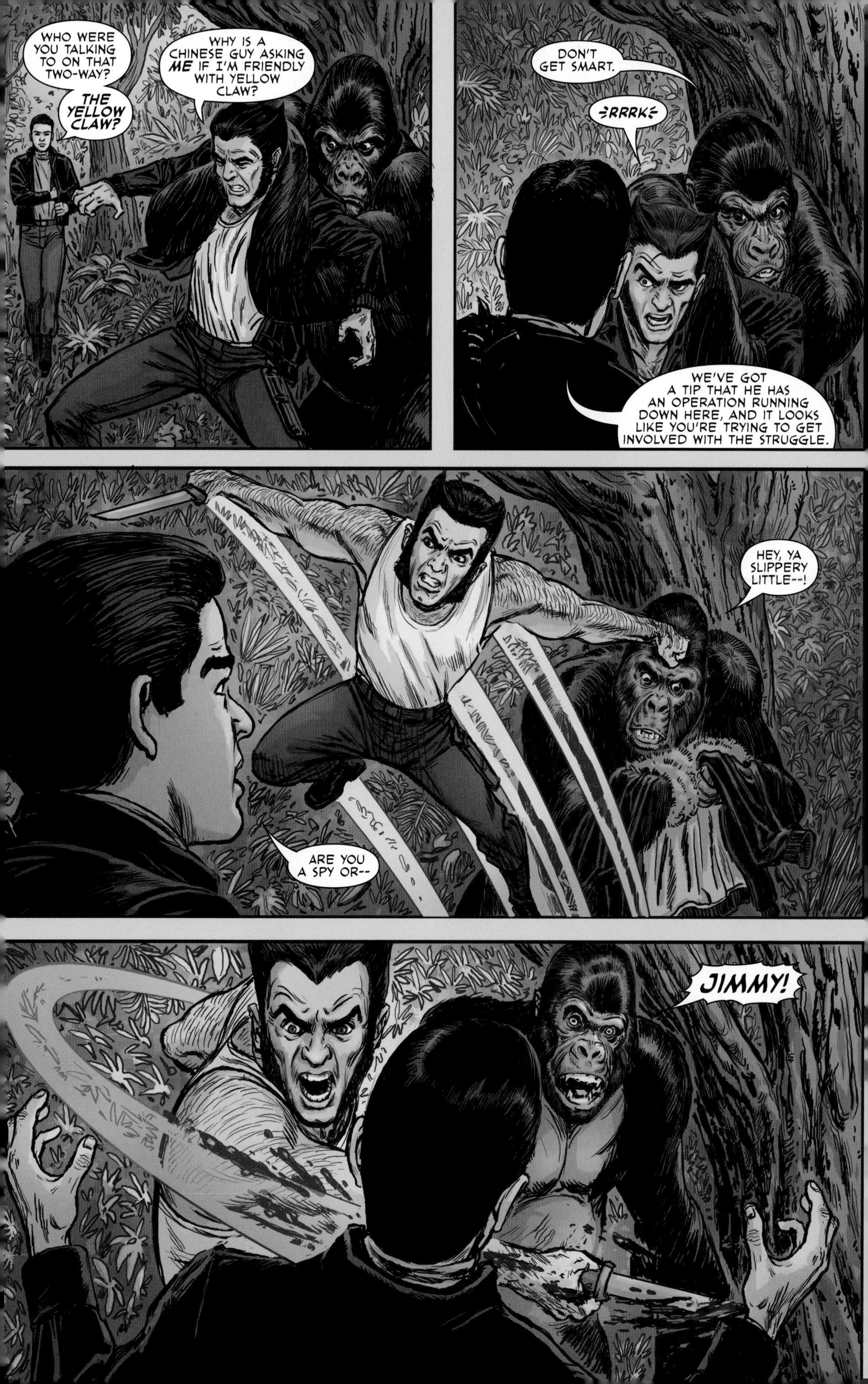
WHO WERE YOU TALKING TO ON THAT TWO-WAY?
THE YELLOW CLAW?
WHY IS A CHINESE GUY ASKING ME IF I'M FRIENDLY WITH YELLOW CLAW?
DON'T GET SMART.
RRRK
WE'VE GOT A TIP THAT HE HAS AN OPERATION RUNNING DOWN HERE, AND IT LOOKS LIKE YOU'RE TRYING TO GET INVOLVED WITH THE STRUGGLE.
HEY, YA SLIPPERY LITTLE--!
ARE YOU A SPY OR--
JIMMY!

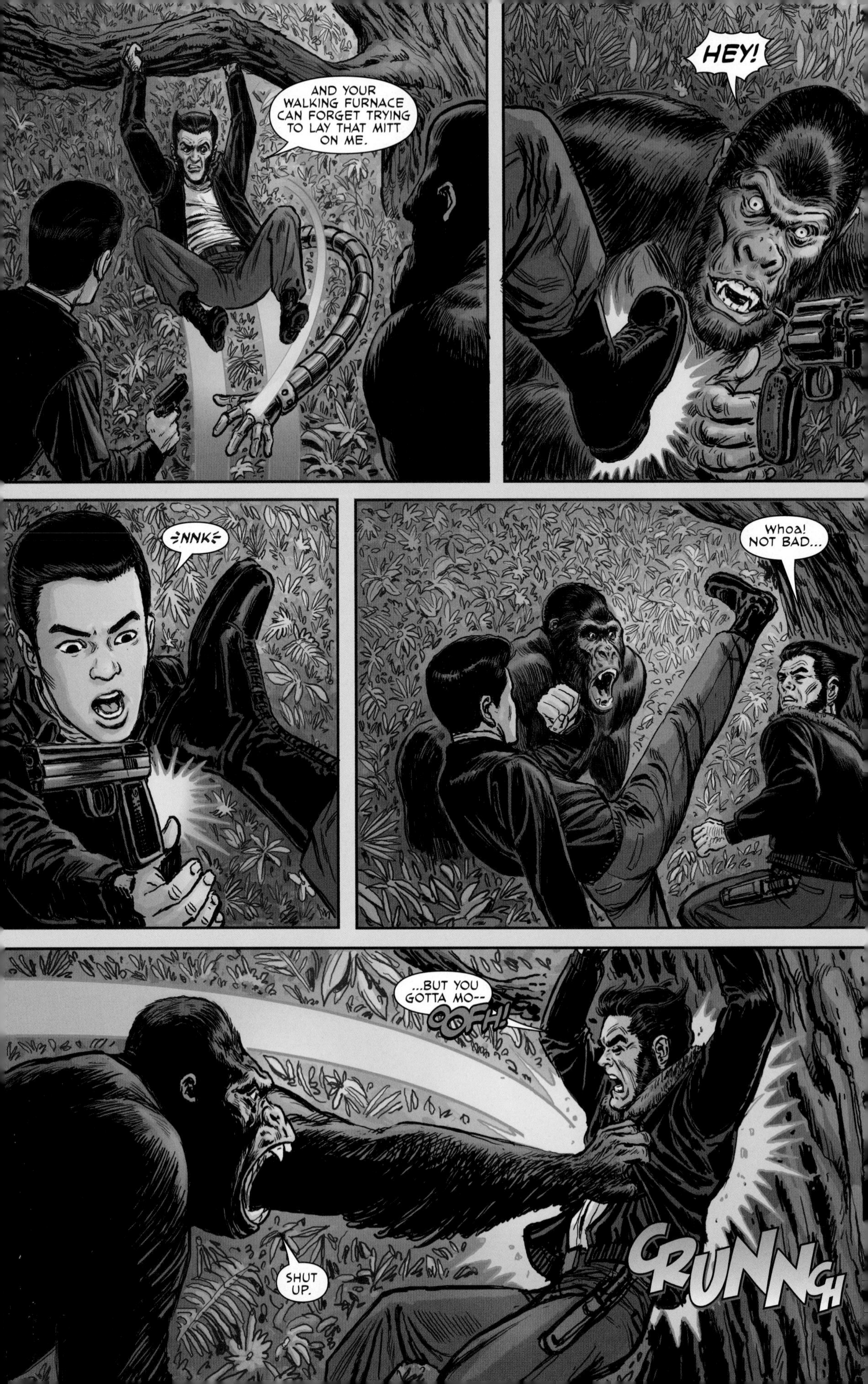
AND YOUR WALKING FURNACE CAN FORGET TRYING TO LAY THAT MITT ON ME.
HEY!
NNK
Whoa! NOT BAD...
...BUT YOU GOTTA MO--
OOFH!
SHUT UP.
CRUNNGH

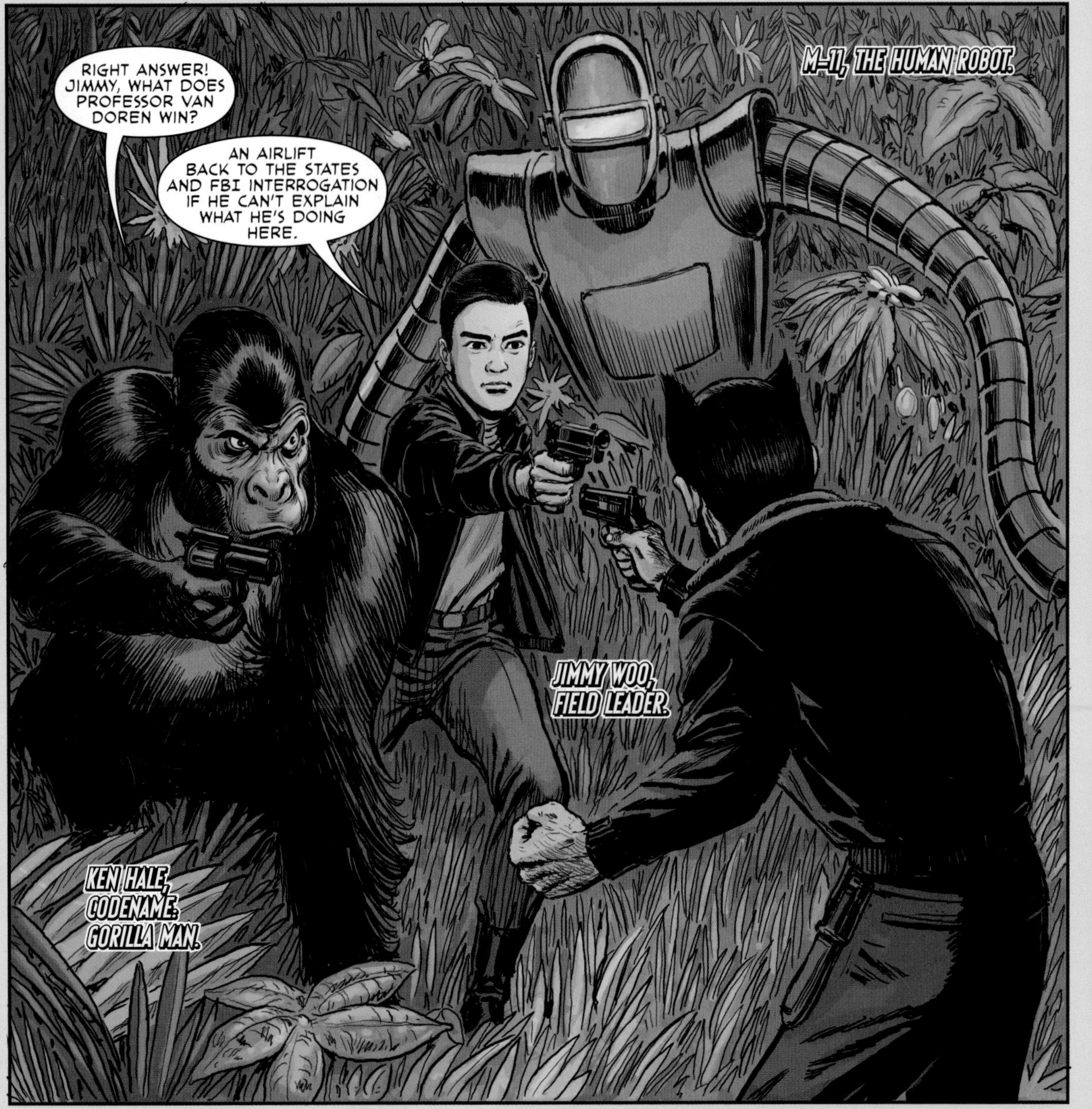

RIGHT ANSWER! JIMMY, WHAT DOES PROFESSOR VAN DOREN WIN?
AN AIRLIFT BACK TO THE STATES AND FBI INTERROGATION IF HE CAN'T EXPLAIN WHAT HE'S DOING HERE.
M-11, THE HUMAN ROBOT.
JIMMY WOO, FIELD LEADER.
KEN HALE, CODENAME: GORILLA MAN.

WOLVERINE AGENT OF ATLAS

WORDS–JEFF PARKER ART–BENTON JEW
COLORS–ELIZABETH DISMANG BREITWEISER
LETTERS–BLAMBOT'S NATE PIEKOS
PRODUCTION–RANDALL MILLER
ASST. EDITORS–COSBY & SANKOVITCH
EDITOR–MARK PANICCIA
EDITOR IN CHIEF–JOE QUESADA
PUBLISHER–DAN BUCKLEY

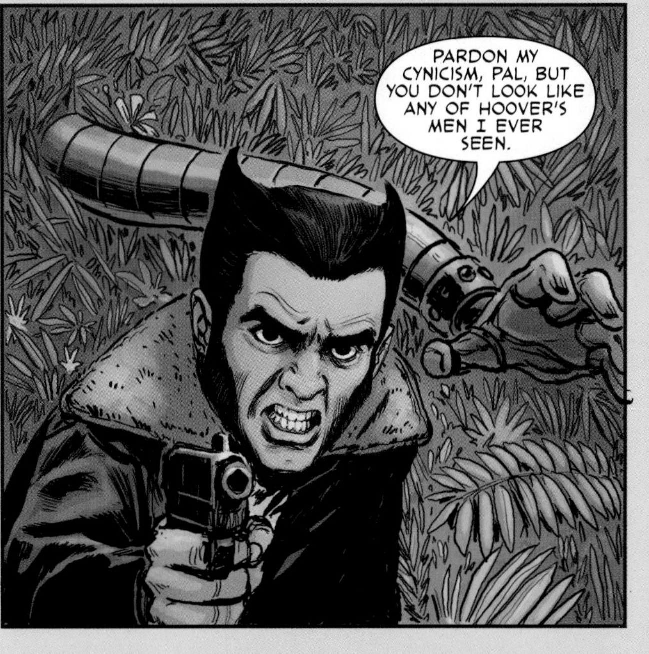

PARDON MY CYNICISM, PAL, BUT YOU DON'T LOOK LIKE ANY OF HOOVER'S MEN I EVER SEEN.

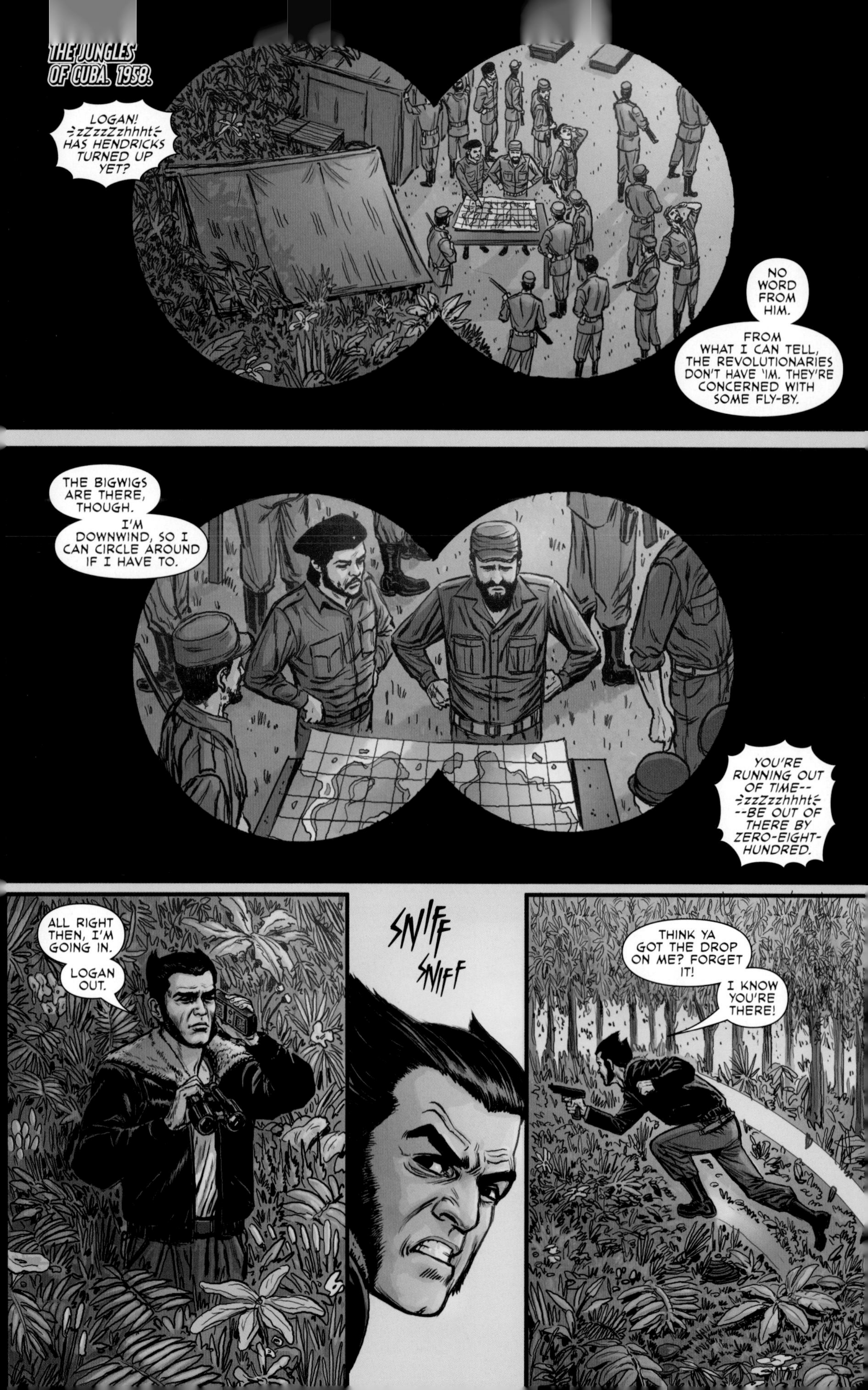
THE JUNGLES OF CUBA. 1958.
LOGAN! zZzzZzhhht HAS HENDRICKS TURNED UP YET?
NO WORD FROM HIM.
FROM WHAT I CAN TELL, THE REVOLUTIONARIES DON'T HAVE 'IM. THEY'RE CONCERNED WITH SOME FLY-BY.
THE BIGWIGS ARE THERE, THOUGH.
I'M DOWNWIND, SO I CAN CIRCLE AROUND IF I HAVE TO.
YOU'RE RUNNING OUT OF TIME-- zzZzzhhht --BE OUT OF THERE BY ZERO-EIGHT-HUNDRED.
ALL RIGHT THEN, I'M GOING IN.
LOGAN OUT.
SNIFF
SNIFF
THINK YA GOT THE DROP ON ME? FORGET IT!
I KNOW YOU'RE THERE!

CLASSIFIED DOCUMENT / FEDERAL BUREAU OF
INVESTIGATION

CASE 7-A / JAMES WOO- HEAD OF WEST COAST SPECIAL
DEPARTMENT ZERO

Transcribed by Agent Angela Wellington,
San Francisco Adjunct

May 3rd, 1958/ CUBA

CLASSIFIED

As with all other transcriptions of Agent Woo's DEPART-
MENT ZERO group, I have received audio recordings from
the automaton known as M-11, supplemented with ac-
counts from the other members of the team. This was
particularly necessary in this instance as M-11's files
are exceptionally unreliable near mission's end, for
causes which will become apparent. Also supplied is
aerial photography from Bob Grayson's craft The Silver
Bullet.

-A. Wellington

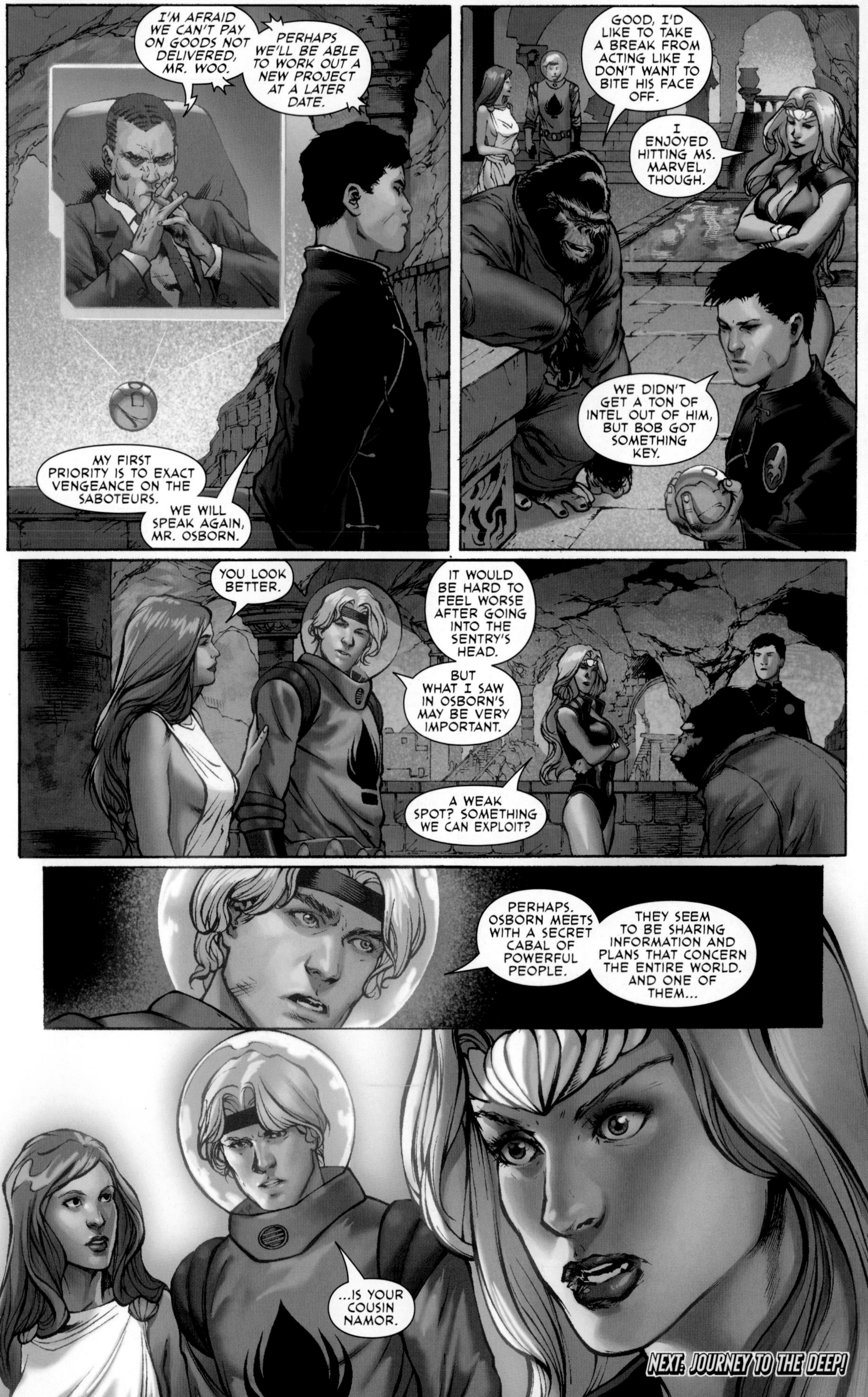
I'M AFRAID WE CAN'T PAY ON GOODS NOT DELIVERED, MR. WOO.
PERHAPS WE'LL BE ABLE TO WORK OUT A NEW PROJECT AT A LATER DATE.
MY FIRST PRIORITY IS TO EXACT VENGEANCE ON THE SABOTEURS.
WE WILL SPEAK AGAIN, MR. OSBORN.
GOOD, I'D LIKE TO TAKE A BREAK FROM ACTING LIKE I DON'T WANT TO BITE HIS FACE OFF.
I ENJOYED HITTING MS. MARVEL, THOUGH.
WE DIDN'T GET A TON OF INTEL OUT OF HIM, BUT BOB GOT SOMETHING KEY.
YOU LOOK BETTER.
IT WOULD BE HARD TO FEEL WORSE AFTER GOING INTO THE SENTRY'S HEAD.
BUT WHAT I SAW IN OSBORN'S MAY BE VERY IMPORTANT.
A WEAK SPOT? SOMETHING WE CAN EXPLOIT?
PERHAPS. OSBORN MEETS WITH A SECRET CABAL OF POWERFUL PEOPLE.
THEY SEEM TO BE SHARING INFORMATION AND PLANS THAT CONCERN THE ENTIRE WORLD. AND ONE OF THEM...
...IS YOUR COUSIN NAMOR.
NEXT: JOURNEY TO THE DEEP!

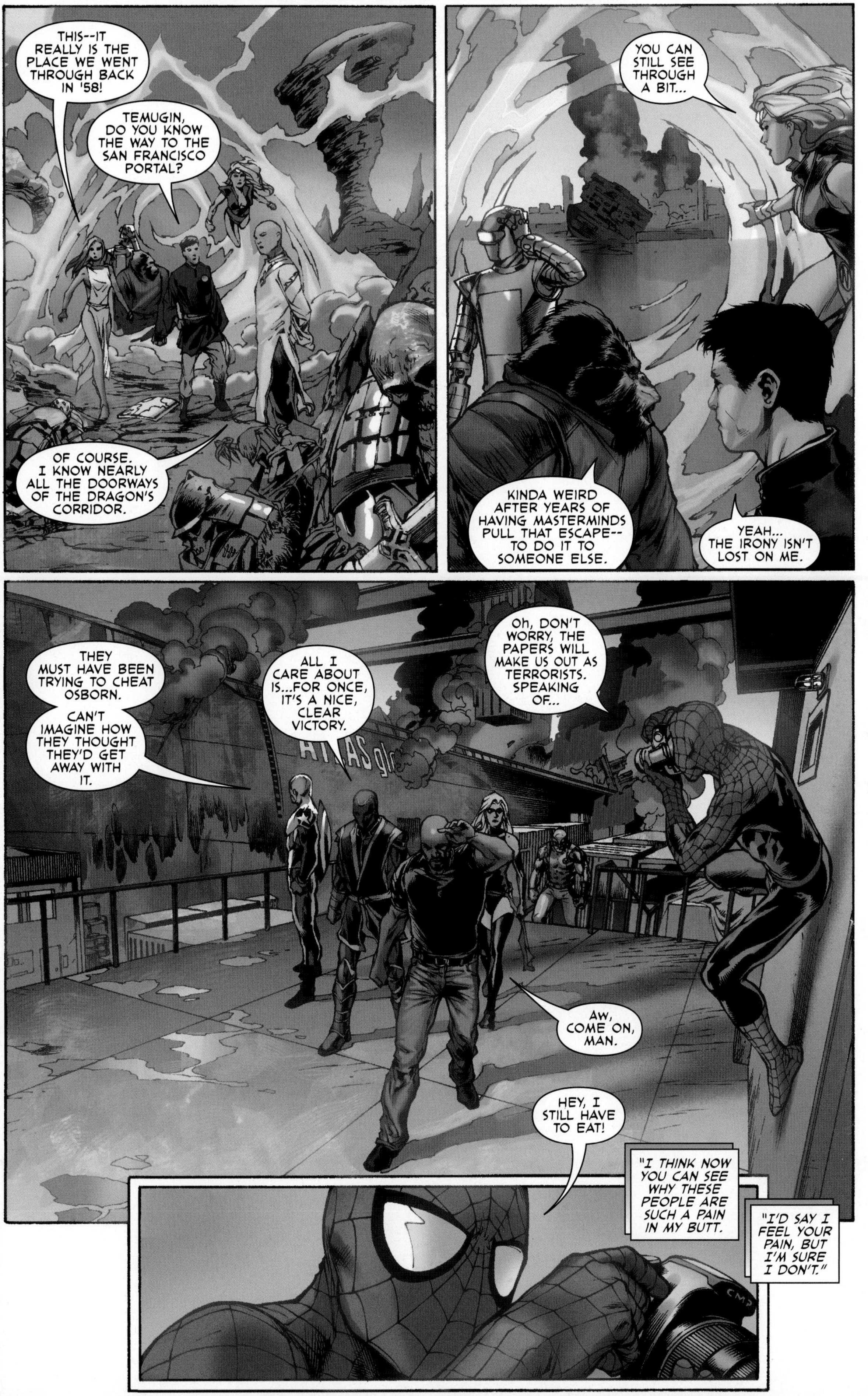
THIS--IT REALLY IS THE PLACE WE WENT THROUGH BACK IN '58!
TEMUGIN, DO YOU KNOW THE WAY TO THE SAN FRANCISCO PORTAL?
OF COURSE. I KNOW NEARLY ALL THE DOORWAYS OF THE DRAGON'S CORRIDOR.
YOU CAN STILL SEE THROUGH A BIT...
KINDA WEIRD AFTER YEARS OF HAVING MASTERMINDS PULL THAT ESCAPE--TO DO IT TO SOMEONE ELSE.
YEAH... THE IRONY ISN'T LOST ON ME.
THEY MUST HAVE BEEN TRYING TO CHEAT OSBORN.
CAN'T IMAGINE HOW THEY THOUGHT THEY'D GET AWAY WITH IT.
ALL I CARE ABOUT IS...FOR ONCE, IT'S A NICE, CLEAR VICTORY.
Oh, DON'T WORRY, THE PAPERS WILL MAKE US OUT AS TERRORISTS. SPEAKING OF...
AW, COME ON, MAN.
HEY, I STILL HAVE TO EAT!
"I THINK NOW YOU CAN SEE WHY THESE PEOPLE ARE SUCH A PAIN IN MY BUTT.
"I'D SAY I FEEL YOUR PAIN, BUT I'M SURE I DON'T."

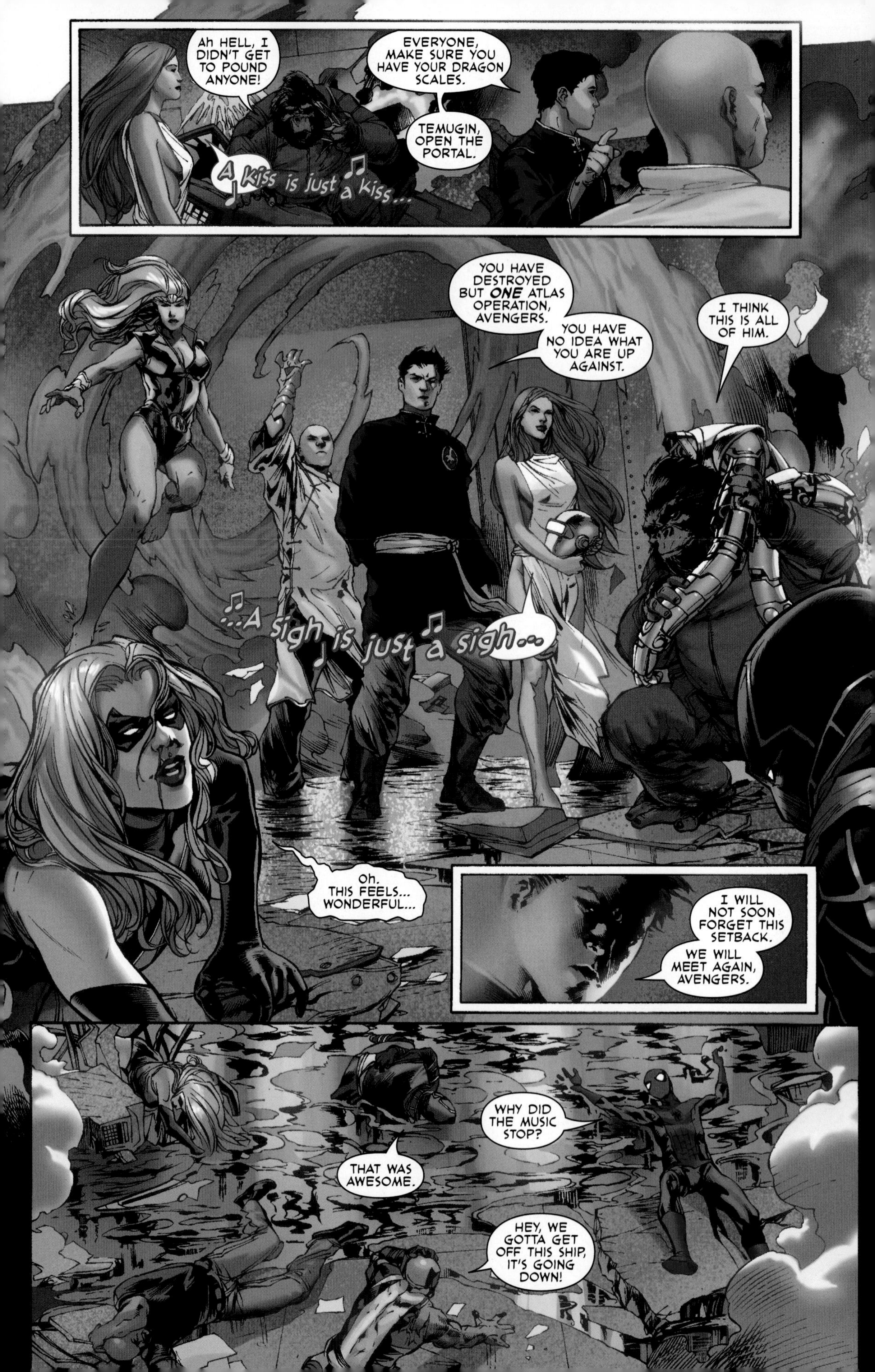

Ah HELL, I DIDN'T GET TO POUND ANYONE!
EVERYONE, MAKE SURE YOU HAVE YOUR DRAGON SCALES.
TEMUGIN, OPEN THE PORTAL.
A Kiss is just a kiss...
YOU HAVE DESTROYED BUT ONE ATLAS OPERATION, AVENGERS.
YOU HAVE NO IDEA WHAT YOU ARE UP AGAINST.
I THINK THIS IS ALL OF HIM.
...A sigh is just a sigh...
Oh. THIS FEELS... WONDERFUL...
I WILL NOT SOON FORGET THIS SETBACK.
WE WILL MEET AGAIN, AVENGERS.
WHY DID THE MUSIC STOP?
THAT WAS AWESOME.
HEY, WE GOTTA GET OFF THIS SHIP, IT'S GOING DOWN!

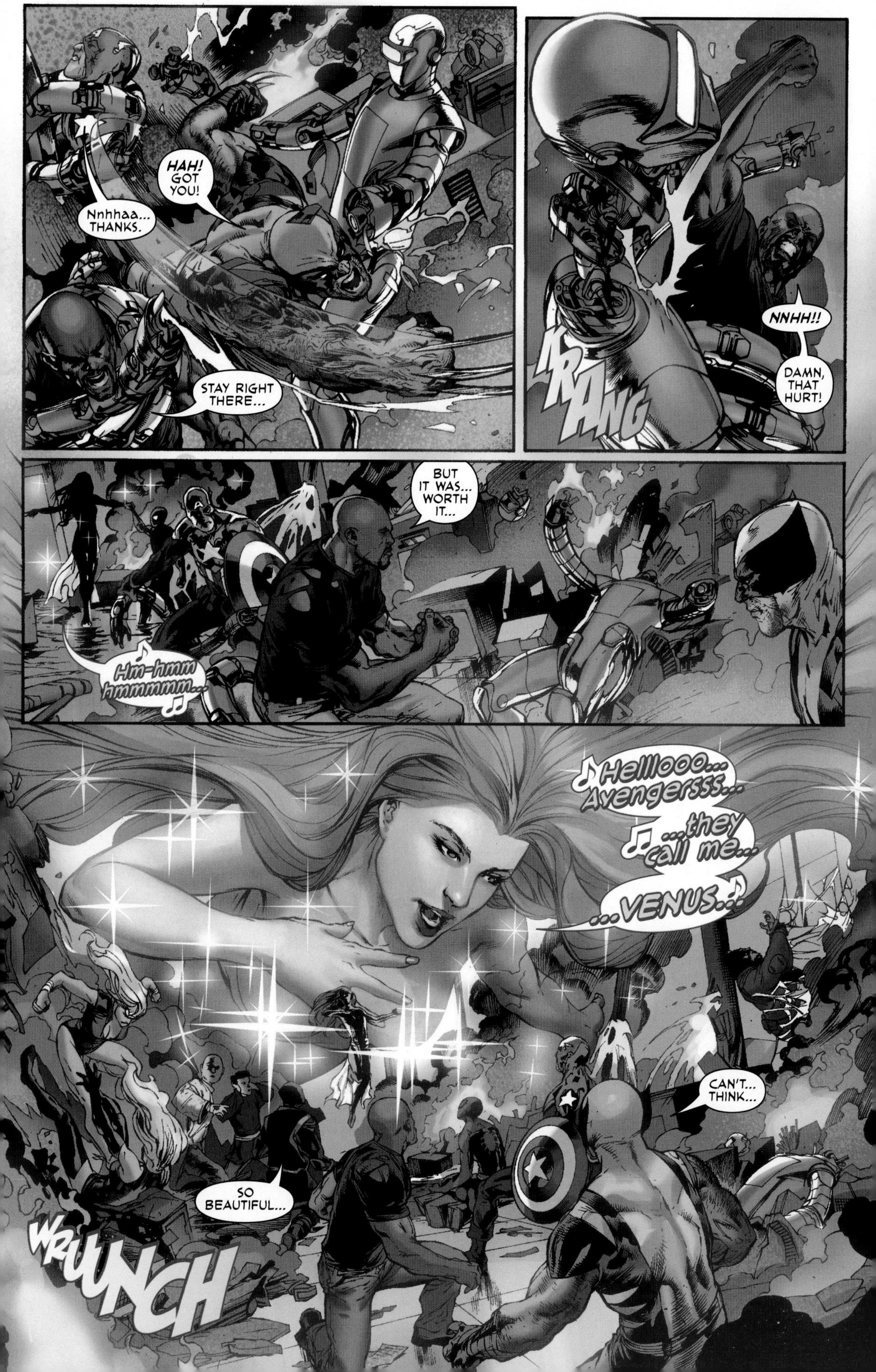
HAH! GOT YOU!
Nnhhaa... THANKS.
STAY RIGHT THERE...
KRANG
NNHH!!
DAMN, THAT HURT!
BUT IT WAS... WORTH IT...
♪ Hm-hmm hmmmmm... ♫
♪ Hellllooo... Avengersss...
♫ ...they call me...
...VENUS...♪
CAN'T... THINK...
SO BEAUTIFUL...
WRUUNCH

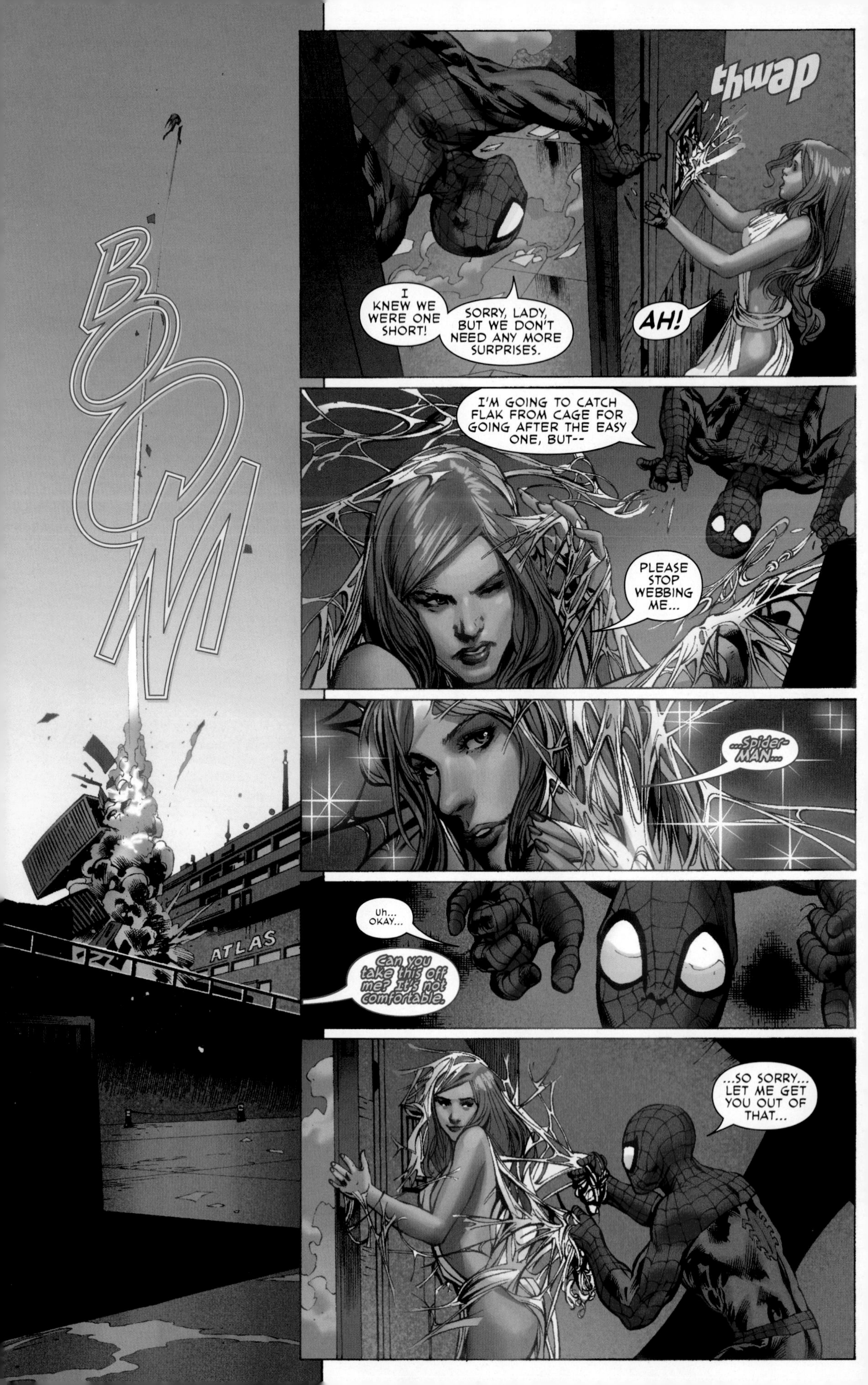
BOOM
thwap
I KNEW WE WERE ONE SHORT!
SORRY, LADY, BUT WE DON'T NEED ANY MORE SURPRISES.
AH!
I'M GOING TO CATCH FLAK FROM CAGE FOR GOING AFTER THE EASY ONE, BUT--
PLEASE STOP WEBBING ME...
...Spider-MAN...
Uh... OKAY...
Can you take this off me? It's not comfortable.
...SO SORRY... LET ME GET YOU OUT OF THAT...
ATLAS

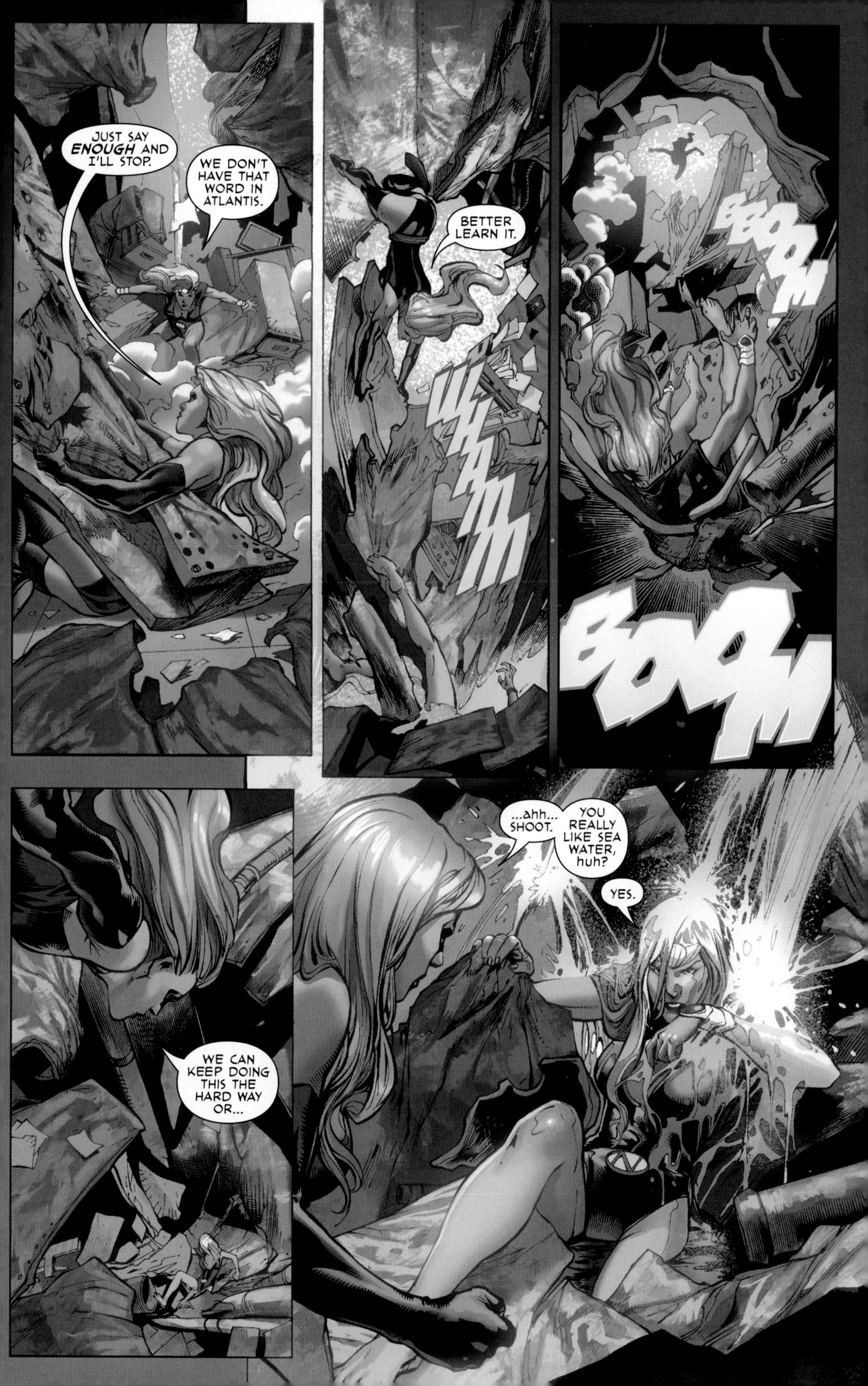

JUST SAY ENOUGH AND I'LL STOP.
WE DON'T HAVE THAT WORD IN ATLANTIS.
BETTER LEARN IT.
WHAM
BBOOM
BOOM
WE CAN KEEP DOING THIS THE HARD WAY OR...
...ahh... SHOOT.
YOU REALLY LIKE SEA WATER, huh?
YES.

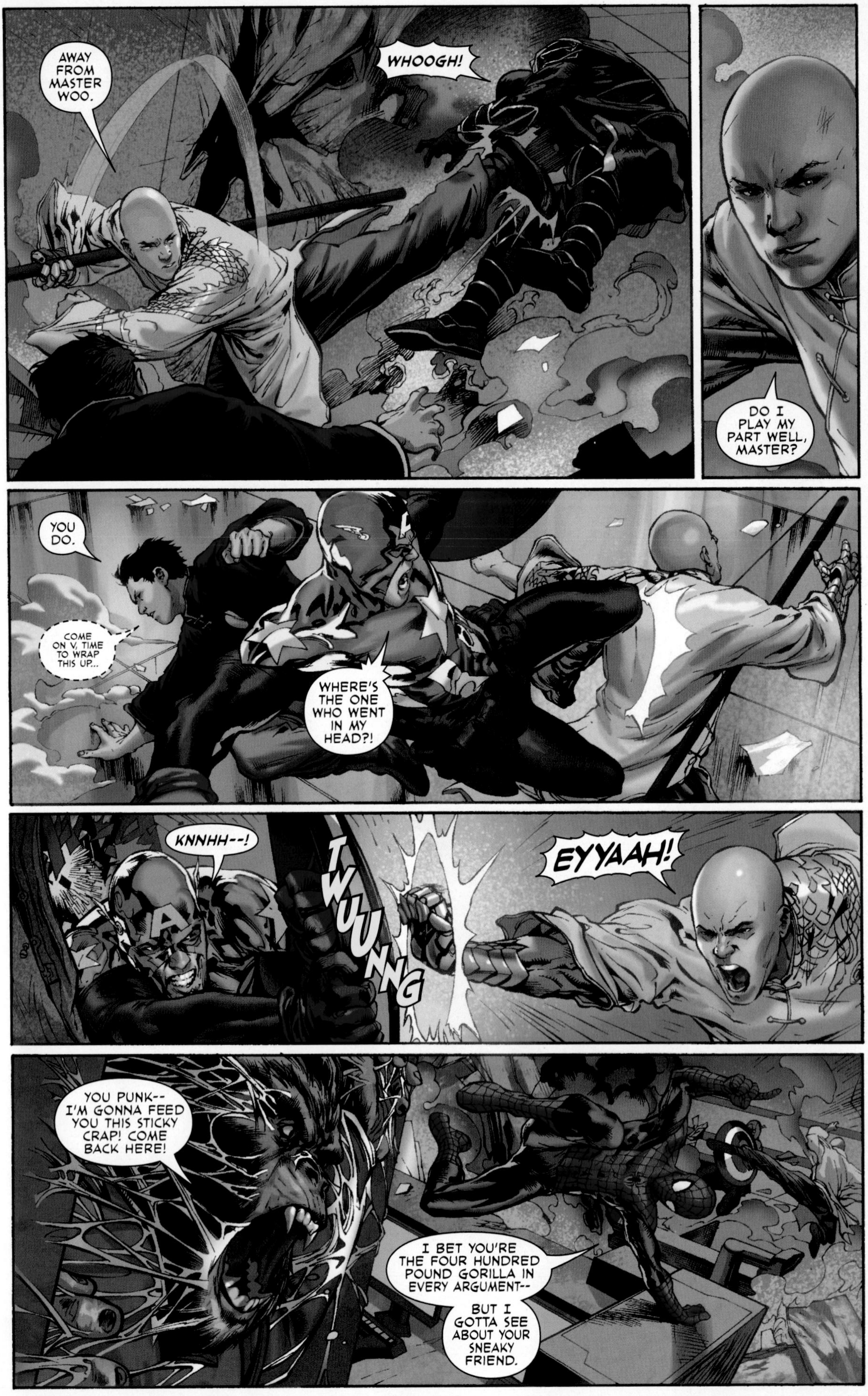
AWAY FROM MASTER WOO.
WHOOGH!
DO I PLAY MY PART WELL, MASTER?
YOU DO.
COME ON V, TIME TO WRAP THIS UP...
WHERE'S THE ONE WHO WENT IN MY HEAD?!
KNNHH--!
TWUUUNNG
EYYAAH!
YOU PUNK-- I'M GONNA FEED YOU THIS STICKY CRAP! COME BACK HERE!
I BET YOU'RE THE FOUR HUNDRED POUND GORILLA IN EVERY ARGUMENT--
BUT I GOTTA SEE ABOUT YOUR SNEAKY FRIEND.

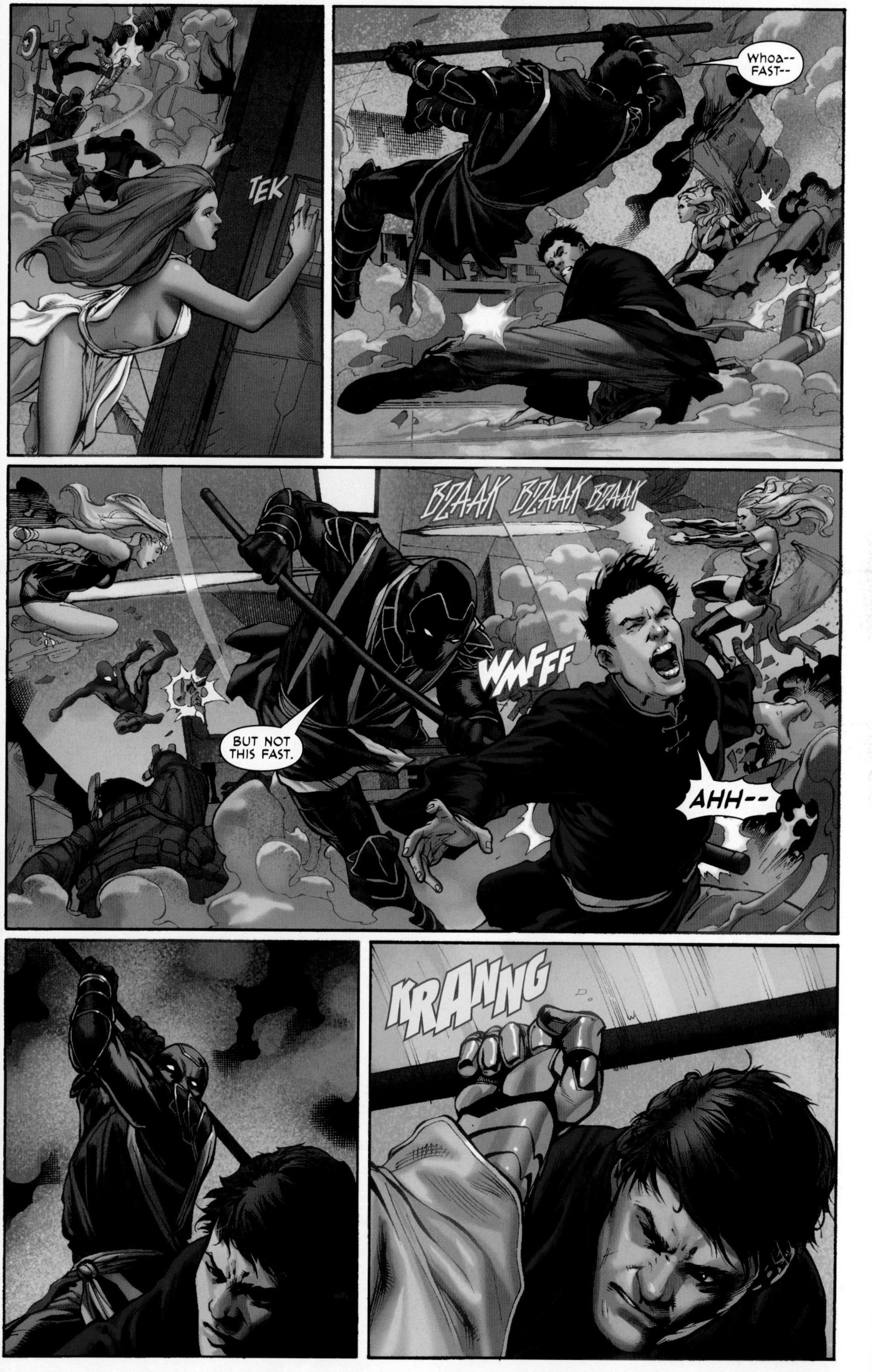
TEK
Whoa-- FAST--
BZAAK BZAAK BZAAK
WMFFF
BUT NOT THIS FAST.
AHH--
KRANNG

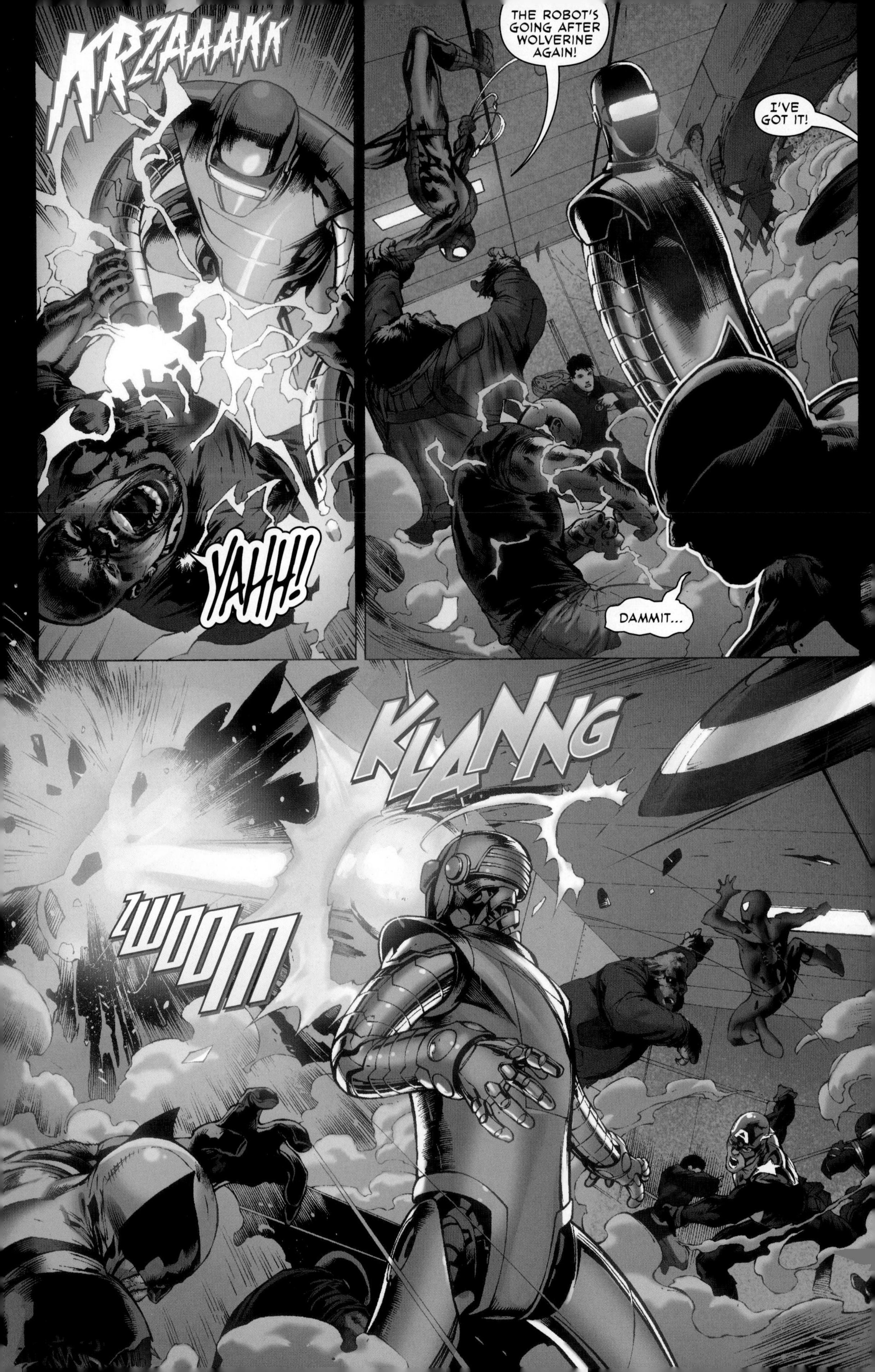
KRZAAAKK
YAHH!
THE ROBOT'S GOING AFTER WOLVERINE AGAIN!
I'VE GOT IT!
DAMMIT...
KLANNG
ZWOOM

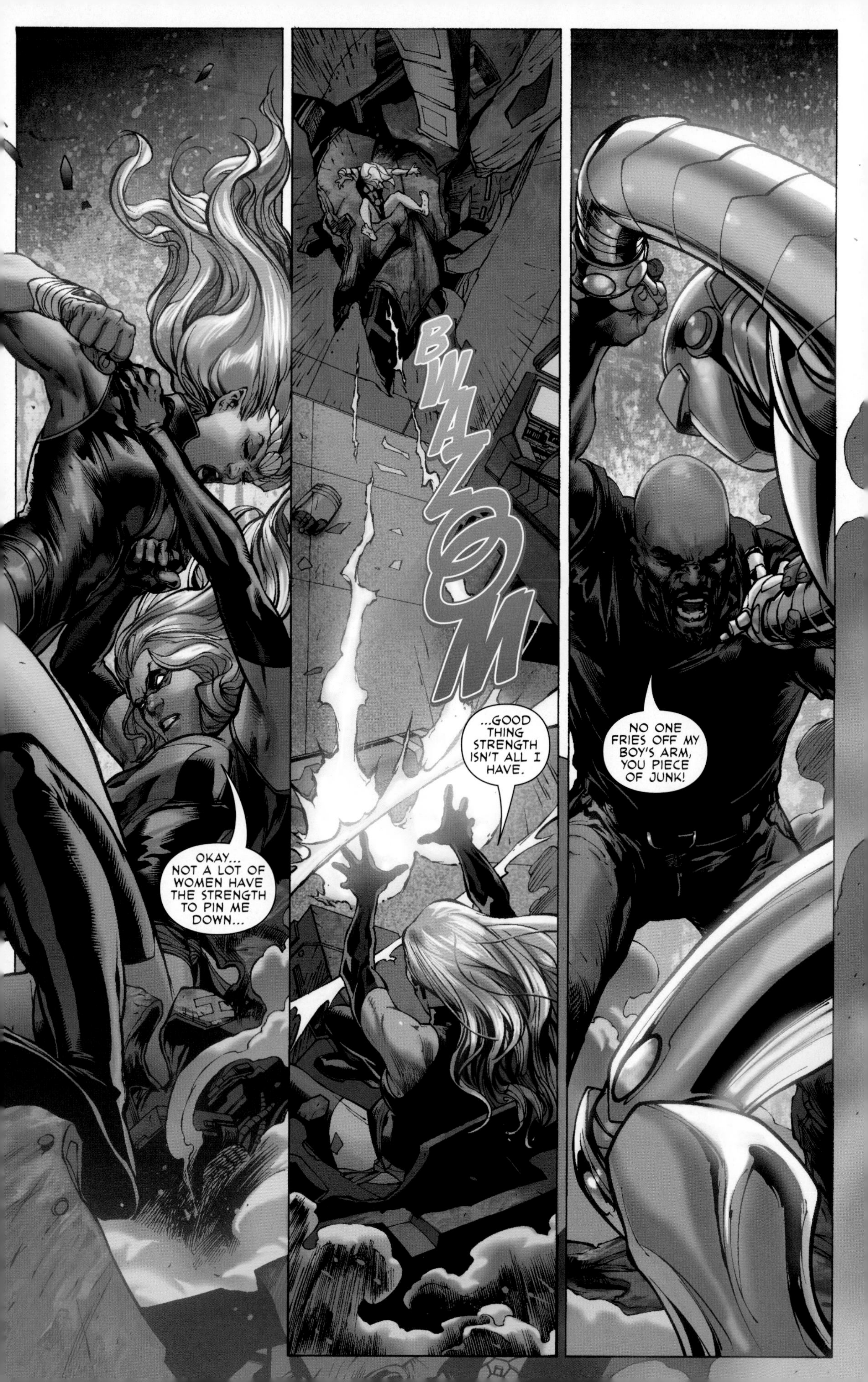
OKAY... NOT A LOT OF WOMEN HAVE THE STRENGTH TO PIN ME DOWN...
BWAZOOM
...GOOD THING STRENGTH ISN'T ALL I HAVE.
NO ONE FRIES OFF MY BOY'S ARM, YOU PIECE OF JUNK!

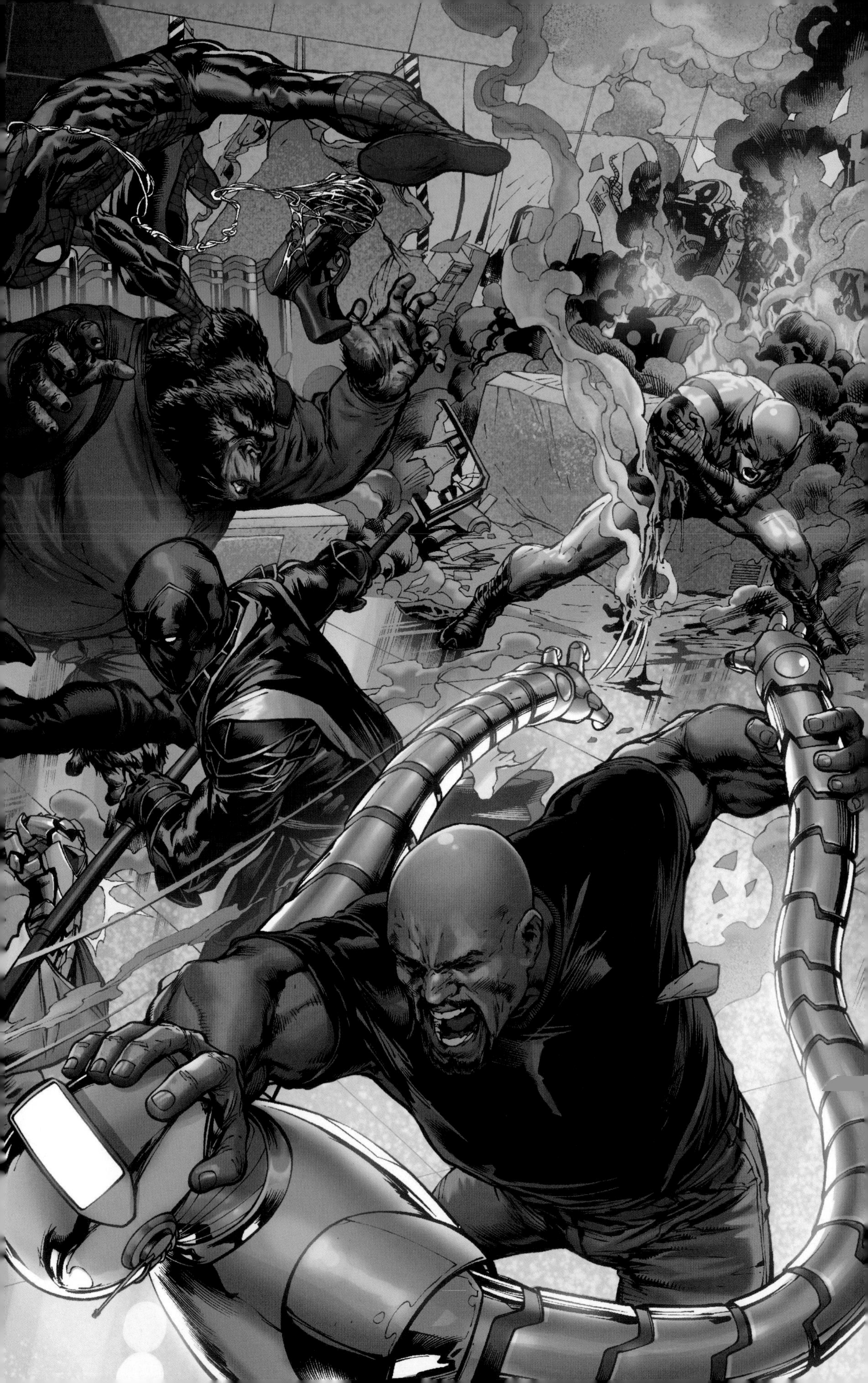

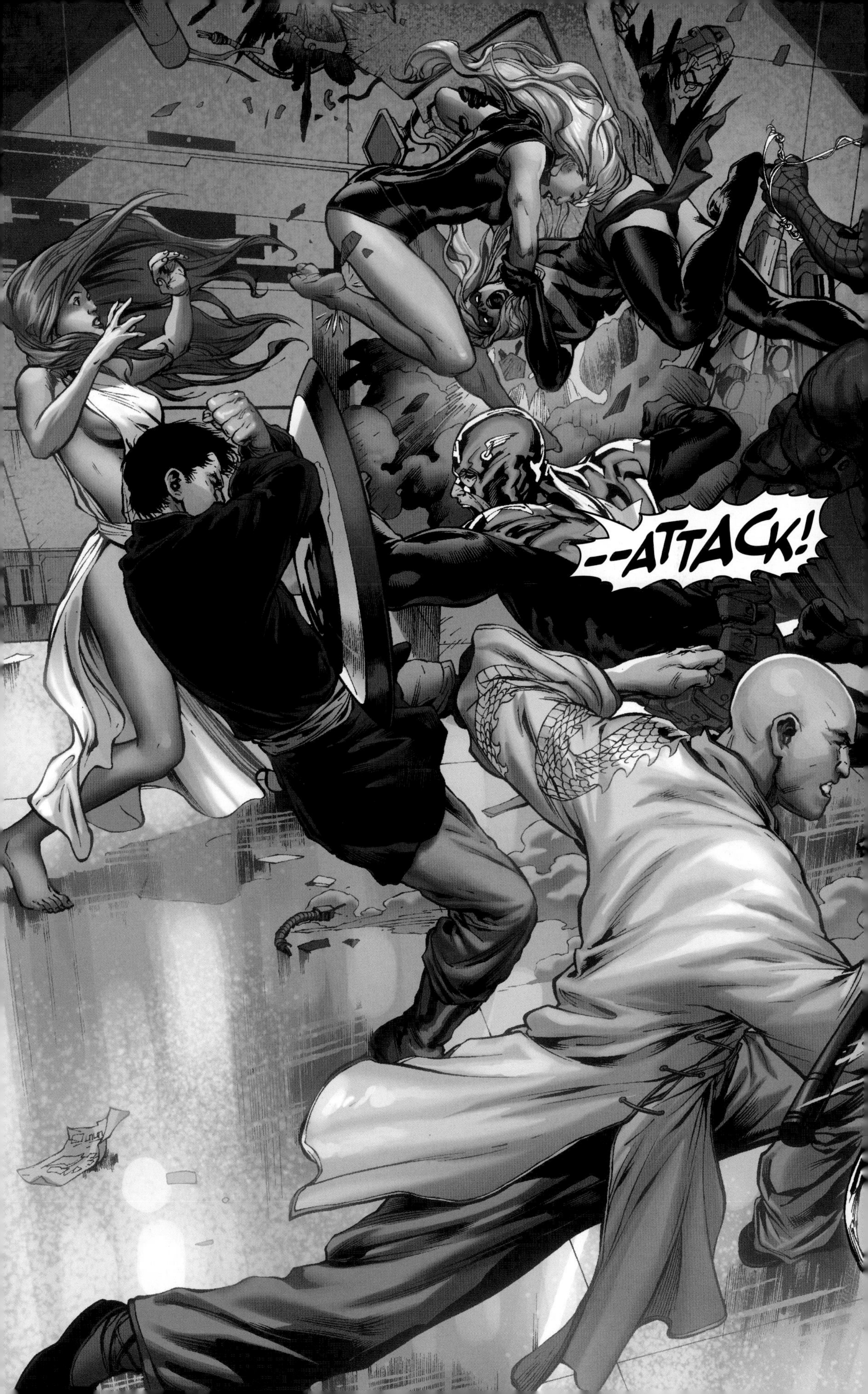
--ATTACK!

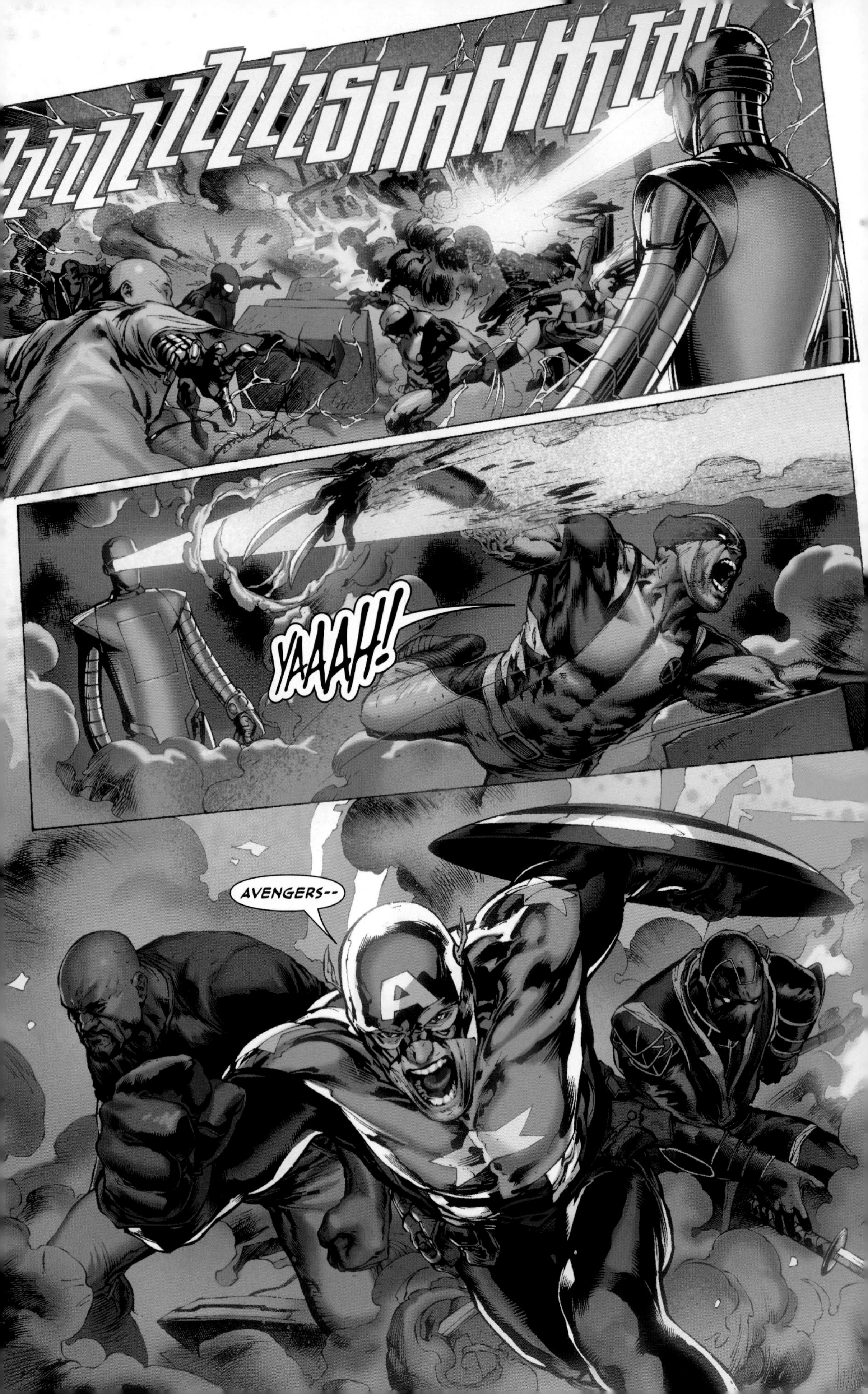
ZZZZZZZZZZZSHHHHHTTT!!
YAAAH!
AVENGERS--

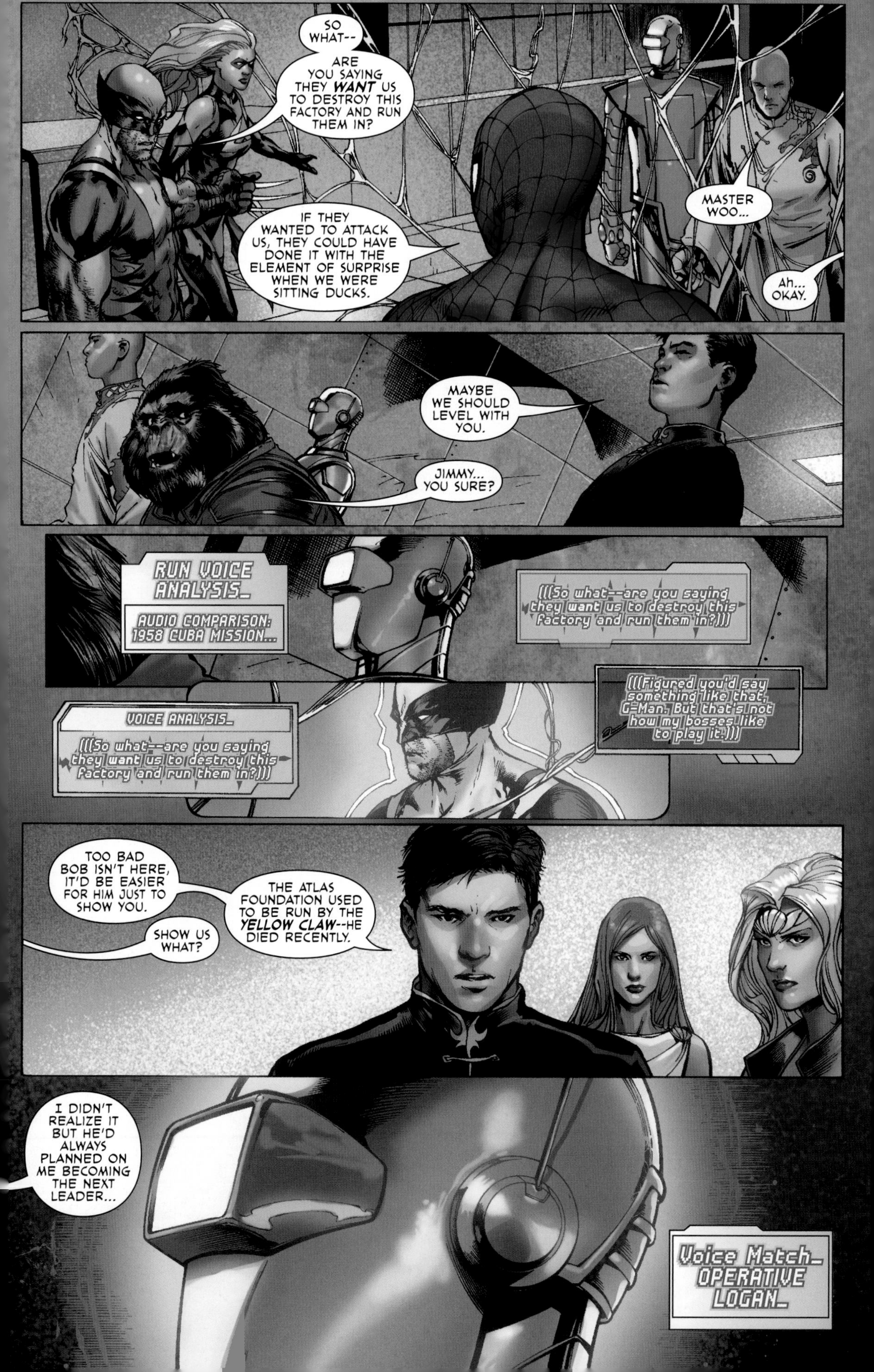
SO WHAT-- ARE YOU SAYING THEY WANT US TO DESTROY THIS FACTORY AND RUN THEM IN?
IF THEY WANTED TO ATTACK US, THEY COULD HAVE DONE IT WITH THE ELEMENT OF SURPRISE WHEN WE WERE SITTING DUCKS.
MASTER WOO...
Ah... OKAY.
MAYBE WE SHOULD LEVEL WITH YOU.
JIMMY... YOU SURE?
RUN VOICE ANALYSIS_
AUDIO COMPARISON: 1958 CUBA MISSION...
(((So what--are you saying they want us to destroy this factory and run them in?)))
VOICE ANALYSIS_
(((So what--are you saying they want us to destroy this factory and run them in?)))
(((Figured you'd say something like that, G-Man. But that's not how my bosses like to play it.)))
TOO BAD BOB ISN'T HERE, IT'D BE EASIER FOR HIM JUST TO SHOW YOU.
SHOW US WHAT?
THE ATLAS FOUNDATION USED TO BE RUN BY THE YELLOW CLAW--HE DIED RECENTLY.
I DIDN'T REALIZE IT BUT HE'D ALWAYS PLANNED ON ME BECOMING THE NEXT LEADER...
Voice Match_ OPERATIVE LOGAN_

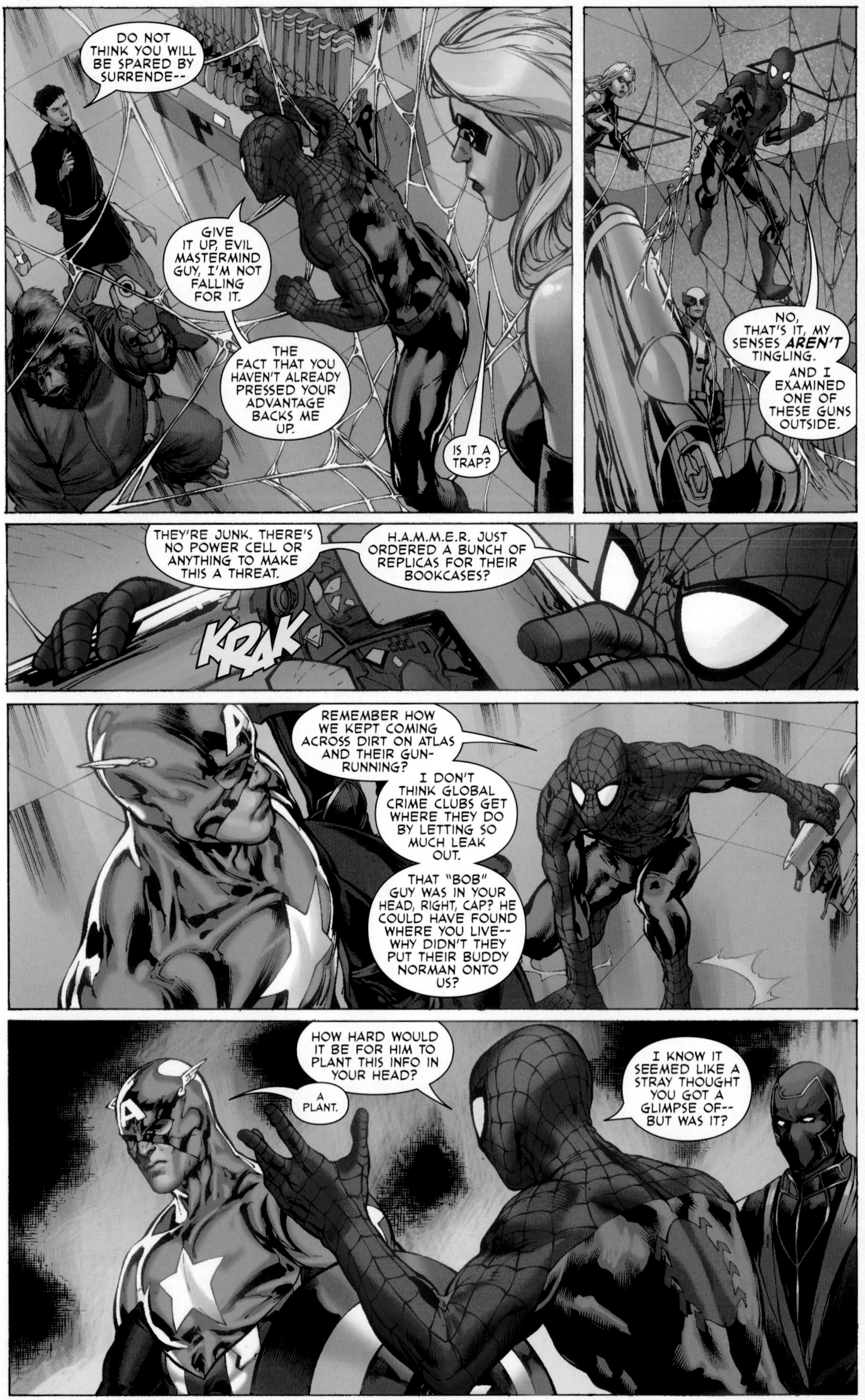
DO NOT THINK YOU WILL BE SPARED BY SURRENDE--
GIVE IT UP, EVIL MASTERMIND GUY, I'M NOT FALLING FOR IT.
THE FACT THAT YOU HAVEN'T ALREADY PRESSED YOUR ADVANTAGE BACKS ME UP.
IS IT A TRAP?
NO, THAT'S IT, MY SENSES AREN'T TINGLING.
AND I EXAMINED ONE OF THESE GUNS OUTSIDE.
THEY'RE JUNK. THERE'S NO POWER CELL OR ANYTHING TO MAKE THIS A THREAT.
H.A.M.M.E.R. JUST ORDERED A BUNCH OF REPLICAS FOR THEIR BOOKCASES?
KRAK
REMEMBER HOW WE KEPT COMING ACROSS DIRT ON ATLAS AND THEIR GUN-RUNNING?
I DON'T THINK GLOBAL CRIME CLUBS GET WHERE THEY DO BY LETTING SO MUCH LEAK OUT.
THAT "BOB" GUY WAS IN YOUR HEAD, RIGHT, CAP? HE COULD HAVE FOUND WHERE YOU LIVE-- WHY DIDN'T THEY PUT THEIR BUDDY NORMAN ONTO US?
HOW HARD WOULD IT BE FOR HIM TO PLANT THIS INFO IN YOUR HEAD?
A PLANT.
I KNOW IT SEEMED LIKE A STRAY THOUGHT YOU GOT A GLIMPSE OF-- BUT WAS IT?

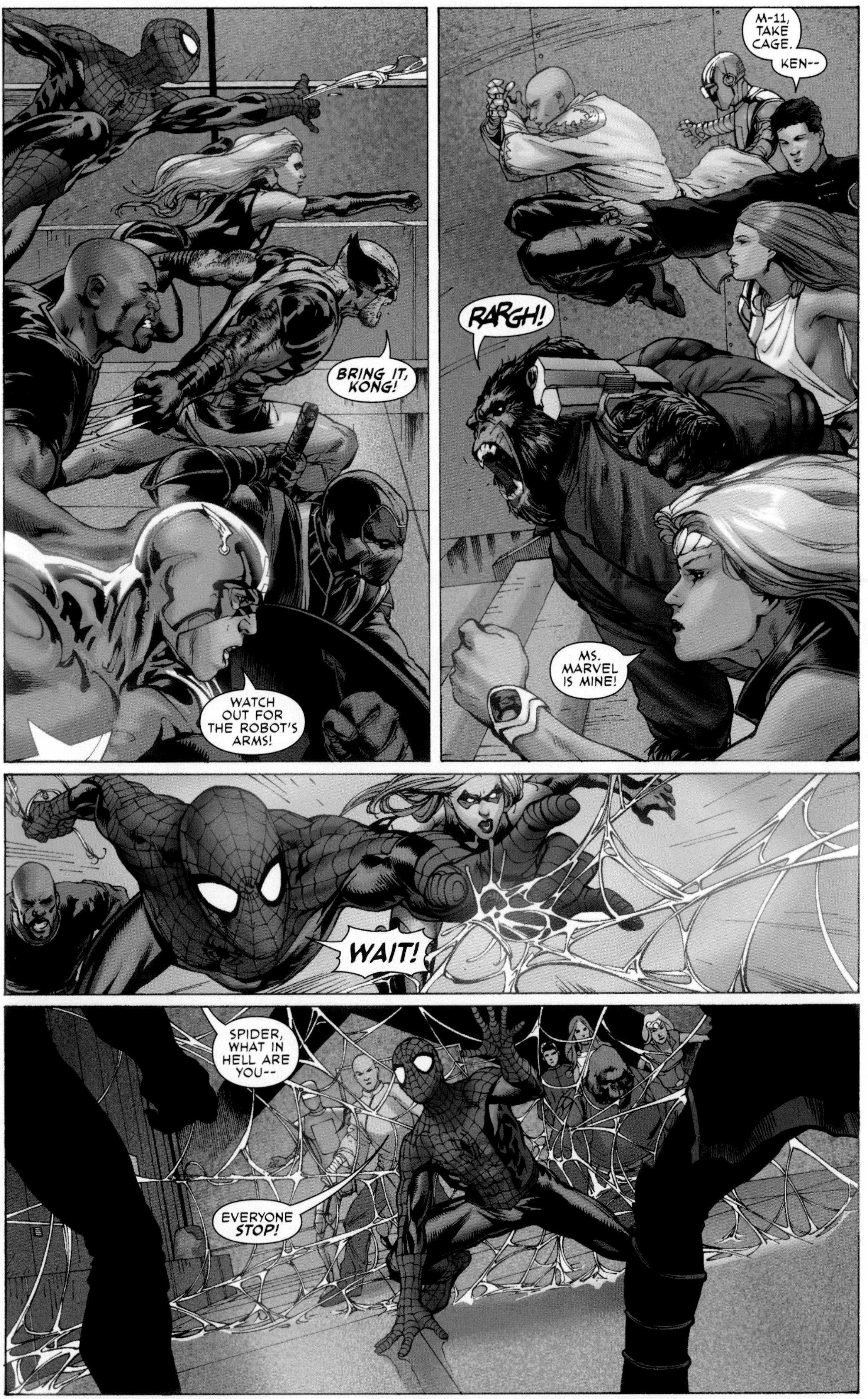
BRING IT, KONG!
WATCH OUT FOR THE ROBOT'S ARMS!
M-11, TAKE CAGE.
KEN--
RARGH!
MS. MARVEL IS MINE!
WAIT!
SPIDER, WHAT IN HELL ARE YOU--
EVERYONE STOP!

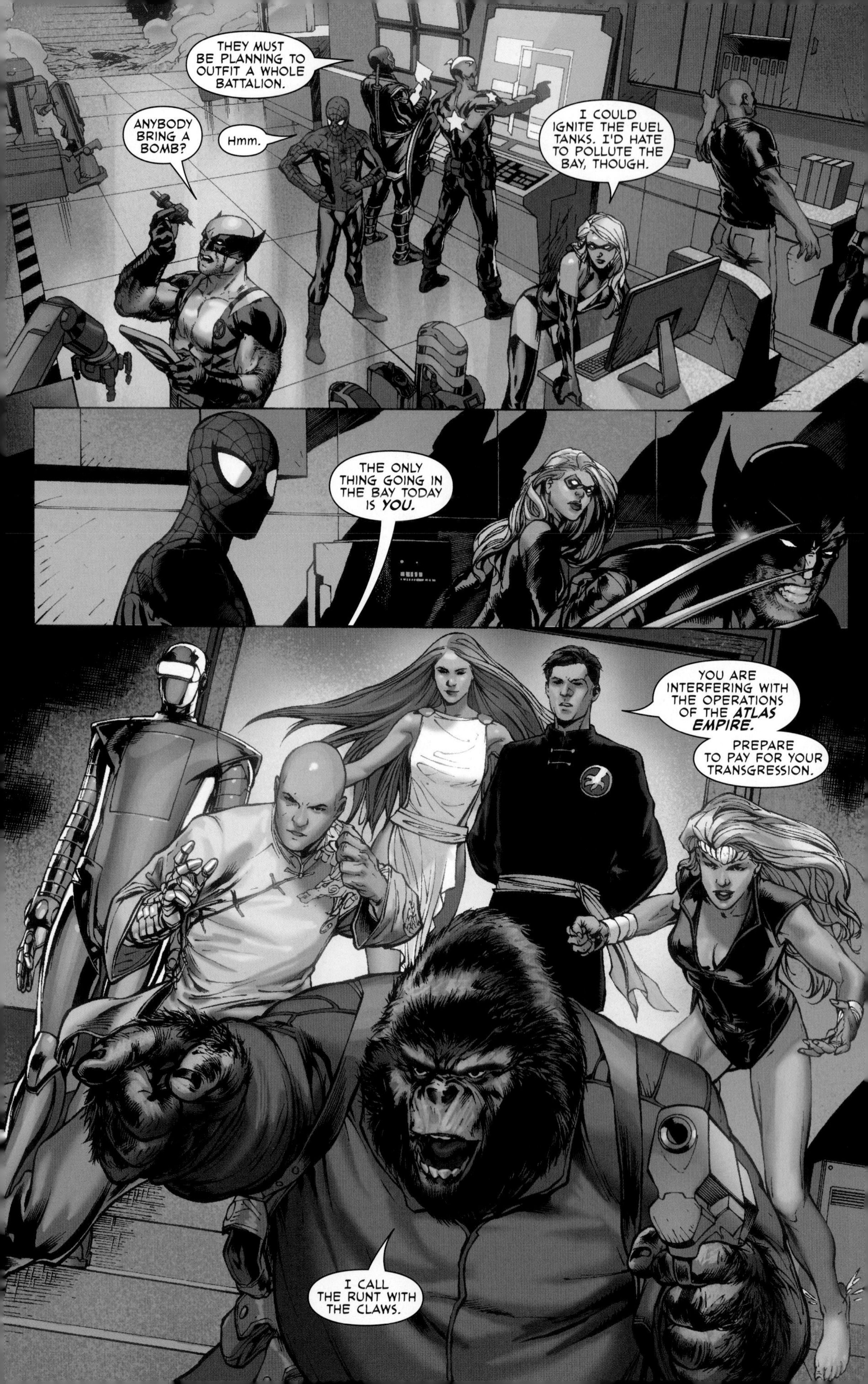
THEY MUST BE PLANNING TO OUTFIT A WHOLE BATTALION.
ANYBODY BRING A BOMB?
Hmm.
I COULD IGNITE THE FUEL TANKS. I'D HATE TO POLLUTE THE BAY, THOUGH.
THE ONLY THING GOING IN THE BAY TODAY IS YOU.
YOU ARE INTERFERING WITH THE OPERATIONS OF THE ATLAS EMPIRE.
PREPARE TO PAY FOR YOUR TRANSGRESSION.
I CALL THE RUNT WITH THE CLAWS.

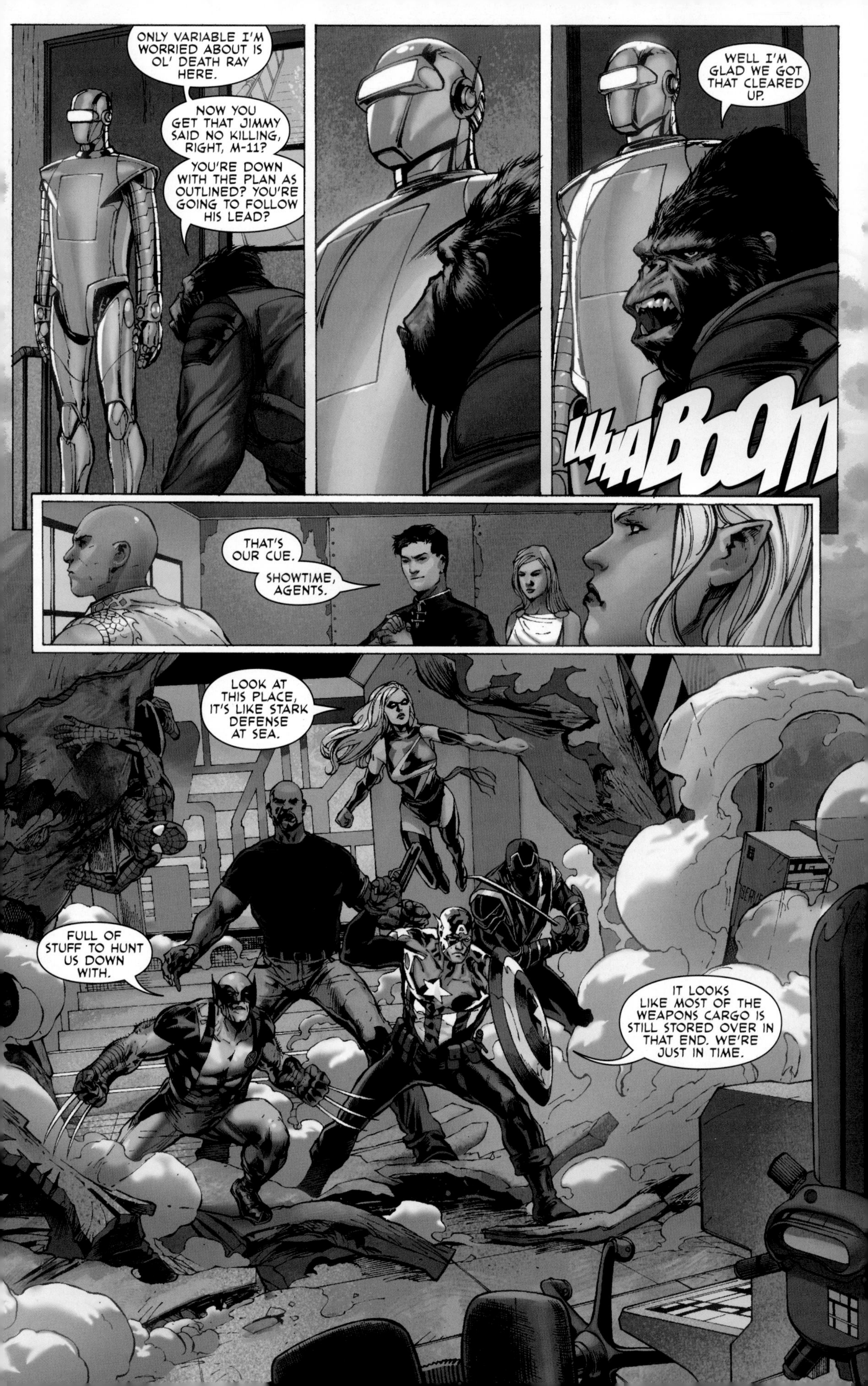
ONLY VARIABLE I'M WORRIED ABOUT IS OL' DEATH RAY HERE.
NOW YOU GET THAT JIMMY SAID NO KILLING, RIGHT, M-11?
YOU'RE DOWN WITH THE PLAN AS OUTLINED? YOU'RE GOING TO FOLLOW HIS LEAD?
WELL I'M GLAD WE GOT THAT CLEARED UP.
WHABOOM
THAT'S OUR CUE.
SHOWTIME, AGENTS.
LOOK AT THIS PLACE, IT'S LIKE STARK DEFENSE AT SEA.
FULL OF STUFF TO HUNT US DOWN WITH.
IT LOOKS LIKE MOST OF THE WEAPONS CARGO IS STILL STORED OVER IN THAT END. WE'RE JUST IN TIME.

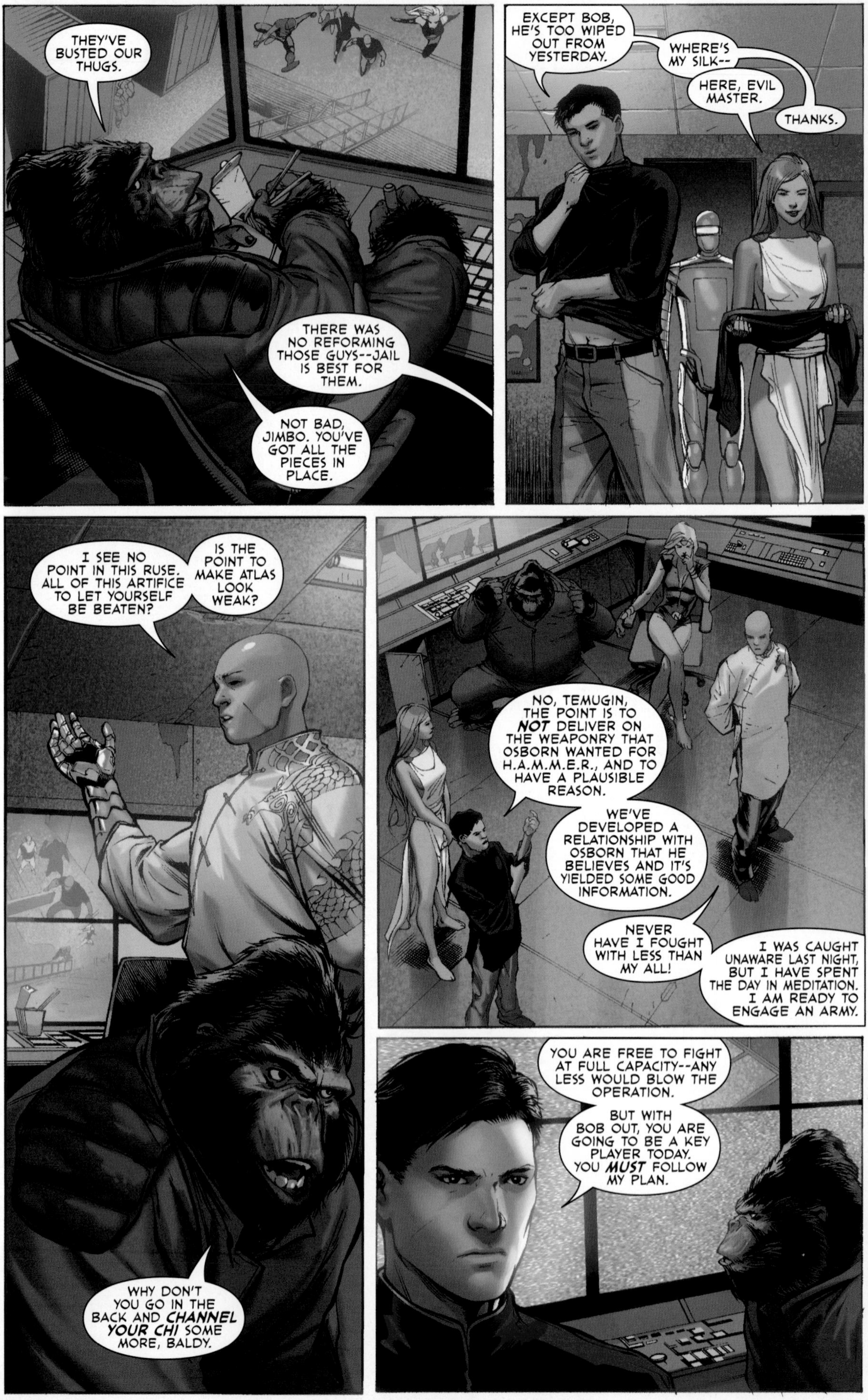

THEY'VE BUSTED OUR THUGS.
THERE WAS NO REFORMING THOSE GUYS--JAIL IS BEST FOR THEM.
NOT BAD, JIMBO. YOU'VE GOT ALL THE PIECES IN PLACE.
EXCEPT BOB, HE'S TOO WIPED OUT FROM YESTERDAY.
WHERE'S MY SILK--
HERE, EVIL MASTER.
THANKS.
I SEE NO POINT IN THIS RUSE. ALL OF THIS ARTIFICE TO LET YOURSELF BE BEATEN?
IS THE POINT TO MAKE ATLAS LOOK WEAK?
WHY DON'T YOU GO IN THE BACK AND CHANNEL YOUR CHI SOME MORE, BALDY.
NO, TEMUGIN, THE POINT IS TO NOT DELIVER ON THE WEAPONRY THAT OSBORN WANTED FOR H.A.M.M.E.R., AND TO HAVE A PLAUSIBLE REASON.
WE'VE DEVELOPED A RELATIONSHIP WITH OSBORN THAT HE BELIEVES AND IT'S YIELDED SOME GOOD INFORMATION.
NEVER HAVE I FOUGHT WITH LESS THAN MY ALL!
I WAS CAUGHT UNAWARE LAST NIGHT, BUT I HAVE SPENT THE DAY IN MEDITATION. I AM READY TO ENGAGE AN ARMY.
YOU ARE FREE TO FIGHT AT FULL CAPACITY--ANY LESS WOULD BLOW THE OPERATION.
BUT WITH BOB OUT, YOU ARE GOING TO BE A KEY PLAYER TODAY. YOU MUST FOLLOW MY PLAN.

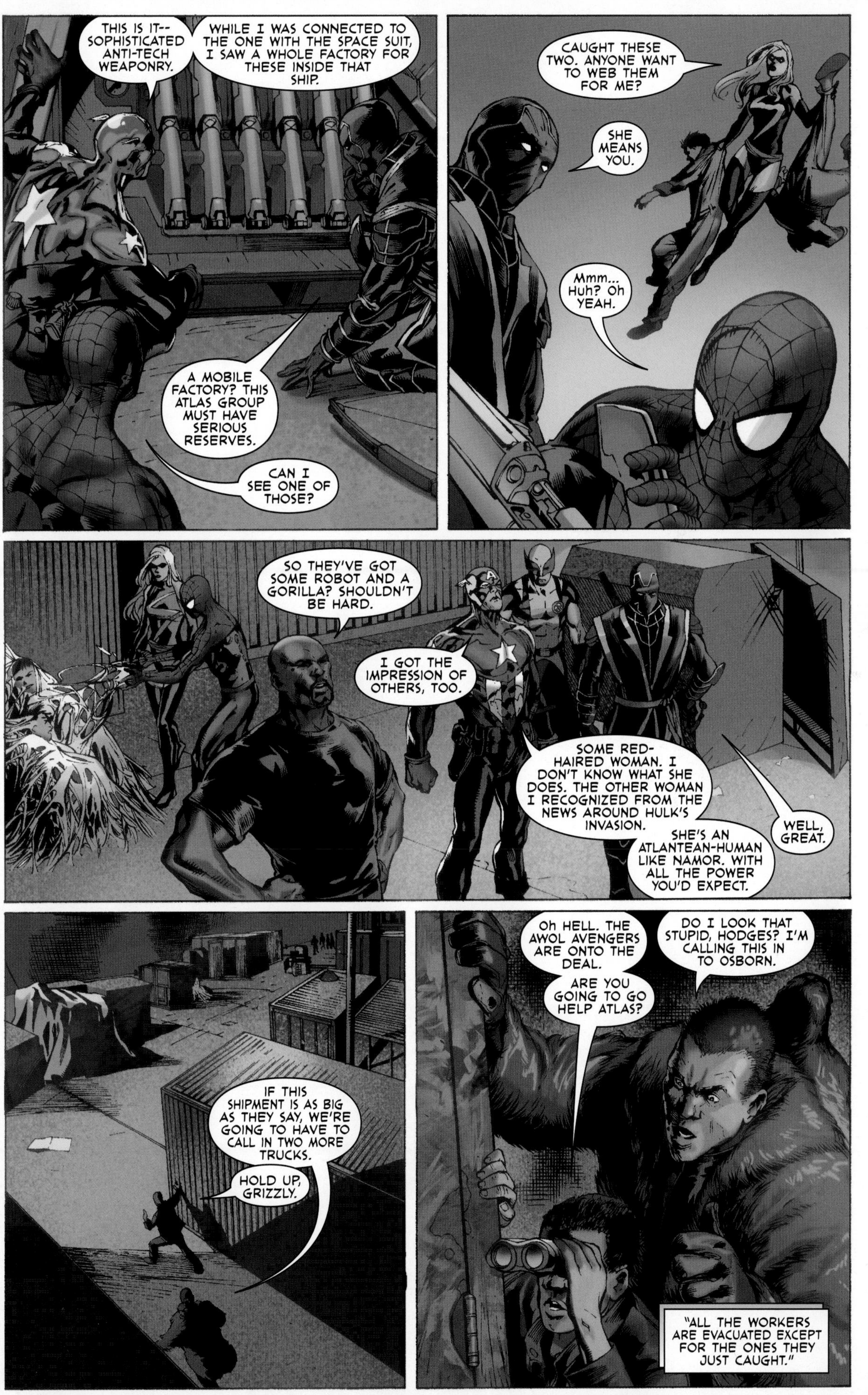

THIS IS IT-- SOPHISTICATED ANTI-TECH WEAPONRY.
WHILE I WAS CONNECTED TO THE ONE WITH THE SPACE SUIT, I SAW A WHOLE FACTORY FOR THESE INSIDE THAT SHIP.
A MOBILE FACTORY? THIS ATLAS GROUP MUST HAVE SERIOUS RESERVES.
CAN I SEE ONE OF THOSE?
CAUGHT THESE TWO. ANYONE WANT TO WEB THEM FOR ME?
SHE MEANS YOU.
Mmm... Huh? Oh YEAH.
SO THEY'VE GOT SOME ROBOT AND A GORILLA? SHOULDN'T BE HARD.
I GOT THE IMPRESSION OF OTHERS, TOO.
SOME RED-HAIRED WOMAN. I DON'T KNOW WHAT SHE DOES. THE OTHER WOMAN I RECOGNIZED FROM THE NEWS AROUND HULK'S INVASION.
SHE'S AN ATLANTEAN-HUMAN LIKE NAMOR. WITH ALL THE POWER YOU'D EXPECT.
WELL, GREAT.
IF THIS SHIPMENT IS AS BIG AS THEY SAY, WE'RE GOING TO HAVE TO CALL IN TWO MORE TRUCKS.
HOLD UP, GRIZZLY.
Oh HELL. THE AWOL AVENGERS ARE ONTO THE DEAL.
ARE YOU GOING TO GO HELP ATLAS?
DO I LOOK THAT STUPID, HODGES? I'M CALLING THIS IN TO OSBORN.
"ALL THE WORKERS ARE EVACUATED EXCEPT FOR THE ONES THEY JUST CAUGHT."

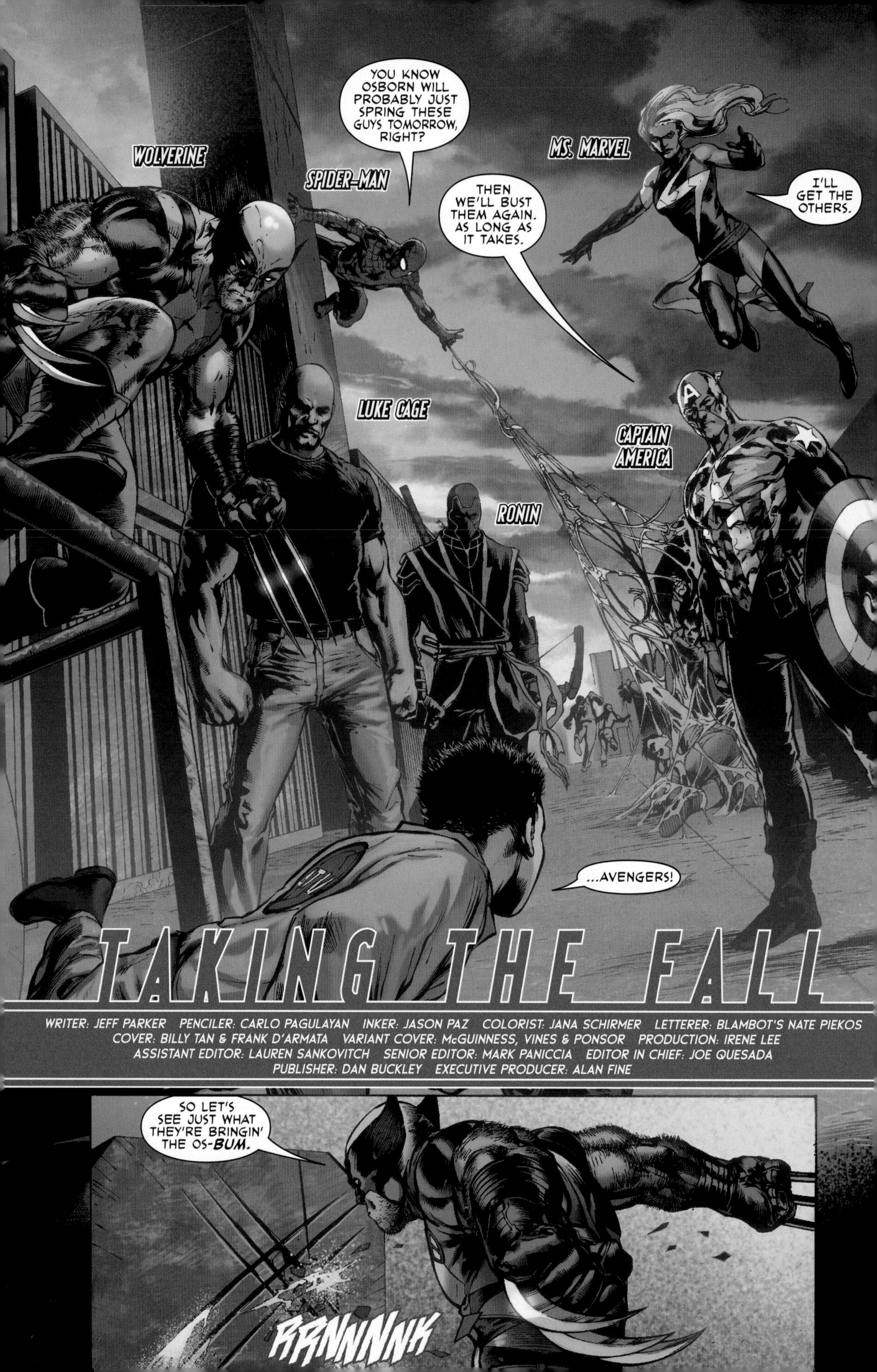
WOLVERINE
SPIDER-MAN
YOU KNOW OSBORN WILL PROBABLY JUST SPRING THESE GUYS TOMORROW, RIGHT?
MS. MARVEL
THEN WE'LL BUST THEM AGAIN. AS LONG AS IT TAKES.
I'LL GET THE OTHERS.
LUKE CAGE
CAPTAIN AMERICA
RONIN
...AVENGERS!
TAKING THE FALL
WRITER: JEFF PARKER PENCILER: CARLO PAGULAYAN INKER: JASON PAZ COLORIST: JANA SCHIRMER LETTERER: BLAMBOT'S NATE PIEKOS
COVER: BILLY TAN & FRANK D'ARMATA VARIANT COVER: McGUINNESS, VINES & PONSOR PRODUCTION: IRENE LEE
ASSISTANT EDITOR: LAUREN SANKOVITCH SENIOR EDITOR: MARK PANICCIA EDITOR IN CHIEF: JOE QUESADA
PUBLISHER: DAN BUCKLEY EXECUTIVE PRODUCER: ALAN FINE
SO LET'S SEE JUST WHAT THEY'RE BRINGIN' THE OS-BUM.
RRNNNNK

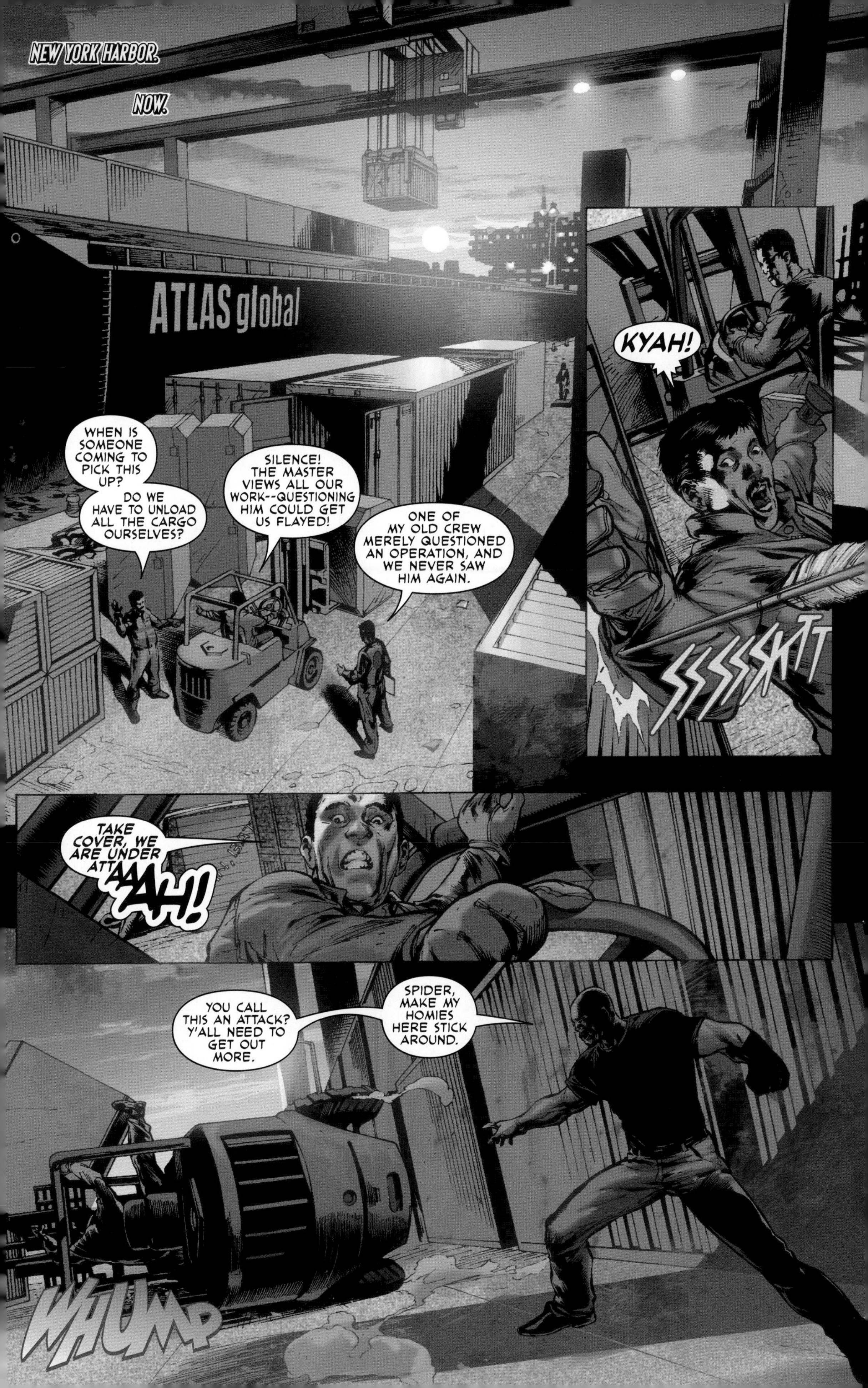
NEW YORK HARBOR.
NOW.
ATLAS global
WHEN IS SOMEONE COMING TO PICK THIS UP? DO WE HAVE TO UNLOAD ALL THE CARGO OURSELVES?
SILENCE! THE MASTER VIEWS ALL OUR WORK--QUESTIONING HIM COULD GET US FLAYED!
ONE OF MY OLD CREW MERELY QUESTIONED AN OPERATION, AND WE NEVER SAW HIM AGAIN.
KYAH!
SSSSSKTT
TAKE COVER, WE ARE UNDER ATT
AAAAH!
YOU CALL THIS AN ATTACK? Y'ALL NEED TO GET OUT MORE.
SPIDER, MAKE MY HOMIES HERE STICK AROUND.
WHUMP

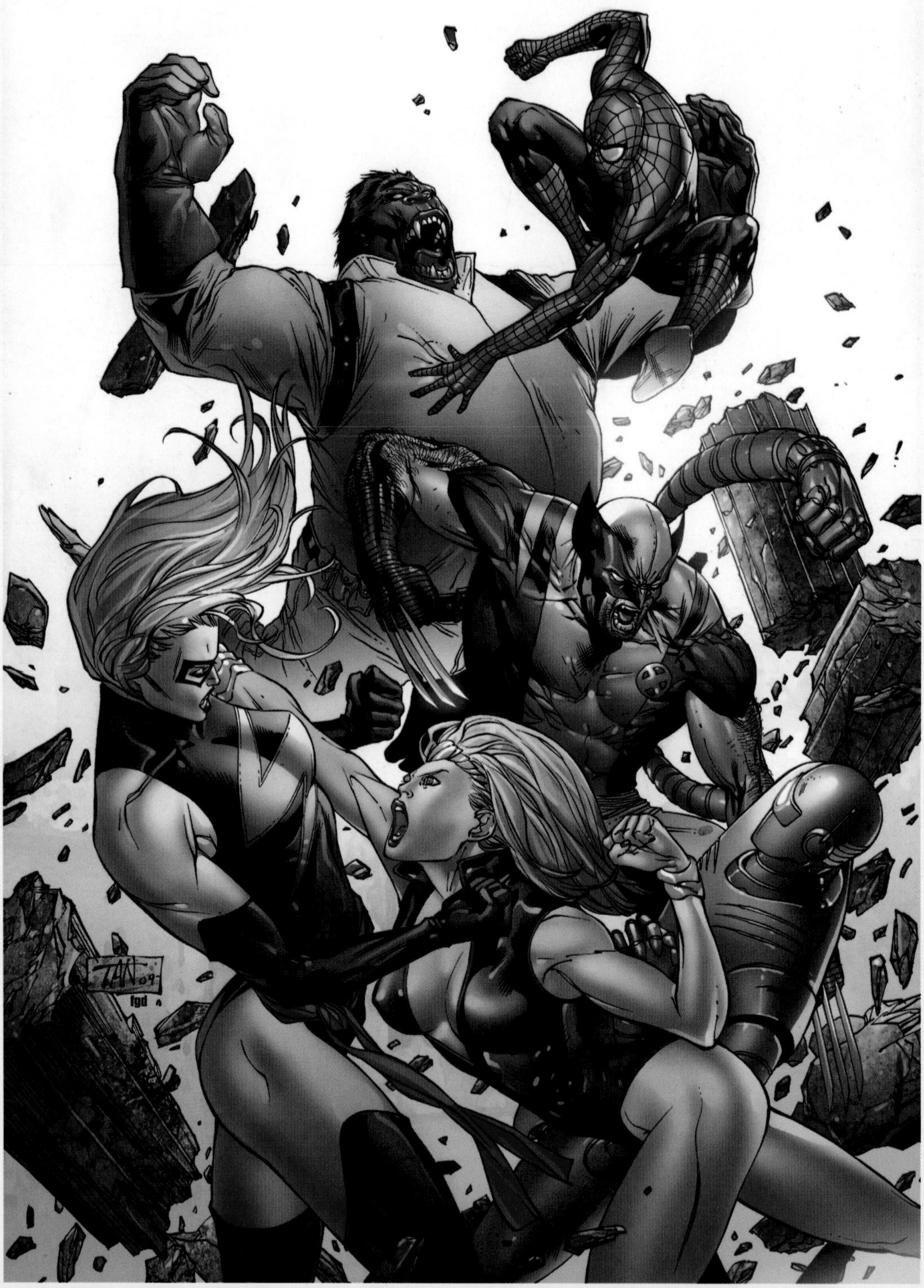

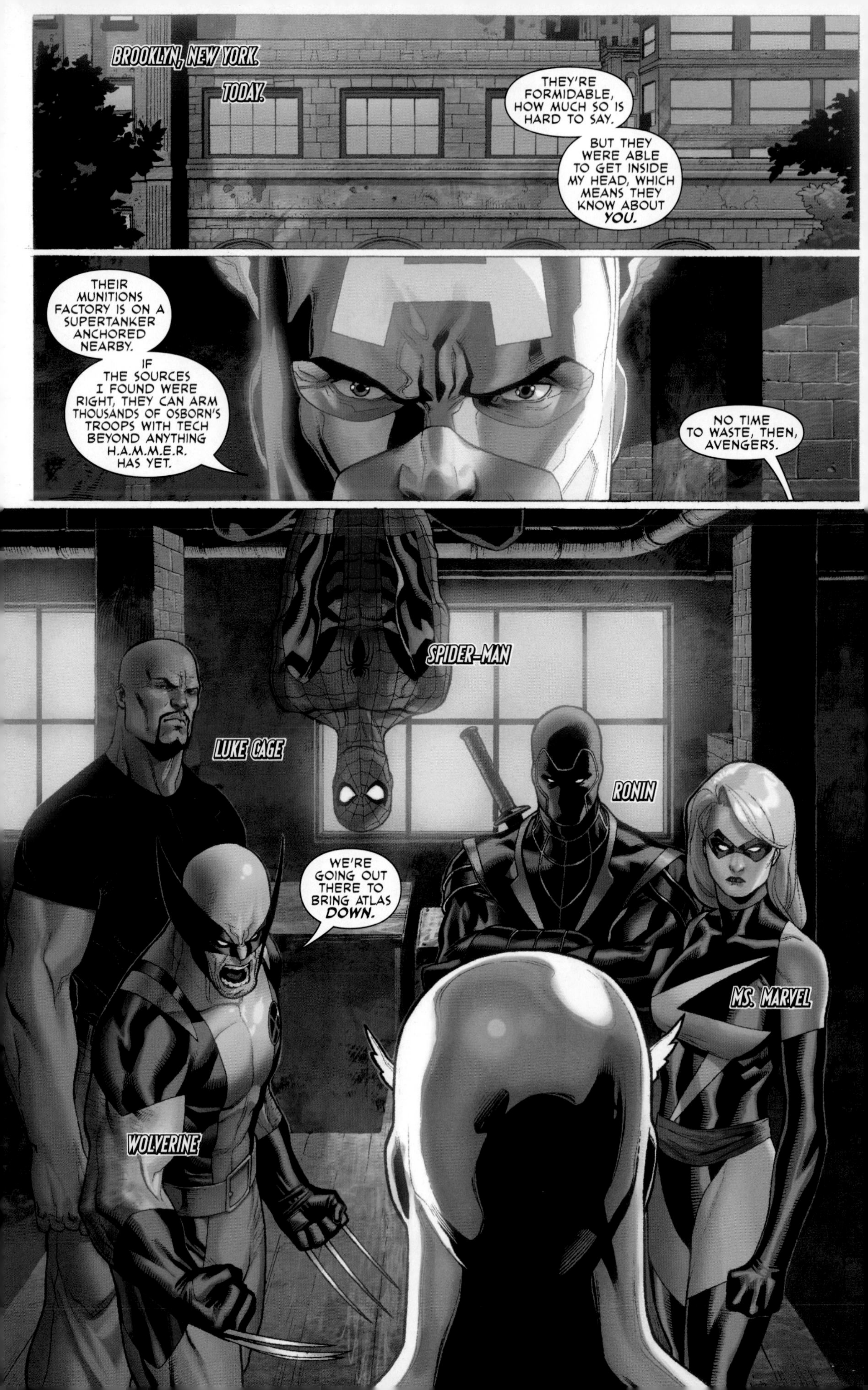

BROOKLYN, NEW YORK.
TODAY.
THEY'RE FORMIDABLE, HOW MUCH SO IS HARD TO SAY.
BUT THEY WERE ABLE TO GET INSIDE MY HEAD, WHICH MEANS THEY KNOW ABOUT YOU.
THEIR MUNITIONS FACTORY IS ON A SUPERTANKER ANCHORED NEARBY.
IF THE SOURCES I FOUND WERE RIGHT, THEY CAN ARM THOUSANDS OF OSBORN'S TROOPS WITH TECH BEYOND ANYTHING H.A.M.M.E.R. HAS YET.
NO TIME TO WASTE, THEN, AVENGERS.
SPIDER-MAN
LUKE CAGE
RONIN
WE'RE GOING OUT THERE TO BRING ATLAS DOWN.
MS. MARVEL
WOLVERINE

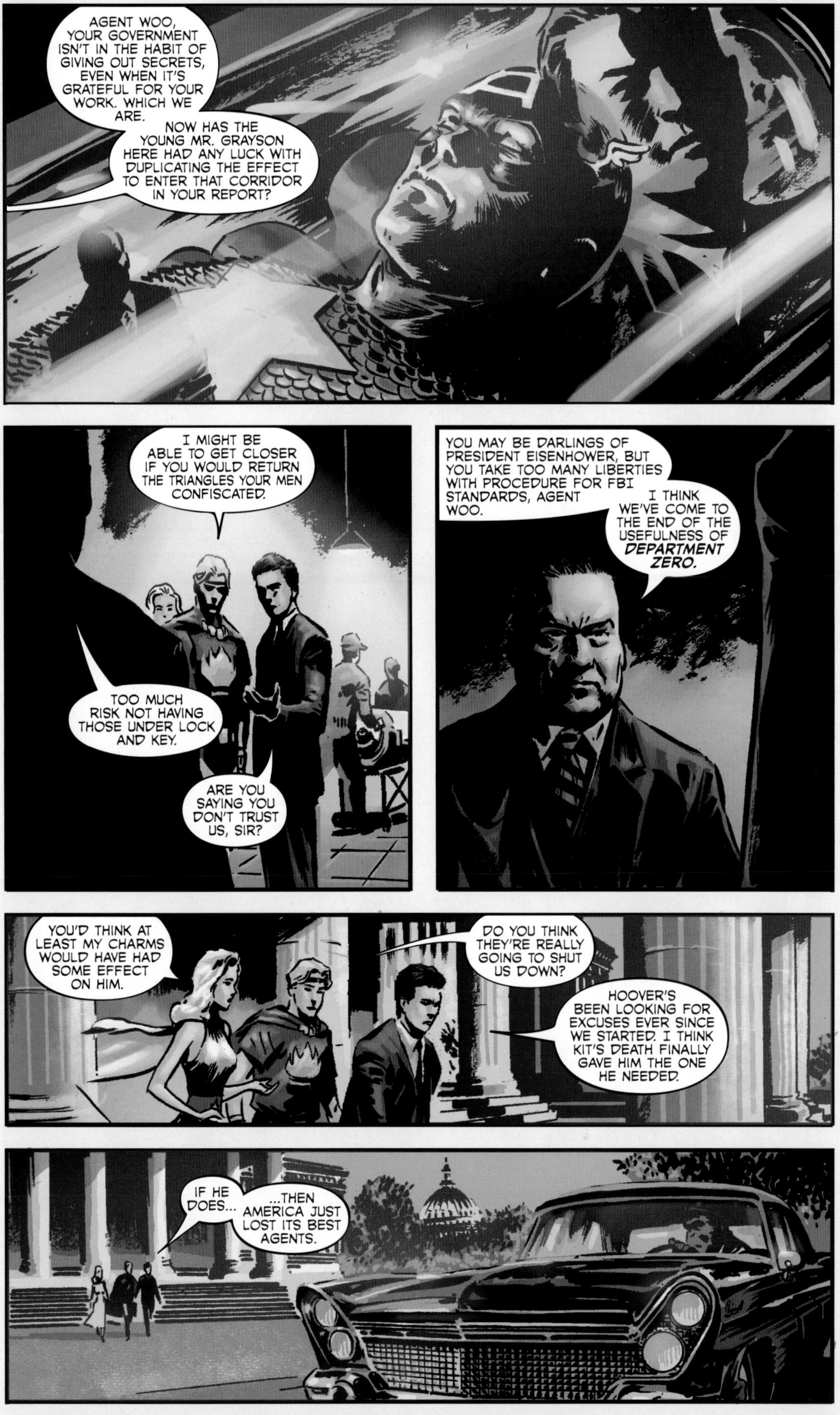
AGENT WOO, YOUR GOVERNMENT ISN'T IN THE HABIT OF GIVING OUT SECRETS, EVEN WHEN IT'S GRATEFUL FOR YOUR WORK. WHICH WE ARE.
NOW HAS THE YOUNG MR. GRAYSON HERE HAD ANY LUCK WITH DUPLICATING THE EFFECT TO ENTER THAT CORRIDOR IN YOUR REPORT?
I MIGHT BE ABLE TO GET CLOSER IF YOU WOULD RETURN THE TRIANGLES YOUR MEN CONFISCATED.
TOO MUCH RISK NOT HAVING THOSE UNDER LOCK AND KEY.
ARE YOU SAYING YOU DON'T TRUST US, SIR?
YOU MAY BE DARLINGS OF PRESIDENT EISENHOWER, BUT YOU TAKE TOO MANY LIBERTIES WITH PROCEDURE FOR FBI STANDARDS, AGENT WOO.
I THINK WE'VE COME TO THE END OF THE USEFULNESS OF *DEPARTMENT ZERO.*
YOU'D THINK AT LEAST MY CHARMS WOULD HAVE HAD SOME EFFECT ON HIM.
DO YOU THINK THEY'RE REALLY GOING TO SHUT US DOWN?
HOOVER'S BEEN LOOKING FOR EXCUSES EVER SINCE WE STARTED. I THINK KIT'S DEATH FINALLY GAVE HIM THE ONE HE NEEDED.
IF HE DOES...
...THEN AMERICA JUST LOST ITS BEST AGENTS.

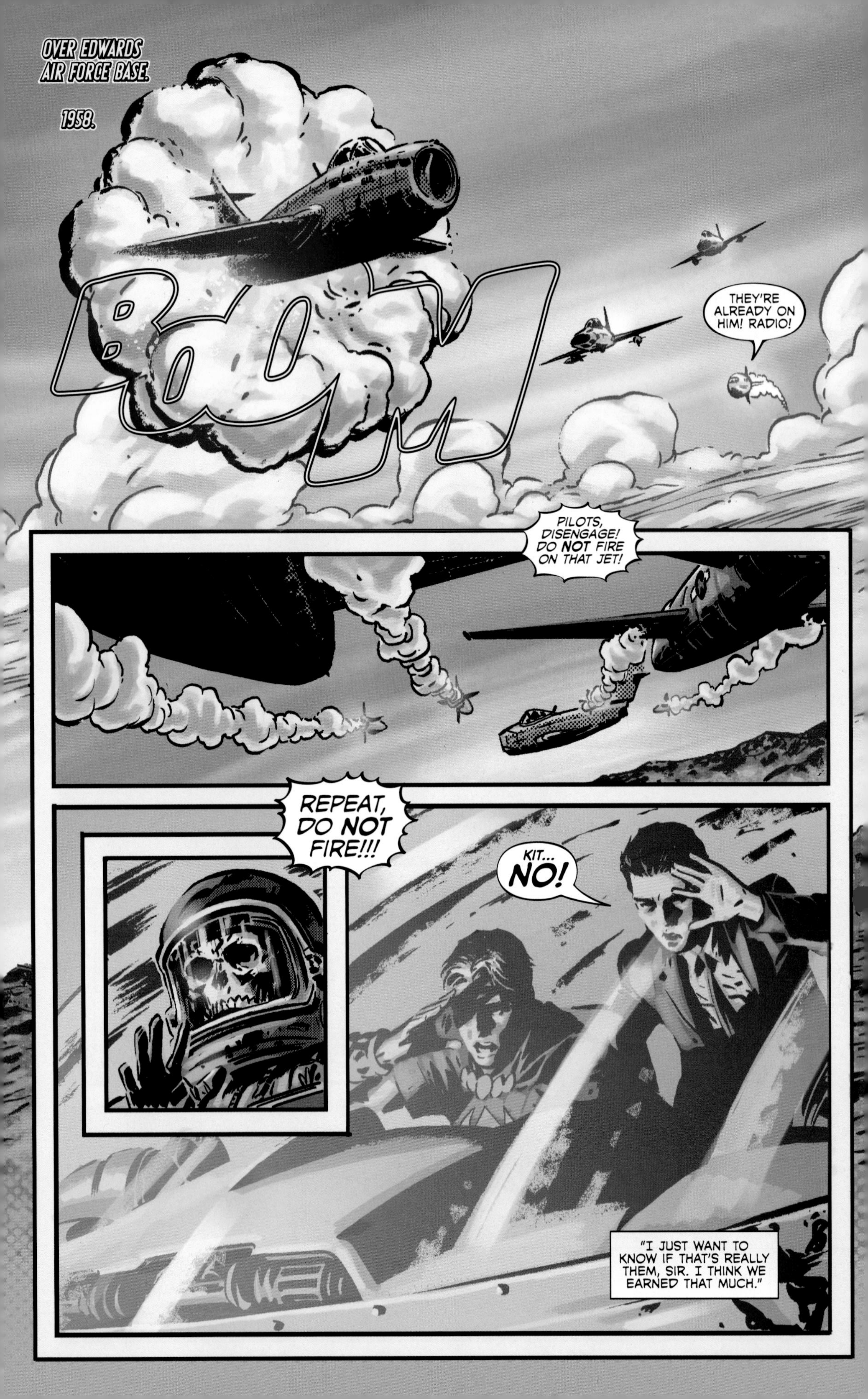
OVER EDWARDS AIR FORCE BASE.
1958.
BOOM
THEY'RE ALREADY ON HIM! RADIO!
PILOTS, DISENGAGE! DO NOT FIRE ON THAT JET!
REPEAT, DO NOT FIRE!!!
KIT... NO!
"I JUST WANT TO KNOW IF THAT'S REALLY THEM, SIR. I THINK WE EARNED THAT MUCH."

YOUR TRIP INTO THE SENTRY'S MIND DRAINED YOU... ...AND YOU PASSED OUT WHILE CONNECTING US. I THINK IF YOU TAKE OFF YOUR HEADBAND...

ARE YOU SUGGESTING THAT WE'RE TRAPPED IN A...

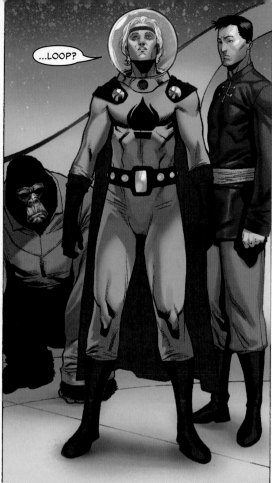

...LOOP?

LATER.

YOU SURE HE DIDN'T LEARN ANYTHING ABOUT OUR OPERATION?

HE NEVER VENTURED OUTSIDE HIS MEMORIES, BUT I WENT INTO HIS.

HE'S NOT ONLY IN CONTACT WITH THE REAL AVENGERS, HE'S HIDING THEM.

PERFECT.

I LEFT THE INFORMATION YOU WANTED IN HIS MIND.

GOOD.

THEN IT'S TIME FOR THE SHOWDOWN.

"WE'RE ALMOST THERE! IF I GO ANY FASTER, WE'LL OVERSHOOT THE WHOLE VALLEY!"

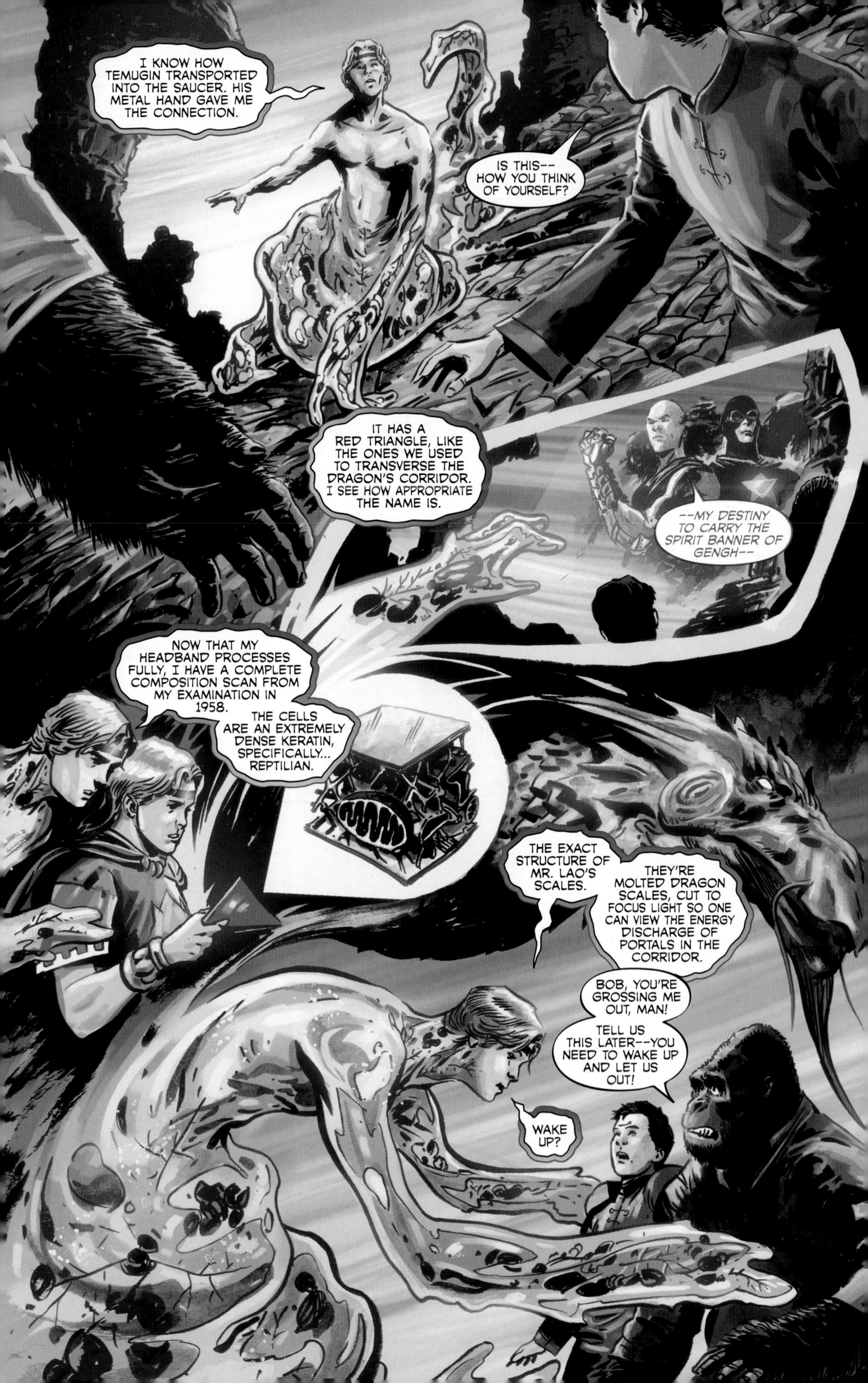
I KNOW HOW TEMUGIN TRANSPORTED INTO THE SAUCER. HIS METAL HAND GAVE ME THE CONNECTION.
IS THIS-- HOW YOU THINK OF YOURSELF?
IT HAS A RED TRIANGLE, LIKE THE ONES WE USED TO TRANSVERSE THE DRAGON'S CORRIDOR. I SEE HOW APPROPRIATE THE NAME IS.
--MY DESTINY TO CARRY THE SPIRIT BANNER OF GENGH--
NOW THAT MY HEADBAND PROCESSES FULLY, I HAVE A COMPLETE COMPOSITION SCAN FROM MY EXAMINATION IN 1958.
THE CELLS ARE AN EXTREMELY DENSE KERATIN, SPECIFICALLY... REPTILIAN.
THE EXACT STRUCTURE OF MR. LAO'S SCALES.
THEY'RE MOLTED DRAGON SCALES, CUT TO FOCUS LIGHT SO ONE CAN VIEW THE ENERGY DISCHARGE OF PORTALS IN THE CORRIDOR.
BOB, YOU'RE GROSSING ME OUT, MAN!
TELL US THIS LATER--YOU NEED TO WAKE UP AND LET US OUT!
WAKE UP?

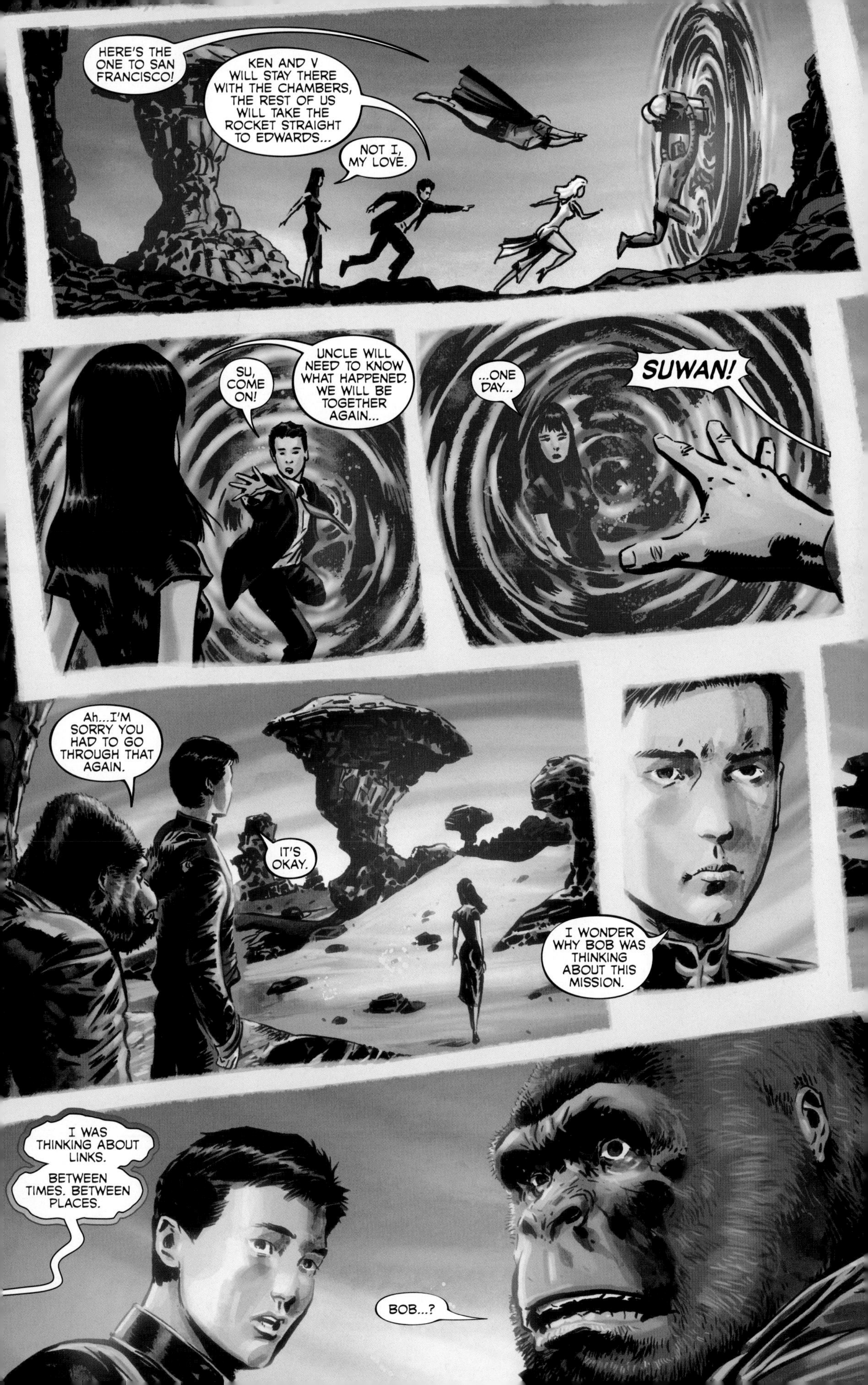
HERE'S THE ONE TO SAN FRANCISCO!
KEN AND V WILL STAY THERE WITH THE CHAMBERS, THE REST OF US WILL TAKE THE ROCKET STRAIGHT TO EDWARDS...
NOT I, MY LOVE.
SU, COME ON!
UNCLE WILL NEED TO KNOW WHAT HAPPENED. WE WILL BE TOGETHER AGAIN...
...ONE DAY...
SUWAN!
Ah...I'M SORRY YOU HAD TO GO THROUGH THAT AGAIN.
IT'S OKAY.
I WONDER WHY BOB WAS THINKING ABOUT THIS MISSION.
I WAS THINKING ABOUT LINKS.
BETWEEN TIMES. BETWEEN PLACES.
BOB...?

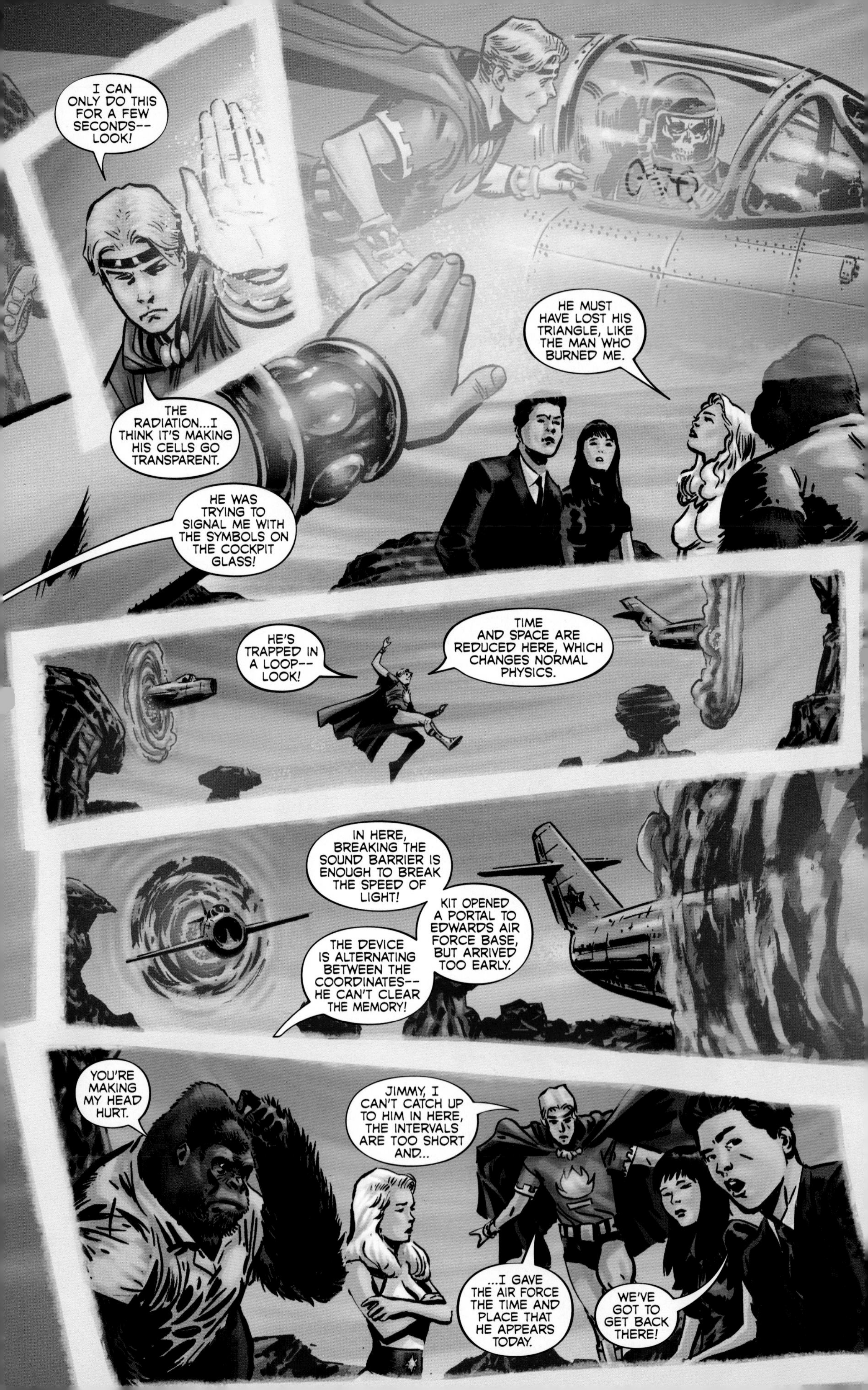
I CAN ONLY DO THIS FOR A FEW SECONDS-- LOOK!
THE RADIATION...I THINK IT'S MAKING HIS CELLS GO TRANSPARENT.
HE WAS TRYING TO SIGNAL ME WITH THE SYMBOLS ON THE COCKPIT GLASS!
HE MUST HAVE LOST HIS TRIANGLE, LIKE THE MAN WHO BURNED ME.
HE'S TRAPPED IN A LOOP-- LOOK!
TIME AND SPACE ARE REDUCED HERE, WHICH CHANGES NORMAL PHYSICS.
IN HERE, BREAKING THE SOUND BARRIER IS ENOUGH TO BREAK THE SPEED OF LIGHT!
KIT OPENED A PORTAL TO EDWARDS AIR FORCE BASE, BUT ARRIVED TOO EARLY.
THE DEVICE IS ALTERNATING BETWEEN THE COORDINATES-- HE CAN'T CLEAR THE MEMORY!
YOU'RE MAKING MY HEAD HURT.
JIMMY, I CAN'T CATCH UP TO HIM IN HERE, THE INTERVALS ARE TOO SHORT AND...
...I GAVE THE AIR FORCE THE TIME AND PLACE THAT HE APPEARS TODAY.
WE'VE GOT TO GET BACK THERE!

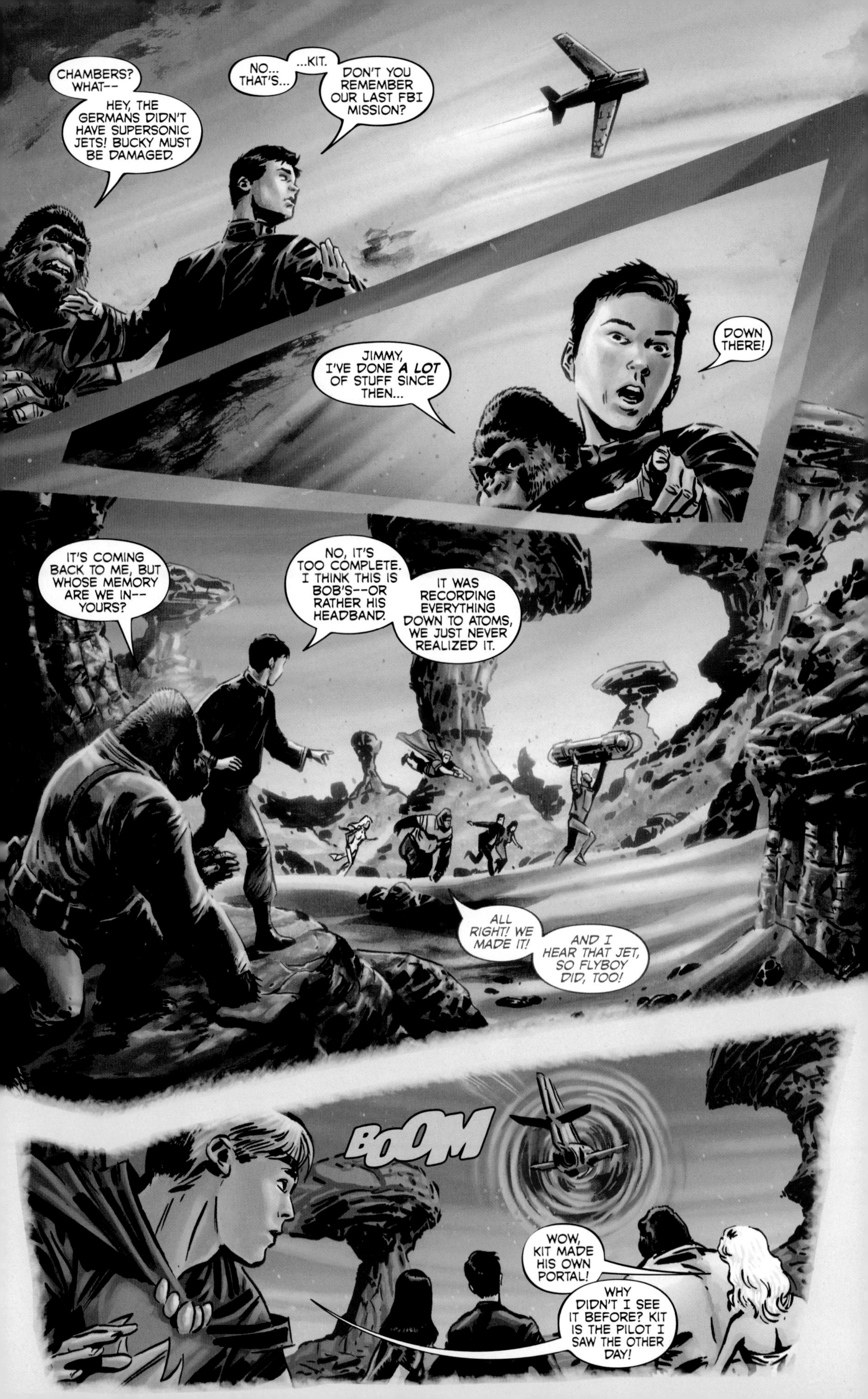
CHAMBERS? WHAT--
NO... THAT'S...
...KIT.
DON'T YOU REMEMBER OUR LAST FBI MISSION?
HEY, THE GERMANS DIDN'T HAVE SUPERSONIC JETS! BUCKY MUST BE DAMAGED.
JIMMY, I'VE DONE A LOT OF STUFF SINCE THEN...
DOWN THERE!
IT'S COMING BACK TO ME, BUT WHOSE MEMORY ARE WE IN--YOURS?
NO, IT'S TOO COMPLETE. I THINK THIS IS BOB'S--OR RATHER HIS HEADBAND.
IT WAS RECORDING EVERYTHING DOWN TO ATOMS, WE JUST NEVER REALIZED IT.
ALL RIGHT! WE MADE IT!
AND I HEAR THAT JET, SO FLYBOY DID, TOO!
BOOM
WOW, KIT MADE HIS OWN PORTAL!
WHY DIDN'T I SEE IT BEFORE? KIT IS THE PILOT I SAW THE OTHER DAY!

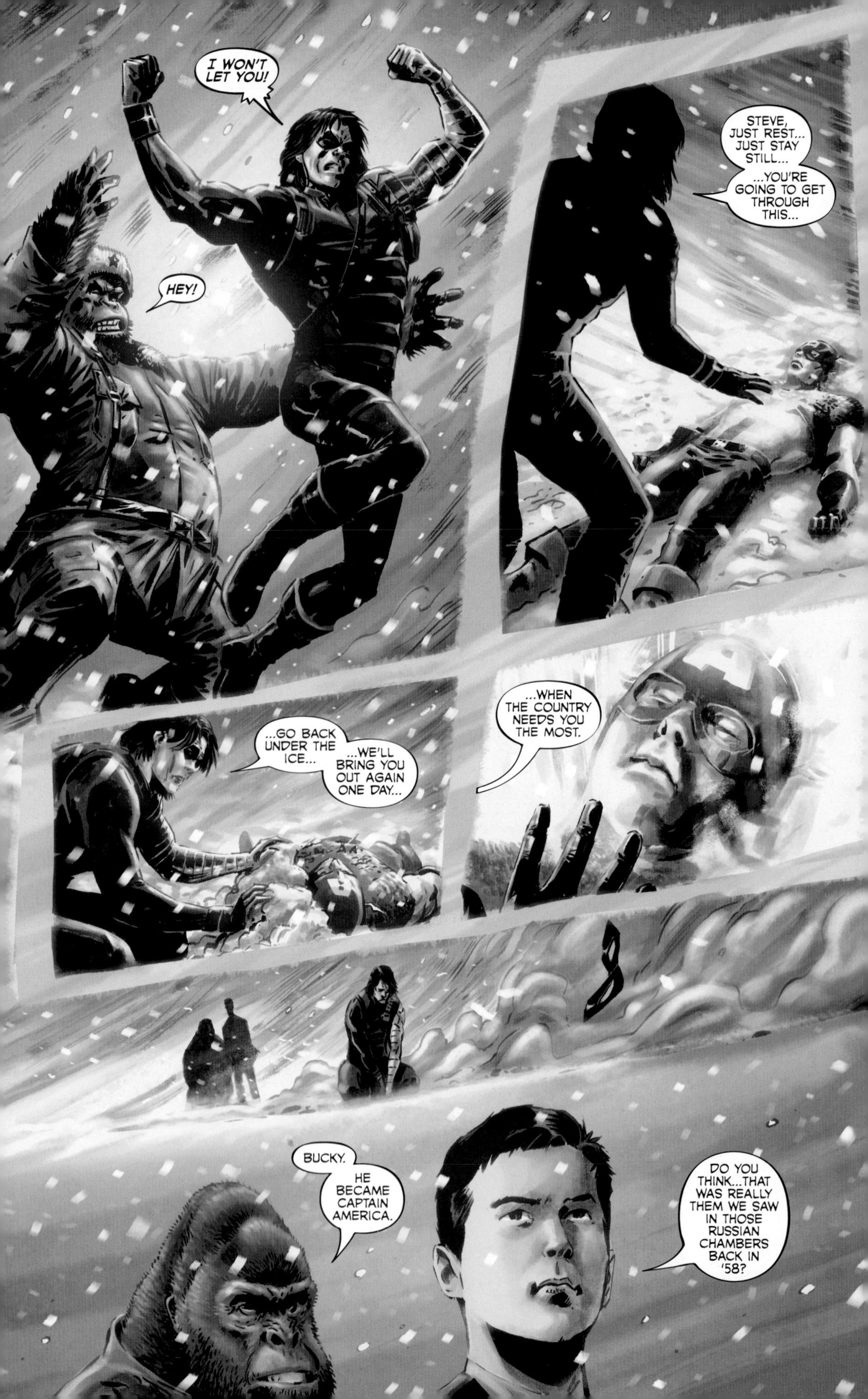
I WON'T LET YOU!
HEY!
STEVE, JUST REST... JUST STAY STILL...
...YOU'RE GOING TO GET THROUGH THIS...
...GO BACK UNDER THE ICE...
...WE'LL BRING YOU OUT AGAIN ONE DAY...
...WHEN THE COUNTRY NEEDS YOU THE MOST.
BUCKY.
HE BECAME CAPTAIN AMERICA.
DO YOU THINK...THAT WAS REALLY THEM WE SAW IN THOSE RUSSIAN CHAMBERS BACK IN '58?

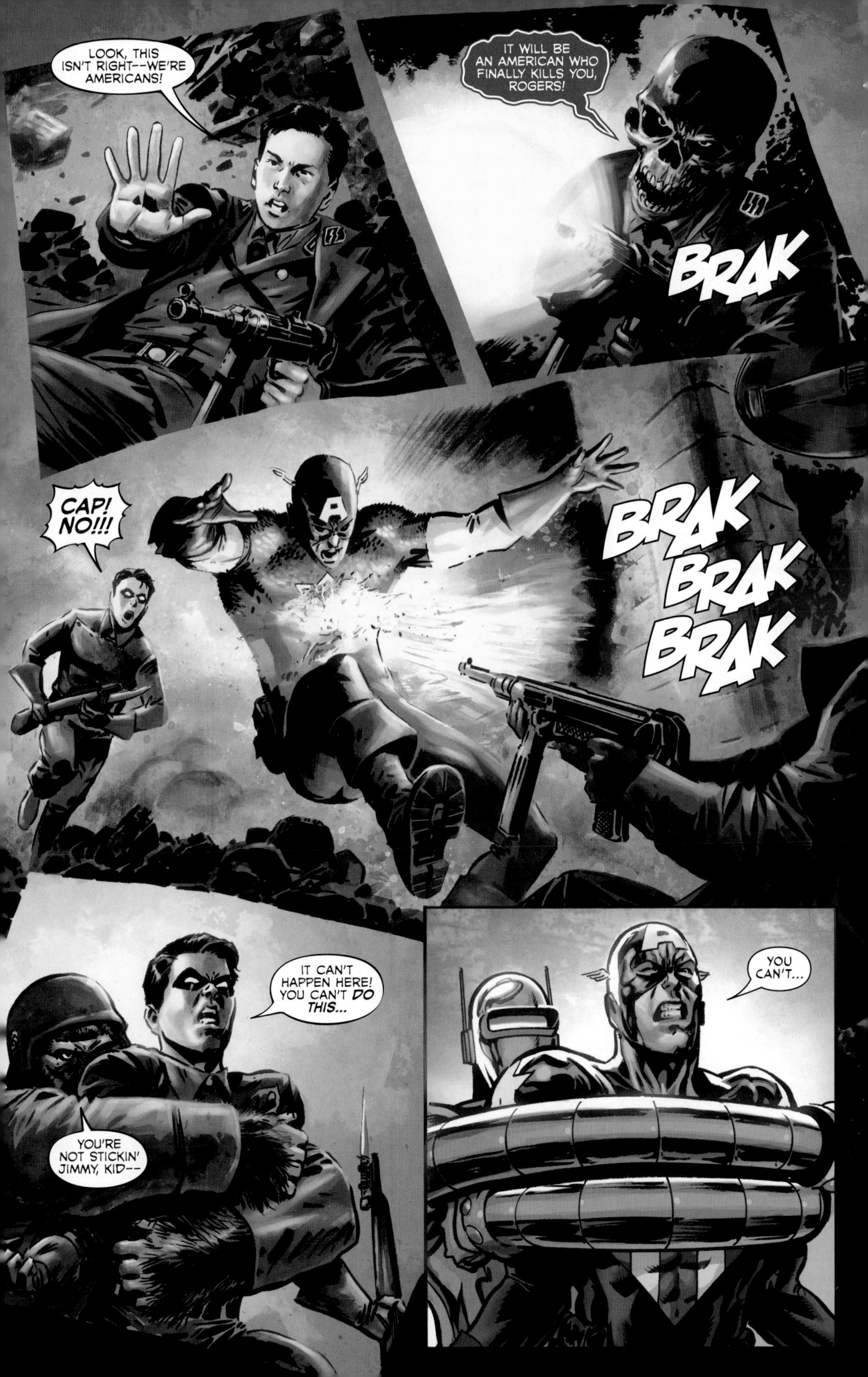
LOOK, THIS ISN'T RIGHT--WE'RE AMERICANS!
IT WILL BE AN AMERICAN WHO FINALLY KILLS YOU, ROGERS!
BRAK
CAP! NO!!!
BRAK
BRAK
BRAK
IT CAN'T HAPPEN HERE! YOU CAN'T *DO THIS...*
YOU'RE NOT STICKIN' JIMMY, KID--
YOU CAN'T...

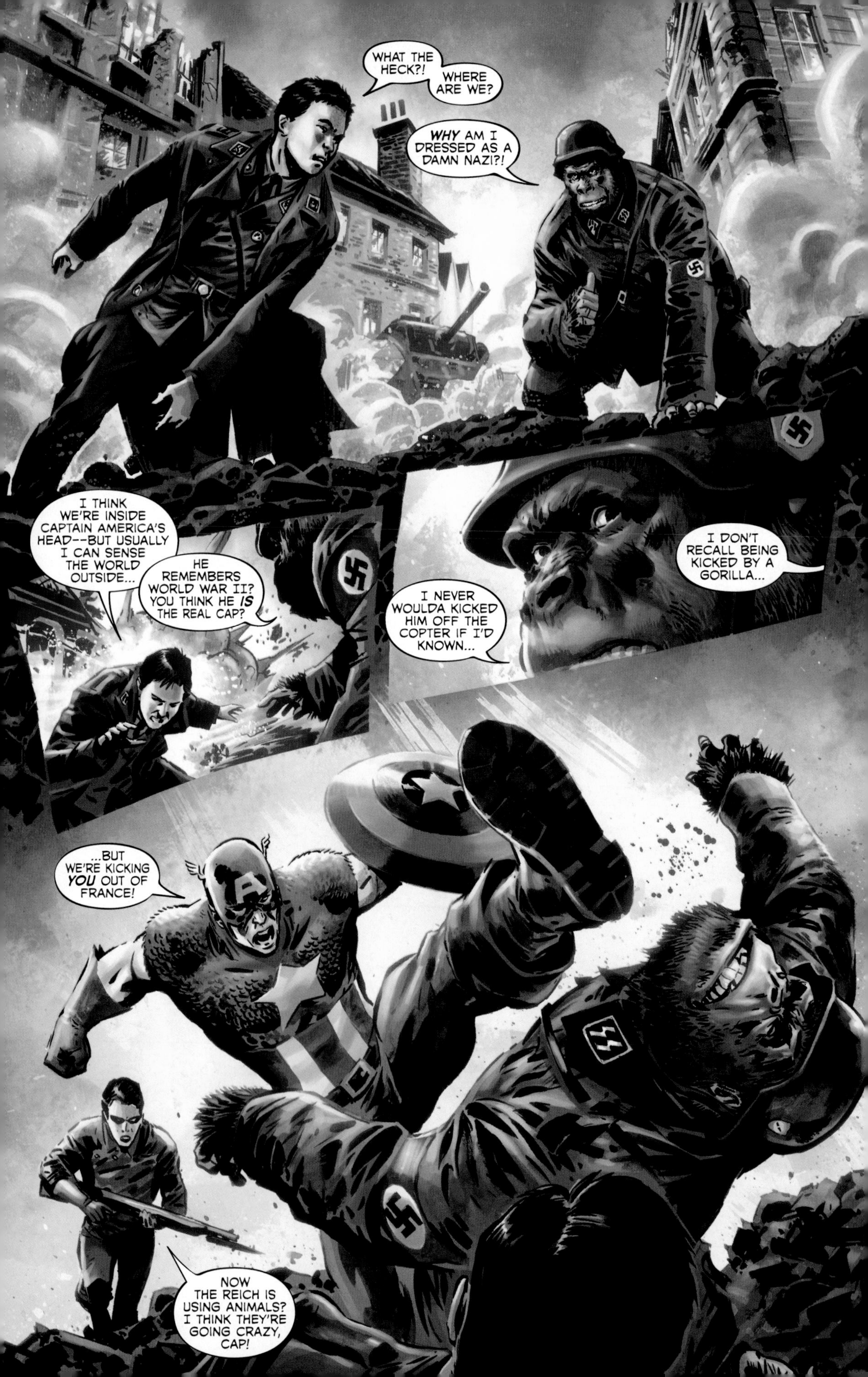
WHAT THE HECK?!
WHERE ARE WE?
WHY AM I DRESSED AS A DAMN NAZI?!
I THINK WE'RE INSIDE CAPTAIN AMERICA'S HEAD--BUT USUALLY I CAN SENSE THE WORLD OUTSIDE...
HE REMEMBERS WORLD WAR II? YOU THINK HE IS THE REAL CAP?
I NEVER WOULDA KICKED HIM OFF THE COPTER IF I'D KNOWN...
I DON'T RECALL BEING KICKED BY A GORILLA...
...BUT WE'RE KICKING YOU OUT OF FRANCE!
NOW THE REICH IS USING ANIMALS? I THINK THEY'RE GOING CRAZY, CAP!

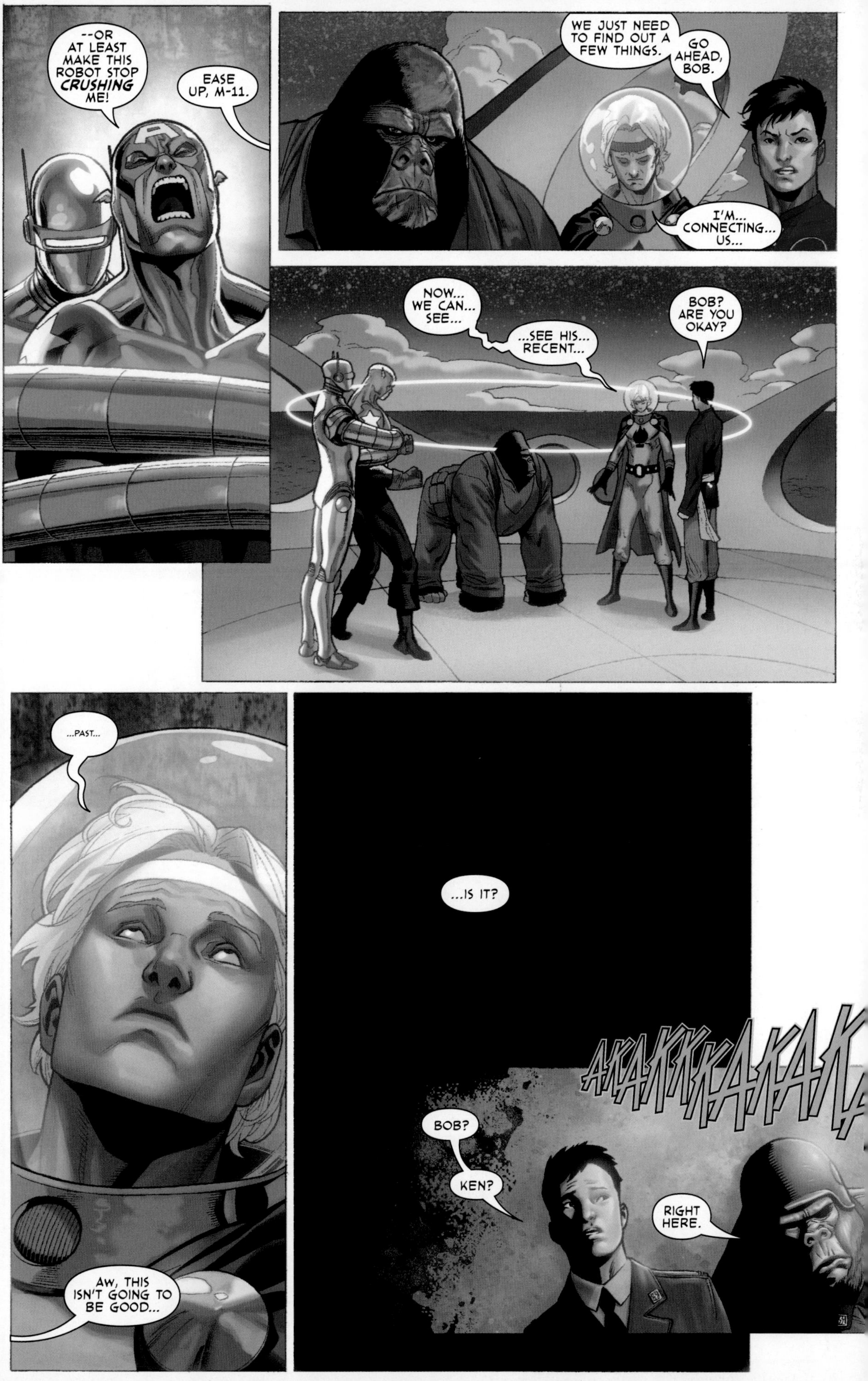
--OR AT LEAST MAKE THIS ROBOT STOP *CRUSHING* ME!
EASE UP, M-11.
WE JUST NEED TO FIND OUT A FEW THINGS.
GO AHEAD, BOB.
I'M... CONNECTING... US...
NOW... WE CAN... SEE...
...SEE HIS... RECENT...
BOB? ARE YOU OKAY?
...PAST...
AW, THIS ISN'T GOING TO BE GOOD...
...IS IT?
AKAKKKAKAKA
BOB?
KEN?
RIGHT HERE.

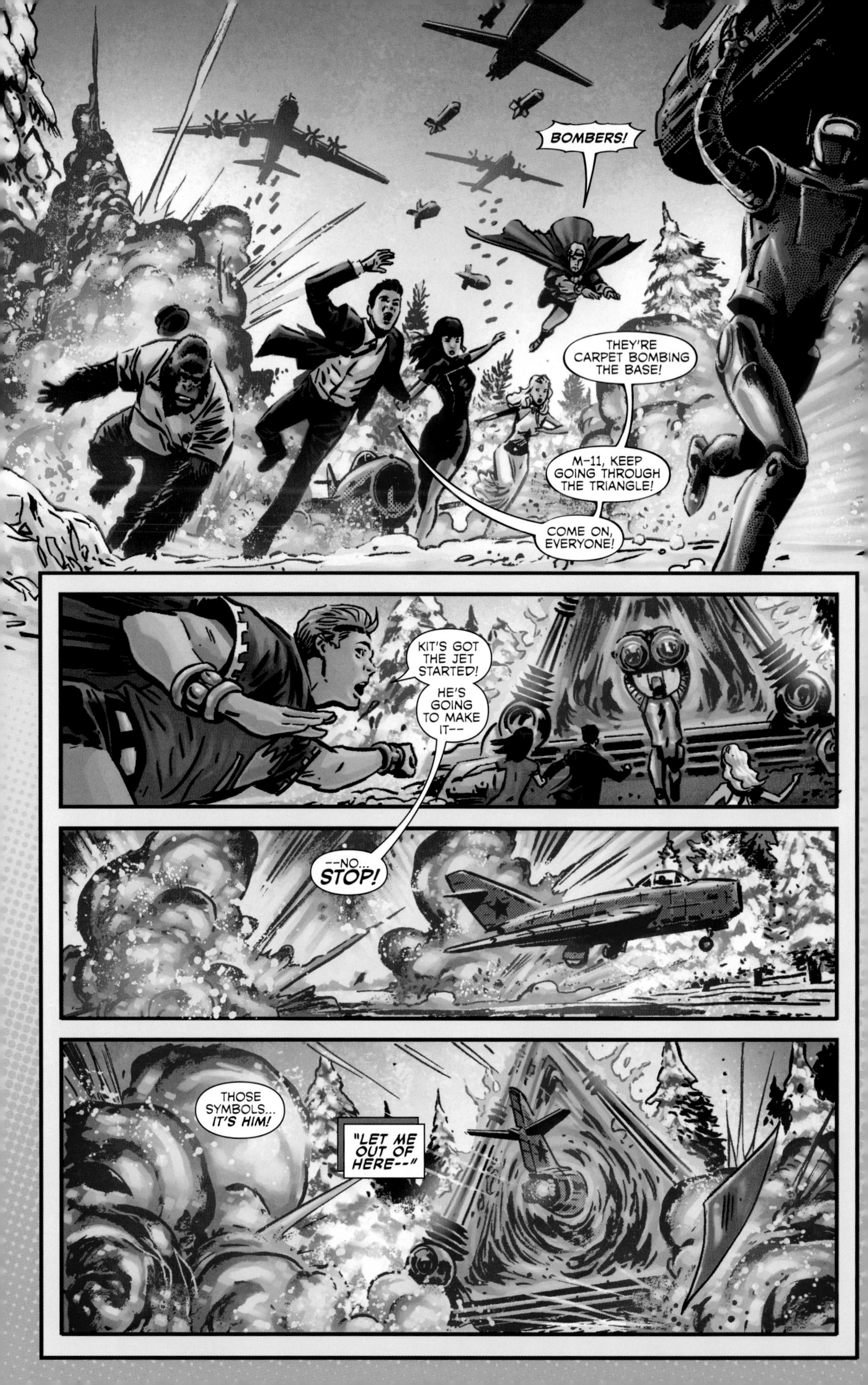
BOMBERS!
THEY'RE CARPET BOMBING THE BASE!
M-11, KEEP GOING THROUGH THE TRIANGLE!
COME ON, EVERYONE!
KIT'S GOT THE JET STARTED!
HE'S GOING TO MAKE IT--
--NO... STOP!
THOSE SYMBOLS... IT'S HIM!
"LET ME OUT OF HERE--"

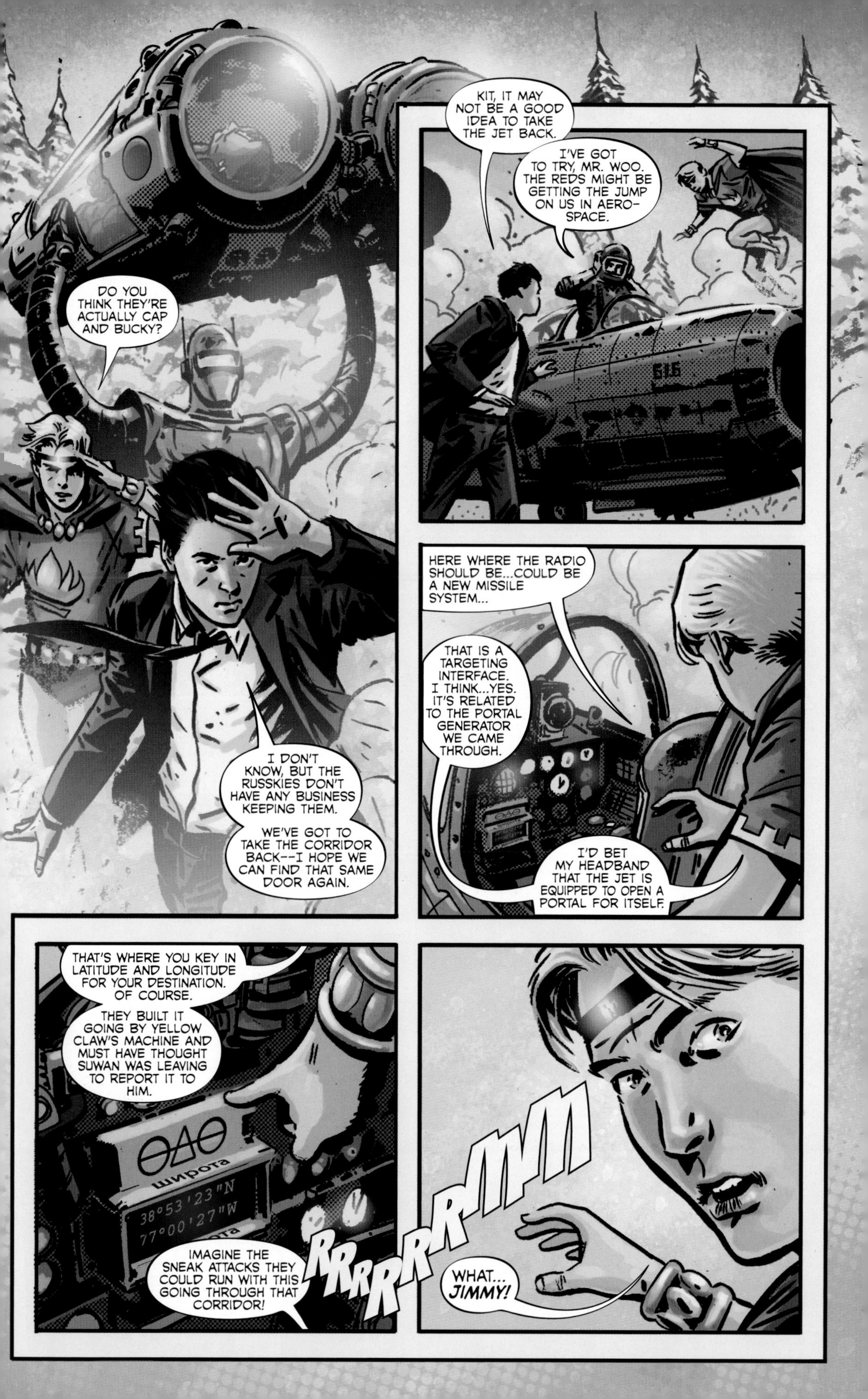
DO YOU THINK THEY'RE ACTUALLY CAP AND BUCKY?
I DON'T KNOW, BUT THE RUSSKIES DON'T HAVE ANY BUSINESS KEEPING THEM.
WE'VE GOT TO TAKE THE CORRIDOR BACK--I HOPE WE CAN FIND THAT SAME DOOR AGAIN.
KIT, IT MAY NOT BE A GOOD IDEA TO TAKE THE JET BACK.
I'VE GOT TO TRY, MR. WOO. THE REDS MIGHT BE GETTING THE JUMP ON US IN AERO-SPACE.
HERE WHERE THE RADIO SHOULD BE...COULD BE A NEW MISSILE SYSTEM...
THAT IS A TARGETING INTERFACE. I THINK...YES. IT'S RELATED TO THE PORTAL GENERATOR WE CAME THROUGH.
I'D BET MY HEADBAND THAT THE JET IS EQUIPPED TO OPEN A PORTAL FOR ITSELF.
THAT'S WHERE YOU KEY IN LATITUDE AND LONGITUDE FOR YOUR DESTINATION. OF COURSE.
THEY BUILT IT GOING BY YELLOW CLAW'S MACHINE AND MUST HAVE THOUGHT SUWAN WAS LEAVING TO REPORT IT TO HIM.
широта
38°53'23"N
77°00'27"W
IMAGINE THE SNEAK ATTACKS THEY COULD RUN WITH THIS GOING THROUGH THAT CORRIDOR!
RRRRRRRMMM
WHAT... JIMMY!

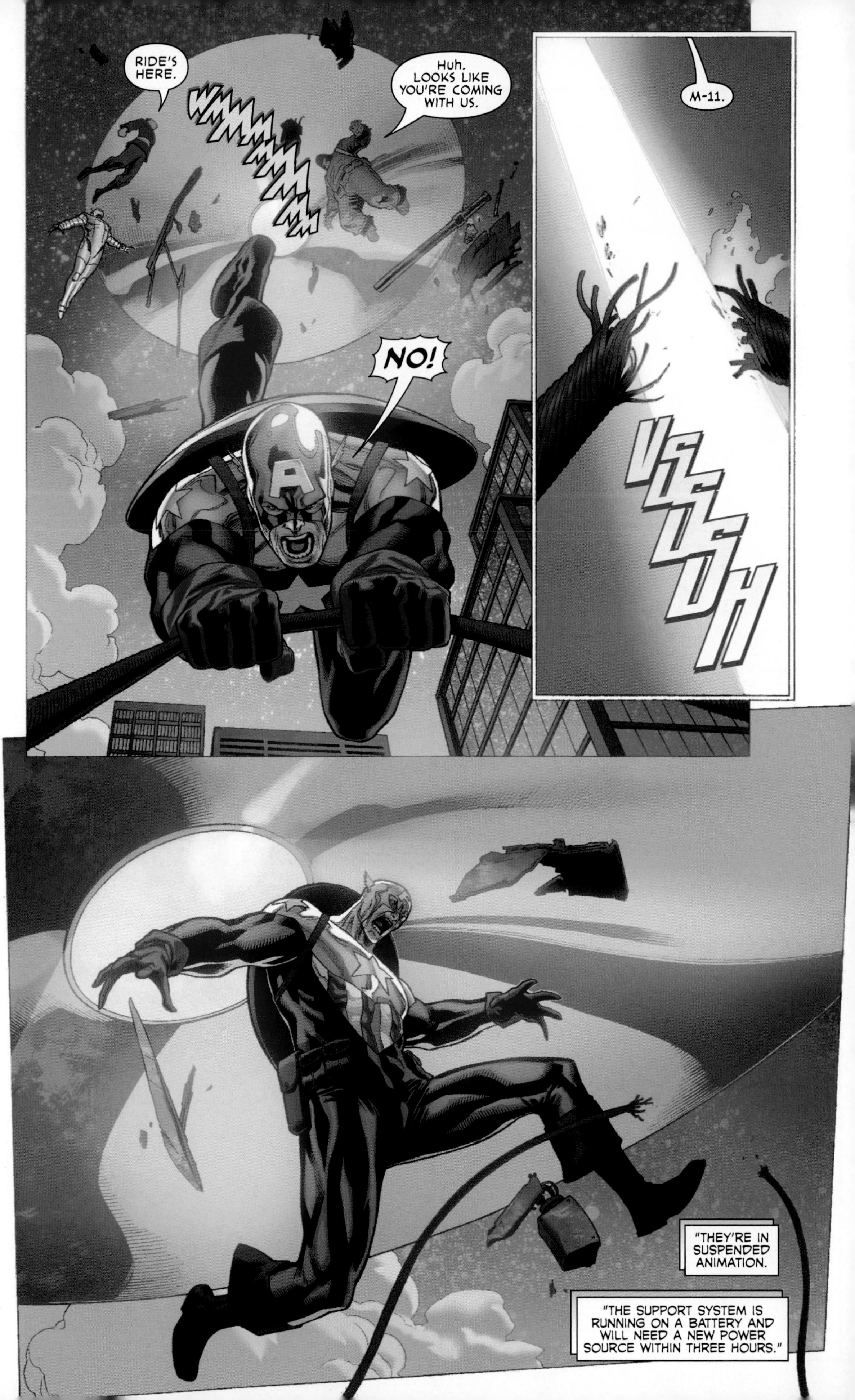
RIDE'S HERE.
WMMMMMMM
Huh. LOOKS LIKE YOU'RE COMING WITH US.
NO!
M-11.
VSSSH
"THEY'RE IN SUSPENDED ANIMATION.
"THE SUPPORT SYSTEM IS RUNNING ON A BATTERY AND WILL NEED A NEW POWER SOURCE WITHIN THREE HOURS."

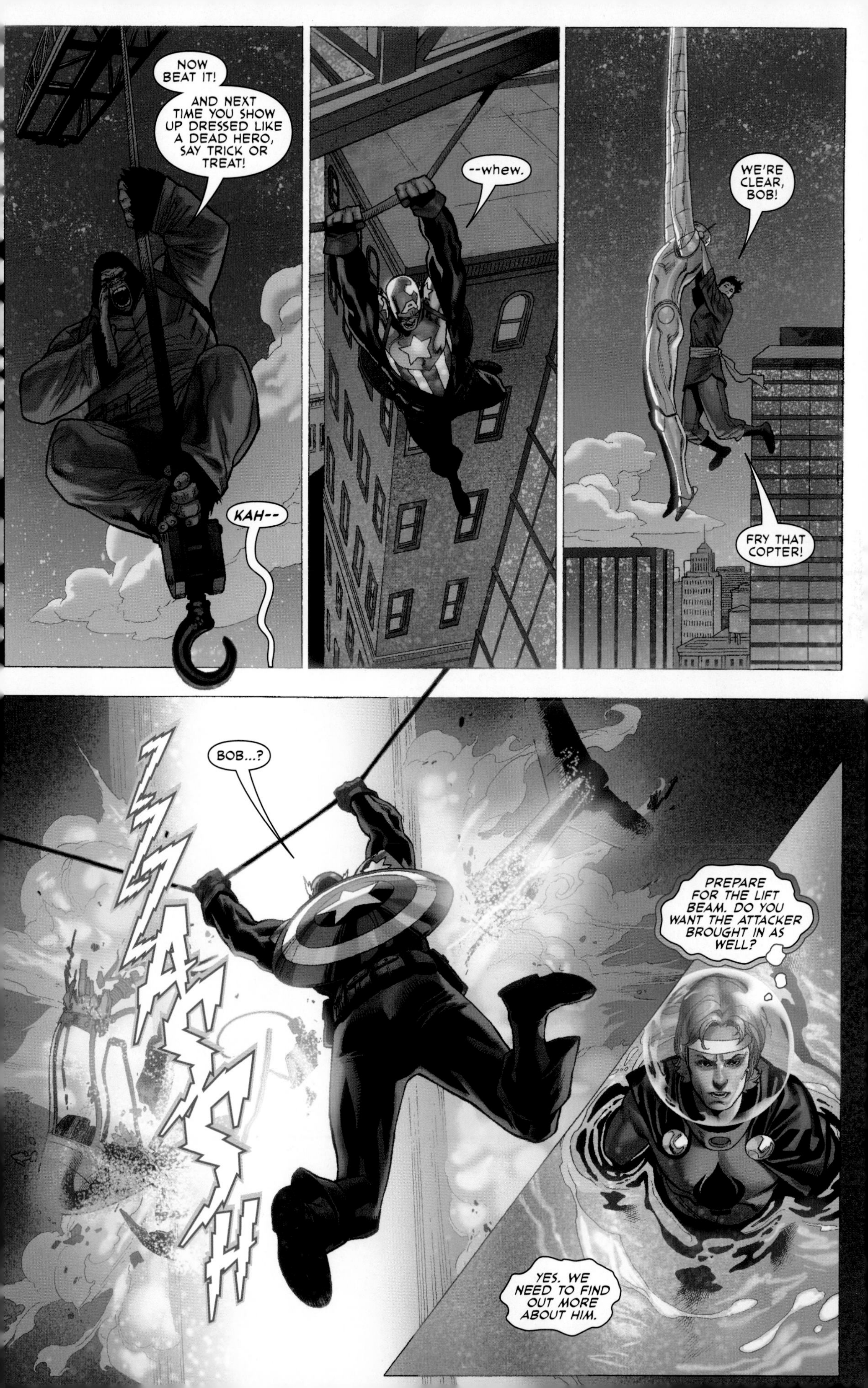
NOW BEAT IT!
AND NEXT TIME YOU SHOW UP DRESSED LIKE A DEAD HERO, SAY TRICK OR TREAT!
KAH--
--whew.
WE'RE CLEAR, BOB!
FRY THAT COPTER!
BOB...?
ZZZAKASSH
PREPARE FOR THE LIFT BEAM. DO YOU WANT THE ATTACKER BROUGHT IN AS WELL?
YES. WE NEED TO FIND OUT MORE ABOUT HIM.

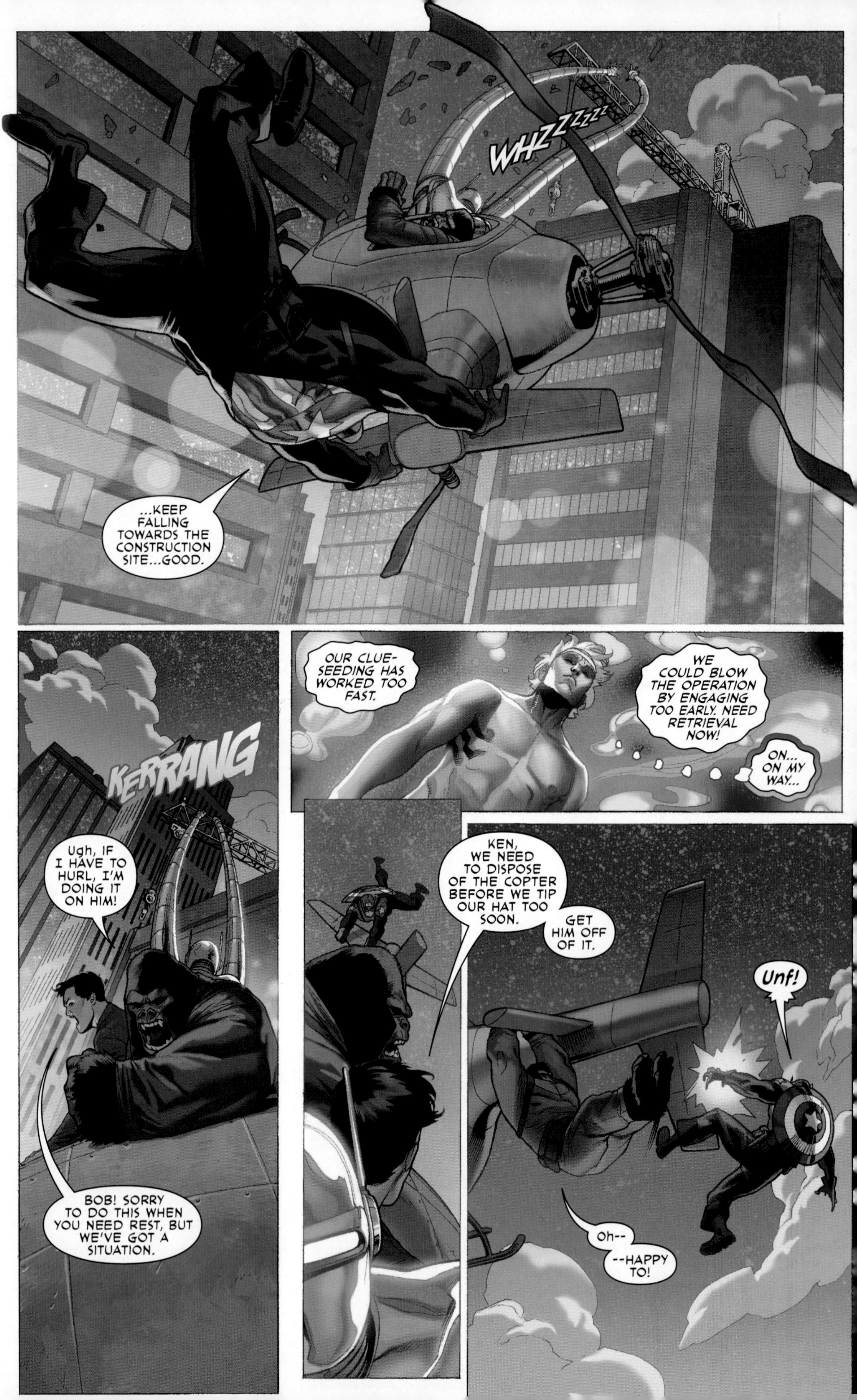
WHZZZZZZ
...KEEP FALLING TOWARDS THE CONSTRUCTION SITE...GOOD.
KERRANG
Ugh, IF I HAVE TO HURL, I'M DOING IT ON HIM!
BOB! SORRY TO DO THIS WHEN YOU NEED REST, BUT WE'VE GOT A SITUATION.
OUR CLUE-SEEDING HAS WORKED TOO FAST.
WE COULD BLOW THE OPERATION BY ENGAGING TOO EARLY. NEED RETRIEVAL NOW!
ON... ON MY WAY...
KEN, WE NEED TO DISPOSE OF THE COPTER BEFORE WE TIP OUR HAT TOO SOON.
GET HIM OFF OF IT.
Unf!
Oh--
--HAPPY TO!

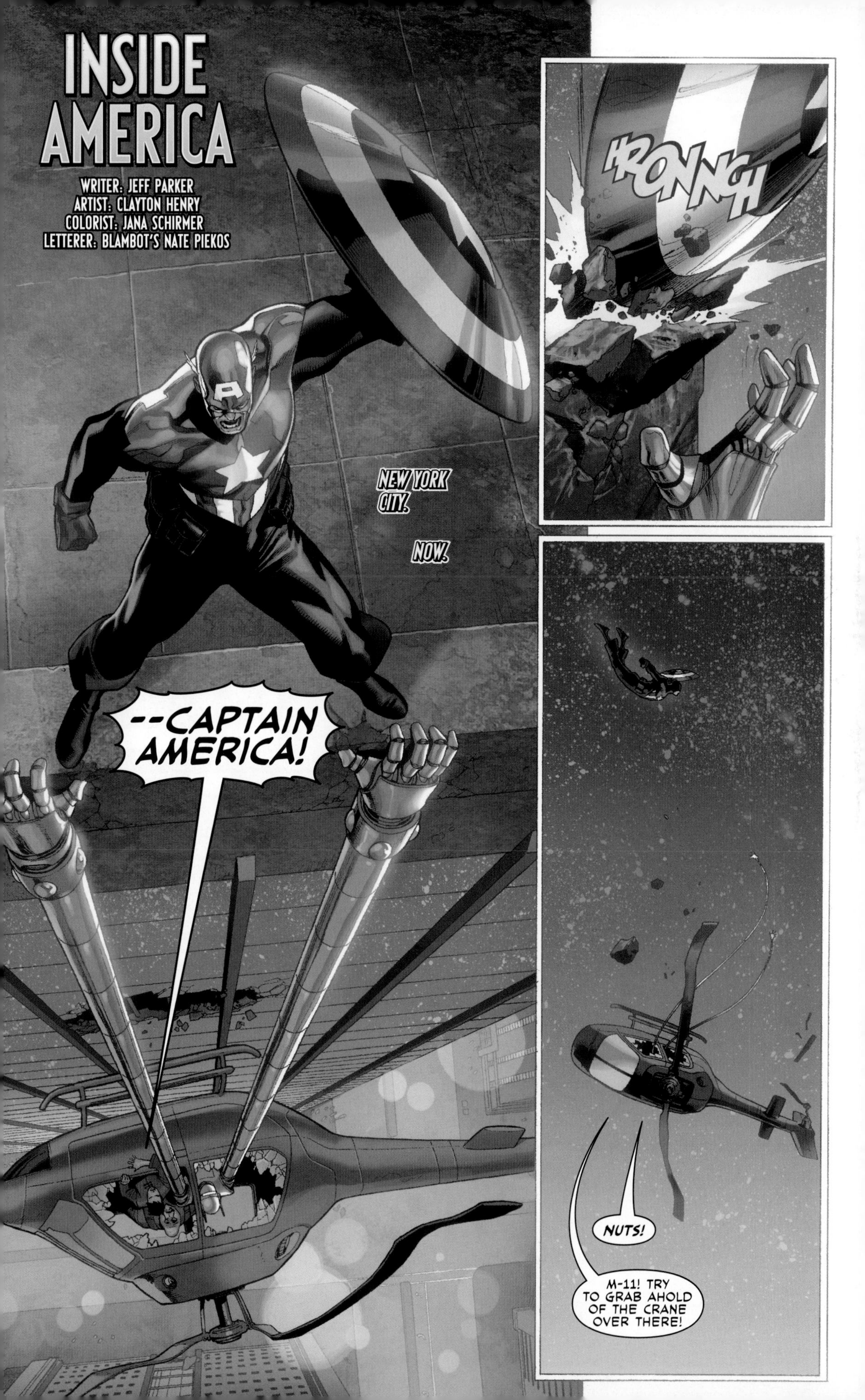
INSIDE AMERICA
WRITER: JEFF PARKER
ARTIST: CLAYTON HENRY
COLORIST: JANA SCHIRMER
LETTERER: BLAMBOT'S NATE PIEKOS
NEW YORK CITY.
NOW.
--CAPTAIN AMERICA!
HRONNGH
NUTS!
M-11! TRY TO GRAB AHOLD OF THE CRANE OVER THERE!

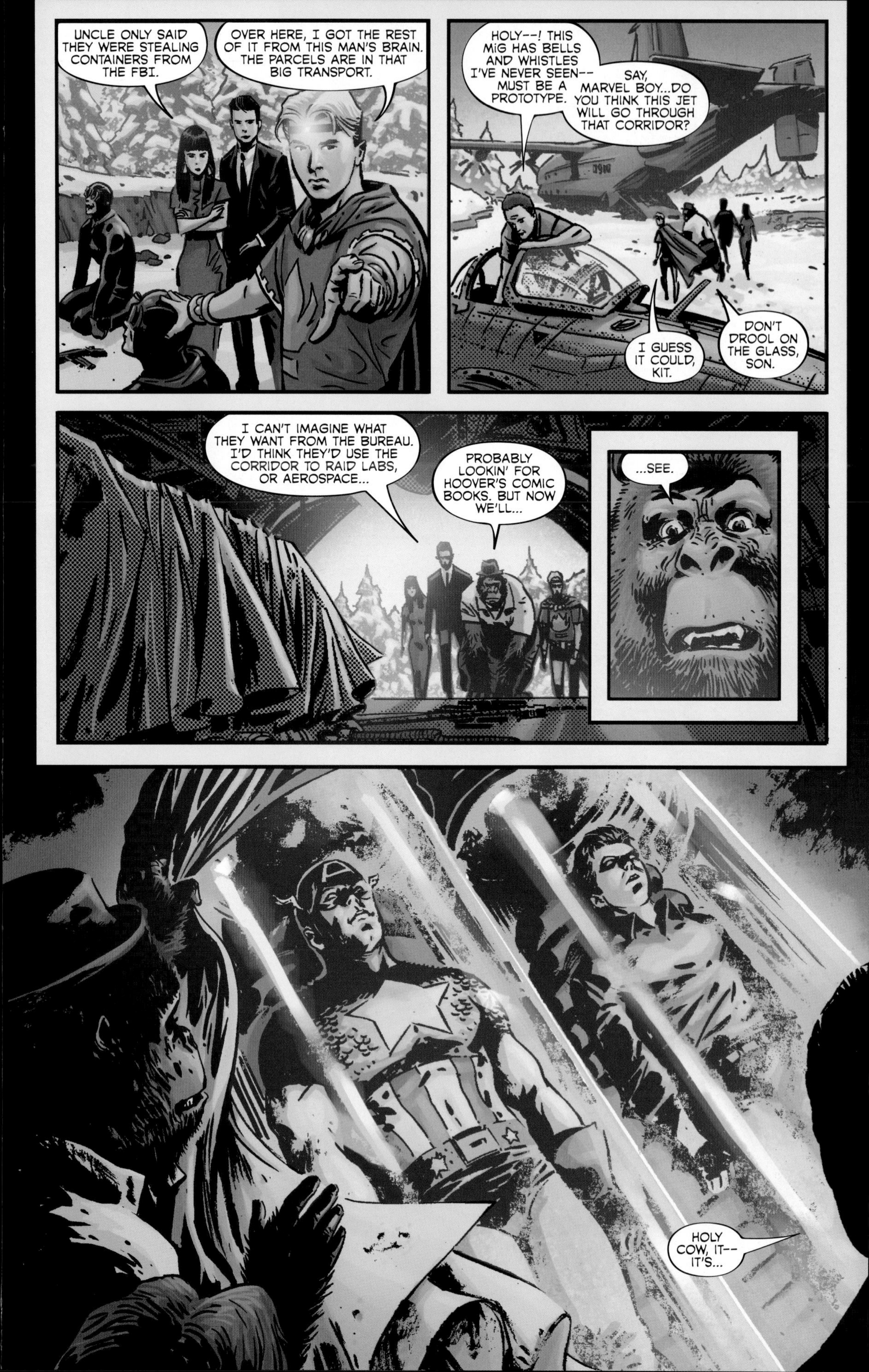
UNCLE ONLY SAID THEY WERE STEALING CONTAINERS FROM THE FBI.
OVER HERE, I GOT THE REST OF IT FROM THIS MAN'S BRAIN. THE PARCELS ARE IN THAT BIG TRANSPORT.
HOLY--! THIS MiG HAS BELLS AND WHISTLES I'VE NEVER SEEN-- MUST BE A PROTOTYPE.
SAY, MARVEL BOY...DO YOU THINK THIS JET WILL GO THROUGH THAT CORRIDOR?
I GUESS IT COULD, KIT.
DON'T DROOL ON THE GLASS, SON.
I CAN'T IMAGINE WHAT THEY WANT FROM THE BUREAU. I'D THINK THEY'D USE THE CORRIDOR TO RAID LABS, OR AEROSPACE...
PROBABLY LOOKIN' FOR HOOVER'S COMIC BOOKS. BUT NOW WE'LL...
...SEE.
HOLY COW, IT-- IT'S...

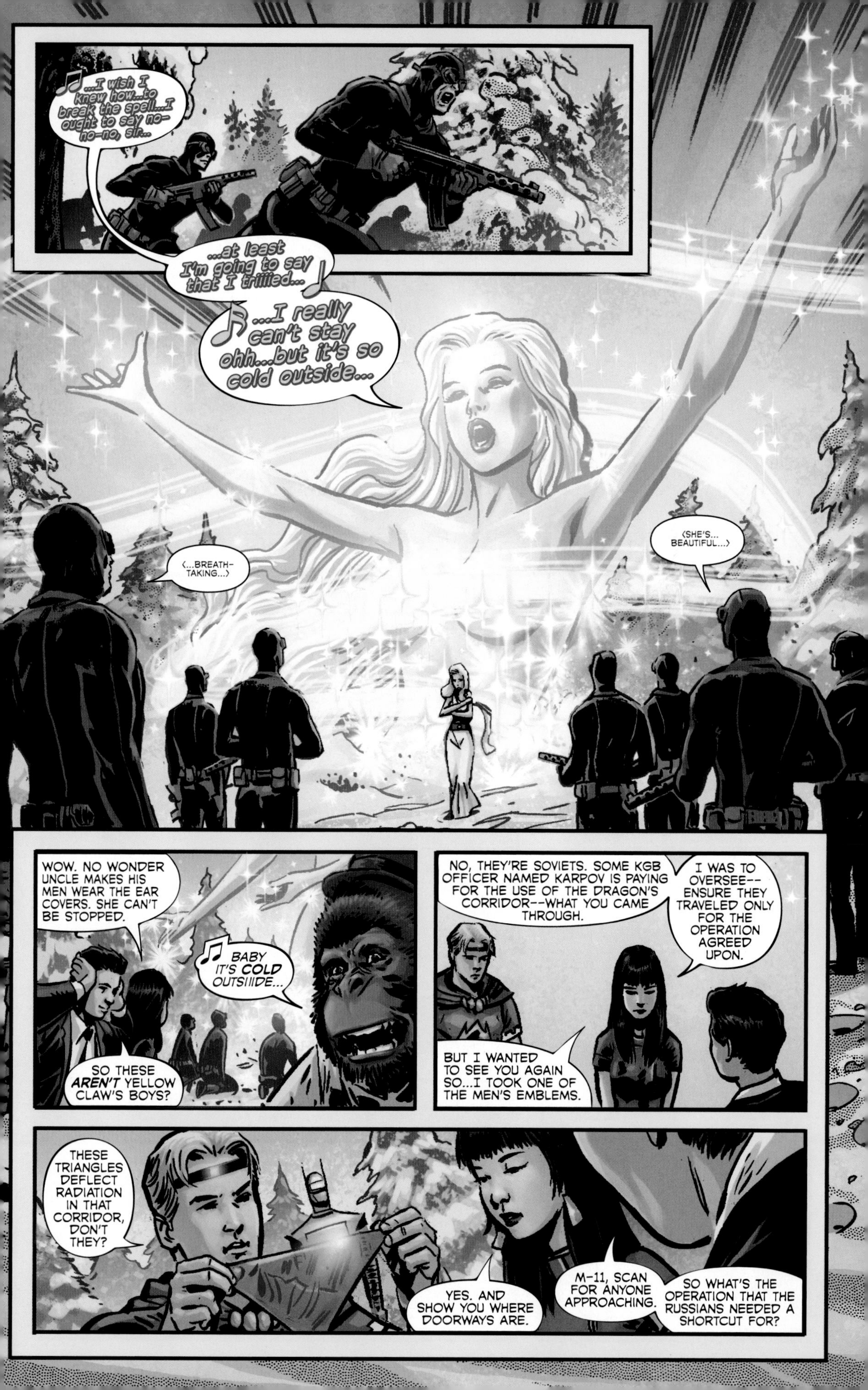
...I wish I knew how...to break the spell...I ought to say no-no-no, sir...
...at least I'm going to say that I triiied...
...I really can't stay ohh...but it's so cold outside...
‹...BREATH-TAKING...›
‹SHE'S... BEAUTIFUL...›
WOW. NO WONDER UNCLE MAKES HIS MEN WEAR THE EAR COVERS. SHE CAN'T BE STOPPED.
BABY IT'S COLD OUTSIIIDE...
SO THESE AREN'T YELLOW CLAW'S BOYS?
NO, THEY'RE SOVIETS. SOME KGB OFFICER NAMED KARPOV IS PAYING FOR THE USE OF THE DRAGON'S CORRIDOR--WHAT YOU CAME THROUGH.
I WAS TO OVERSEE--ENSURE THEY TRAVELED ONLY FOR THE OPERATION AGREED UPON.
BUT I WANTED TO SEE YOU AGAIN SO...I TOOK ONE OF THE MEN'S EMBLEMS.
THESE TRIANGLES DEFLECT RADIATION IN THAT CORRIDOR, DON'T THEY?
YES. AND SHOW YOU WHERE DOORWAYS ARE.
M-11, SCAN FOR ANYONE APPROACHING.
SO WHAT'S THE OPERATION THAT THE RUSSIANS NEEDED A SHORTCUT FOR?

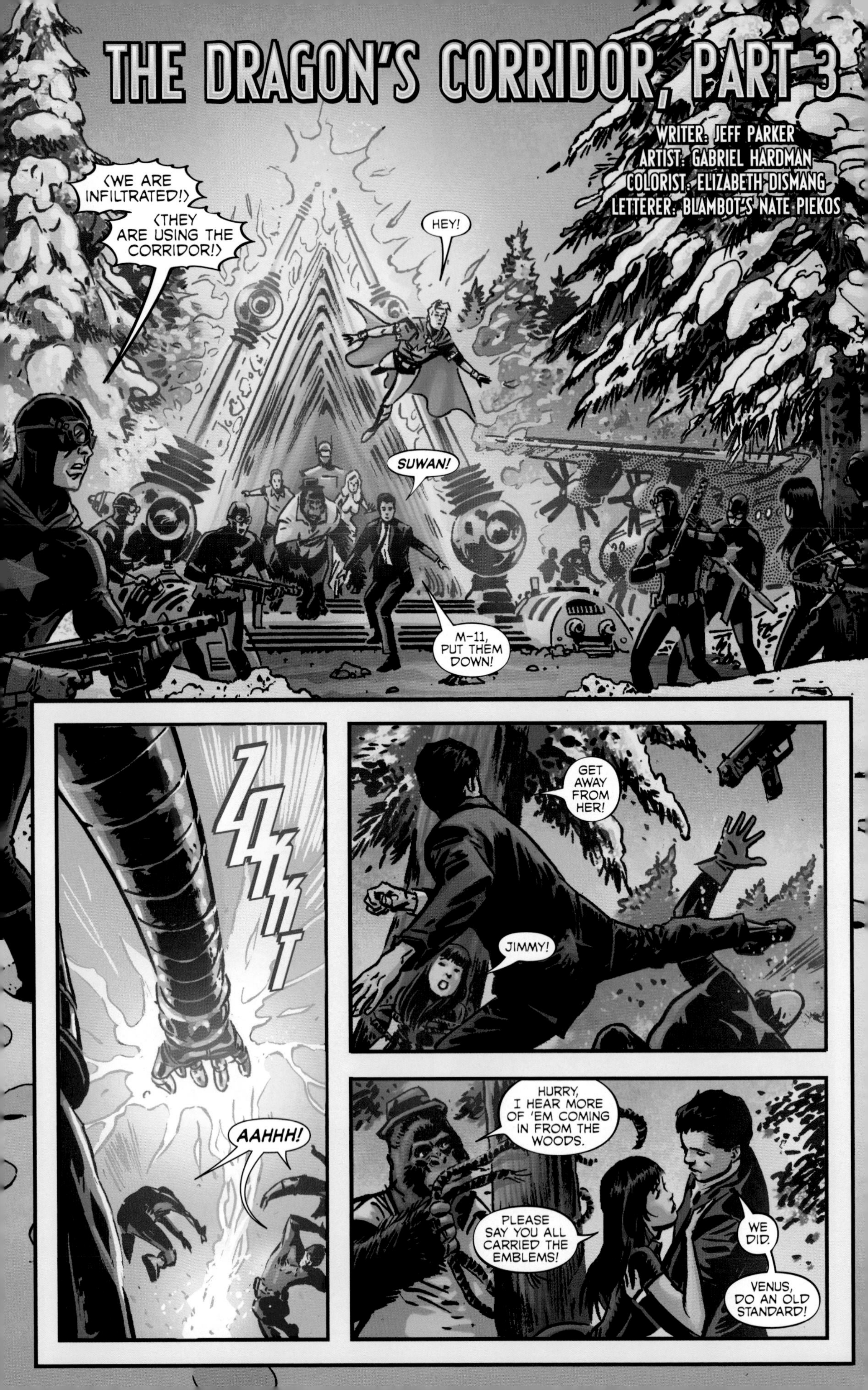
THE DRAGON'S CORRIDOR, PART 3
WRITER: JEFF PARKER
ARTIST: GABRIEL HARDMAN
COLORIST: ELIZABETH DISMANG
LETTERER: BLAMBOT'S NATE PIEKOS
⟨WE ARE INFILTRATED!⟩
⟨THEY ARE USING THE CORRIDOR!⟩
HEY!
SUWAN!
M-11, PUT THEM DOWN!
ZAKT
AAHHH!
GET AWAY FROM HER!
JIMMY!
HURRY, I HEAR MORE OF 'EM COMING IN FROM THE WOODS.
PLEASE SAY YOU ALL CARRIED THE EMBLEMS!
WE DID.
VENUS, DO AN OLD STANDARD!

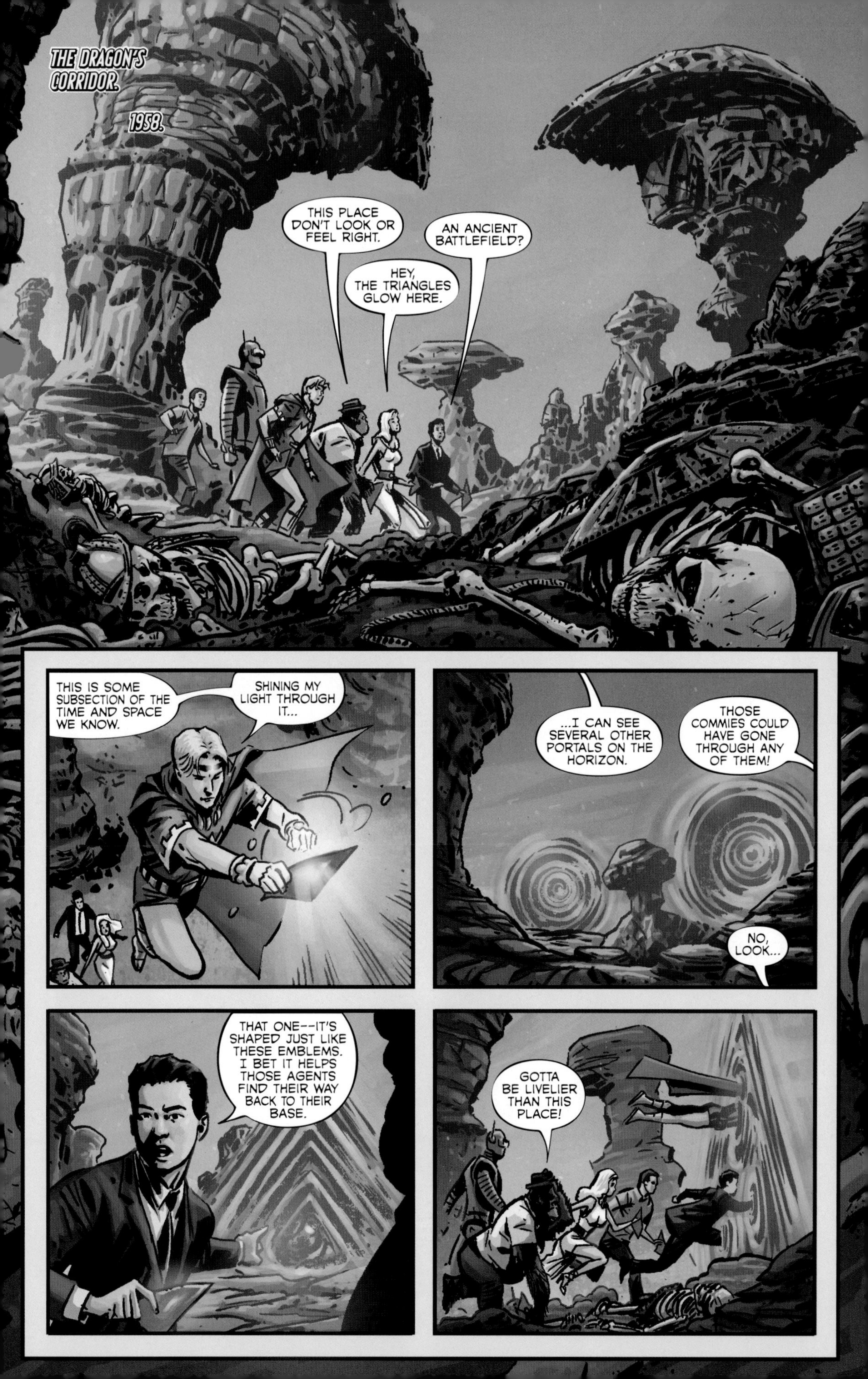
THE DRAGON'S CORRIDOR.
1958.
THIS PLACE DON'T LOOK OR FEEL RIGHT.
AN ANCIENT BATTLEFIELD?
HEY, THE TRIANGLES GLOW HERE.
THIS IS SOME SUBSECTION OF THE TIME AND SPACE WE KNOW.
SHINING MY LIGHT THROUGH IT...
...I CAN SEE SEVERAL OTHER PORTALS ON THE HORIZON.
THOSE COMMIES COULD HAVE GONE THROUGH ANY OF THEM!
NO, LOOK...
THAT ONE--IT'S SHAPED JUST LIKE THESE EMBLEMS. I BET IT HELPS THOSE AGENTS FIND THEIR WAY BACK TO THEIR BASE.
GOTTA BE LIVELIER THAN THIS PLACE!

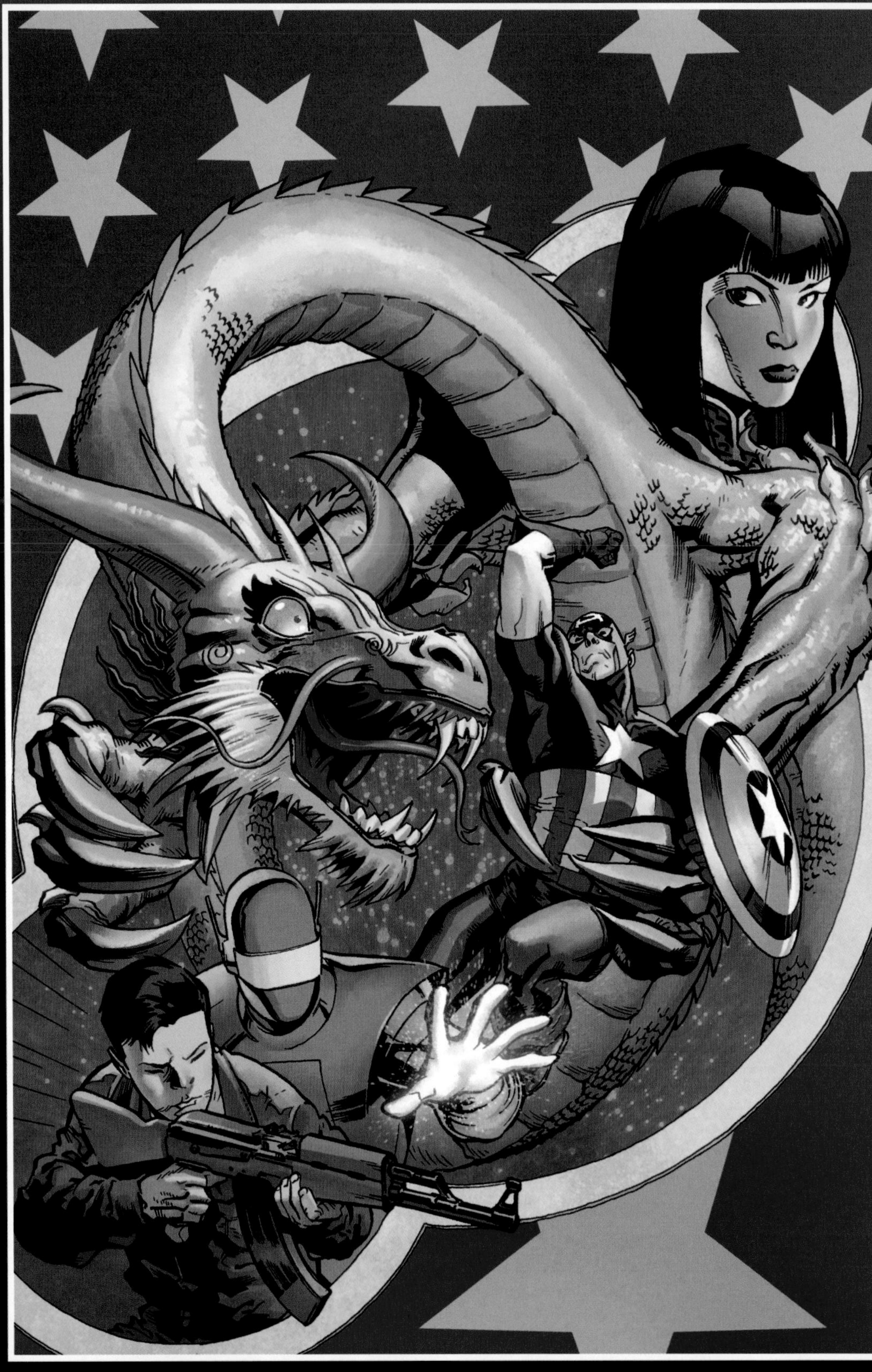

#4

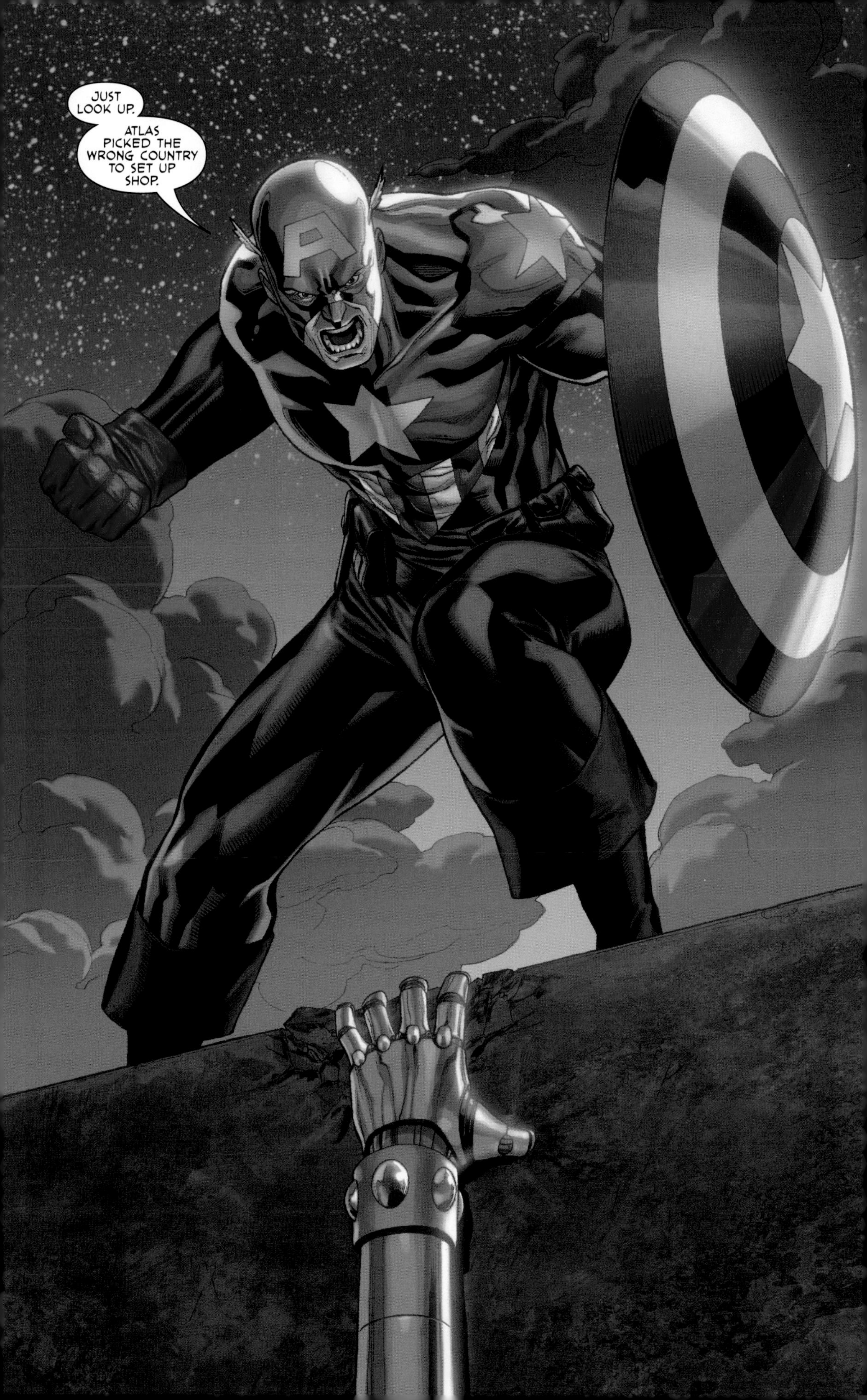
JUST LOOK UP.
ATLAS PICKED THE WRONG COUNTRY TO SET UP SHOP.

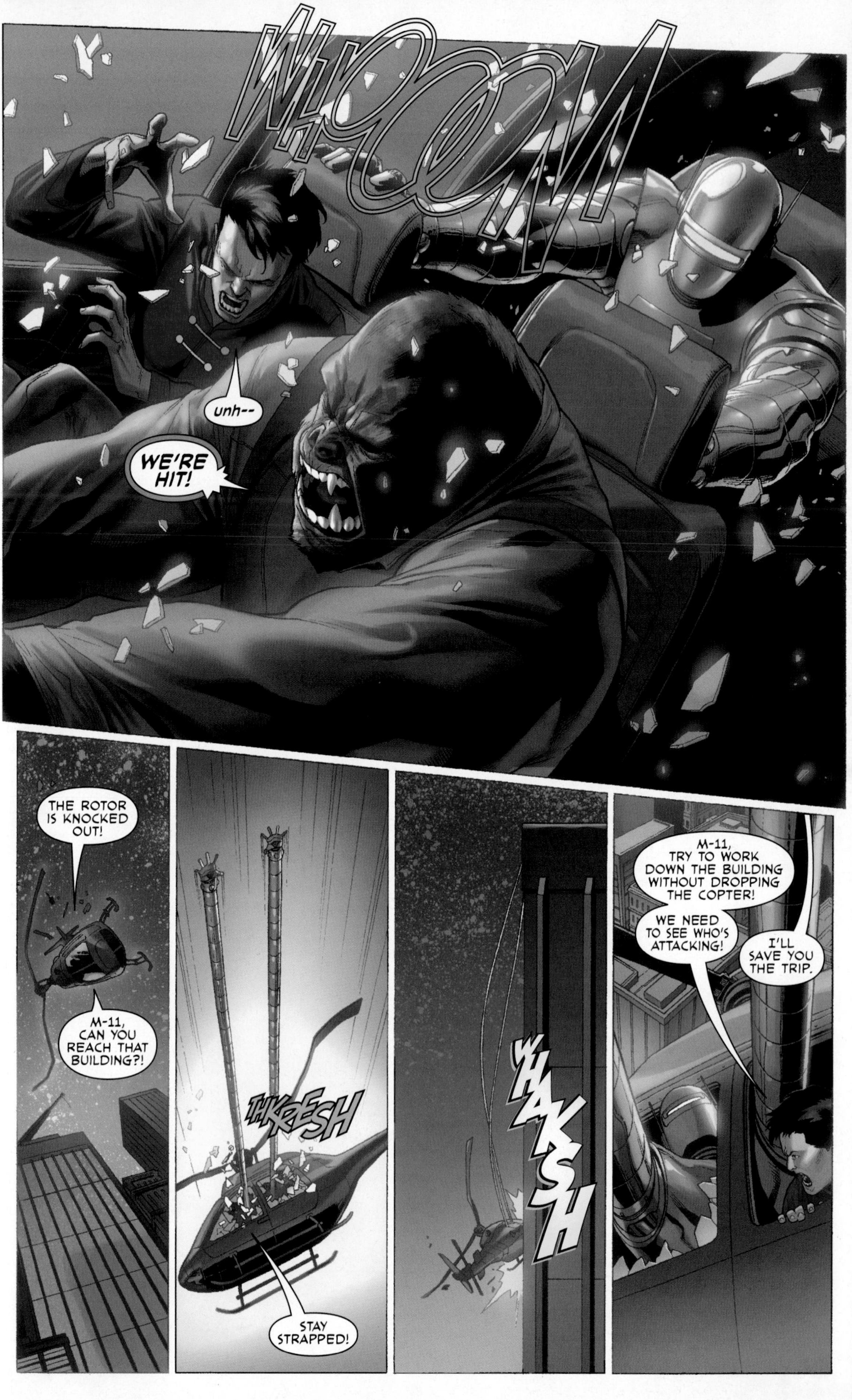
WHOOM
unh--
WE'RE HIT!
THE ROTOR IS KNOCKED OUT!
M-11, CAN YOU REACH THAT BUILDING?!
THKRESH
STAY STRAPPED!
WHAKSH
M-11, TRY TO WORK DOWN THE BUILDING WITHOUT DROPPING THE COPTER!
WE NEED TO SEE WHO'S ATTACKING!
I'LL SAVE YOU THE TRIP.

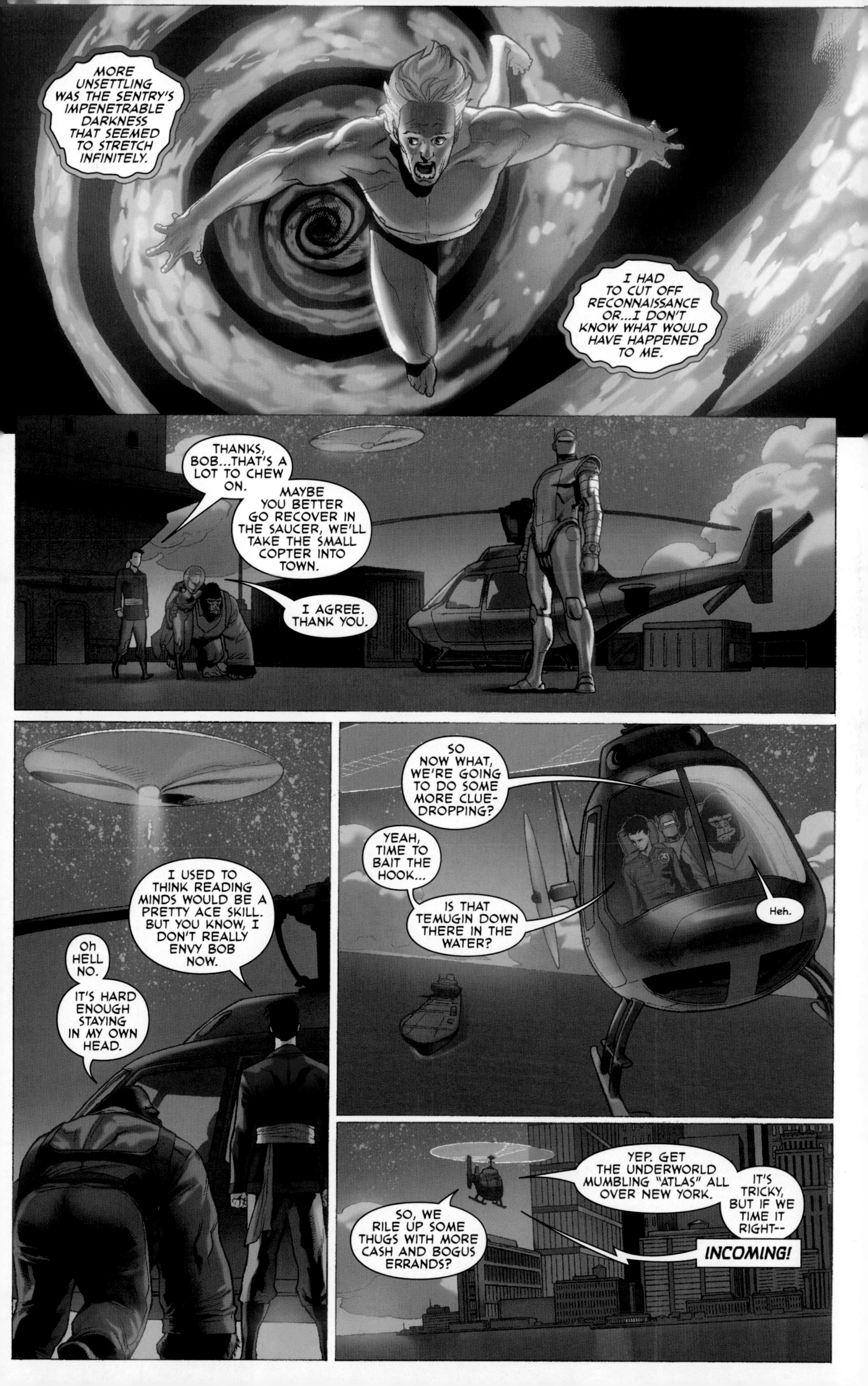
MORE UNSETTLING WAS THE SENTRY'S IMPENETRABLE DARKNESS THAT SEEMED TO STRETCH INFINITELY.
I HAD TO CUT OFF RECONNAISSANCE OR...I DON'T KNOW WHAT WOULD HAVE HAPPENED TO ME.
THANKS, BOB...THAT'S A LOT TO CHEW ON.
MAYBE YOU BETTER GO RECOVER IN THE SAUCER, WE'LL TAKE THE SMALL COPTER INTO TOWN.
I AGREE. THANK YOU.
I USED TO THINK READING MINDS WOULD BE A PRETTY ACE SKILL. BUT YOU KNOW, I DON'T REALLY ENVY BOB NOW.
Oh HELL NO.
IT'S HARD ENOUGH STAYING IN MY OWN HEAD.
SO NOW WHAT, WE'RE GOING TO DO SOME MORE CLUE-DROPPING?
YEAH, TIME TO BAIT THE HOOK...
IS THAT TEMUGIN DOWN THERE IN THE WATER?
Heh.
SO, WE RILE UP SOME THUGS WITH MORE CASH AND BOGUS ERRANDS?
YEP. GET THE UNDERWORLD MUMBLING "ATLAS" ALL OVER NEW YORK.
IT'S TRICKY, BUT IF WE TIME IT RIGHT--
INCOMING!

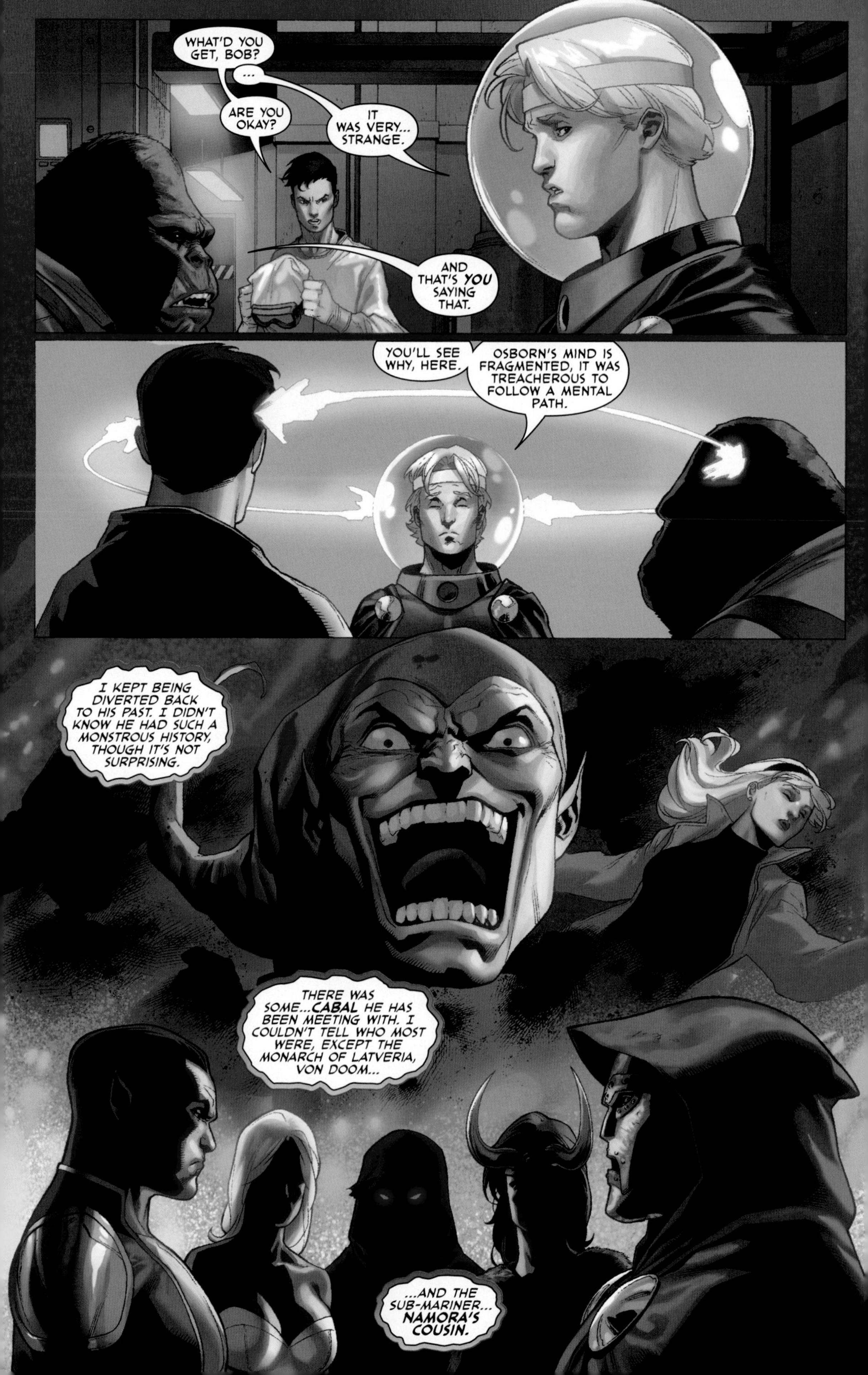
WHAT'D YOU GET, BOB?
...
ARE YOU OKAY?
IT WAS VERY... STRANGE.
AND THAT'S YOU SAYING THAT.
YOU'LL SEE WHY, HERE.
OSBORN'S MIND IS FRAGMENTED, IT WAS TREACHEROUS TO FOLLOW A MENTAL PATH.
I KEPT BEING DIVERTED BACK TO HIS PAST. I DIDN'T KNOW HE HAD SUCH A MONSTROUS HISTORY, THOUGH IT'S NOT SURPRISING.
THERE WAS SOME...CABAL HE HAS BEEN MEETING WITH. I COULDN'T TELL WHO MOST WERE, EXCEPT THE MONARCH OF LATVERIA, VON DOOM...
...AND THE SUB-MARINER... NAMORA'S COUSIN.

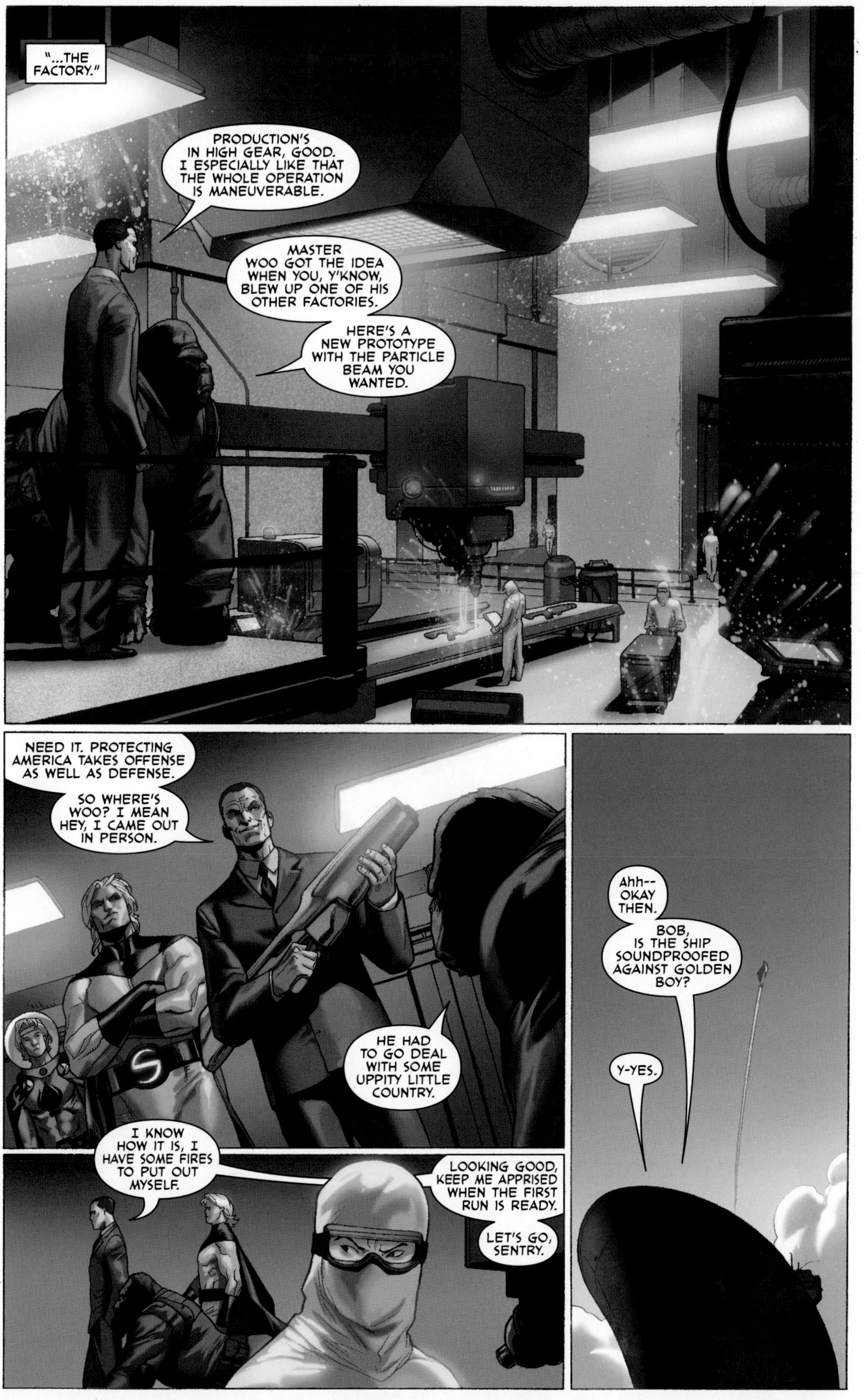
"...THE FACTORY."
PRODUCTION'S IN HIGH GEAR, GOOD. I ESPECIALLY LIKE THAT THE WHOLE OPERATION IS MANEUVERABLE.
MASTER WOO GOT THE IDEA WHEN YOU, Y'KNOW, BLEW UP ONE OF HIS OTHER FACTORIES.
HERE'S A NEW PROTOTYPE WITH THE PARTICLE BEAM YOU WANTED.
NEED IT. PROTECTING AMERICA TAKES OFFENSE AS WELL AS DEFENSE.
SO WHERE'S WOO? I MEAN HEY, I CAME OUT IN PERSON.
HE HAD TO GO DEAL WITH SOME UPPITY LITTLE COUNTRY.
I KNOW HOW IT IS, I HAVE SOME FIRES TO PUT OUT MYSELF.
LOOKING GOOD, KEEP ME APPRISED WHEN THE FIRST RUN IS READY.
LET'S GO, SENTRY.
Ahh-- OKAY THEN.
BOB, IS THE SHIP SOUNDPROOFED AGAINST GOLDEN BOY?
Y-YES.

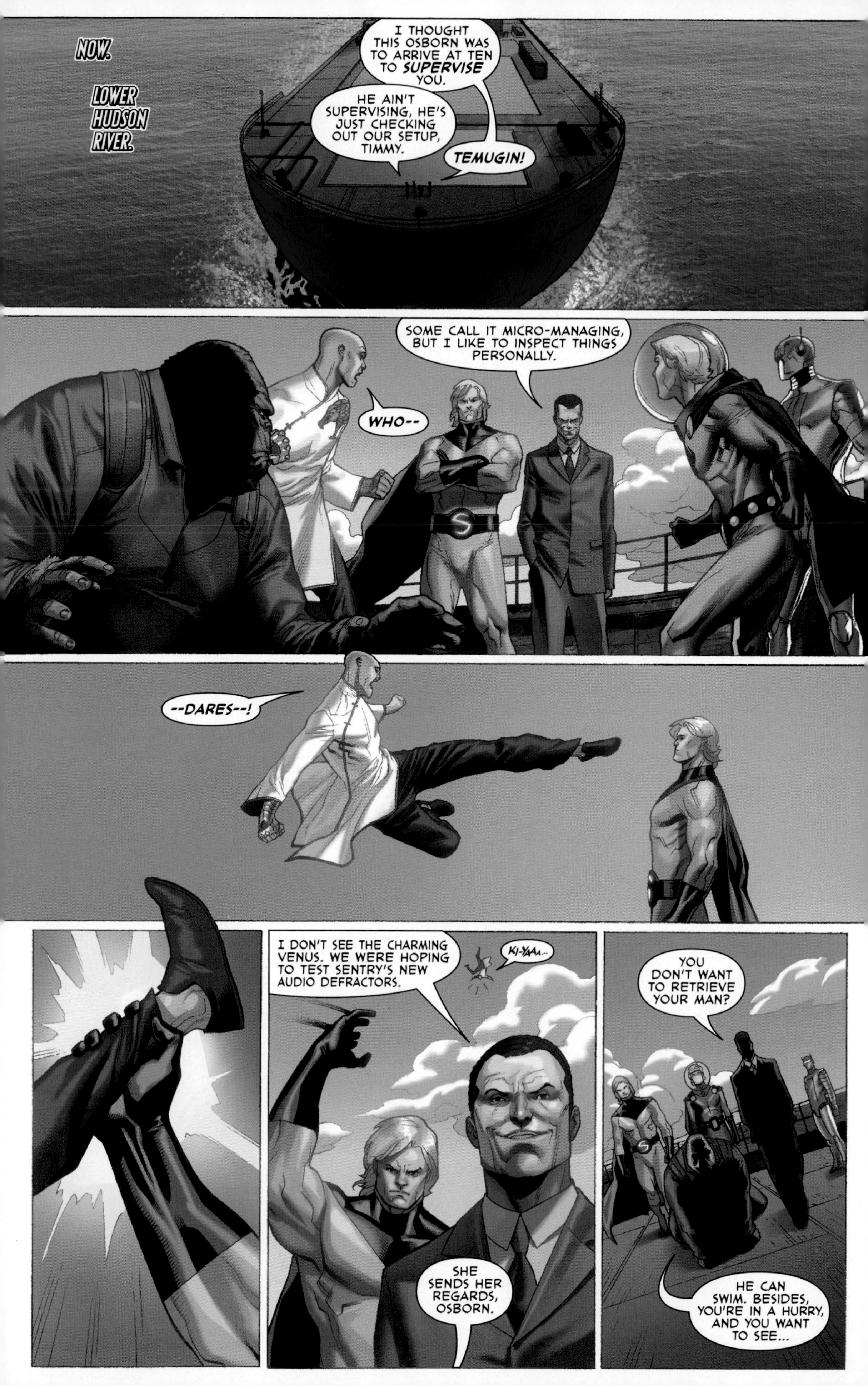
NOW.
LOWER HUDSON RIVER.
I THOUGHT THIS OSBORN WAS TO ARRIVE AT TEN TO SUPERVISE YOU.
HE AIN'T SUPERVISING, HE'S JUST CHECKING OUT OUR SETUP, TIMMY.
TEMUGIN!
SOME CALL IT MICRO-MANAGING, BUT I LIKE TO INSPECT THINGS PERSONALLY.
WHO--
--DARES--!
I DON'T SEE THE CHARMING VENUS. WE WERE HOPING TO TEST SENTRY'S NEW AUDIO DEFRACTORS.
KI-YAAA...
SHE SENDS HER REGARDS, OSBORN.
YOU DON'T WANT TO RETRIEVE YOUR MAN?
HE CAN SWIM. BESIDES, YOU'RE IN A HURRY, AND YOU WANT TO SEE...

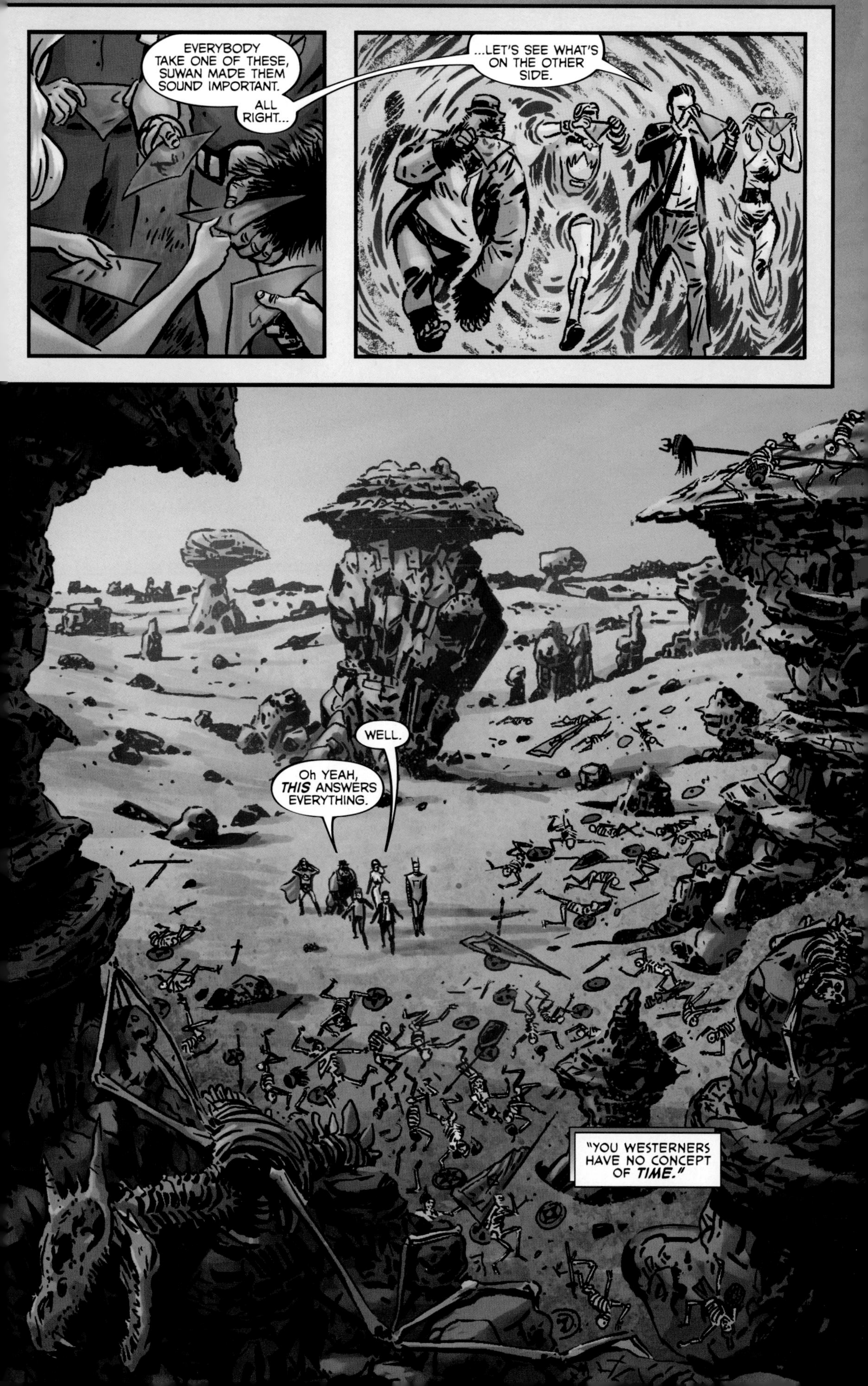
EVERYBODY TAKE ONE OF THESE, SUWAN MADE THEM SOUND IMPORTANT.
ALL RIGHT...
...LET'S SEE WHAT'S ON THE OTHER SIDE.
WELL.
Oh YEAH, *THIS* ANSWERS EVERYTHING.
"YOU WESTERNERS HAVE NO CONCEPT OF *TIME*."

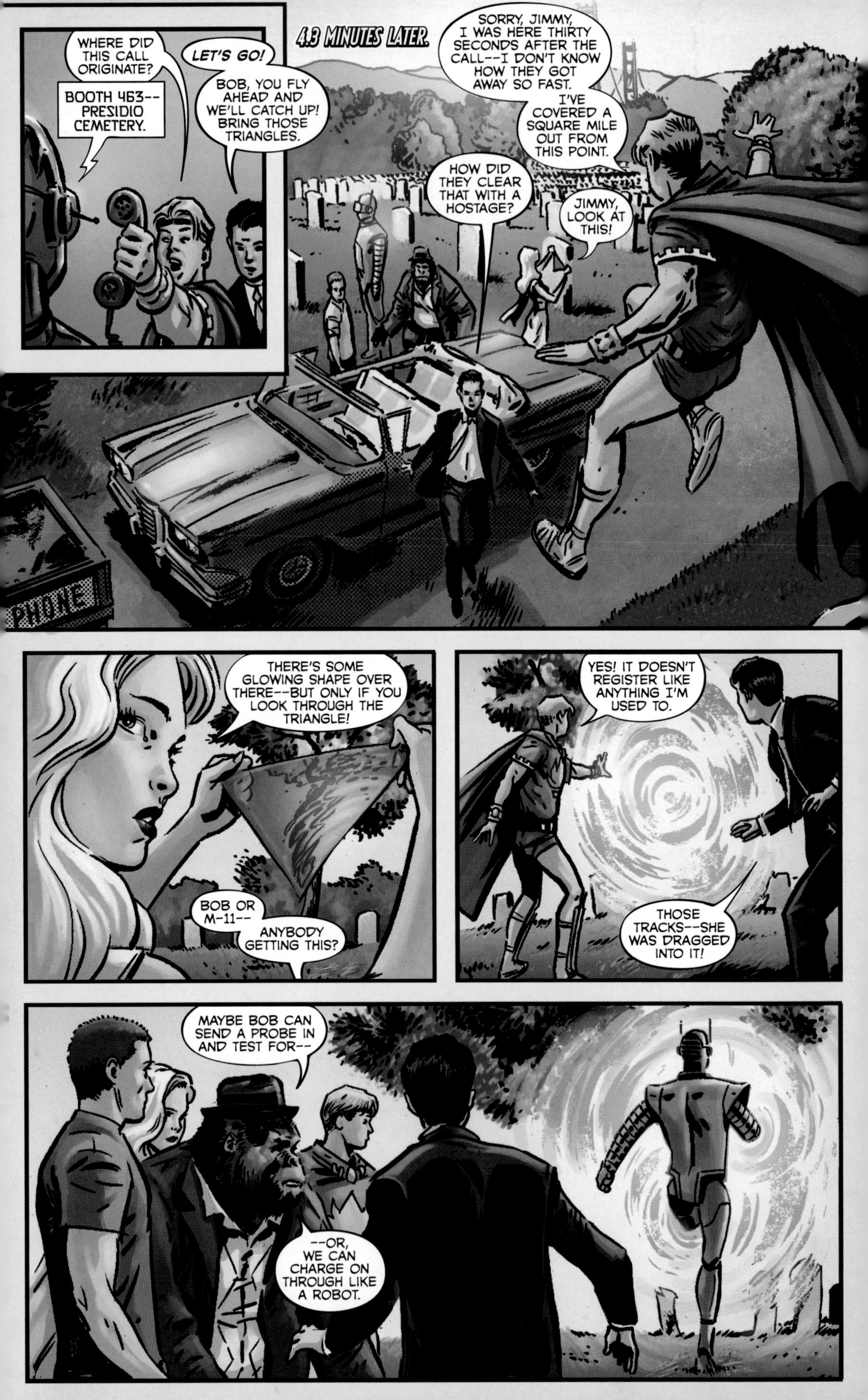
WHERE DID THIS CALL ORIGINATE?
BOOTH 463-- PRESIDIO CEMETERY.
LET'S GO!
BOB, YOU FLY AHEAD AND WE'LL CATCH UP! BRING THOSE TRIANGLES.
4.3 MINUTES LATER.
SORRY, JIMMY, I WAS HERE THIRTY SECONDS AFTER THE CALL--I DON'T KNOW HOW THEY GOT AWAY SO FAST.
I'VE COVERED A SQUARE MILE OUT FROM THIS POINT.
HOW DID THEY CLEAR THAT WITH A HOSTAGE?
JIMMY, LOOK AT THIS!
PHONE
THERE'S SOME GLOWING SHAPE OVER THERE--BUT ONLY IF YOU LOOK THROUGH THE TRIANGLE!
BOB OR M-11--
ANYBODY GETTING THIS?
YES! IT DOESN'T REGISTER LIKE ANYTHING I'M USED TO.
THOSE TRACKS--SHE WAS DRAGGED INTO IT!
MAYBE BOB CAN SEND A PROBE IN AND TEST FOR--
--OR, WE CAN CHARGE ON THROUGH LIKE A ROBOT.

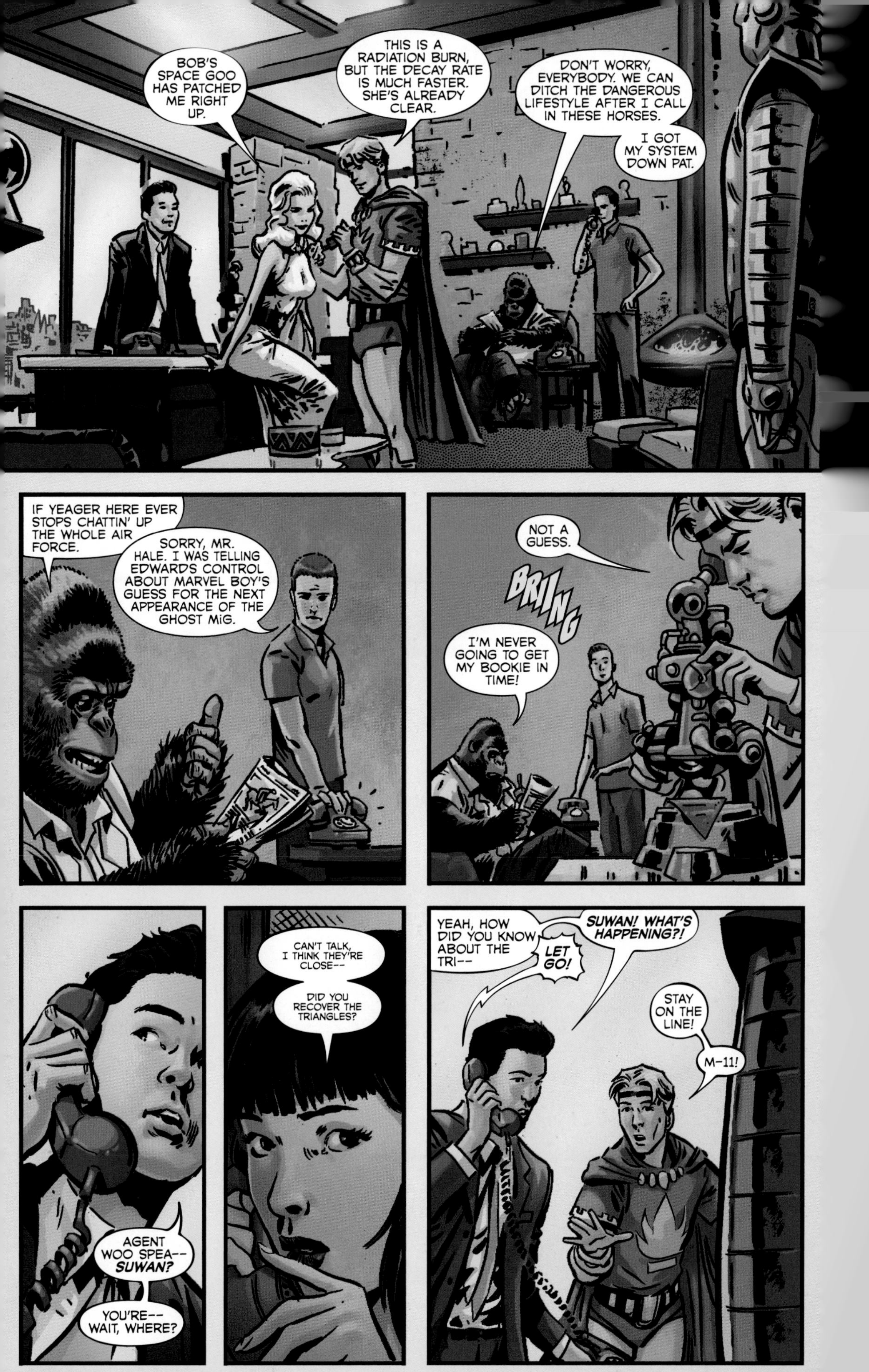
BOB'S SPACE GOO HAS PATCHED ME RIGHT UP.
THIS IS A RADIATION BURN, BUT THE DECAY RATE IS MUCH FASTER. SHE'S ALREADY CLEAR.
DON'T WORRY, EVERYBODY. WE CAN DITCH THE DANGEROUS LIFESTYLE AFTER I CALL IN THESE HORSES.
I GOT MY SYSTEM DOWN PAT.
IF YEAGER HERE EVER STOPS CHATTIN' UP THE WHOLE AIR FORCE.
SORRY, MR. HALE. I WAS TELLING EDWARDS CONTROL ABOUT MARVEL BOY'S GUESS FOR THE NEXT APPEARANCE OF THE GHOST MiG.
NOT A GUESS.
BRING
I'M NEVER GOING TO GET MY BOOKIE IN TIME!
AGENT WOO SPEA-- SUWAN?
YOU'RE-- WAIT, WHERE?
CAN'T TALK, I THINK THEY'RE CLOSE--
DID YOU RECOVER THE TRIANGLES?
YEAH, HOW DID YOU KNOW ABOUT THE TRI--
LET GO!
SUWAN! WHAT'S HAPPENING?!
STAY ON THE LINE!
M-11!

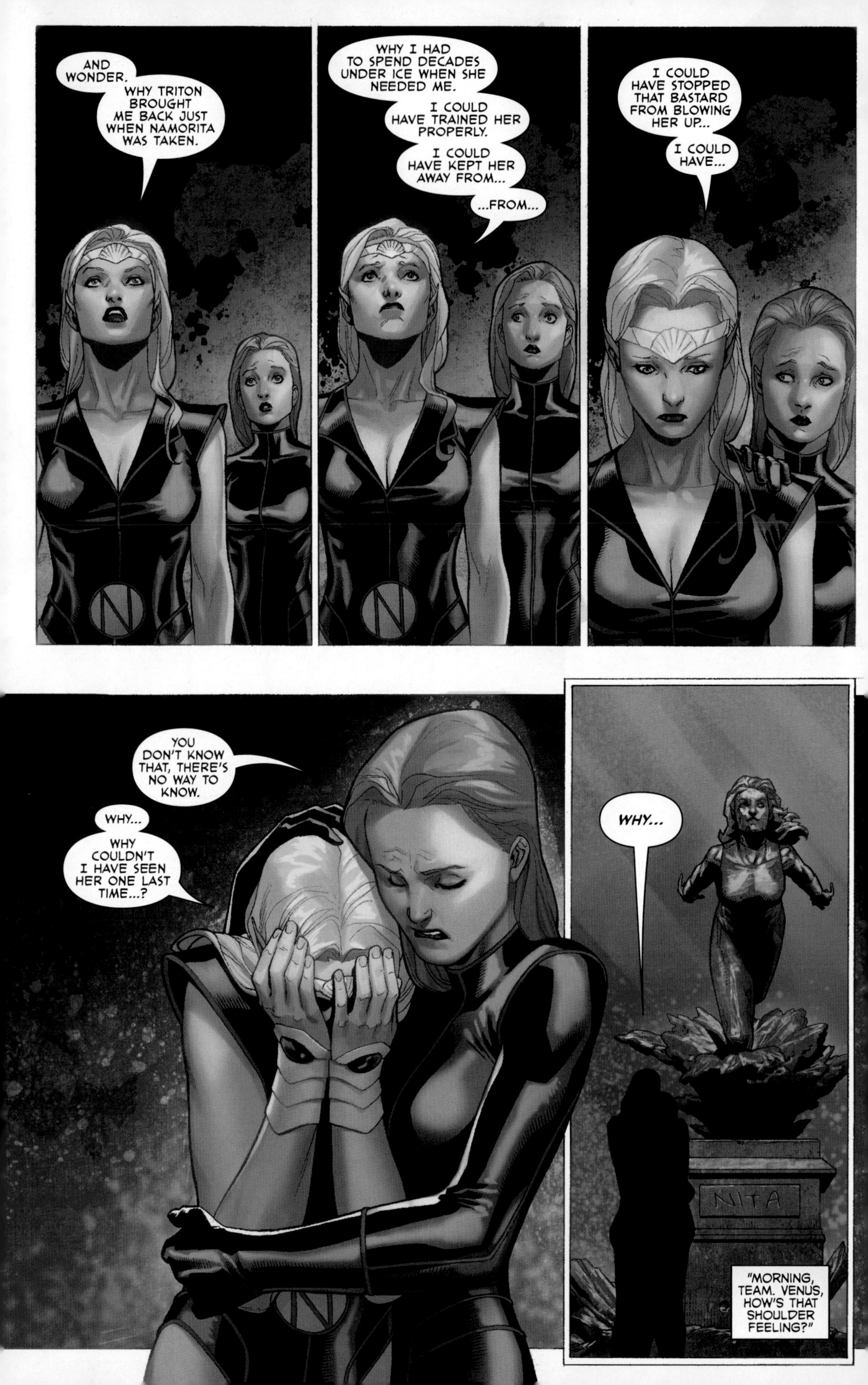
AND WONDER.
WHY TRITON BROUGHT ME BACK JUST WHEN NAMORITA WAS TAKEN.
WHY I HAD TO SPEND DECADES UNDER ICE WHEN SHE NEEDED ME.
I COULD HAVE TRAINED HER PROPERLY.
I COULD HAVE KEPT HER AWAY FROM...
...FROM...
I COULD HAVE STOPPED THAT BASTARD FROM BLOWING HER UP...
I COULD HAVE...
YOU DON'T KNOW THAT, THERE'S NO WAY TO KNOW.
WHY...
WHY COULDN'T I HAVE SEEN HER ONE LAST TIME...?
WHY...
NITA
"MORNING, TEAM. VENUS, HOW'S THAT SHOULDER FEELING?"

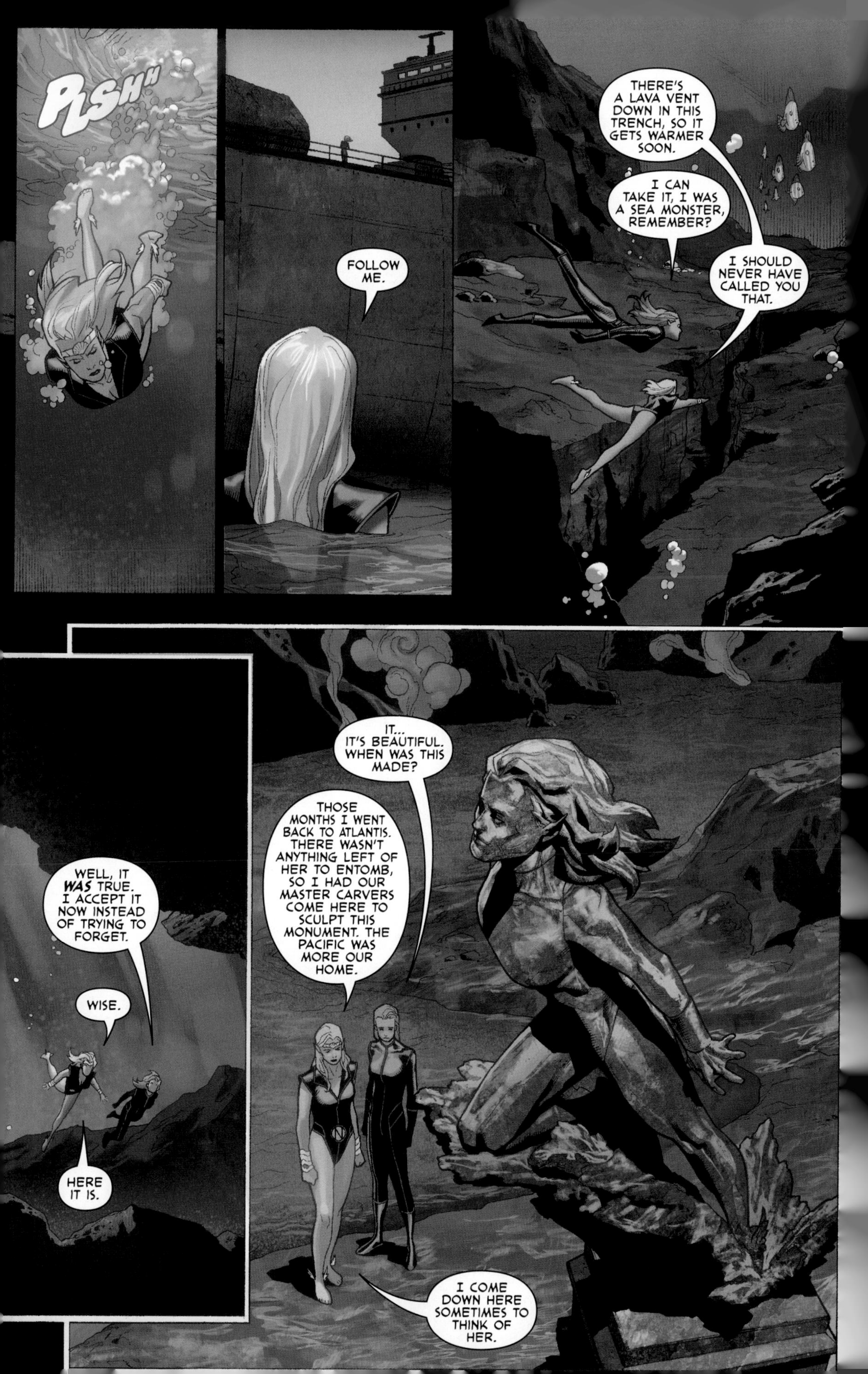
PLSHH
FOLLOW ME.
THERE'S A LAVA VENT DOWN IN THIS TRENCH, SO IT GETS WARMER SOON.
I CAN TAKE IT, I WAS A SEA MONSTER, REMEMBER?
I SHOULD NEVER HAVE CALLED YOU THAT.
WELL, IT WAS TRUE. I ACCEPT IT NOW INSTEAD OF TRYING TO FORGET.
WISE.
HERE IT IS.
IT... IT'S BEAUTIFUL. WHEN WAS THIS MADE?
THOSE MONTHS I WENT BACK TO ATLANTIS. THERE WASN'T ANYTHING LEFT OF HER TO ENTOMB, SO I HAD OUR MASTER CARVERS COME HERE TO SCULPT THIS MONUMENT. THE PACIFIC WAS MORE OUR HOME.
I COME DOWN HERE SOMETIMES TO THINK OF HER.

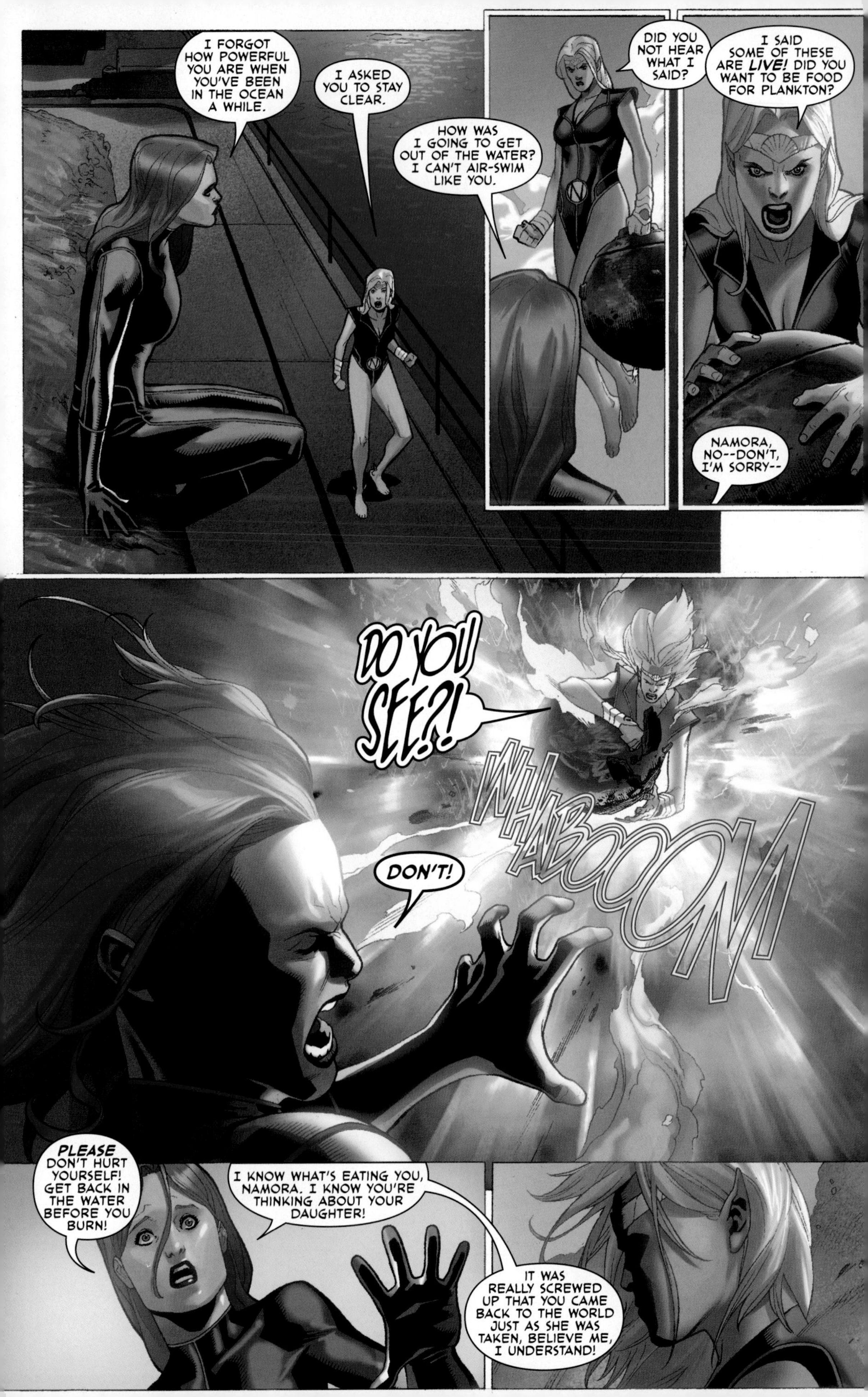
I FORGOT HOW POWERFUL YOU ARE WHEN YOU'VE BEEN IN THE OCEAN A WHILE.
I ASKED YOU TO STAY CLEAR.
HOW WAS I GOING TO GET OUT OF THE WATER? I CAN'T AIR-SWIM LIKE YOU.
DID YOU NOT HEAR WHAT I SAID?
I SAID SOME OF THESE ARE LIVE! DID YOU WANT TO BE FOOD FOR PLANKTON?
NAMORA, NO--DON'T, I'M SORRY--
DO YOU SEE?!
WHABOOOM
DON'T!
PLEASE DON'T HURT YOURSELF! GET BACK IN THE WATER BEFORE YOU BURN!
I KNOW WHAT'S EATING YOU, NAMORA. I KNOW YOU'RE THINKING ABOUT YOUR DAUGHTER!
IT WAS REALLY SCREWED UP THAT YOU CAME BACK TO THE WORLD JUST AS SHE WAS TAKEN, BELIEVE ME, I UNDERSTAND!

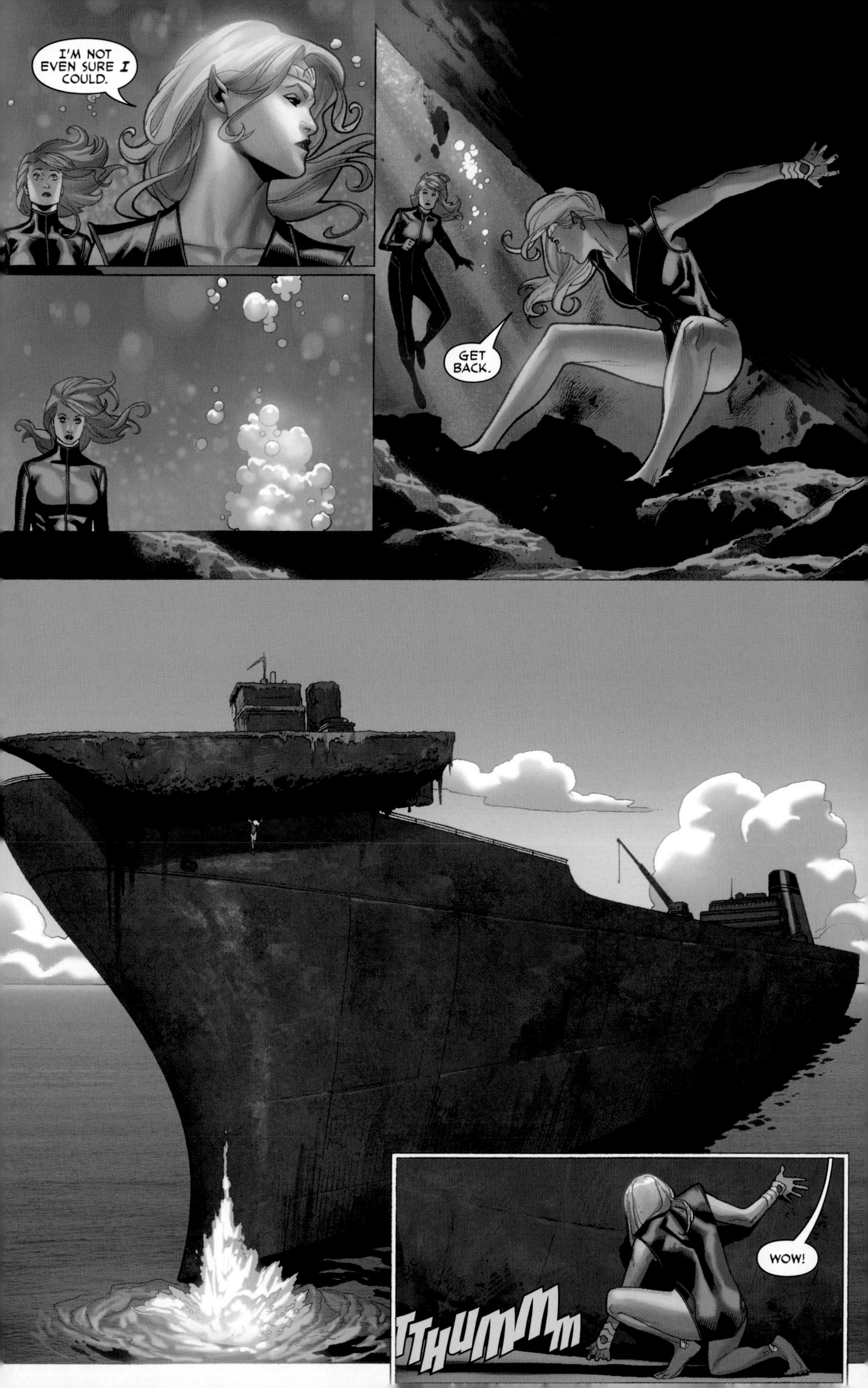
I'M NOT EVEN SURE *I* COULD.
GET BACK.
WOW!
TTHUMMMM

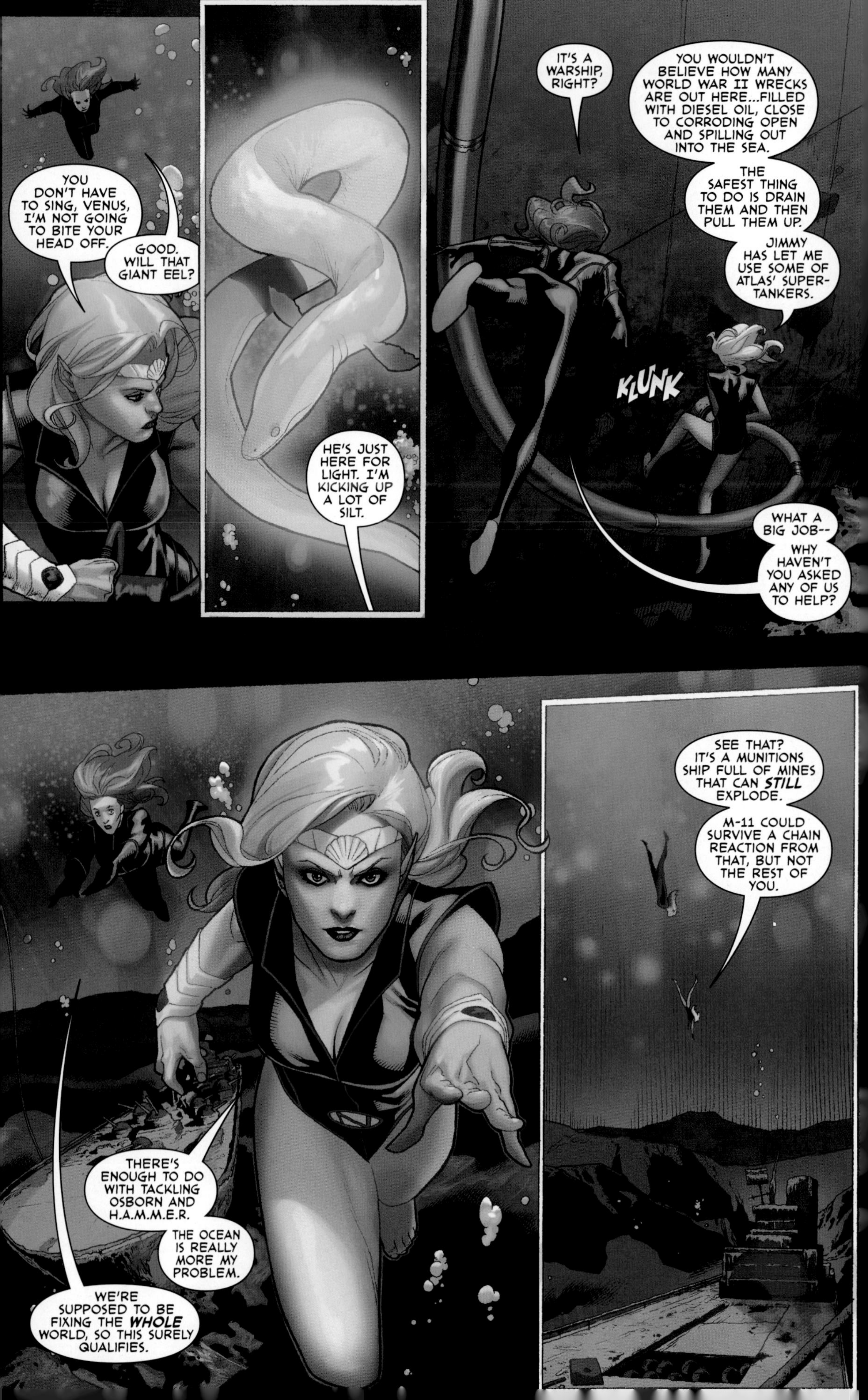

YOU DON'T HAVE TO SING, VENUS, I'M NOT GOING TO BITE YOUR HEAD OFF.
GOOD. WILL THAT GIANT EEL?
HE'S JUST HERE FOR LIGHT. I'M KICKING UP A LOT OF SILT.
IT'S A WARSHIP, RIGHT?
YOU WOULDN'T BELIEVE HOW MANY WORLD WAR II WRECKS ARE OUT HERE...FILLED WITH DIESEL OIL, CLOSE TO CORRODING OPEN AND SPILLING OUT INTO THE SEA.
THE SAFEST THING TO DO IS DRAIN THEM AND THEN PULL THEM UP.
JIMMY HAS LET ME USE SOME OF ATLAS' SUPER-TANKERS.
KLUNK
WHAT A BIG JOB--
WHY HAVEN'T YOU ASKED ANY OF US TO HELP?
THERE'S ENOUGH TO DO WITH TACKLING OSBORN AND H.A.M.M.E.R.
THE OCEAN IS REALLY MORE MY PROBLEM.
WE'RE SUPPOSED TO BE FIXING THE WHOLE WORLD, SO THIS SURELY QUALIFIES.
SEE THAT? IT'S A MUNITIONS SHIP FULL OF MINES THAT CAN STILL EXPLODE.
M-11 COULD SURVIVE A CHAIN REACTION FROM THAT, BUT NOT THE REST OF YOU.

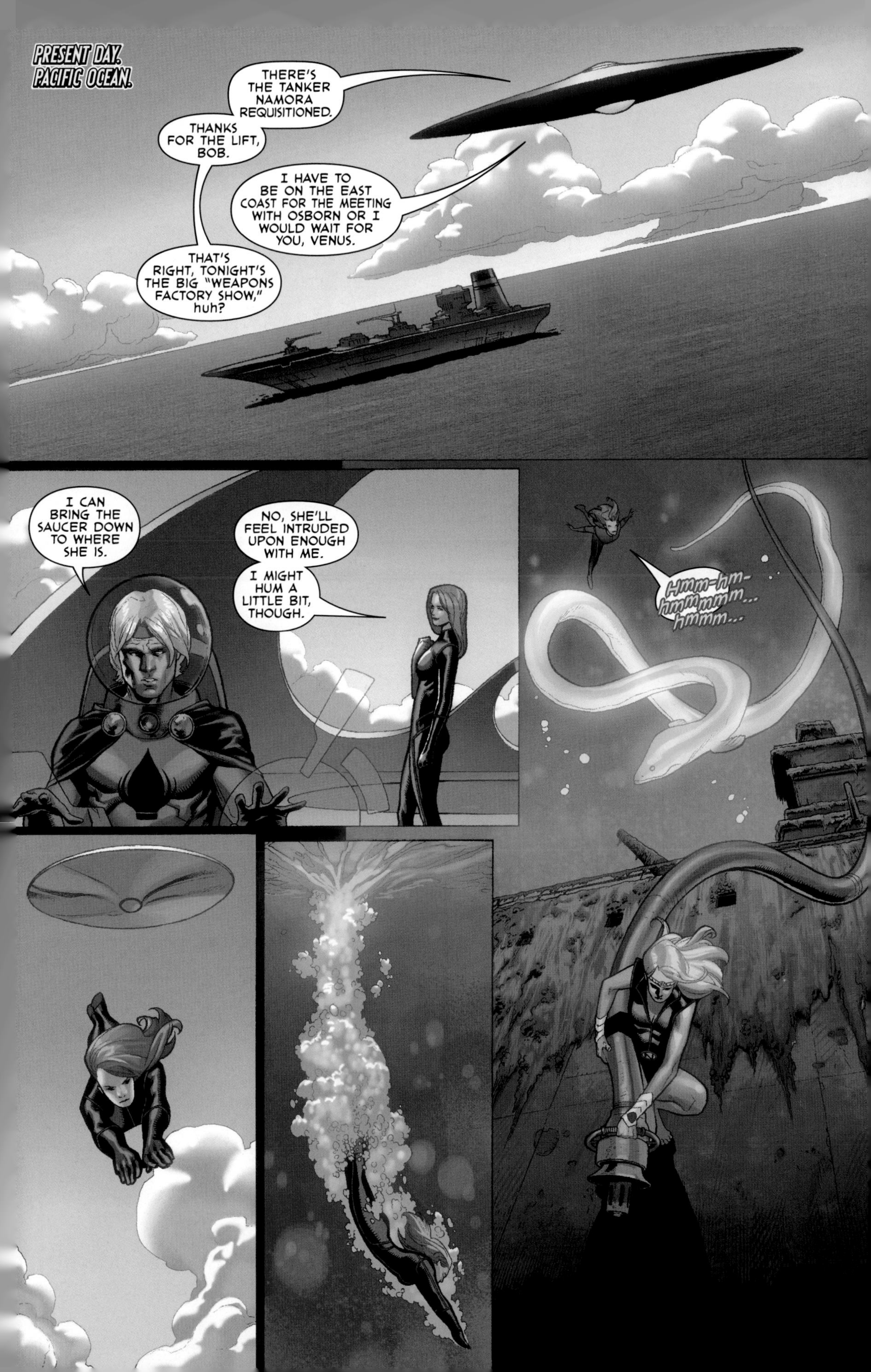
PRESENT DAY. PACIFIC OCEAN.
THERE'S THE TANKER NAMORA REQUISITIONED.
THANKS FOR THE LIFT, BOB.
I HAVE TO BE ON THE EAST COAST FOR THE MEETING WITH OSBORN OR I WOULD WAIT FOR YOU, VENUS.
THAT'S RIGHT, TONIGHT'S THE BIG "WEAPONS FACTORY SHOW," huh?
I CAN BRING THE SAUCER DOWN TO WHERE SHE IS.
NO, SHE'LL FEEL INTRUDED UPON ENOUGH WITH ME.
I MIGHT HUM A LITTLE BIT, THOUGH.
Hmm-hm-hmmmmm... hmmm...

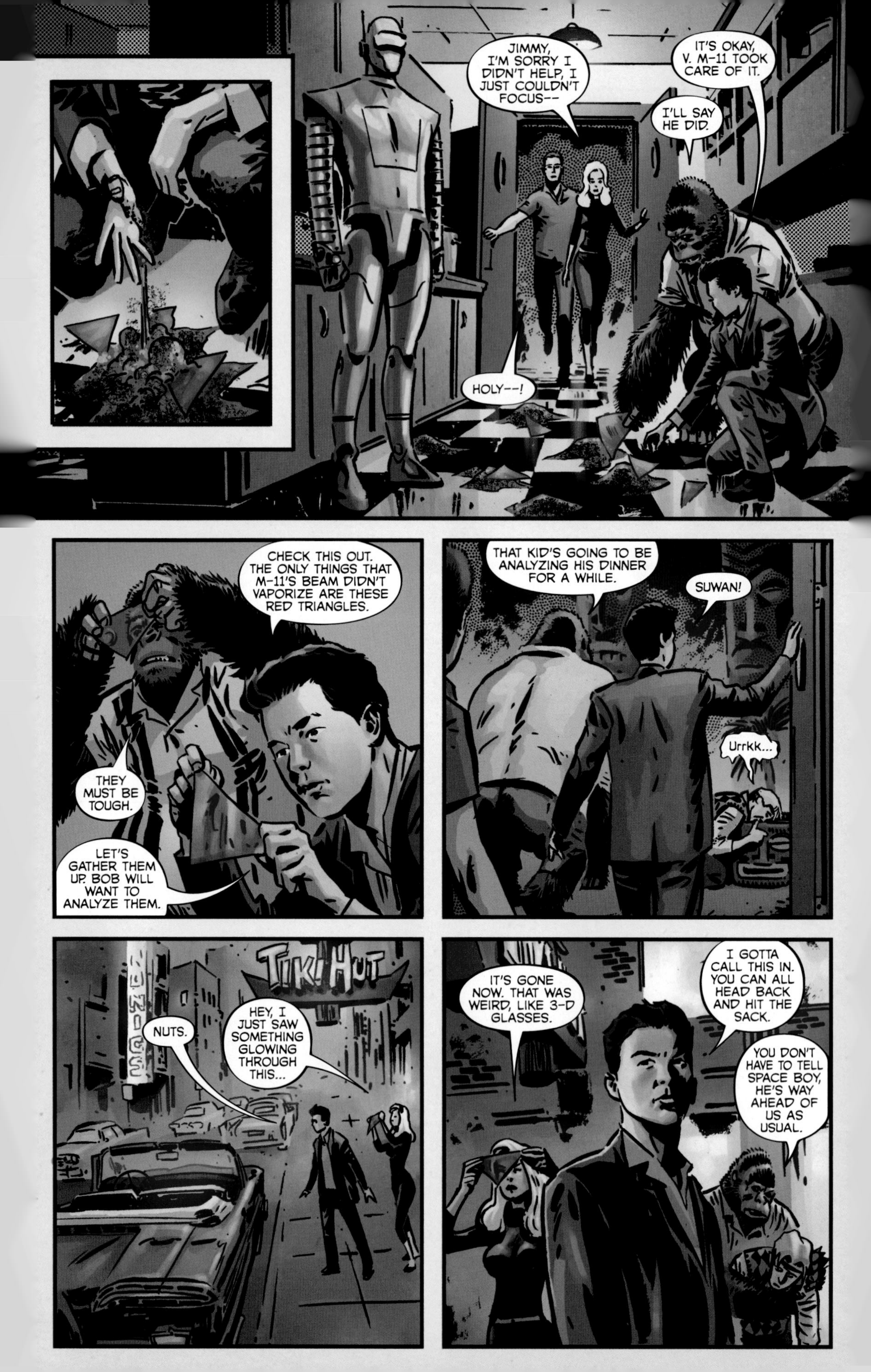
JIMMY, I'M SORRY I DIDN'T HELP, I JUST COULDN'T FOCUS--
IT'S OKAY, V. M-11 TOOK CARE OF IT.
I'LL SAY HE DID.
HOLY--!
CHECK THIS OUT. THE ONLY THINGS THAT M-11'S BEAM DIDN'T VAPORIZE ARE THESE RED TRIANGLES.
THEY MUST BE TOUGH.
LET'S GATHER THEM UP. BOB WILL WANT TO ANALYZE THEM.
THAT KID'S GOING TO BE ANALYZING HIS DINNER FOR A WHILE.
SUWAN!
Urrkk...
TIKI HUT
NUTS.
HEY, I JUST SAW SOMETHING GLOWING THROUGH THIS...
IT'S GONE NOW. THAT WAS WEIRD, LIKE 3-D GLASSES.
I GOTTA CALL THIS IN. YOU CAN ALL HEAD BACK AND HIT THE SACK.
YOU DON'T HAVE TO TELL SPACE BOY, HE'S WAY AHEAD OF US AS USUAL.

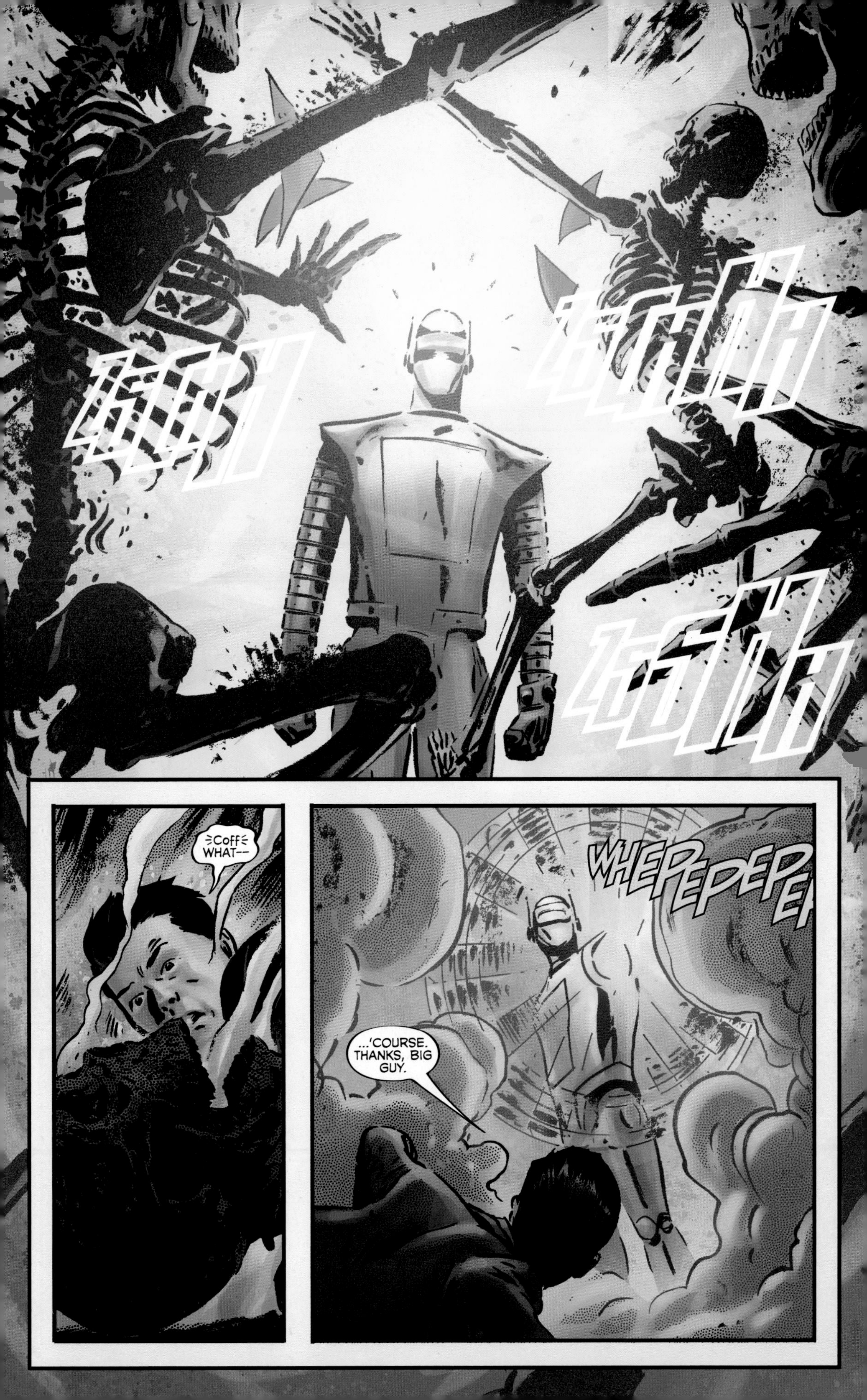
Coff WHAT--
WHEPEPEPEP
...'COURSE. THANKS, BIG GUY.

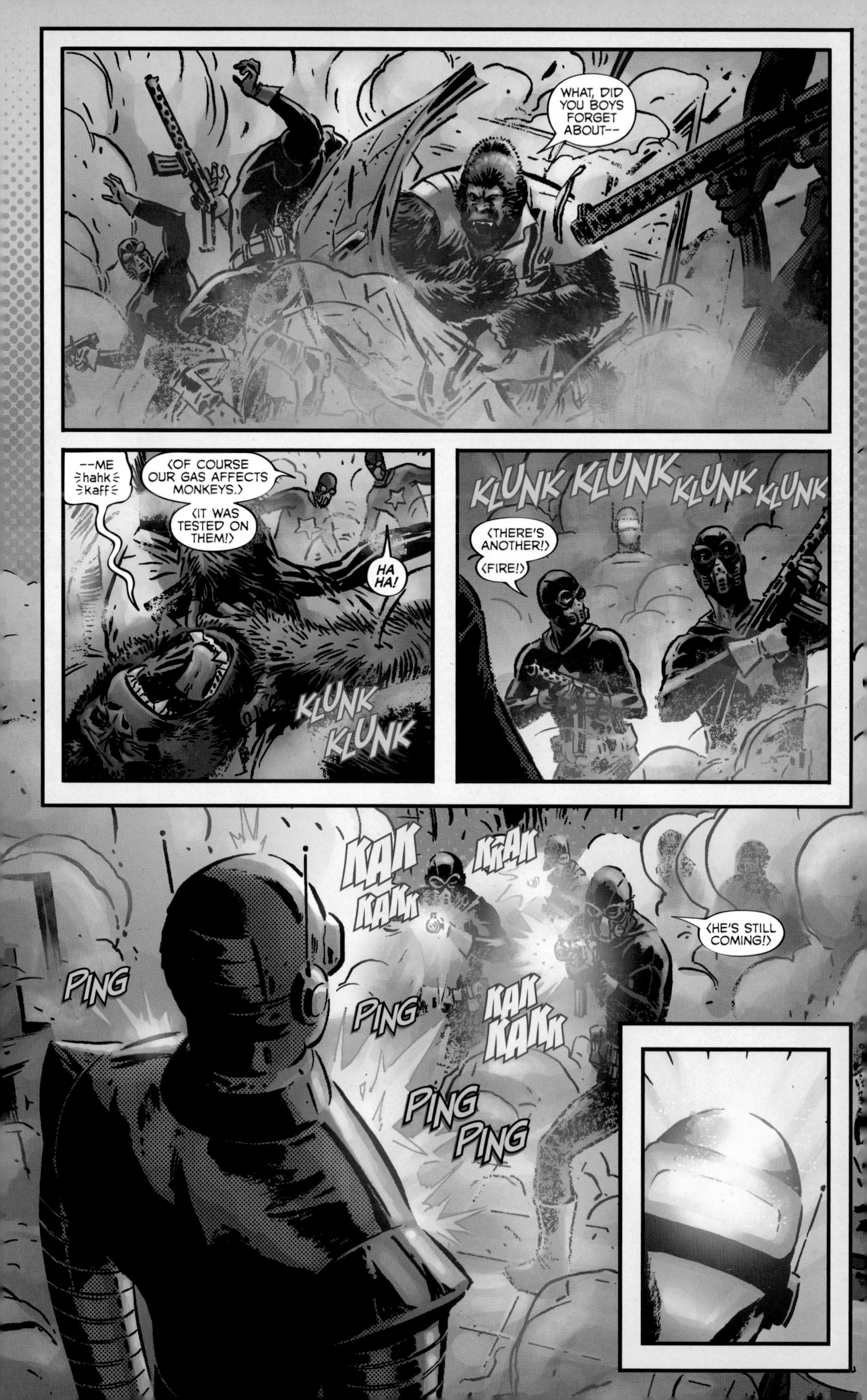
WHAT, DID YOU BOYS FORGET ABOUT--
--ME hahk kaff
(OF COURSE OUR GAS AFFECTS MONKEYS.)
(IT WAS TESTED ON THEM!)
HA HA!
KLUNK KLUNK
KLUNK KLUNK KLUNK KLUNK
(THERE'S ANOTHER!)
(FIRE!)
KAK KAKK
KRAK
(HE'S STILL COMING!)
PING
PING
KAK KAKK
PING PING

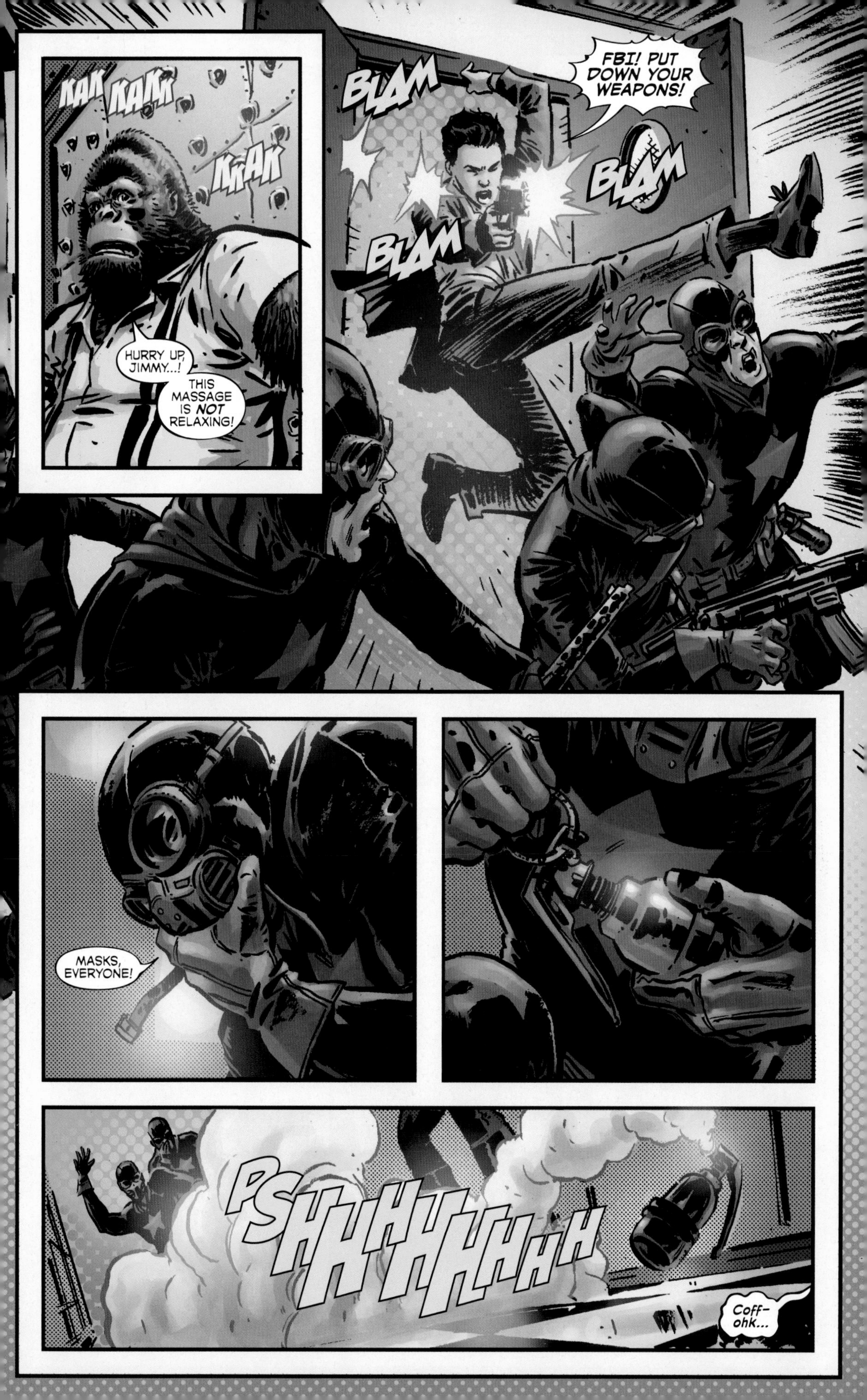
KAK KAKK
KRAK
HURRY UP, JIMMY...!
THIS MASSAGE IS *NOT* RELAXING!
BLAM
FBI! PUT DOWN YOUR WEAPONS!
BLAM
BLAM
MASKS, EVERYONE!
PSHHHHHHHHH
Coff-ohk...

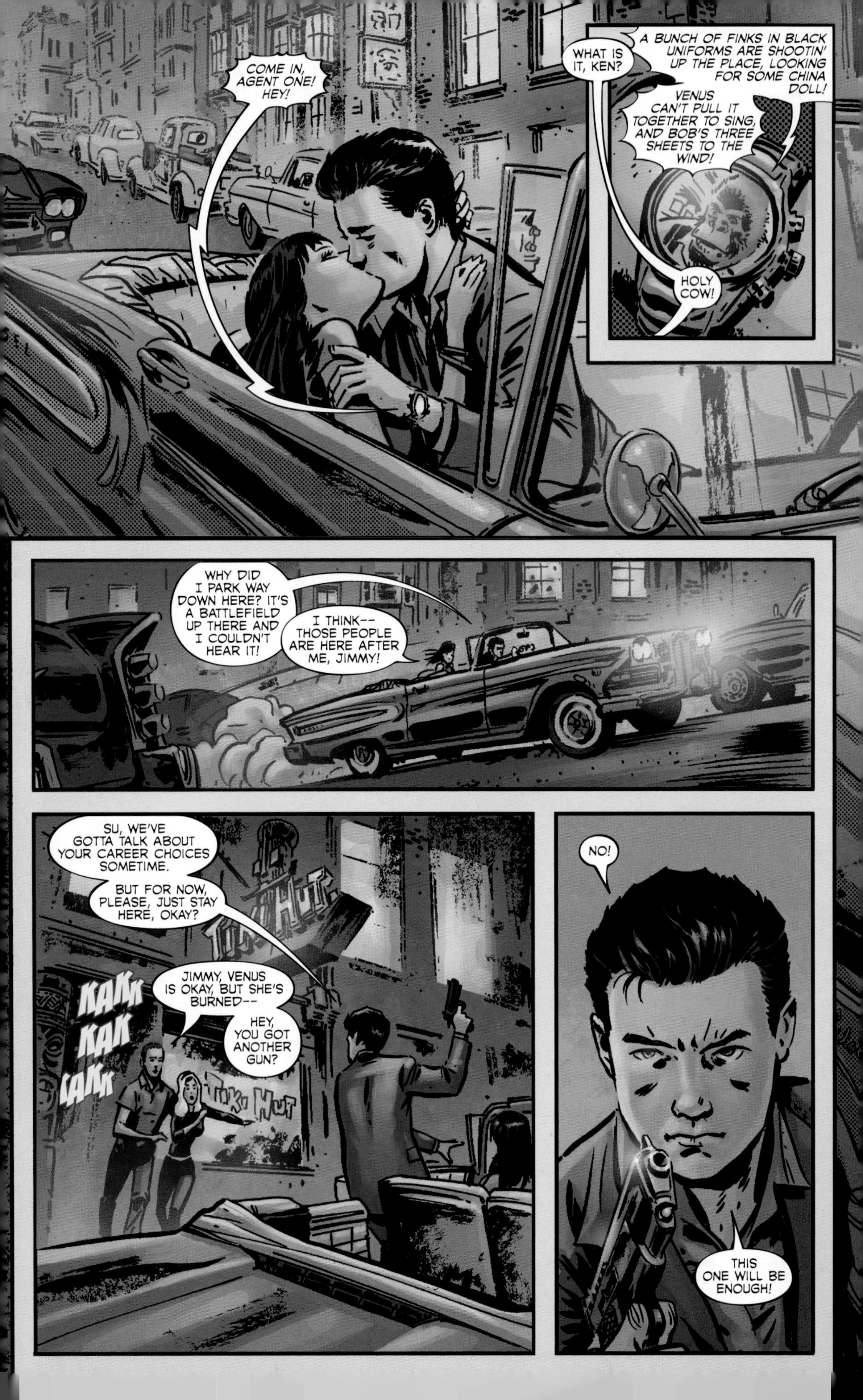
COME IN, AGENT ONE! HEY!
WHAT IS IT, KEN?
A BUNCH OF FINKS IN BLACK UNIFORMS ARE SHOOTIN' UP THE PLACE, LOOKING FOR SOME CHINA DOLL!
VENUS CAN'T PULL IT TOGETHER TO SING, AND BOB'S THREE SHEETS TO THE WIND!
HOLY COW!
WHY DID I PARK WAY DOWN HERE? IT'S A BATTLEFIELD UP THERE AND I COULDN'T HEAR IT!
I THINK-- THOSE PEOPLE ARE HERE AFTER ME, JIMMY!
SU, WE'VE GOTTA TALK ABOUT YOUR CAREER CHOICES SOMETIME.
BUT FOR NOW, PLEASE, JUST STAY HERE, OKAY?
JIMMY, VENUS IS OKAY, BUT SHE'S BURNED--
HEY, YOU GOT ANOTHER GUN?
KAKK KAK KAKK
TIKI HUT
NO!
THIS ONE WILL BE ENOUGH!

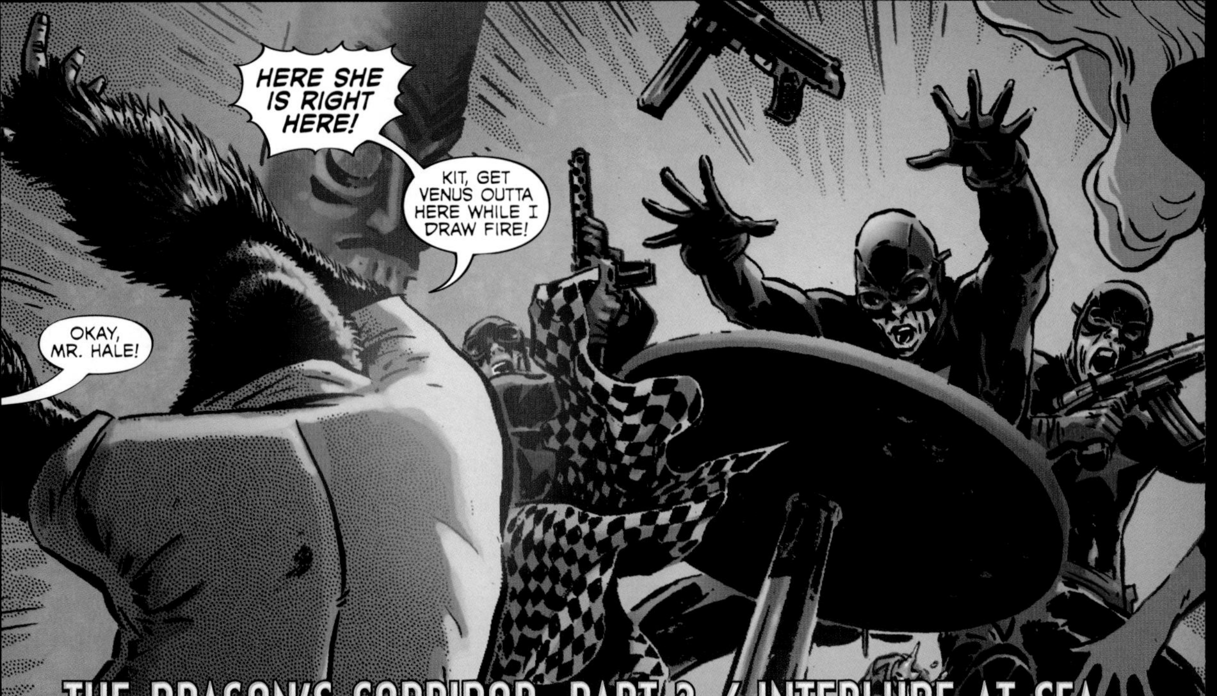
HERE SHE IS RIGHT HERE!
KIT, GET VENUS OUTTA HERE WHILE I DRAW FIRE!
OKAY, MR. HALE!

THE DRAGON'S CORRIDOR, PART 2 / INTERLUDE AT SEA

ARTISTS, STORY 1: GABRIEL HARDMAN & ELIZABETH DISMANG ARTISTS, STORY 2: CLAYTON HENRY & JANA SCHIRMER LETTERER: BLAMBOT'S NATE PIEKOS
COVER: ADI GRANOV VARIANT COVER: McGUINNESS, VINES & PONSOR WOLVERINE VARIANT: GERALD PAREL PRODUCTION: IRENE LEE
ASST. EDITOR: LAUREN SANKOVITCH EDITOR: MARK PANICCIA EDITOR IN CHIEF: JOE QUESADA PUBLISHER: DAN BUCKLEY EXEC. PRODUCER: ALAN FINE

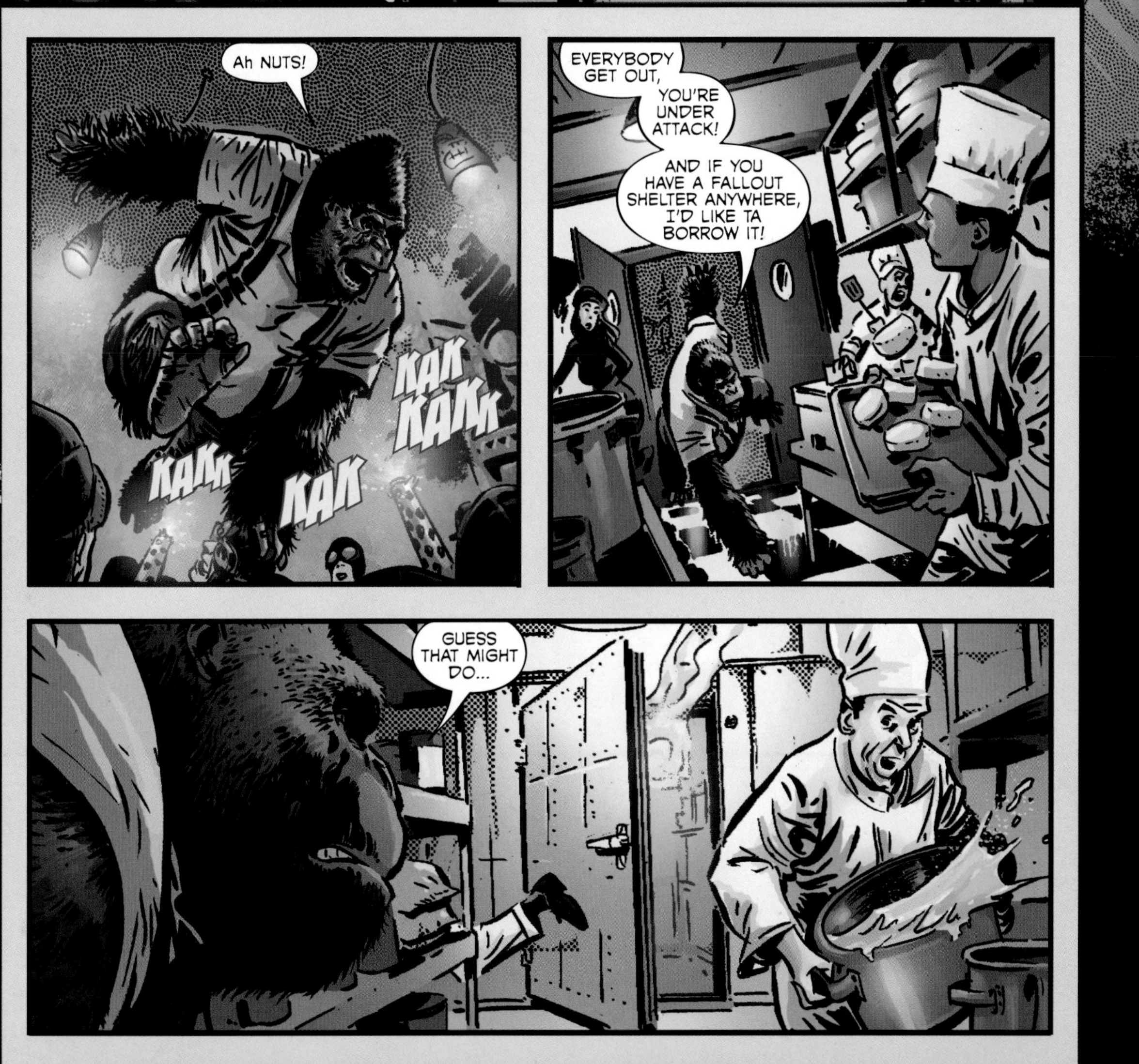
Ah NUTS!
KAK KAKK
KAKK
KAK
EVERYBODY GET OUT,
YOU'RE UNDER ATTACK!
AND IF YOU HAVE A FALLOUT SHELTER ANYWHERE, I'D LIKE TA BORROW IT!
GUESS THAT MIGHT DO...

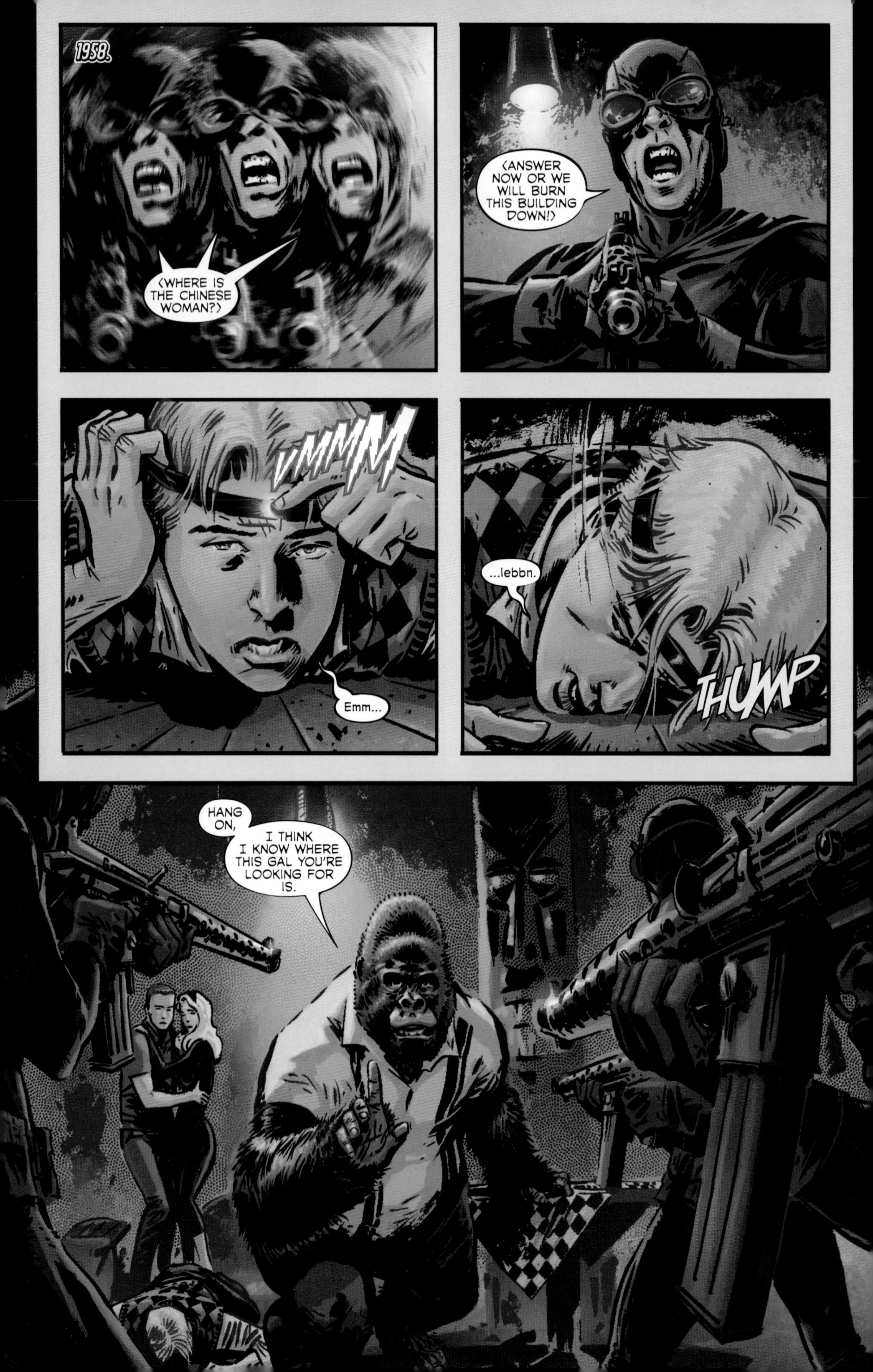
1958.
‹WHERE IS THE CHINESE WOMAN?›
‹ANSWER NOW OR WE WILL BURN THIS BUILDING DOWN!›
VMMM
Emm...
...lebbn.
THUMP
HANG ON,
I THINK I KNOW WHERE THIS GAL YOU'RE LOOKING FOR IS.

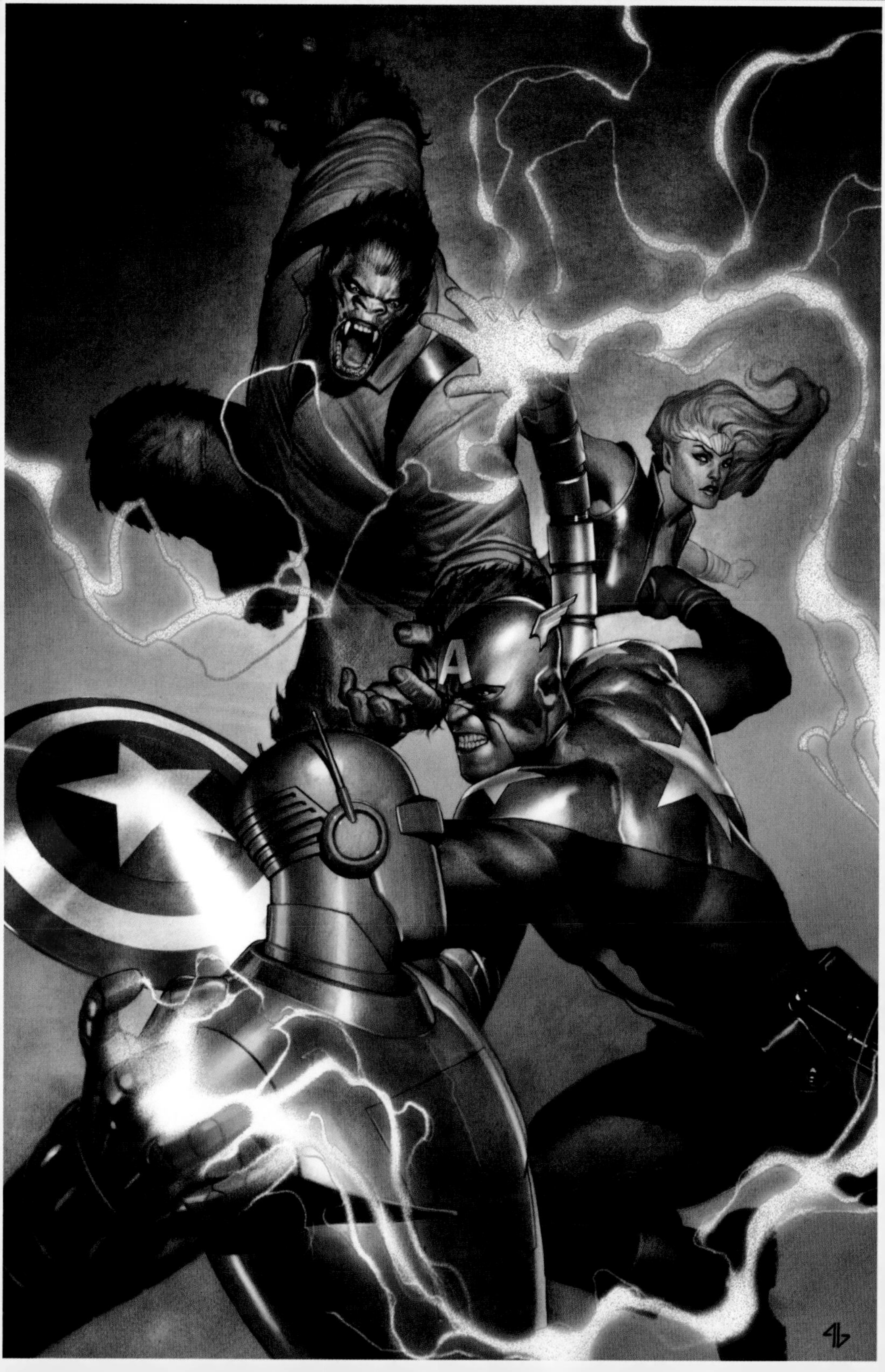

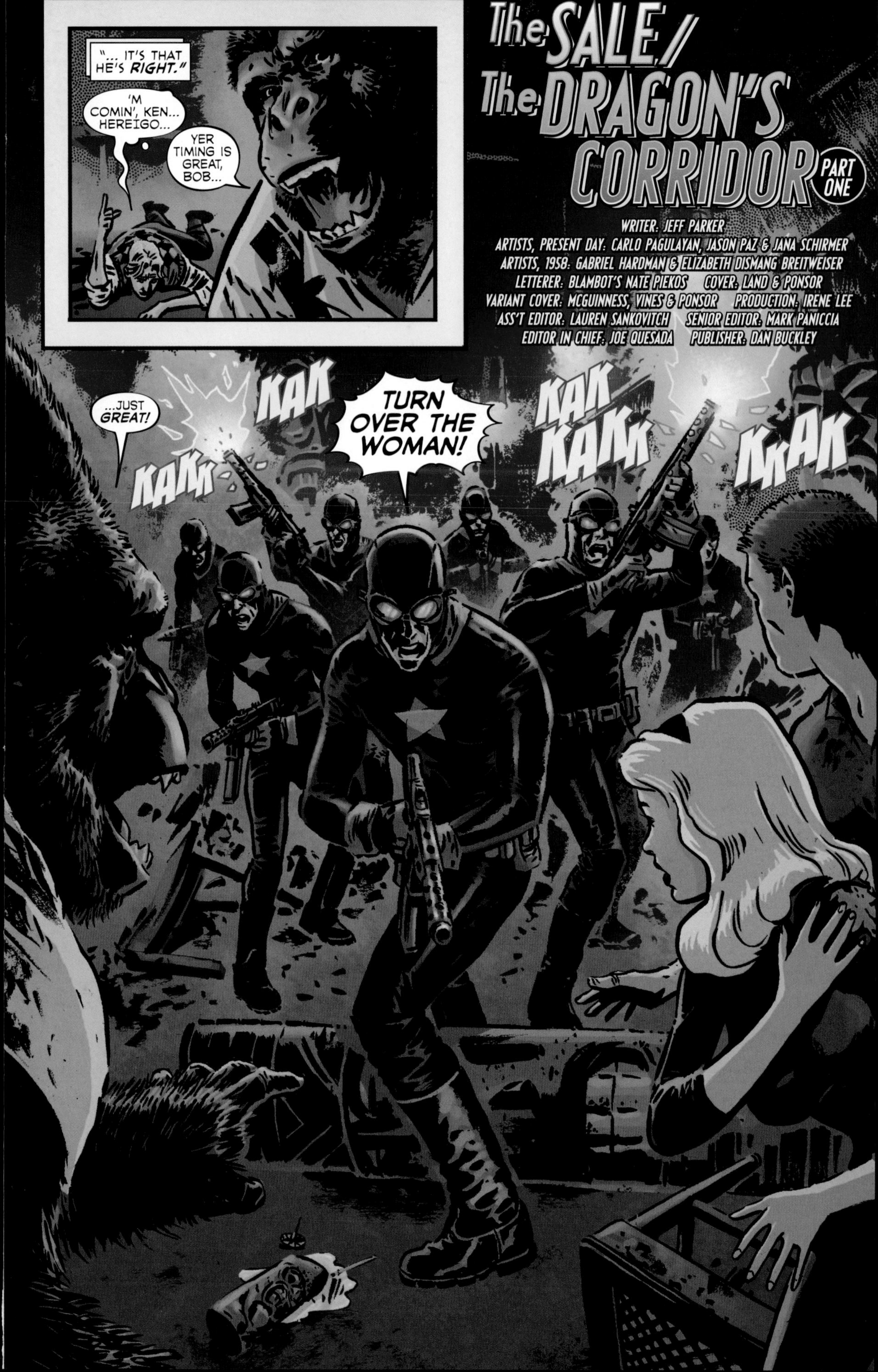
"... IT'S THAT HE'S *RIGHT*."
'M COMIN', KEN... HEREIGO...
YER TIMING IS GREAT, BOB...
The SALE/ The DRAGON'S CORRIDOR PART ONE
WRITER: JEFF PARKER
ARTISTS, PRESENT DAY: CARLO PAGULAYAN, JASON PAZ & JANA SCHIRMER
ARTISTS, 1958: GABRIEL HARDMAN & ELIZABETH DISMANG BREITWEISER
LETTERER: BLAMBOT'S NATE PIEKOS COVER: LAND & PONSOR
VARIANT COVER: MCGUINNESS, VINES & PONSOR PRODUCTION: IRENE LEE
ASS'T EDITOR: LAUREN SANKOVITCH SENIOR EDITOR: MARK PANICCIA
EDITOR IN CHIEF: JOE QUESADA PUBLISHER: DAN BUCKLEY
...JUST *GREAT!*
KAK
KAKK
TURN OVER THE WOMAN!
KAK KAKK
KKAK

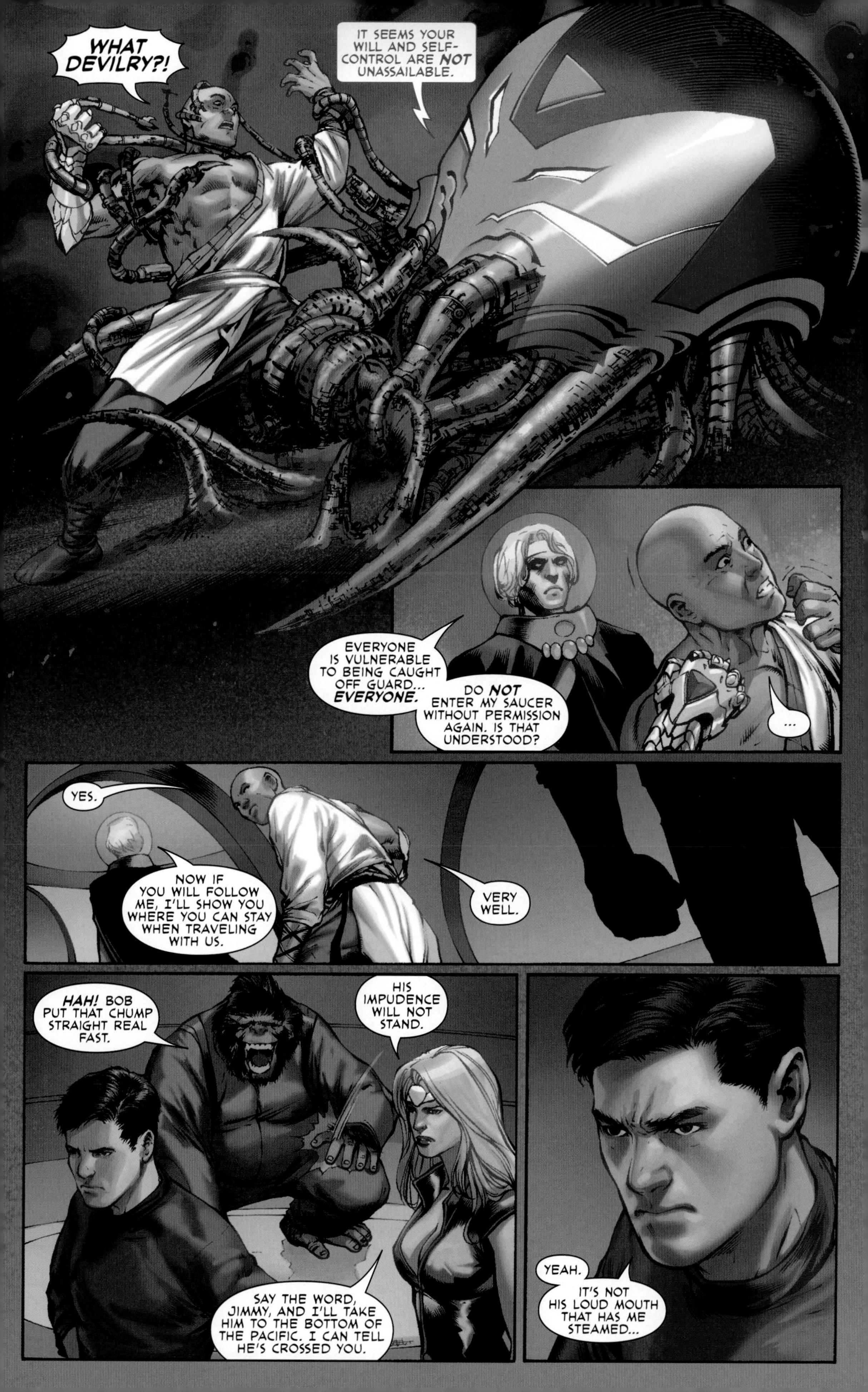
WHAT DEVILRY?!
IT SEEMS YOUR WILL AND SELF-CONTROL ARE NOT UNASSAILABLE.
EVERYONE IS VULNERABLE TO BEING CAUGHT OFF GUARD... EVERYONE.
DO NOT ENTER MY SAUCER WITHOUT PERMISSION AGAIN. IS THAT UNDERSTOOD?
...
YES.
NOW IF YOU WILL FOLLOW ME, I'LL SHOW YOU WHERE YOU CAN STAY WHEN TRAVELING WITH US.
VERY WELL.
HAH! BOB PUT THAT CHUMP STRAIGHT REAL FAST.
HIS IMPUDENCE WILL NOT STAND.
SAY THE WORD, JIMMY, AND I'LL TAKE HIM TO THE BOTTOM OF THE PACIFIC. I CAN TELL HE'S CROSSED YOU.
YEAH.
IT'S NOT HIS LOUD MOUTH THAT HAS ME STEAMED...

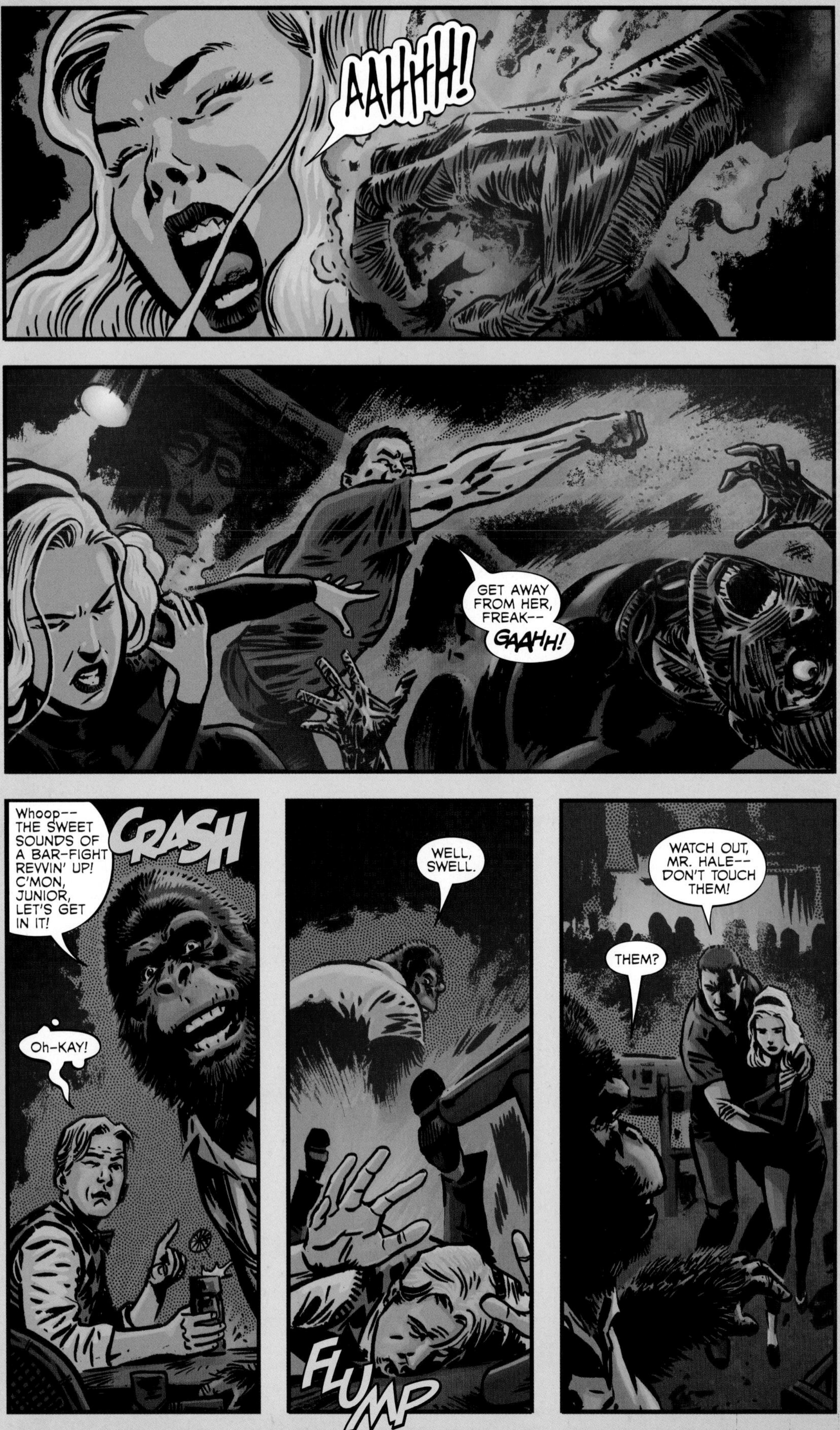
AAHHH!
GET AWAY FROM HER, FREAK--
GAAHH!
Whoop-- THE SWEET SOUNDS OF A BAR-FIGHT REVVIN' UP! C'MON, JUNIOR, LET'S GET IN IT!
CRASH
Oh-KAY!
WELL, SWELL.
FLUMP
WATCH OUT, MR. HALE-- DON'T TOUCH THEM!
THEM?

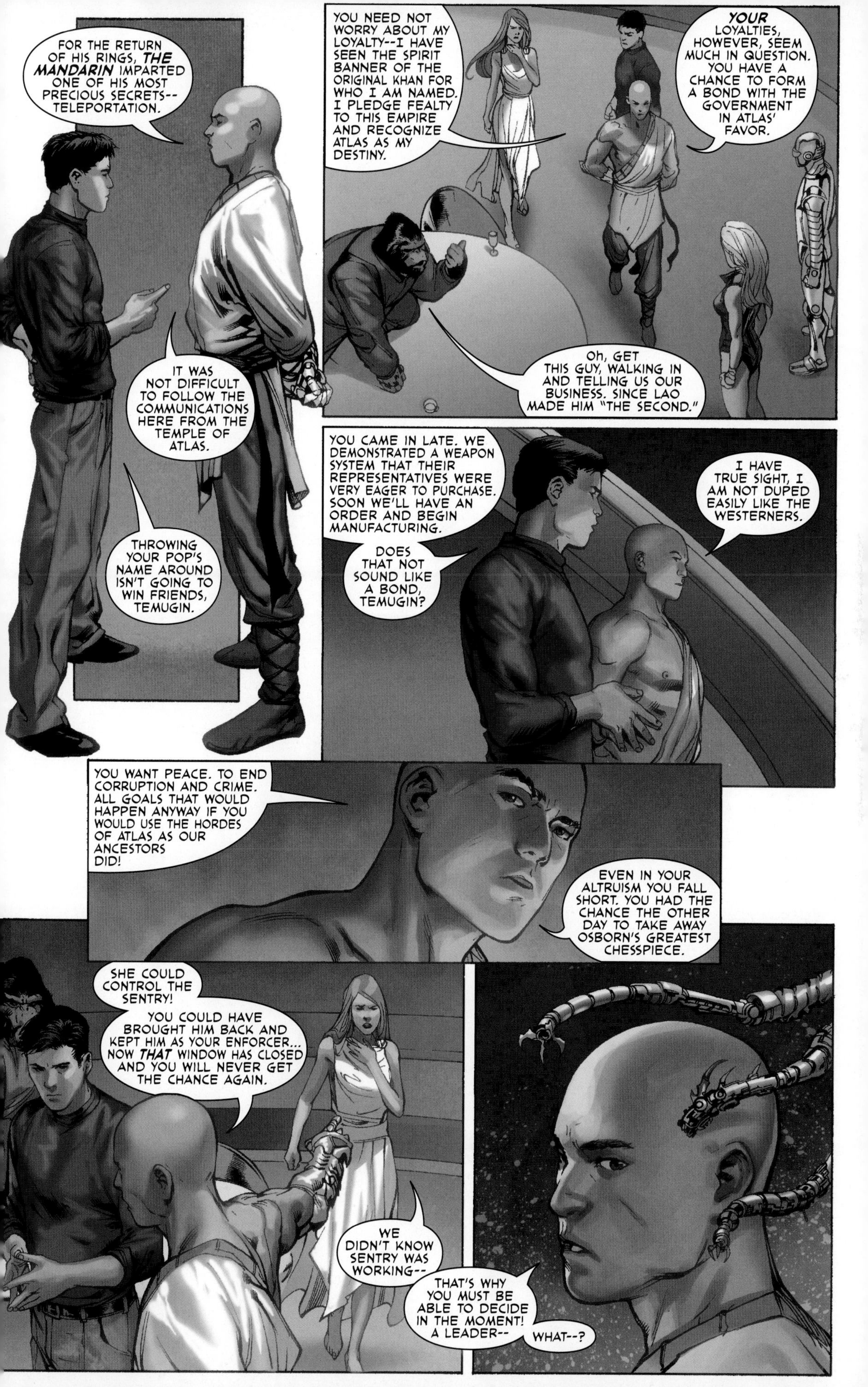
FOR THE RETURN OF HIS RINGS, THE MANDARIN IMPARTED ONE OF HIS MOST PRECIOUS SECRETS-- TELEPORTATION.
IT WAS NOT DIFFICULT TO FOLLOW THE COMMUNICATIONS HERE FROM THE TEMPLE OF ATLAS.
THROWING YOUR POP'S NAME AROUND ISN'T GOING TO WIN FRIENDS, TEMUGIN.
YOU NEED NOT WORRY ABOUT MY LOYALTY--I HAVE SEEN THE SPIRIT BANNER OF THE ORIGINAL KHAN FOR WHO I AM NAMED. I PLEDGE FEALTY TO THIS EMPIRE AND RECOGNIZE ATLAS AS MY DESTINY.
YOUR LOYALTIES, HOWEVER, SEEM MUCH IN QUESTION. YOU HAVE A CHANCE TO FORM A BOND WITH THE GOVERNMENT IN ATLAS' FAVOR.
Oh, GET THIS GUY, WALKING IN AND TELLING US OUR BUSINESS. SINCE LAO MADE HIM "THE SECOND."
YOU CAME IN LATE. WE DEMONSTRATED A WEAPON SYSTEM THAT THEIR REPRESENTATIVES WERE VERY EAGER TO PURCHASE. SOON WE'LL HAVE AN ORDER AND BEGIN MANUFACTURING.
DOES THAT NOT SOUND LIKE A BOND, TEMUGIN?
I HAVE TRUE SIGHT, I AM NOT DUPED EASILY LIKE THE WESTERNERS.
YOU WANT PEACE. TO END CORRUPTION AND CRIME. ALL GOALS THAT WOULD HAPPEN ANYWAY IF YOU WOULD USE THE HORDES OF ATLAS AS OUR ANCESTORS DID!
EVEN IN YOUR ALTRUISM YOU FALL SHORT. YOU HAD THE CHANCE THE OTHER DAY TO TAKE AWAY OSBORN'S GREATEST CHESSPIECE.
SHE COULD CONTROL THE SENTRY!
YOU COULD HAVE BROUGHT HIM BACK AND KEPT HIM AS YOUR ENFORCER... NOW THAT WINDOW HAS CLOSED AND YOU WILL NEVER GET THE CHANCE AGAIN.
WE DIDN'T KNOW SENTRY WAS WORKING--
THAT'S WHY YOU MUST BE ABLE TO DECIDE IN THE MOMENT! A LEADER--
WHAT--?

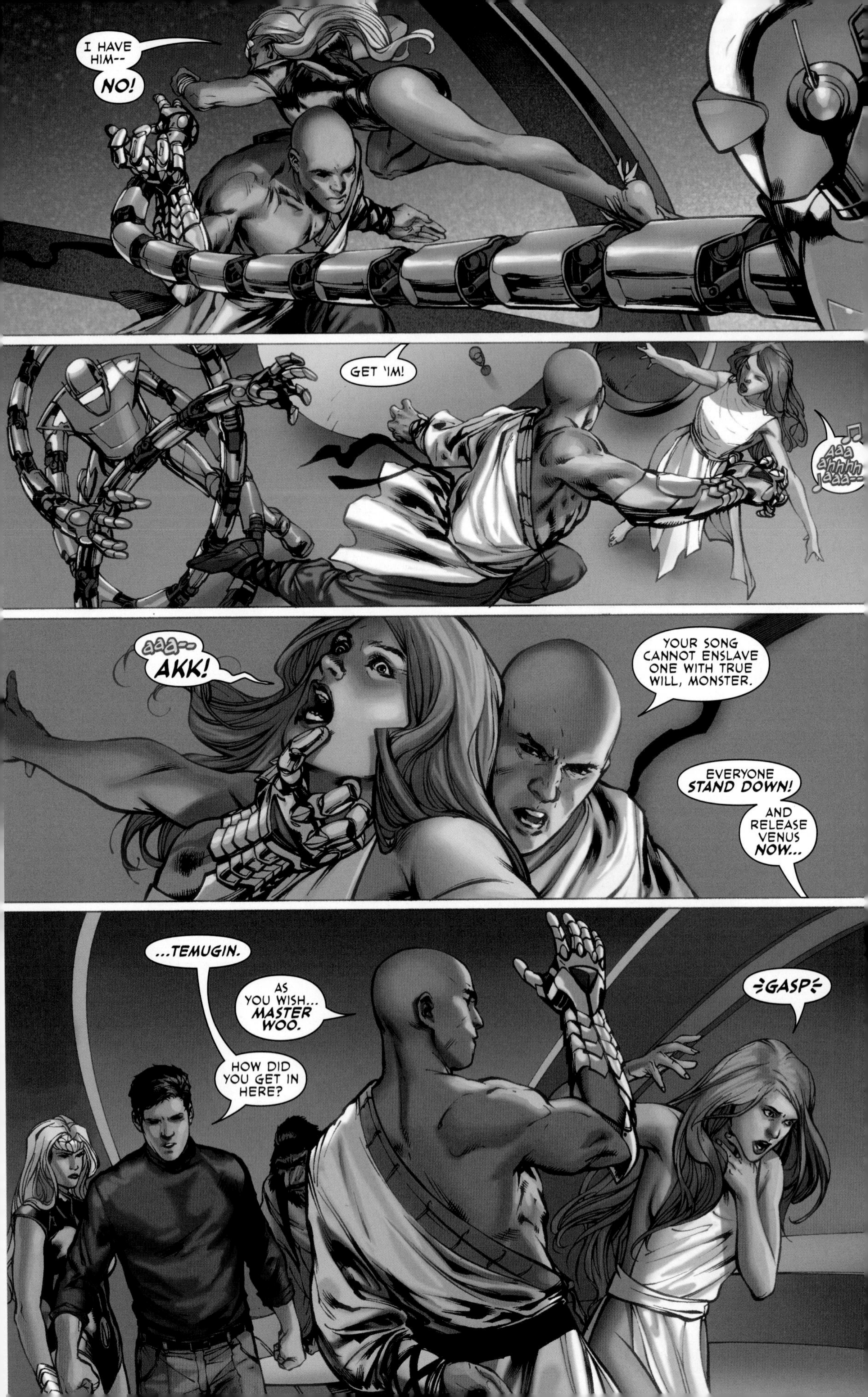

I HAVE HIM-- NO!
GET 'IM!
Aaa ahhhh laaa--
aaa-- AKK!
YOUR SONG CANNOT ENSLAVE ONE WITH TRUE WILL, MONSTER.
EVERYONE STAND DOWN!
AND RELEASE VENUS NOW...
...TEMUGIN.
AS YOU WISH... MASTER WOO.
HOW DID YOU GET IN HERE?
GASP

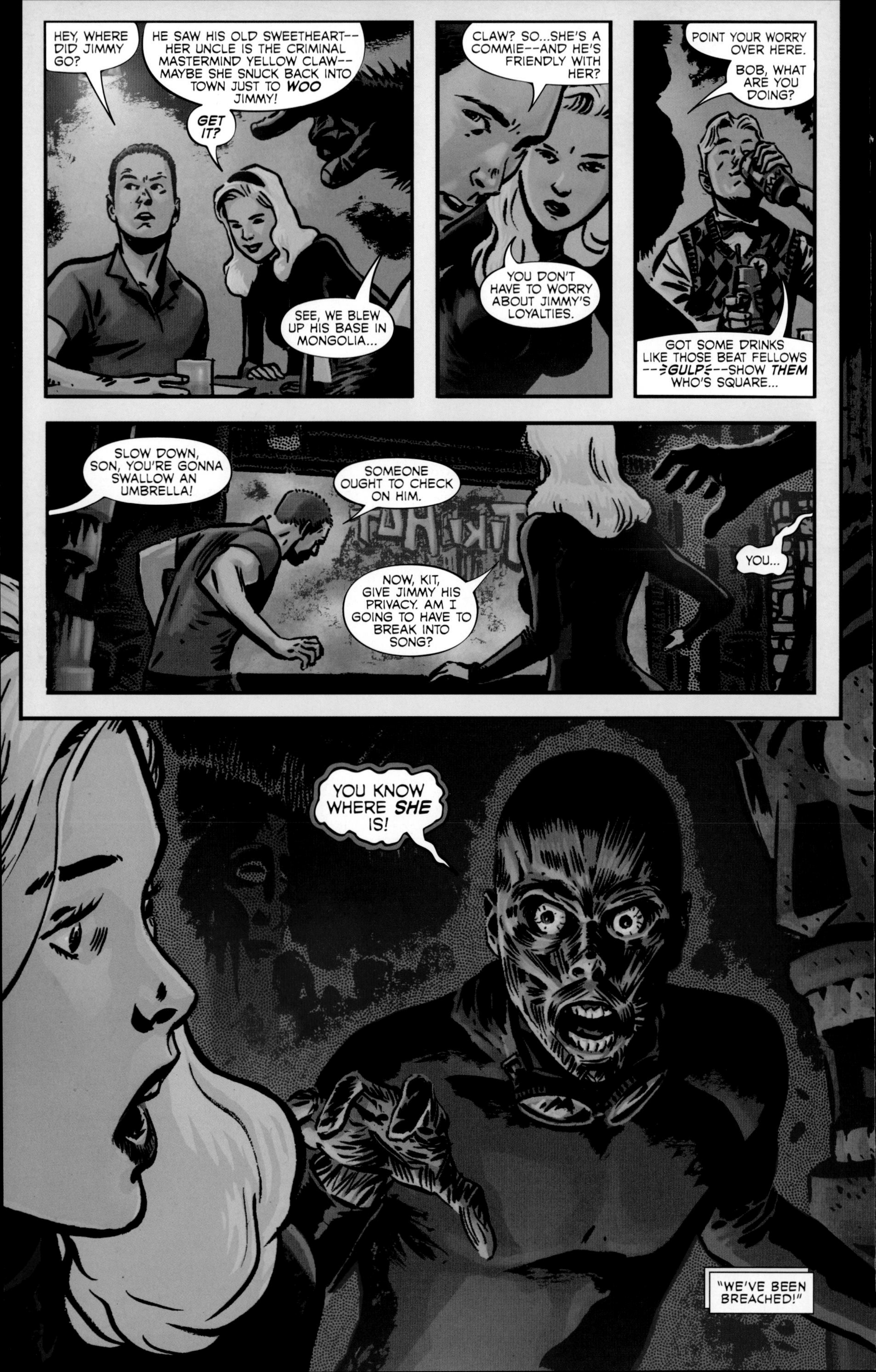
HEY, WHERE DID JIMMY GO?
HE SAW HIS OLD SWEETHEART--HER UNCLE IS THE CRIMINAL MASTERMIND YELLOW CLAW--MAYBE SHE SNUCK BACK INTO TOWN JUST TO WOO JIMMY!
GET IT?
SEE, WE BLEW UP HIS BASE IN MONGOLIA...
CLAW? SO...SHE'S A COMMIE--AND HE'S FRIENDLY WITH HER?
YOU DON'T HAVE TO WORRY ABOUT JIMMY'S LOYALTIES.
POINT YOUR WORRY OVER HERE.
BOB, WHAT ARE YOU DOING?
GOT SOME DRINKS LIKE THOSE BEAT FELLOWS --GULP--SHOW THEM WHO'S SQUARE...
SLOW DOWN, SON, YOU'RE GONNA SWALLOW AN UMBRELLA!
SOMEONE OUGHT TO CHECK ON HIM.
NOW, KIT, GIVE JIMMY HIS PRIVACY. AM I GOING TO HAVE TO BREAK INTO SONG?
YOU...
YOU KNOW WHERE SHE IS!
"WE'VE BEEN BREACHED!"

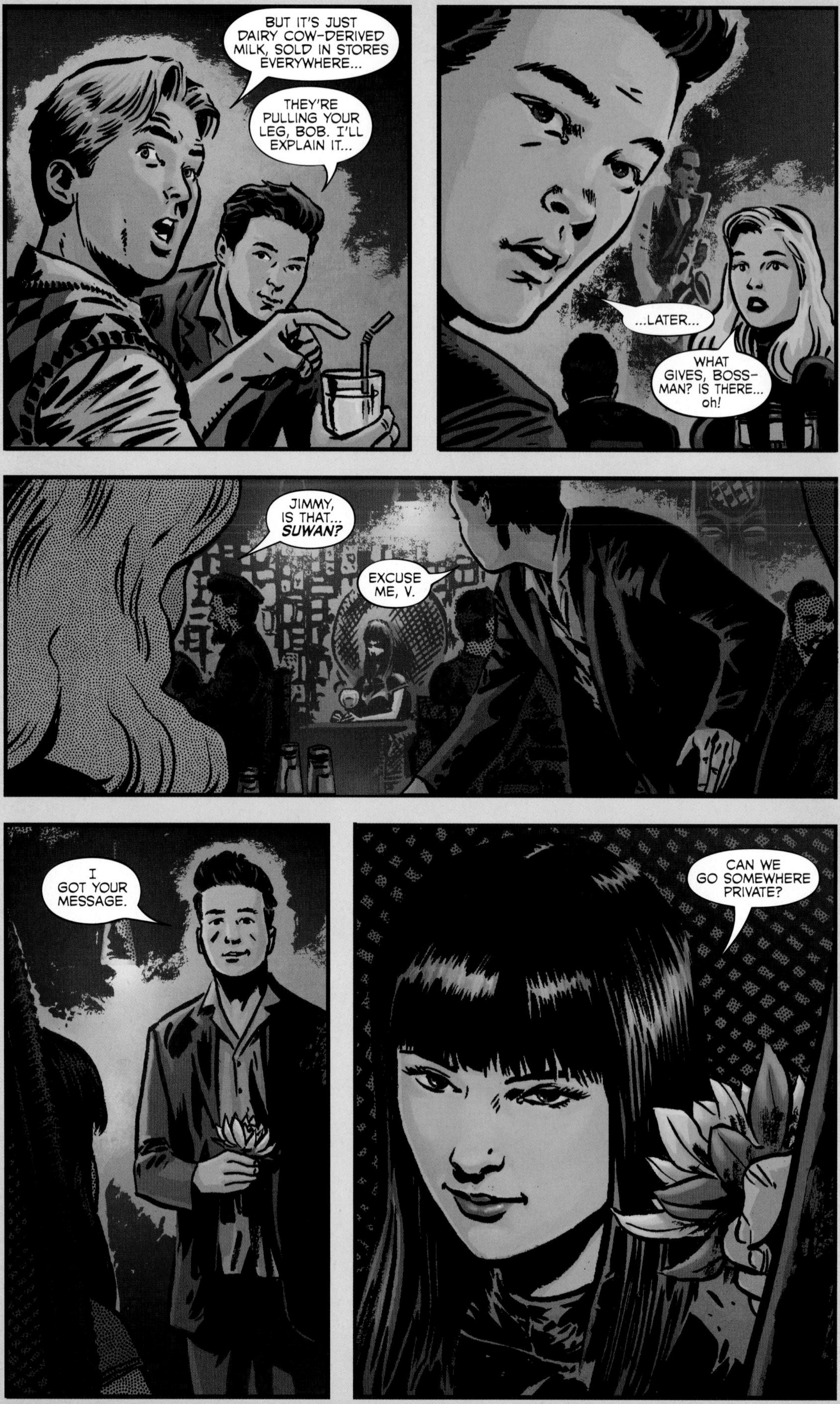
BUT IT'S JUST DAIRY COW-DERIVED MILK, SOLD IN STORES EVERYWHERE...
THEY'RE PULLING YOUR LEG, BOB. I'LL EXPLAIN IT...
...LATER...
WHAT GIVES, BOSS-MAN? IS THERE... oh!
JIMMY, IS THAT... SUWAN?
EXCUSE ME, V.
I GOT YOUR MESSAGE.
CAN WE GO SOMEWHERE PRIVATE?

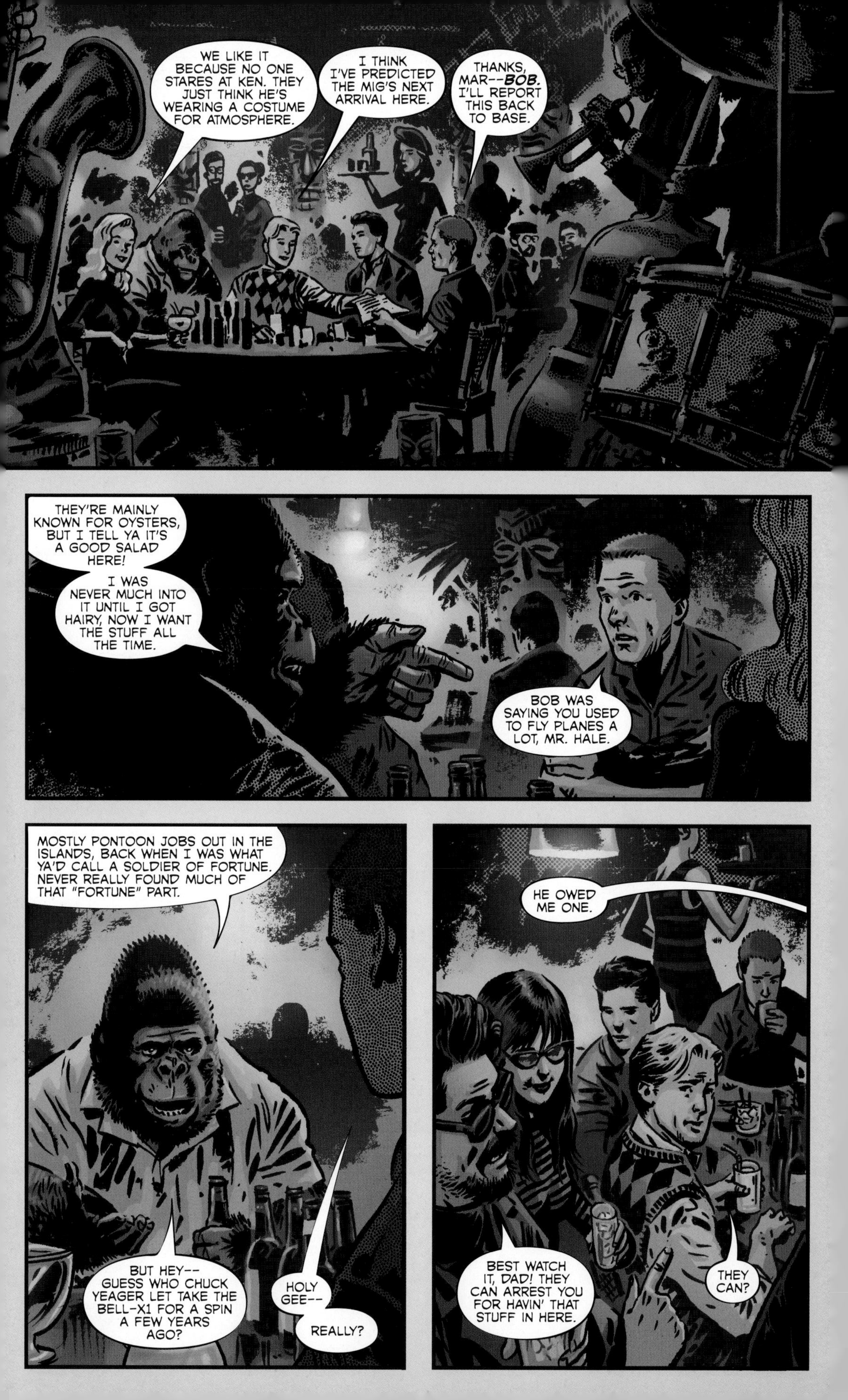
WE LIKE IT BECAUSE NO ONE STARES AT KEN. THEY JUST THINK HE'S WEARING A COSTUME FOR ATMOSPHERE.
I THINK I'VE PREDICTED THE MIG'S NEXT ARRIVAL HERE.
THANKS, MAR--BOB. I'LL REPORT THIS BACK TO BASE.
THEY'RE MAINLY KNOWN FOR OYSTERS, BUT I TELL YA IT'S A GOOD SALAD HERE!
I WAS NEVER MUCH INTO IT UNTIL I GOT HAIRY, NOW I WANT THE STUFF ALL THE TIME.
BOB WAS SAYING YOU USED TO FLY PLANES A LOT, MR. HALE.
MOSTLY PONTOON JOBS OUT IN THE ISLANDS, BACK WHEN I WAS WHAT YA'D CALL A SOLDIER OF FORTUNE. NEVER REALLY FOUND MUCH OF THAT "FORTUNE" PART.
BUT HEY-- GUESS WHO CHUCK YEAGER LET TAKE THE BELL-X1 FOR A SPIN A FEW YEARS AGO?
HOLY GEE--
REALLY?
HE OWED ME ONE.
BEST WATCH IT, DAD! THEY CAN ARREST YOU FOR HAVIN' THAT STUFF IN HERE.
THEY CAN?

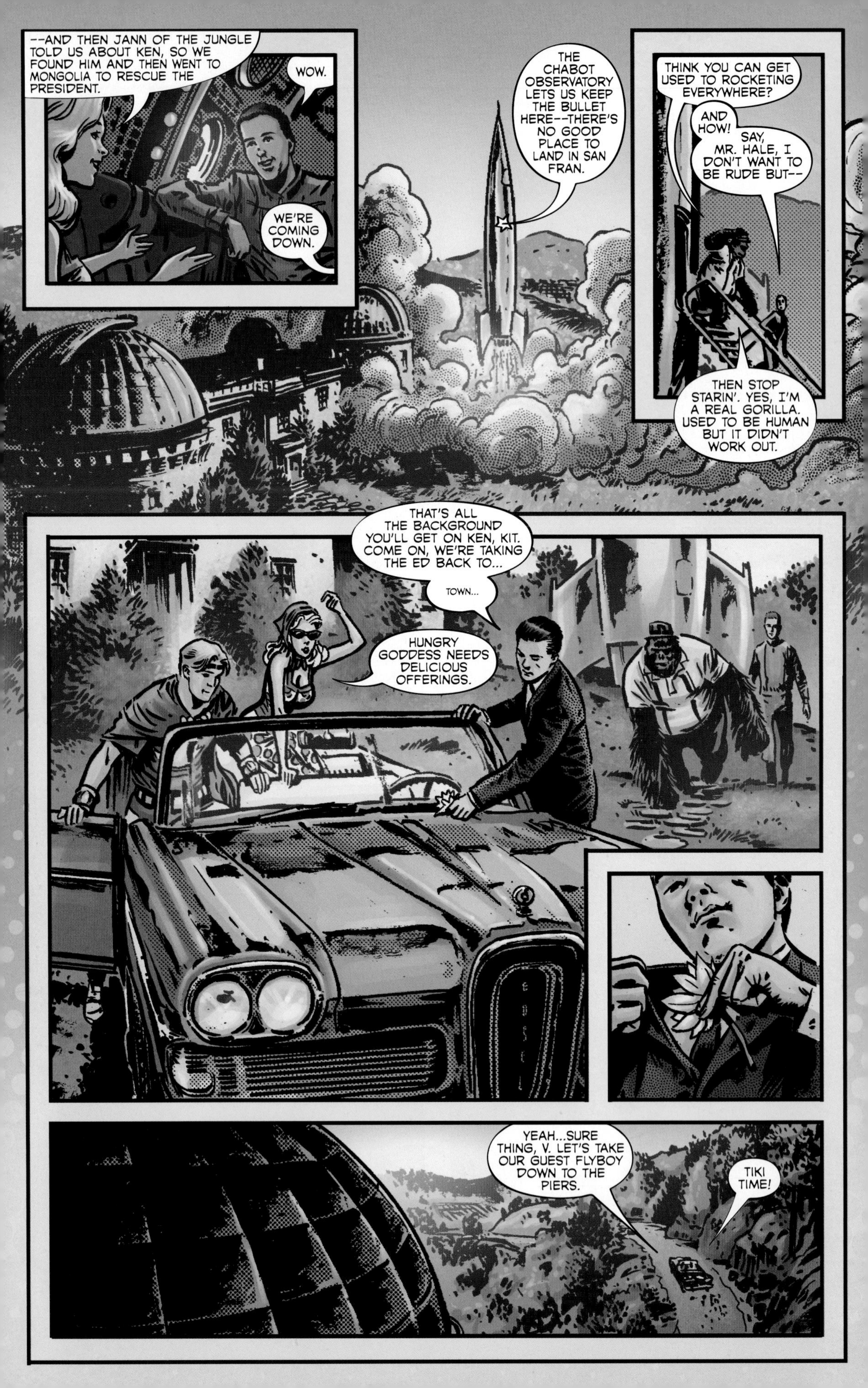
--AND THEN JANN OF THE JUNGLE TOLD US ABOUT KEN, SO WE FOUND HIM AND THEN WENT TO MONGOLIA TO RESCUE THE PRESIDENT.
WOW.
WE'RE COMING DOWN.
THE CHABOT OBSERVATORY LETS US KEEP THE BULLET HERE--THERE'S NO GOOD PLACE TO LAND IN SAN FRAN.
THINK YOU CAN GET USED TO ROCKETING EVERYWHERE?
AND HOW!
SAY, MR. HALE, I DON'T WANT TO BE RUDE BUT--
THEN STOP STARIN'. YES, I'M A REAL GORILLA. USED TO BE HUMAN BUT IT DIDN'T WORK OUT.
THAT'S ALL THE BACKGROUND YOU'LL GET ON KEN, KIT. COME ON, WE'RE TAKING THE ED BACK TO...
TOWN...
HUNGRY GODDESS NEEDS DELICIOUS OFFERINGS.
YEAH...SURE THING, V. LET'S TAKE OUR GUEST FLYBOY DOWN TO THE PIERS.
TIKI TIME!

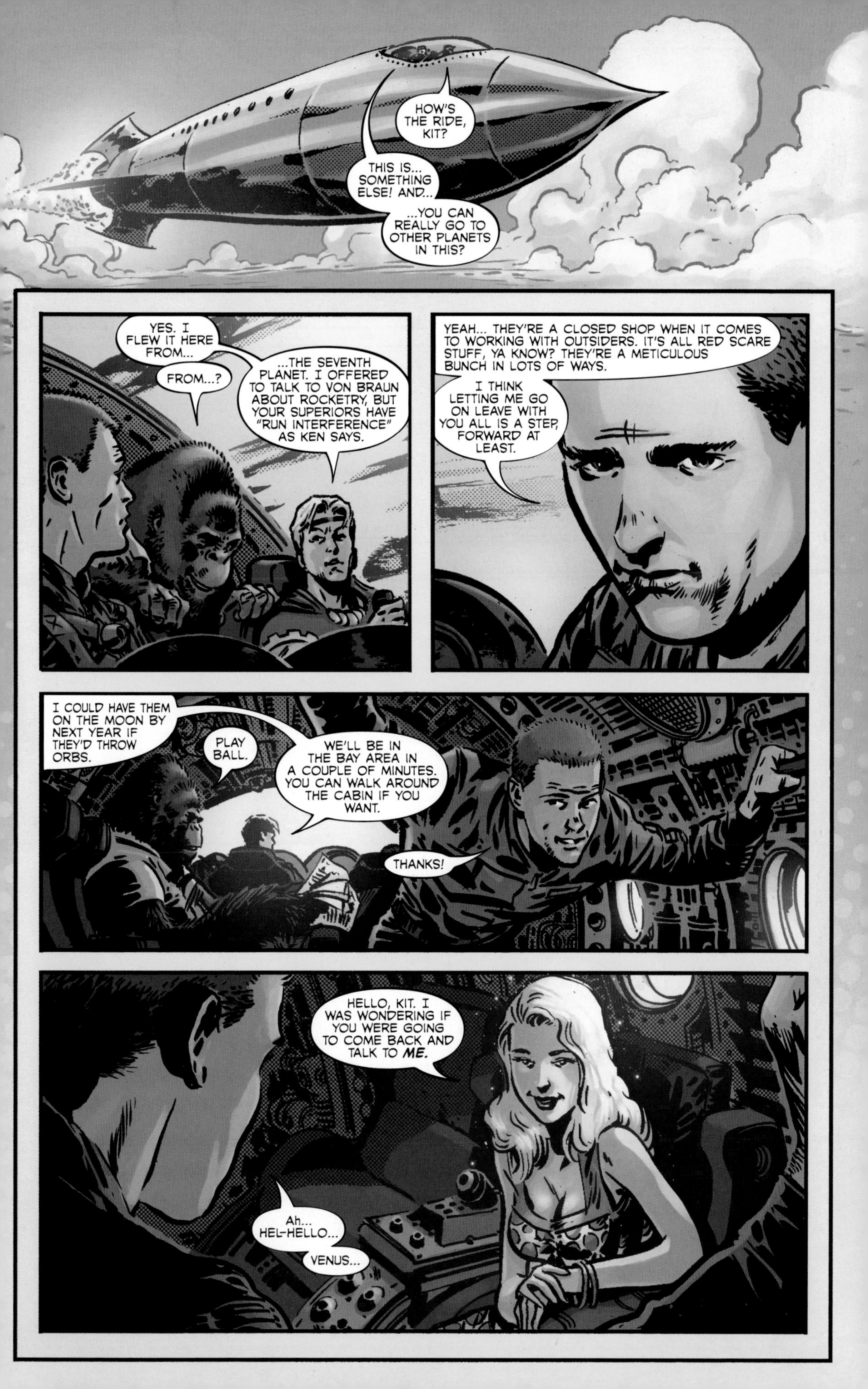
HOW'S THE RIDE, KIT?
THIS IS... SOMETHING ELSE! AND...
...YOU CAN REALLY GO TO OTHER PLANETS IN THIS?
YES. I FLEW IT HERE FROM...
FROM...?
...THE SEVENTH PLANET. I OFFERED TO TALK TO VON BRAUN ABOUT ROCKETRY, BUT YOUR SUPERIORS HAVE "RUN INTERFERENCE" AS KEN SAYS.
YEAH... THEY'RE A CLOSED SHOP WHEN IT COMES TO WORKING WITH OUTSIDERS. IT'S ALL RED SCARE STUFF, YA KNOW? THEY'RE A METICULOUS BUNCH IN LOTS OF WAYS.
I THINK LETTING ME GO ON LEAVE WITH YOU ALL IS A STEP FORWARD AT LEAST.
I COULD HAVE THEM ON THE MOON BY NEXT YEAR IF THEY'D THROW ORBS.
PLAY BALL.
WE'LL BE IN THE BAY AREA IN A COUPLE OF MINUTES. YOU CAN WALK AROUND THE CABIN IF YOU WANT.
THANKS!
HELLO, KIT. I WAS WONDERING IF YOU WERE GOING TO COME BACK AND TALK TO ***ME.***
Ah... HEL-HELLO...
VENUS...

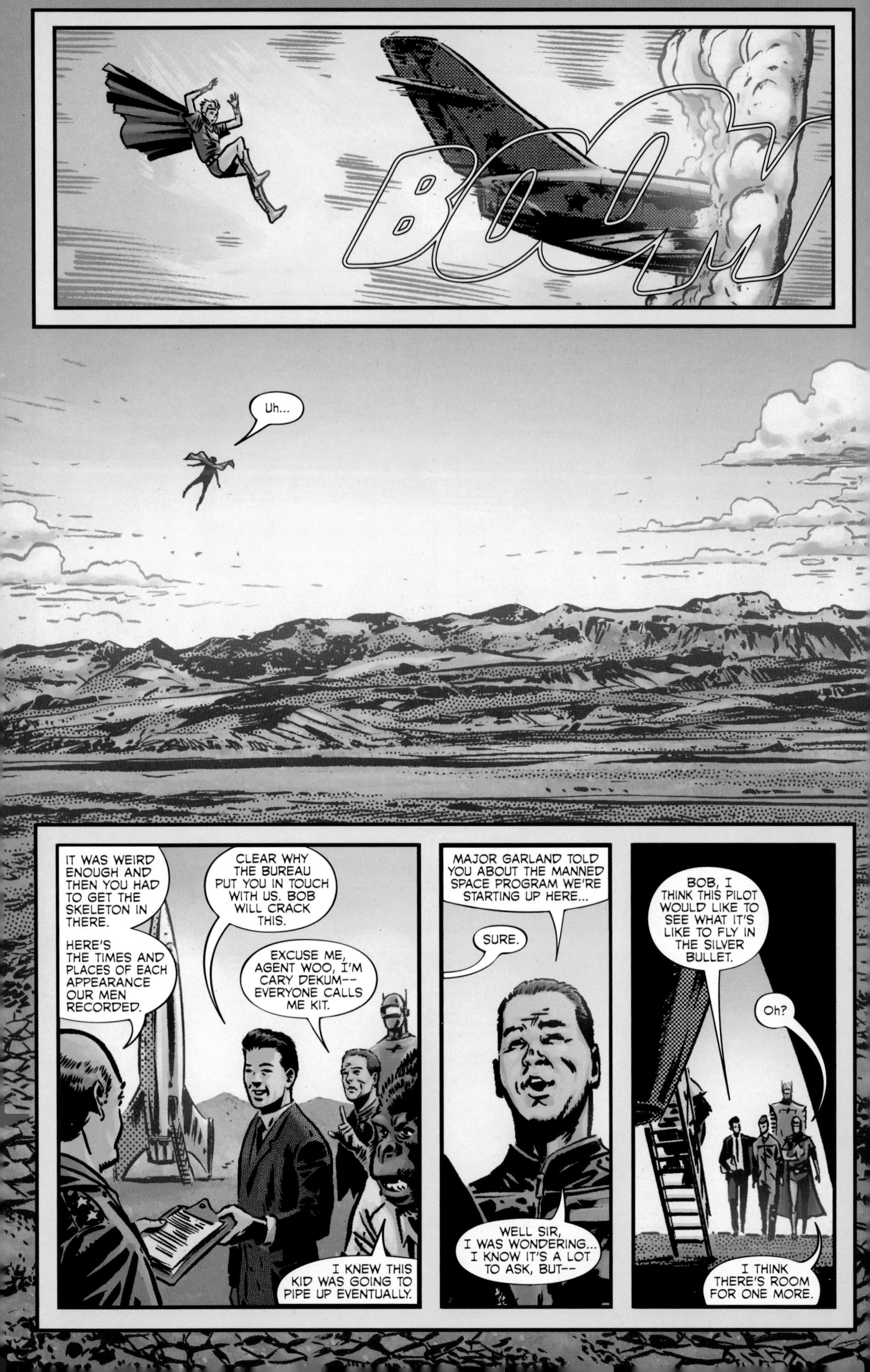
BOOM
Uh...
IT WAS WEIRD ENOUGH AND THEN YOU HAD TO GET THE SKELETON IN THERE.
HERE'S THE TIMES AND PLACES OF EACH APPEARANCE OUR MEN RECORDED.
CLEAR WHY THE BUREAU PUT YOU IN TOUCH WITH US. BOB WILL CRACK THIS.
EXCUSE ME, AGENT WOO, I'M CARY DEKUM-- EVERYONE CALLS ME KIT.
I KNEW THIS KID WAS GOING TO PIPE UP EVENTUALLY.
MAJOR GARLAND TOLD YOU ABOUT THE MANNED SPACE PROGRAM WE'RE STARTING UP HERE...
SURE.
WELL SIR, I WAS WONDERING... I KNOW IT'S A LOT TO ASK, BUT--
BOB, I THINK THIS PILOT WOULD LIKE TO SEE WHAT IT'S LIKE TO FLY IN THE SILVER BULLET.
Oh?
I THINK THERE'S ROOM FOR ONE MORE.

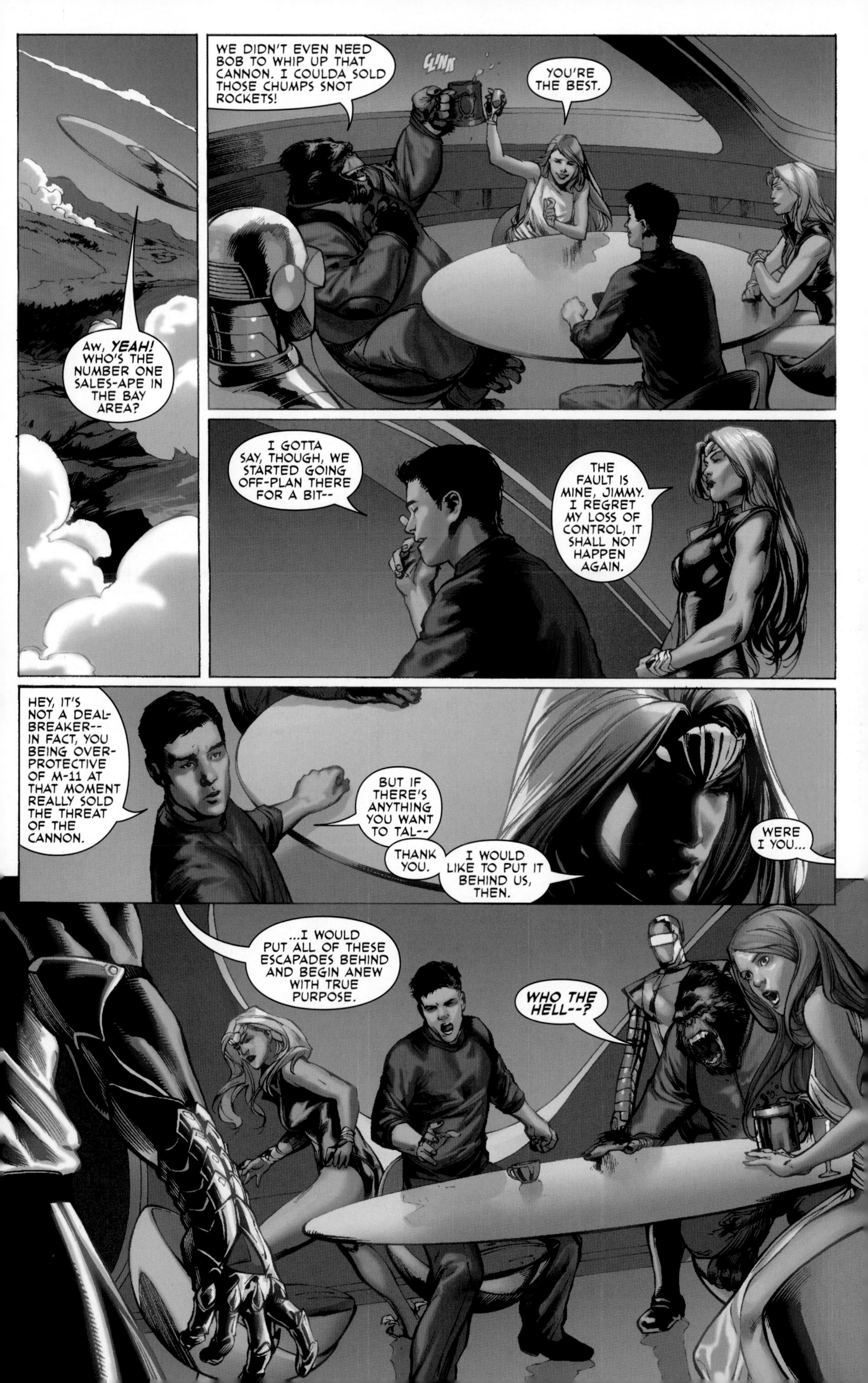

Aw, YEAH! WHO'S THE NUMBER ONE SALES-APE IN THE BAY AREA?
WE DIDN'T EVEN NEED BOB TO WHIP UP THAT CANNON. I COULDA SOLD THOSE CHUMPS SNOT ROCKETS!
CLINK
YOU'RE THE BEST.
I GOTTA SAY, THOUGH, WE STARTED GOING OFF-PLAN THERE FOR A BIT--
THE FAULT IS MINE, JIMMY. I REGRET MY LOSS OF CONTROL, IT SHALL NOT HAPPEN AGAIN.
HEY, IT'S NOT A DEAL-BREAKER-- IN FACT, YOU BEING OVER-PROTECTIVE OF M-11 AT THAT MOMENT REALLY SOLD THE THREAT OF THE CANNON.
BUT IF THERE'S ANYTHING YOU WANT TO TAL--
THANK YOU.
I WOULD LIKE TO PUT IT BEHIND US, THEN.
WERE I YOU...
...I WOULD PUT ALL OF THESE ESCAPADES BEHIND AND BEGIN ANEW WITH TRUE PURPOSE.
WHO THE HELL--?

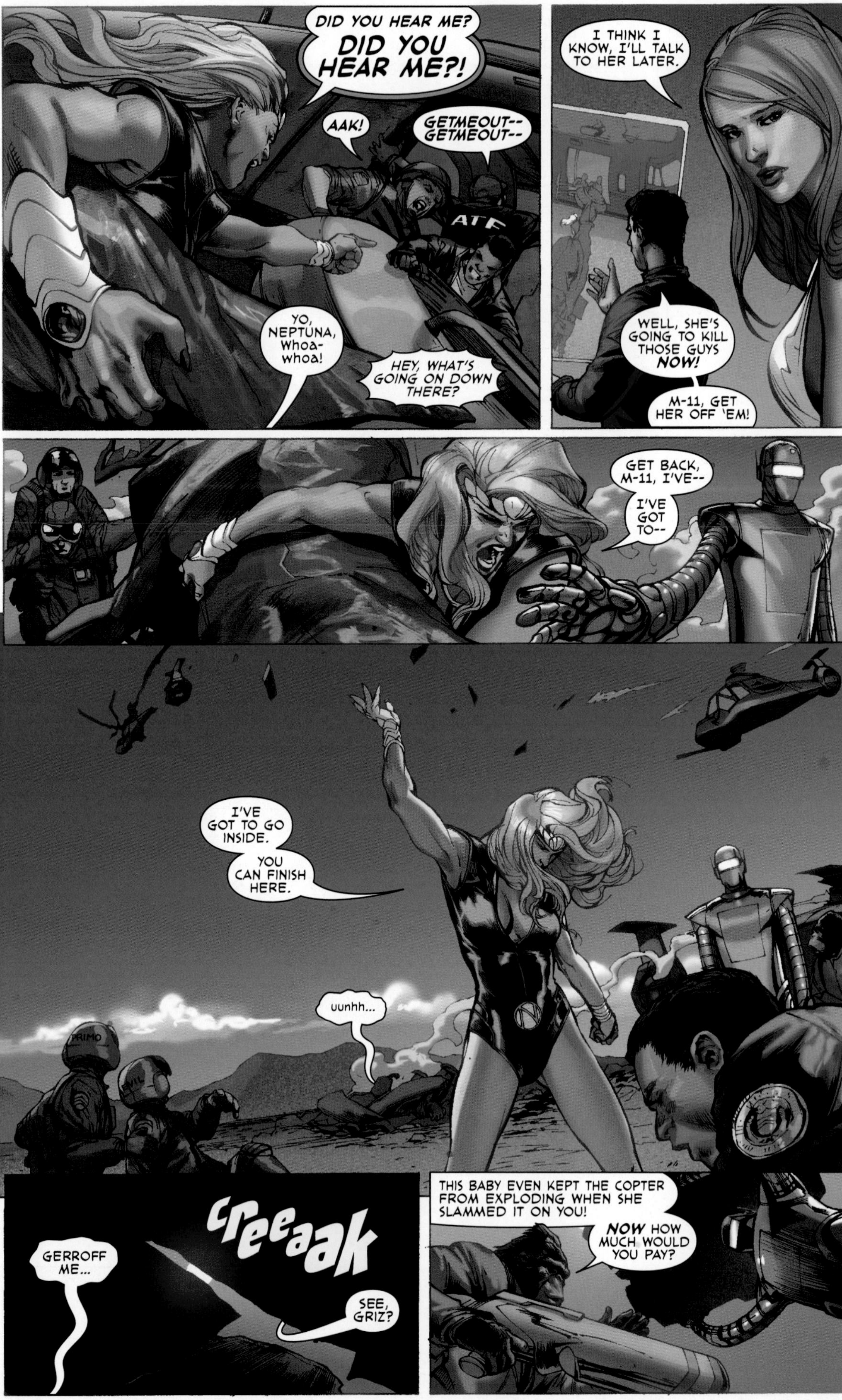
DID YOU HEAR ME? DID YOU HEAR ME?!
AAK!
GETMEOUT-- GETMEOUT--
YO, NEPTUNA, Whoa-whoa!
HEY, WHAT'S GOING ON DOWN THERE?
I THINK I KNOW, I'LL TALK TO HER LATER.
WELL, SHE'S GOING TO KILL THOSE GUYS NOW!
M-11, GET HER OFF 'EM!
GET BACK, M-11, I'VE--
I'VE GOT TO--
I'VE GOT TO GO INSIDE.
YOU CAN FINISH HERE.
uunhh...
creeaak
GERROFF ME...
SEE, GRIZ?
THIS BABY EVEN KEPT THE COPTER FROM EXPLODING WHEN SHE SLAMMED IT ON YOU!
NOW HOW MUCH WOULD YOU PAY?

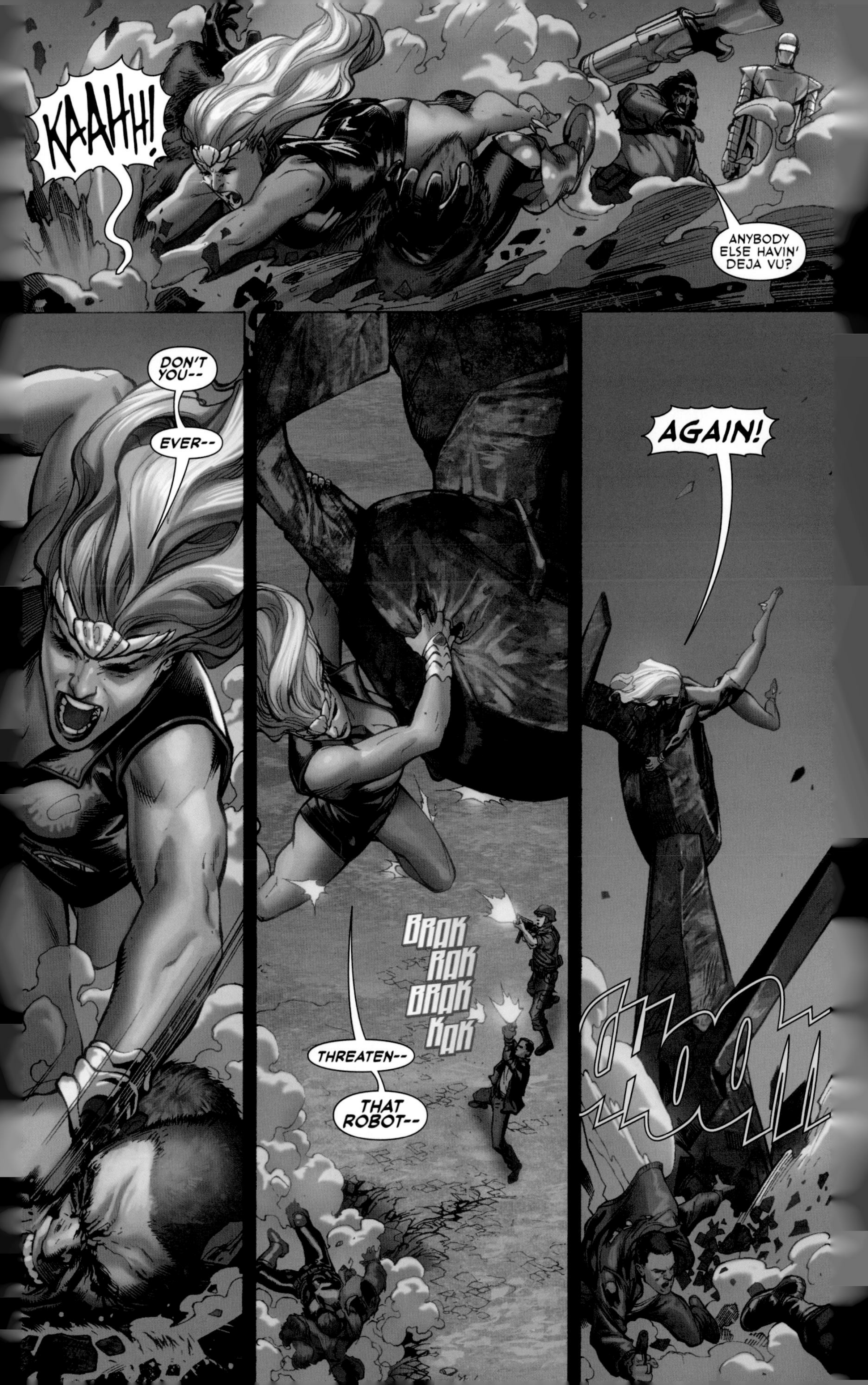
KAAHH!
ANYBODY ELSE HAVIN' DEJA VU?
DON'T YOU--
EVER--
BRAK RAK BRAK KAK
THREATEN--
THAT ROBOT--
AGAIN!

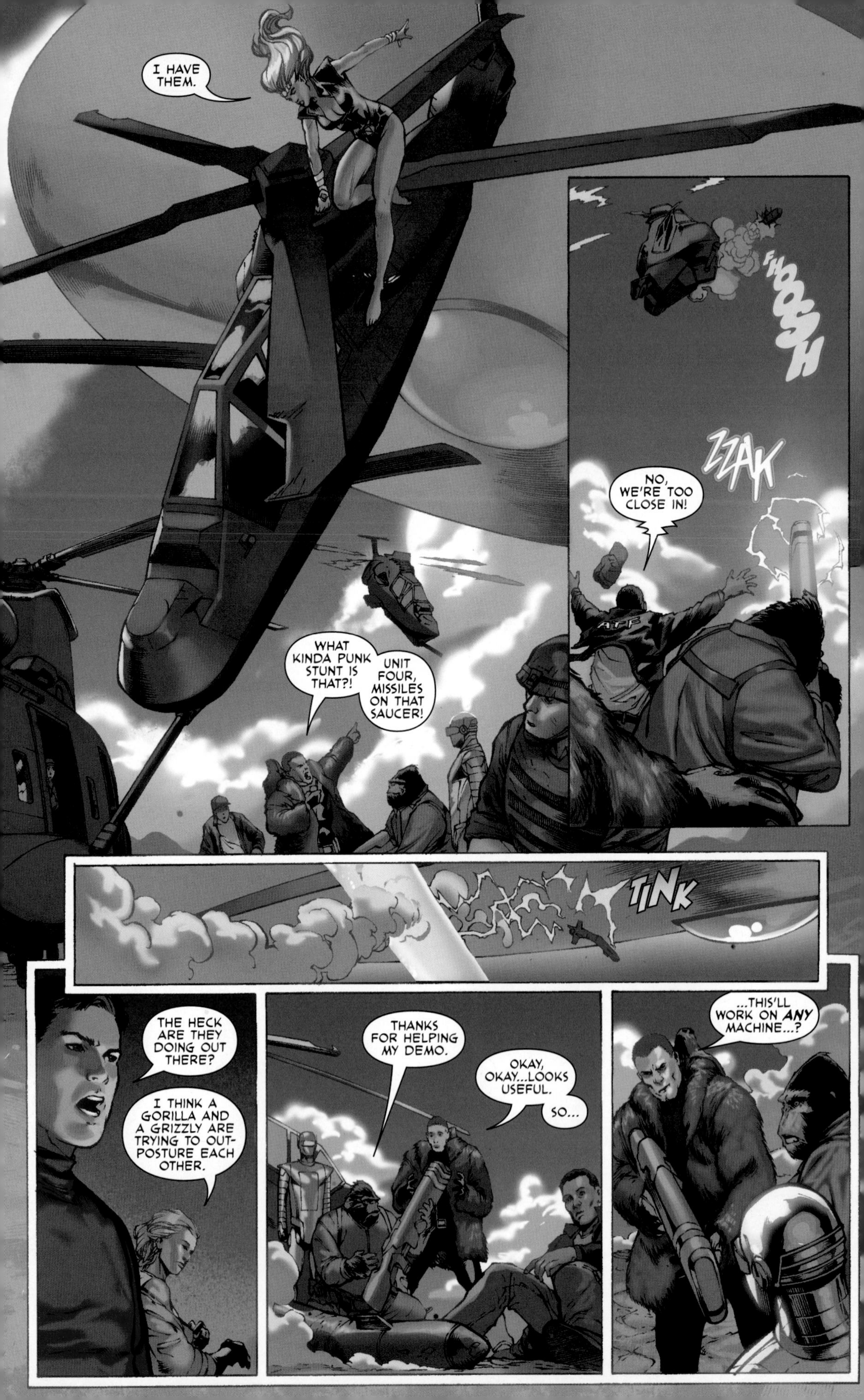
I HAVE THEM.
FHOOSH
ZZAK
NO, WE'RE TOO CLOSE IN!
WHAT KINDA PUNK STUNT IS THAT?!
UNIT FOUR, MISSILES ON THAT SAUCER!
TINK
THE HECK ARE THEY DOING OUT THERE?
I THINK A GORILLA AND A GRIZZLY ARE TRYING TO OUT-POSTURE EACH OTHER.
THANKS FOR HELPING MY DEMO.
OKAY, OKAY...LOOKS USEFUL.
SO...
...THIS'LL WORK ON ANY MACHINE...?

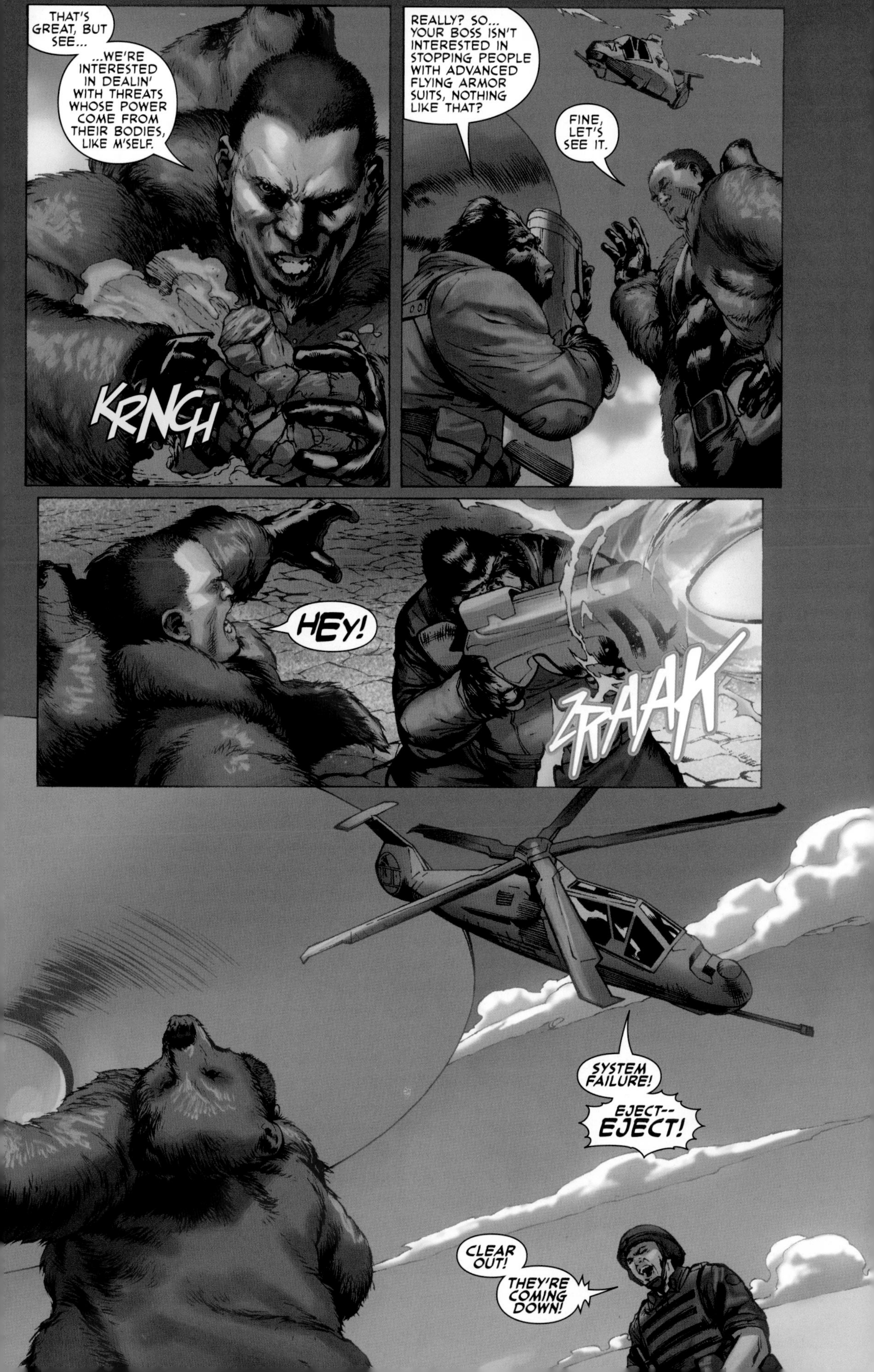
THAT'S GREAT, BUT SEE...
...WE'RE INTERESTED IN DEALIN' WITH THREATS WHOSE POWER COME FROM THEIR BODIES, LIKE M'SELF.
KRNCH
REALLY? SO... YOUR BOSS ISN'T INTERESTED IN STOPPING PEOPLE WITH ADVANCED FLYING ARMOR SUITS, NOTHING LIKE THAT?
FINE, LET'S SEE IT.
HEY!
ZRAAK
SYSTEM FAILURE!
EJECT-- EJECT!
CLEAR OUT!
THEY'RE COMING DOWN!

NOW.

VMMMMMmMMm

AHH!

WHAT THE--?!

ALL RIGHT, LADIES, ON BEHALF OF THE GOVERNMENT TRY NOT TO LOOK ALL RATTLED, HUH?

LOOK AT THIS FREAK SHOW. THIS IS OUR ARMS SUPPLIER?

NOT TO OVERSTEP, MAX, BUT ALL WE'VE GOT OF YOUR PREDECESSOR IS A TORN PIECE OF JACKET WITH TEETH MARKS.

SOME DIPLOMACY, I'M SAYING.

HOWDY.

I'LL CUT TO THE CHASE, EVERYBODY'S GOT WORK TO DO.

WHAT YOU GENTS ARE LOOKING AT HERE IS TECHNOLOGY FROM AN ADVANCED CIVILIZATION THAT NO LONGER EXISTS. THIS FREQUENCY CANNON WAS PRODUCED IN THE ONLY URANIAN WEAPONS LAB STILL OPERATING.

M-11?

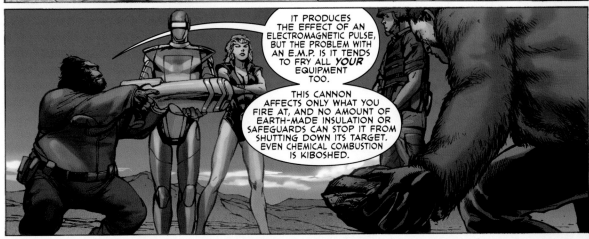

IT PRODUCES THE EFFECT OF AN ELECTROMAGNETIC PULSE, BUT THE PROBLEM WITH AN E.M.P. IS IT TENDS TO FRY ALL *YOUR* EQUIPMENT TOO.

THIS CANNON AFFECTS ONLY WHAT YOU FIRE AT, AND NO AMOUNT OF EARTH-MADE INSULATION OR SAFEGUARDS CAN STOP IT FROM SHUTTING DOWN ITS TARGET. EVEN CHEMICAL COMBUSTION IS KIBOSHED.

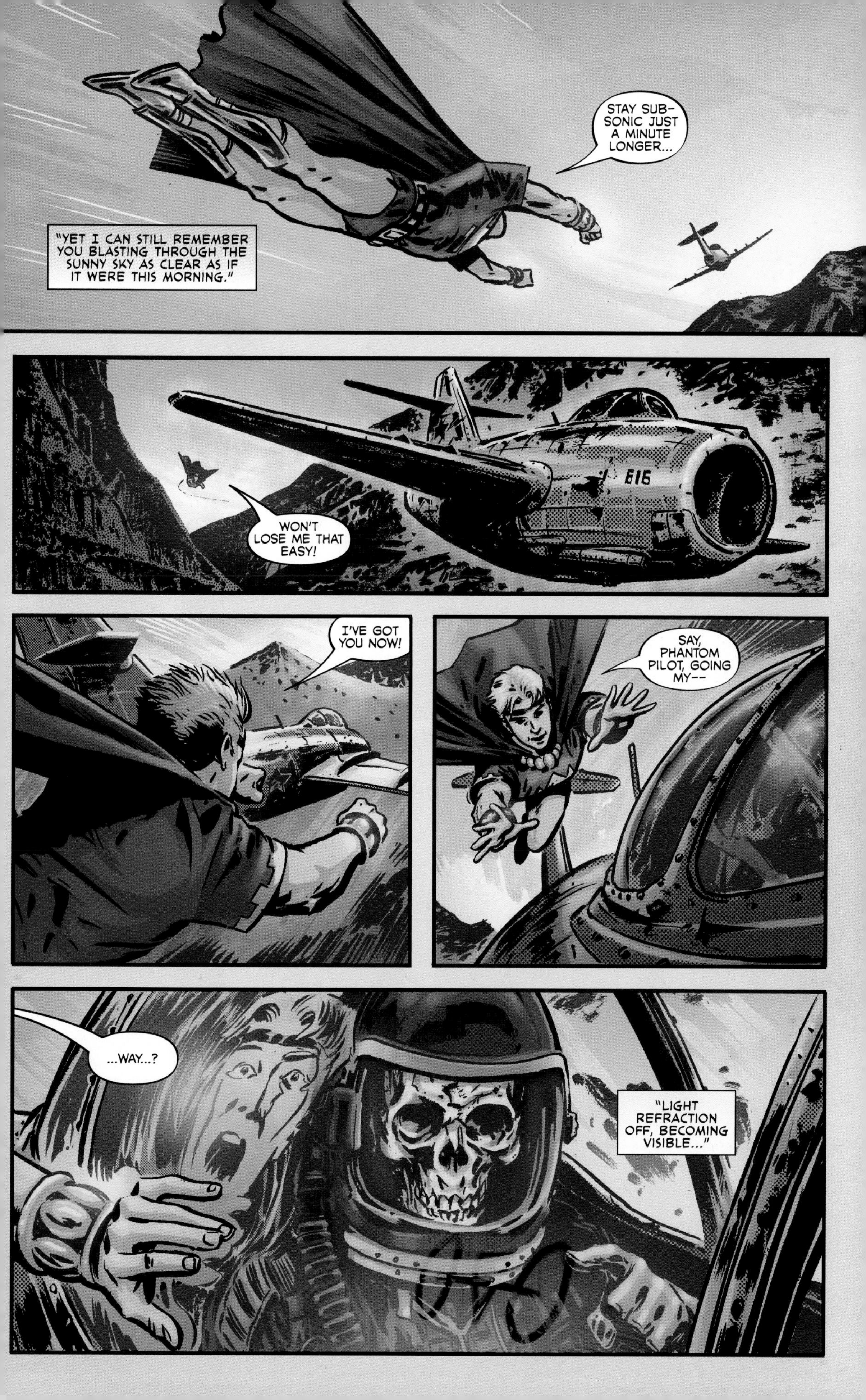
STAY SUB-SONIC JUST A MINUTE LONGER...
"YET I CAN STILL REMEMBER YOU BLASTING THROUGH THE SUNNY SKY AS CLEAR AS IF IT WERE THIS MORNING."
616
WON'T LOSE ME THAT EASY!
I'VE GOT YOU NOW!
SAY, PHANTOM PILOT, GOING MY--
...WAY...?
"LIGHT REFRACTION OFF, BECOMING VISIBLE..."

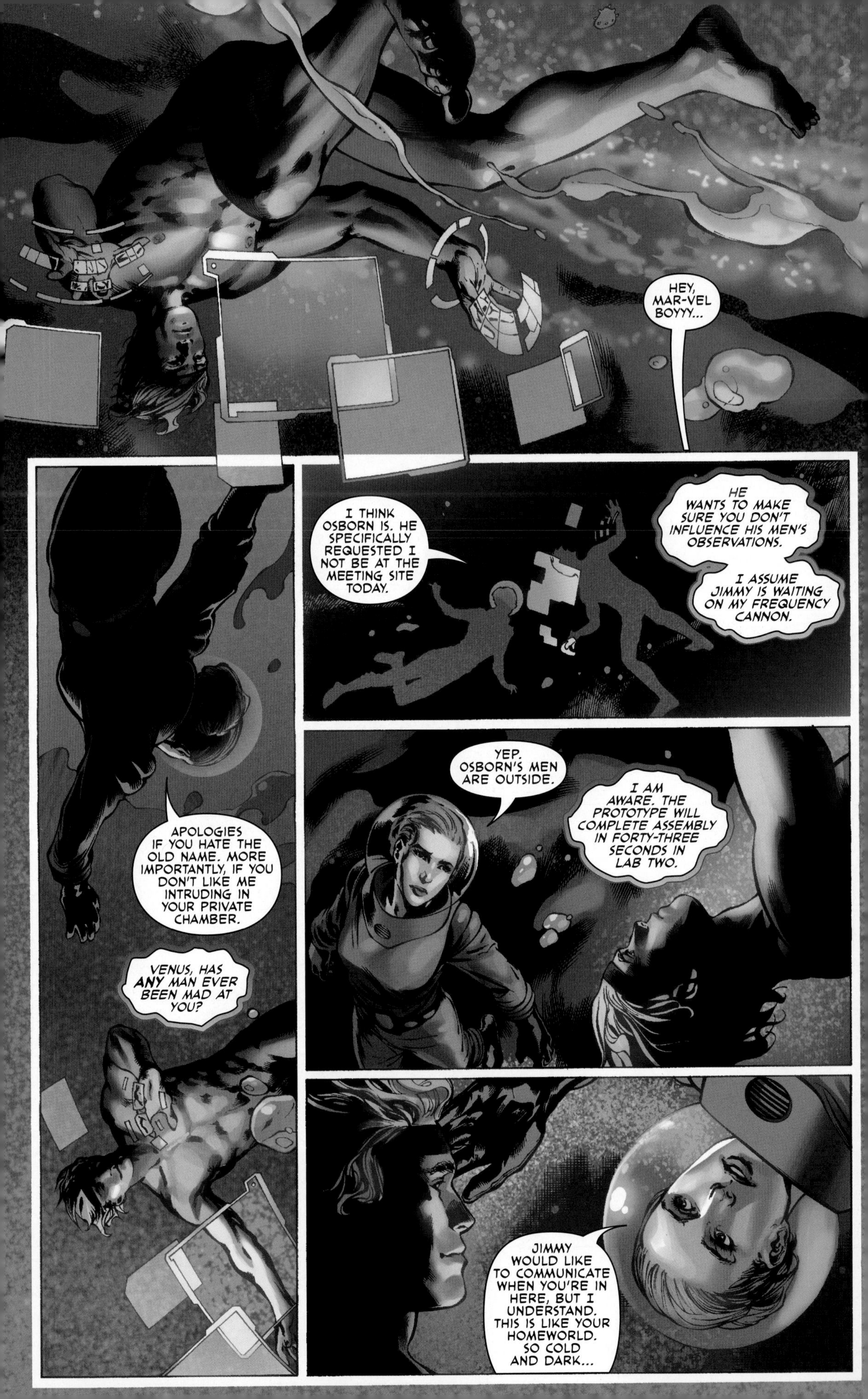
HEY, MAR-VEL BOYYY...
APOLOGIES IF YOU HATE THE OLD NAME. MORE IMPORTANTLY, IF YOU DON'T LIKE ME INTRUDING IN YOUR PRIVATE CHAMBER.
VENUS, HAS ANY MAN EVER BEEN MAD AT YOU?
I THINK OSBORN IS. HE SPECIFICALLY REQUESTED I NOT BE AT THE MEETING SITE TODAY.
HE WANTS TO MAKE SURE YOU DON'T INFLUENCE HIS MEN'S OBSERVATIONS.
I ASSUME JIMMY IS WAITING ON MY FREQUENCY CANNON.
YEP. OSBORN'S MEN ARE OUTSIDE.
I AM AWARE. THE PROTOTYPE WILL COMPLETE ASSEMBLY IN FORTY-THREE SECONDS IN LAB TWO.
JIMMY WOULD LIKE TO COMMUNICATE WHEN YOU'RE IN HERE, BUT I UNDERSTAND. THIS IS LIKE YOUR HOMEWORLD. SO COLD AND DARK...

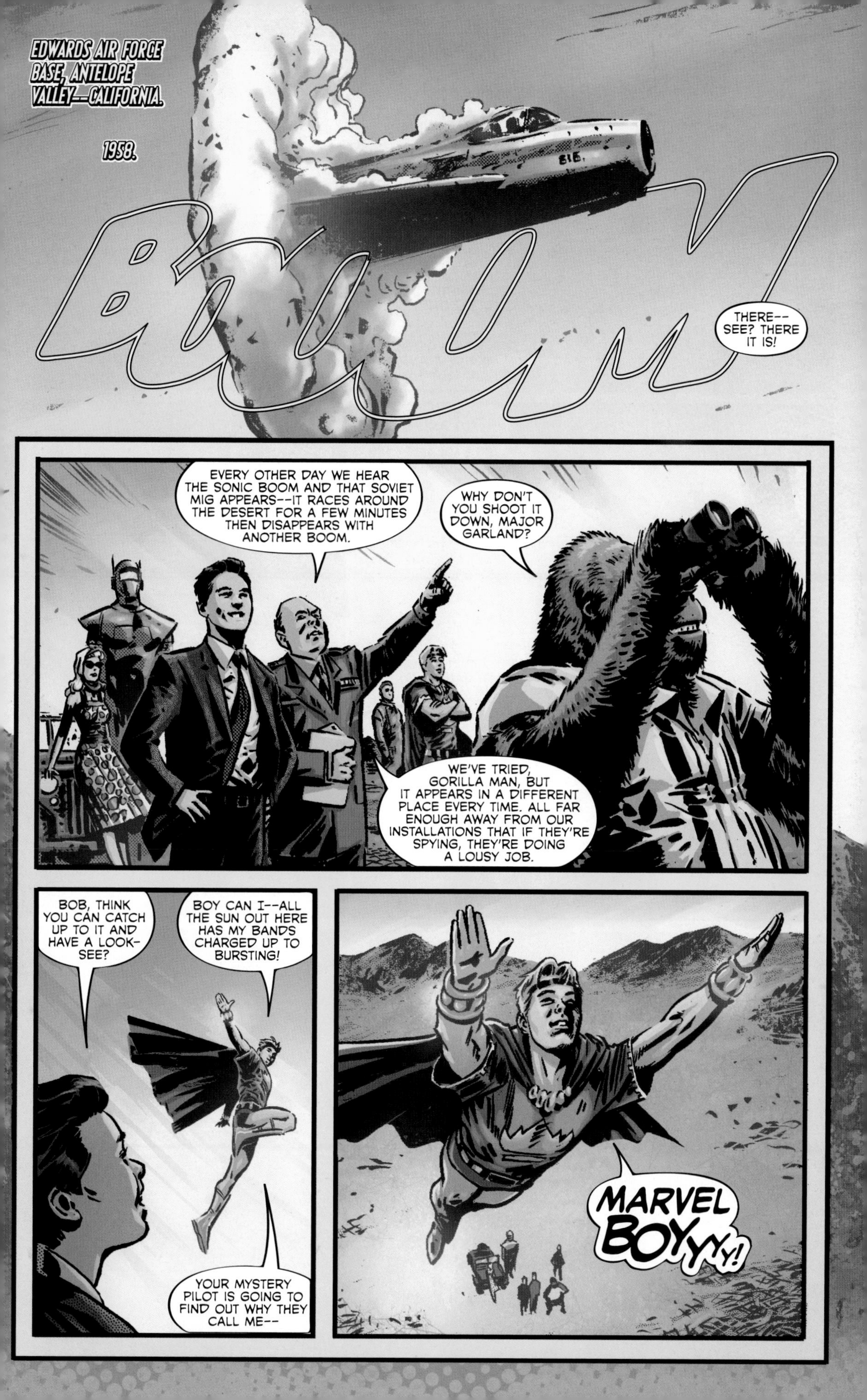
EDWARDS AIR FORCE BASE, ANTELOPE VALLEY--CALIFORNIA.
1958.
THERE-- SEE? THERE IT IS!
EVERY OTHER DAY WE HEAR THE SONIC BOOM AND THAT SOVIET MIG APPEARS--IT RACES AROUND THE DESERT FOR A FEW MINUTES THEN DISAPPEARS WITH ANOTHER BOOM.
WHY DON'T YOU SHOOT IT DOWN, MAJOR GARLAND?
WE'VE TRIED, GORILLA MAN, BUT IT APPEARS IN A DIFFERENT PLACE EVERY TIME. ALL FAR ENOUGH AWAY FROM OUR INSTALLATIONS THAT IF THEY'RE SPYING, THEY'RE DOING A LOUSY JOB.
BOB, THINK YOU CAN CATCH UP TO IT AND HAVE A LOOK-SEE?
BOY CAN I--ALL THE SUN OUT HERE HAS MY BANDS CHARGED UP TO BURSTING!
YOUR MYSTERY PILOT IS GOING TO FIND OUT WHY THEY CALL ME--
MARVEL BOYYY!

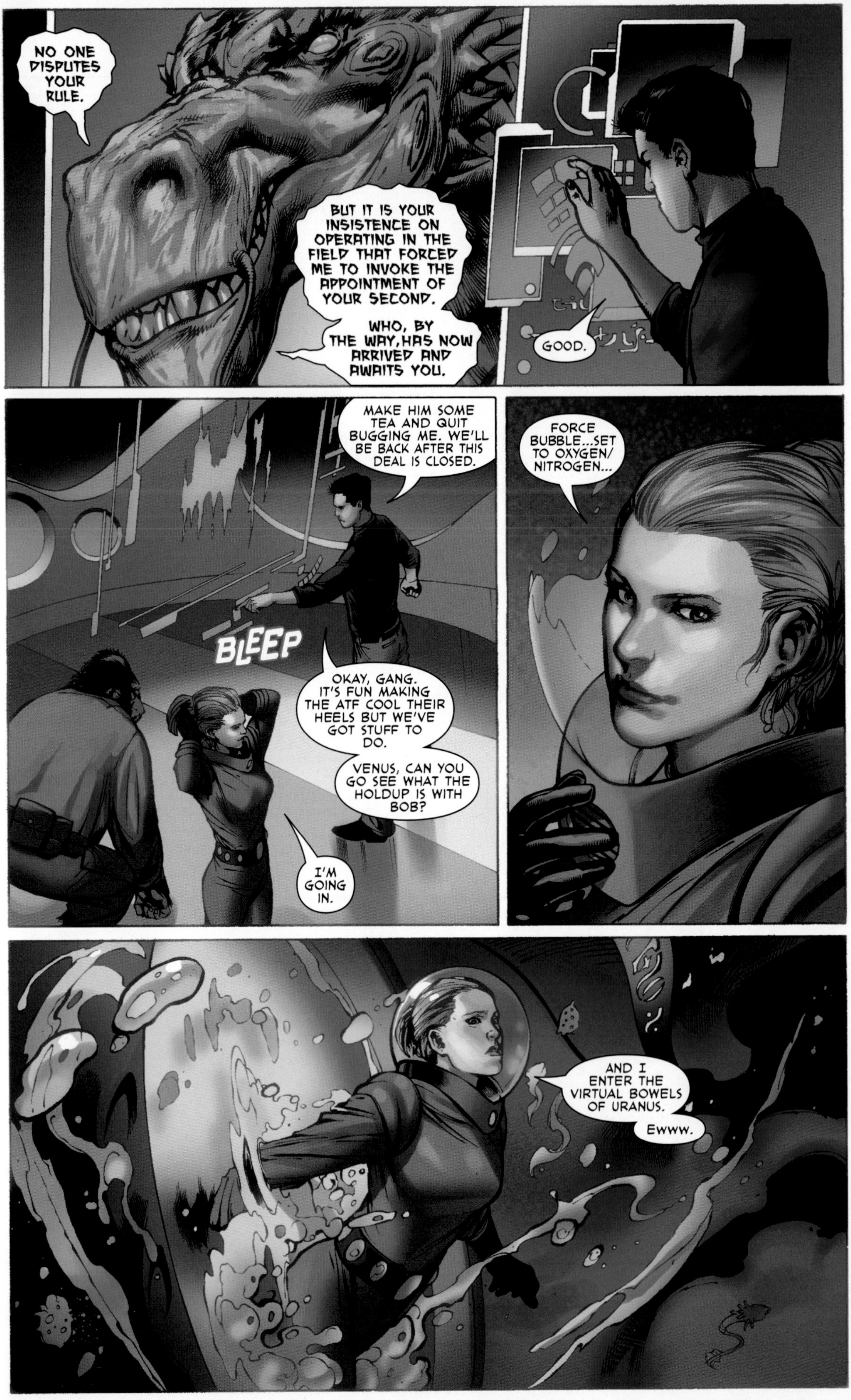
NO ONE DISPUTES YOUR RULE.
BUT IT IS YOUR INSISTENCE ON OPERATING IN THE FIELD THAT FORCED ME TO INVOKE THE APPOINTMENT OF YOUR SECOND.
WHO, BY THE WAY, HAS NOW ARRIVED AND AWAITS YOU.
GOOD.
MAKE HIM SOME TEA AND QUIT BUGGING ME. WE'LL BE BACK AFTER THIS DEAL IS CLOSED.
BLEEP
OKAY, GANG. IT'S FUN MAKING THE ATF COOL THEIR HEELS BUT WE'VE GOT STUFF TO DO.
VENUS, CAN YOU GO SEE WHAT THE HOLDUP IS WITH BOB?
I'M GOING IN.
FORCE BUBBLE...SET TO OXYGEN/NITROGEN...
AND I ENTER THE VIRTUAL BOWELS OF URANUS.
Ewww.

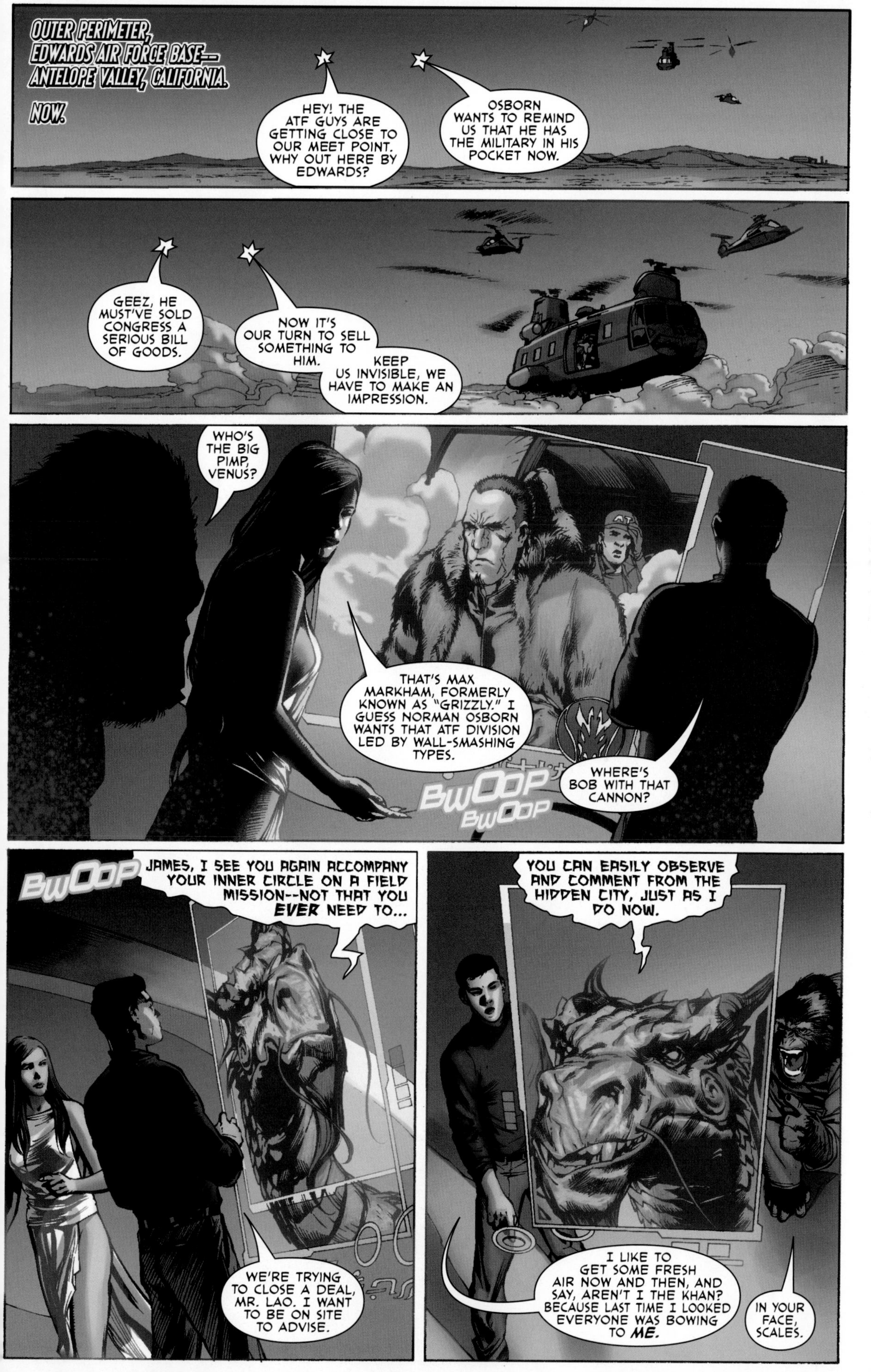
OUTER PERIMETER, EDWARDS AIR FORCE BASE-- ANTELOPE VALLEY, CALIFORNIA.
NOW.
HEY! THE ATF GUYS ARE GETTING CLOSE TO OUR MEET POINT. WHY OUT HERE BY EDWARDS?
OSBORN WANTS TO REMIND US THAT HE HAS THE MILITARY IN HIS POCKET NOW.
GEEZ, HE MUST'VE SOLD CONGRESS A SERIOUS BILL OF GOODS.
NOW IT'S OUR TURN TO SELL SOMETHING TO HIM.
KEEP US INVISIBLE, WE HAVE TO MAKE AN IMPRESSION.
WHO'S THE BIG PIMP, VENUS?
THAT'S MAX MARKHAM, FORMERLY KNOWN AS "GRIZZLY." I GUESS NORMAN OSBORN WANTS THAT ATF DIVISION LED BY WALL-SMASHING TYPES.
WHERE'S BOB WITH THAT CANNON?
BWOOP BWOOP
BWOOP
JAMES, I SEE YOU AGAIN ACCOMPANY YOUR INNER CIRCLE ON A FIELD MISSION--NOT THAT YOU EVER NEED TO...
WE'RE TRYING TO CLOSE A DEAL, MR. LAO. I WANT TO BE ON SITE TO ADVISE.
YOU CAN EASILY OBSERVE AND COMMENT FROM THE HIDDEN CITY, JUST AS I DO NOW.
I LIKE TO GET SOME FRESH AIR NOW AND THEN, AND SAY, AREN'T I THE KHAN? BECAUSE LAST TIME I LOOKED EVERYONE WAS BOWING TO ME.
IN YOUR FACE, SCALES.

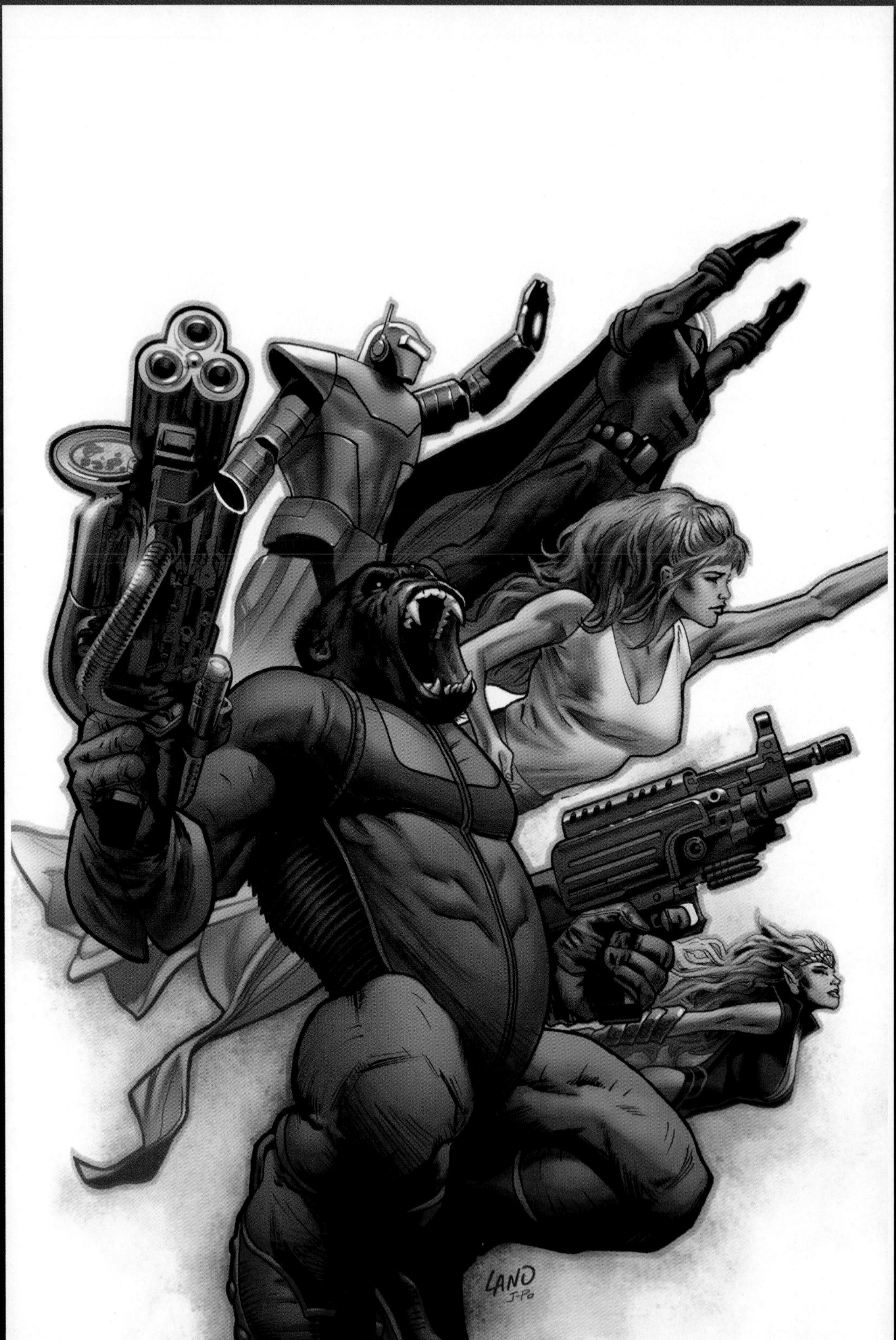
LAND
J-Po

#2

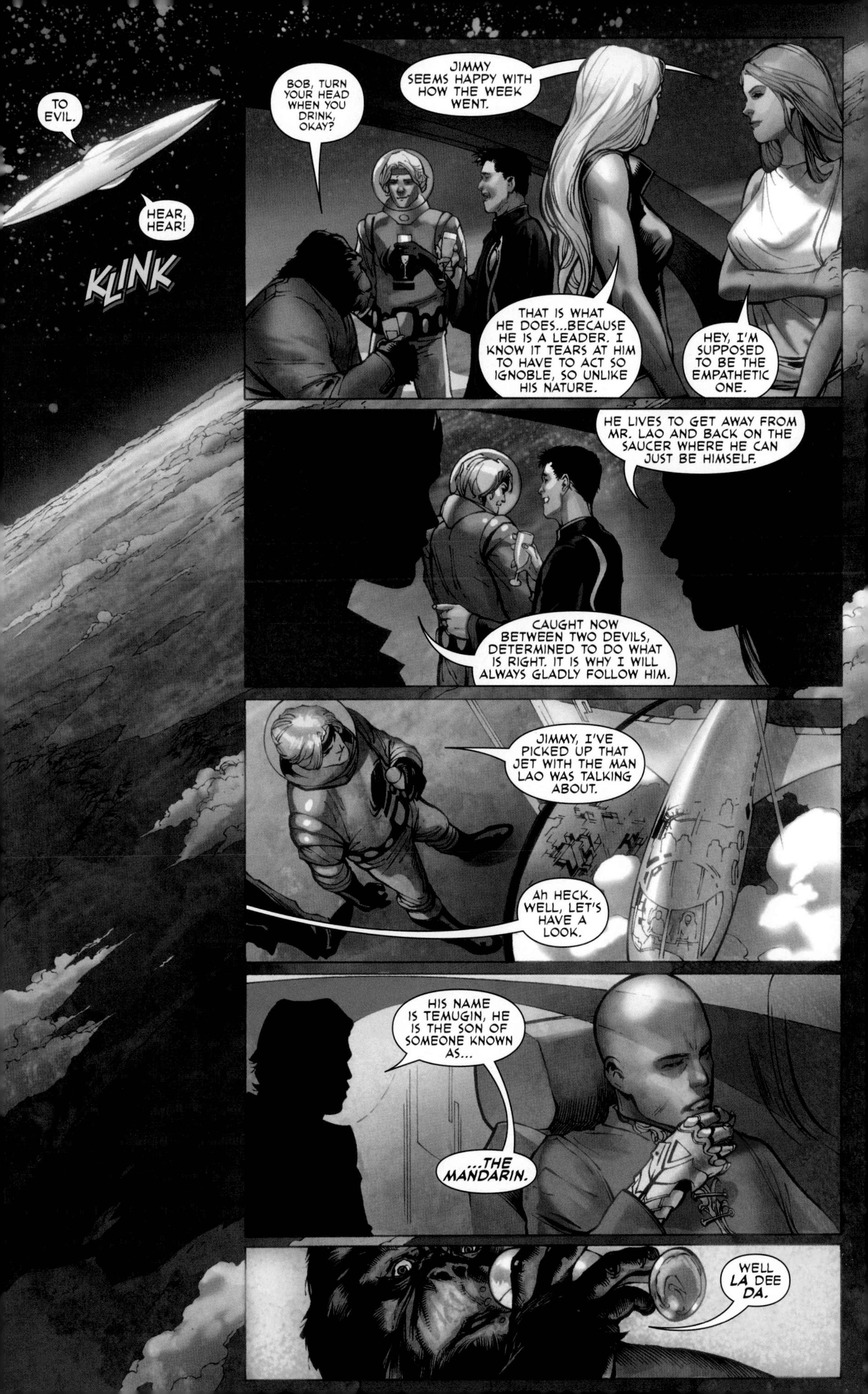
TO EVIL.
HEAR, HEAR!
KLINK
BOB, TURN YOUR HEAD WHEN YOU DRINK, OKAY?
JIMMY SEEMS HAPPY WITH HOW THE WEEK WENT.
THAT IS WHAT HE DOES...BECAUSE HE IS A LEADER. I KNOW IT TEARS AT HIM TO HAVE TO ACT SO IGNOBLE, SO UNLIKE HIS NATURE.
HEY, I'M SUPPOSED TO BE THE EMPATHETIC ONE.
HE LIVES TO GET AWAY FROM MR. LAO AND BACK ON THE SAUCER WHERE HE CAN JUST BE HIMSELF.
CAUGHT NOW BETWEEN TWO DEVILS, DETERMINED TO DO WHAT IS RIGHT. IT IS WHY I WILL ALWAYS GLADLY FOLLOW HIM.
JIMMY, I'VE PICKED UP THAT JET WITH THE MAN LAO WAS TALKING ABOUT.
Ah HECK. WELL, LET'S HAVE A LOOK.
HIS NAME IS TEMUGIN, HE IS THE SON OF SOMEONE KNOWN AS...
...THE MANDARIN.
WELL LA DEE DA.

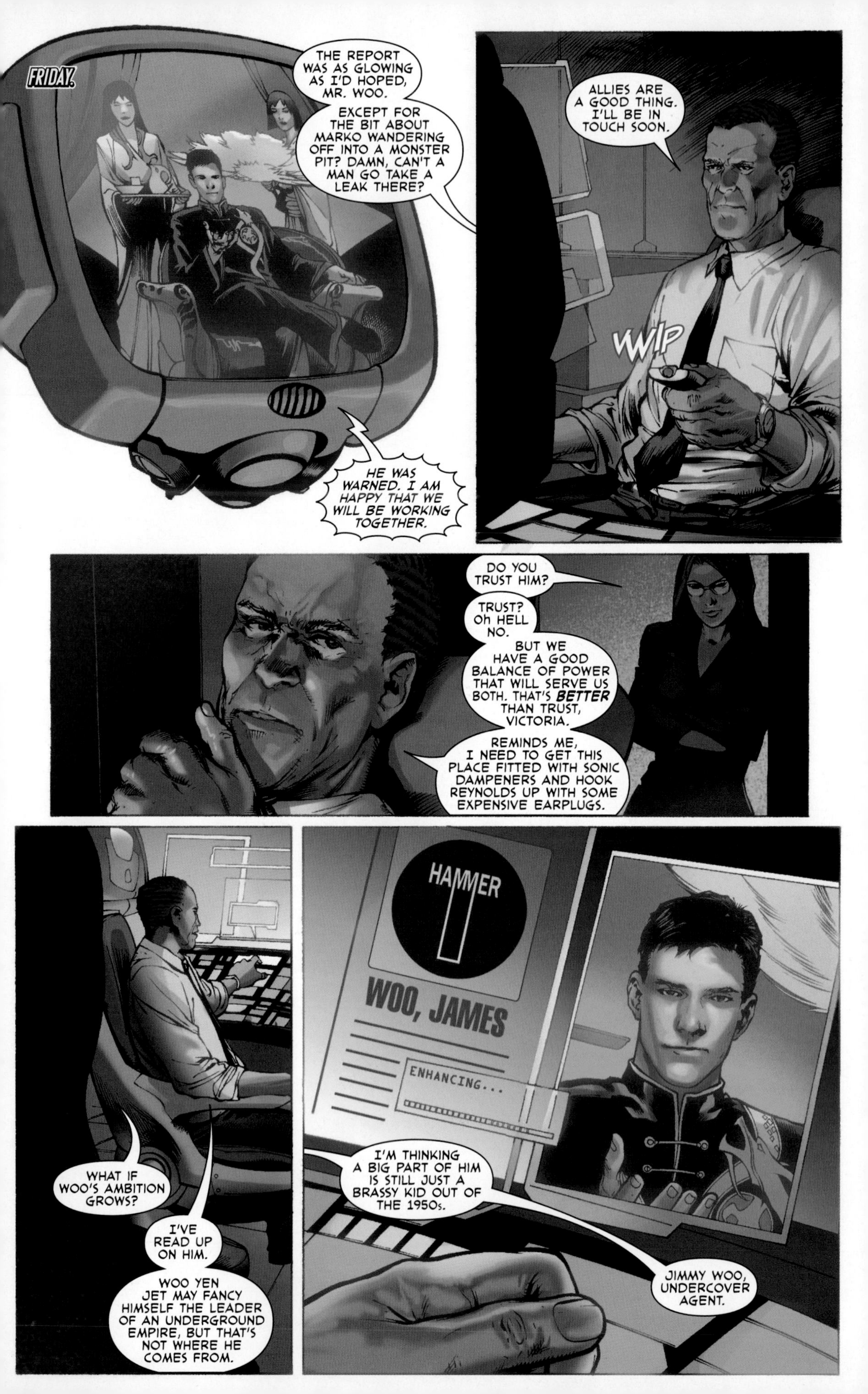
FRIDAY.
THE REPORT WAS AS GLOWING AS I'D HOPED, MR. WOO.
EXCEPT FOR THE BIT ABOUT MARKO WANDERING OFF INTO A MONSTER PIT? DAMN, CAN'T A MAN GO TAKE A LEAK THERE?
HE WAS WARNED. I AM HAPPY THAT WE WILL BE WORKING TOGETHER.
ALLIES ARE A GOOD THING. I'LL BE IN TOUCH SOON.
VWIP
DO YOU TRUST HIM?
TRUST? Oh HELL NO.
BUT WE HAVE A GOOD BALANCE OF POWER THAT WILL SERVE US BOTH. THAT'S BETTER THAN TRUST, VICTORIA.
REMINDS ME, I NEED TO GET THIS PLACE FITTED WITH SONIC DAMPENERS AND HOOK REYNOLDS UP WITH SOME EXPENSIVE EARPLUGS.
WHAT IF WOO'S AMBITION GROWS?
I'VE READ UP ON HIM.
WOO YEN JET MAY FANCY HIMSELF THE LEADER OF AN UNDERGROUND EMPIRE, BUT THAT'S NOT WHERE HE COMES FROM.
HAMMER
WOO, JAMES
ENHANCING...
I'M THINKING A BIG PART OF HIM IS STILL JUST A BRASSY KID OUT OF THE 1950s.
JIMMY WOO, UNDERCOVER AGENT.

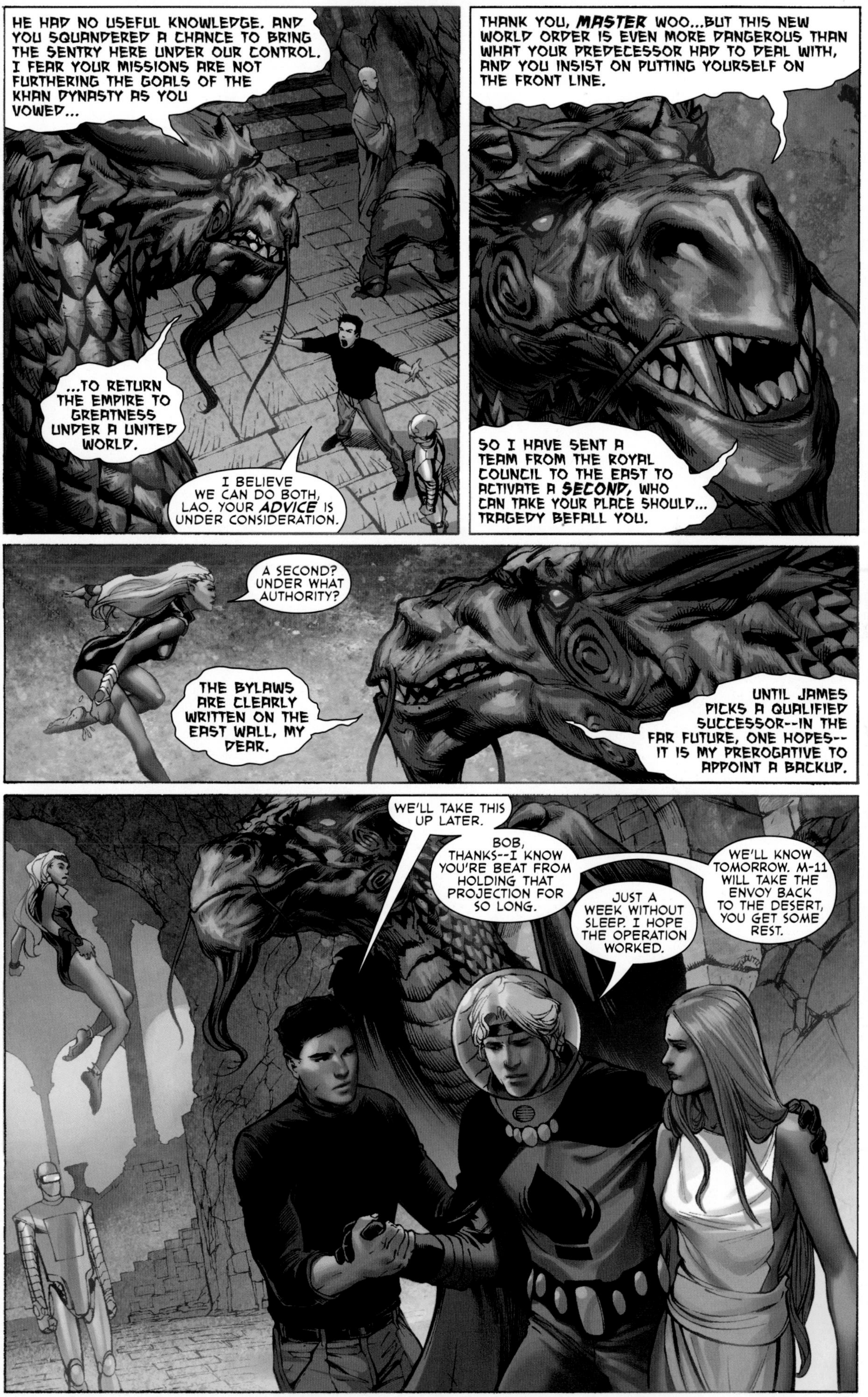
HE HAD NO USEFUL KNOWLEDGE. AND YOU SQUANDERED A CHANCE TO BRING THE SENTRY HERE UNDER OUR CONTROL. I FEAR YOUR MISSIONS ARE NOT FURTHERING THE GOALS OF THE KHAN DYNASTY AS YOU VOWED...
...TO RETURN THE EMPIRE TO GREATNESS UNDER A UNITED WORLD.
I BELIEVE WE CAN DO BOTH, LAO. YOUR ADVICE IS UNDER CONSIDERATION.
THANK YOU, MASTER WOO...BUT THIS NEW WORLD ORDER IS EVEN MORE DANGEROUS THAN WHAT YOUR PREDECESSOR HAD TO DEAL WITH, AND YOU INSIST ON PUTTING YOURSELF ON THE FRONT LINE.
SO I HAVE SENT A TEAM FROM THE ROYAL COUNCIL TO THE EAST TO ACTIVATE A SECOND, WHO CAN TAKE YOUR PLACE SHOULD... TRAGEDY BEFALL YOU.
A SECOND? UNDER WHAT AUTHORITY?
THE BYLAWS ARE CLEARLY WRITTEN ON THE EAST WALL, MY DEAR.
UNTIL JAMES PICKS A QUALIFIED SUCCESSOR--IN THE FAR FUTURE, ONE HOPES-- IT IS MY PREROGATIVE TO APPOINT A BACKUP.
WE'LL TAKE THIS UP LATER.
BOB, THANKS--I KNOW YOU'RE BEAT FROM HOLDING THAT PROJECTION FOR SO LONG.
JUST A WEEK WITHOUT SLEEP. I HOPE THE OPERATION WORKED.
WE'LL KNOW TOMORROW. M-11 WILL TAKE THE ENVOY BACK TO THE DESERT, YOU GET SOME REST.

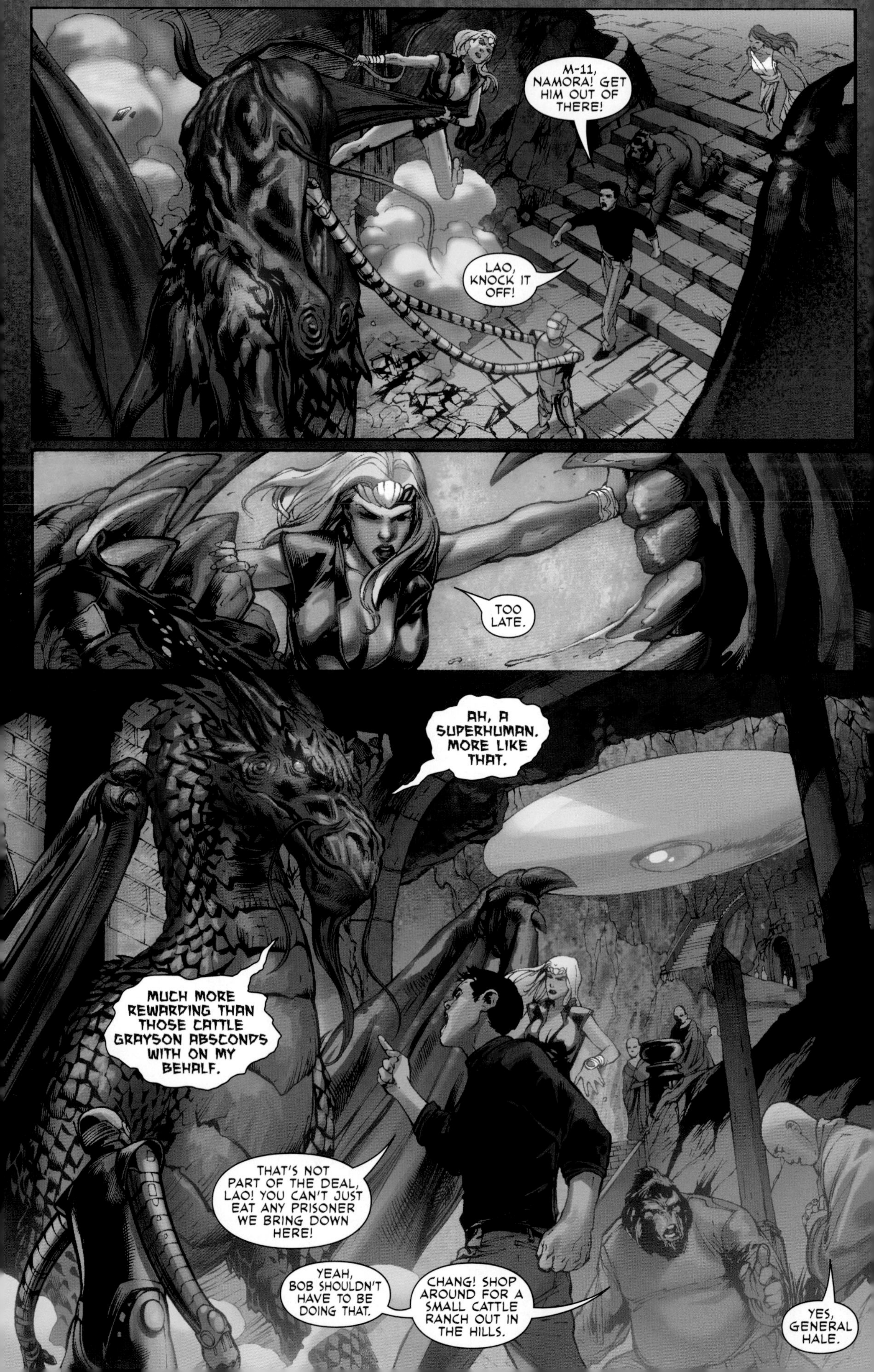
M-11, NAMORA! GET HIM OUT OF THERE!
LAO, KNOCK IT OFF!
TOO LATE.
AH, A SUPERHUMAN. MORE LIKE THAT.
MUCH MORE REWARDING THAN THOSE CATTLE GRAYSON ABSCONDS WITH ON MY BEHALF.
THAT'S NOT PART OF THE DEAL, LAO! YOU CAN'T JUST EAT ANY PRISONER WE BRING DOWN HERE!
YEAH, BOB SHOULDN'T HAVE TO BE DOING THAT.
CHANG! SHOP AROUND FOR A SMALL CATTLE RANCH OUT IN THE HILLS.
YES, GENERAL HALE.

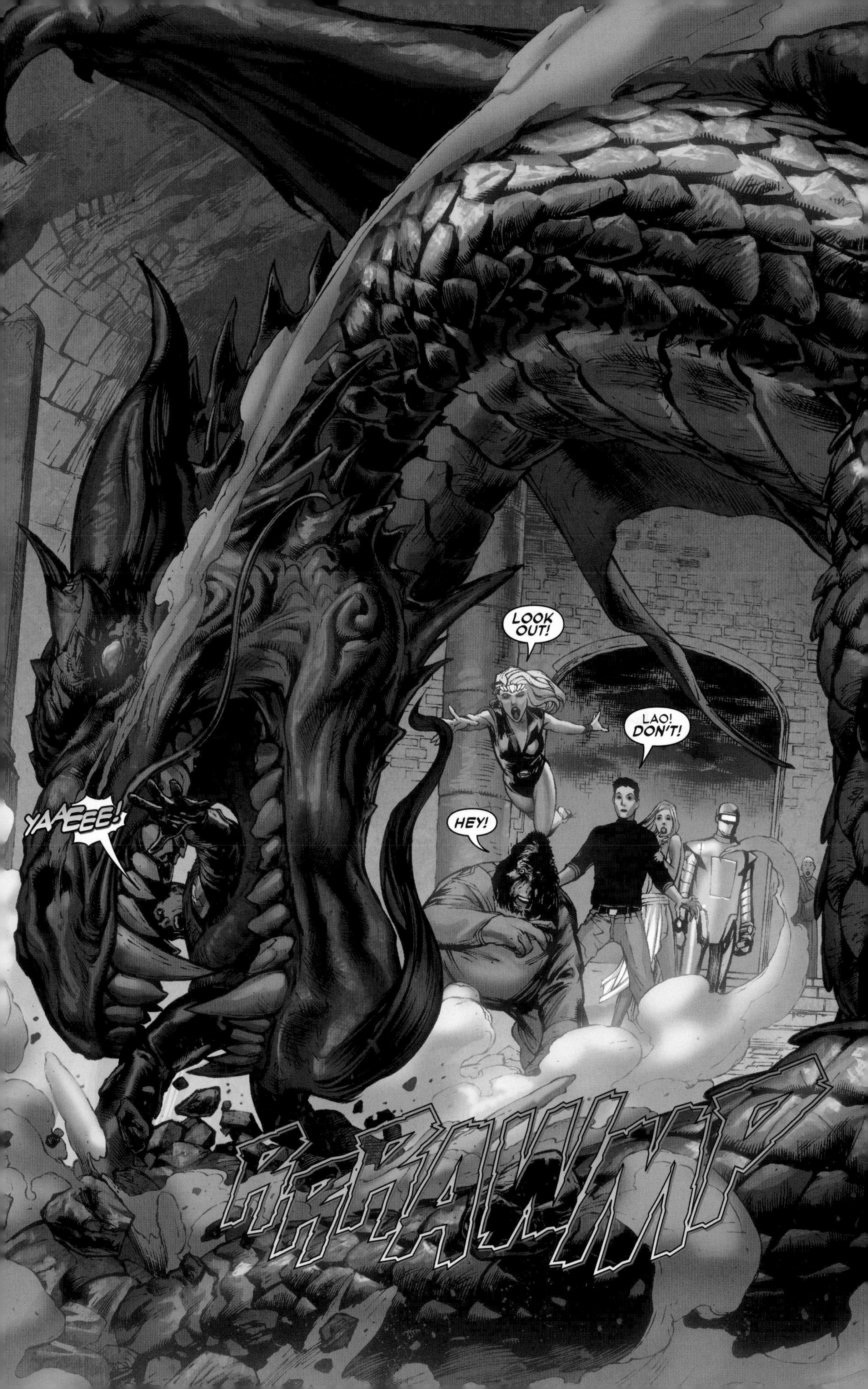
YAAEEE!
LOOK OUT!
LAO! DON'T!
HEY!

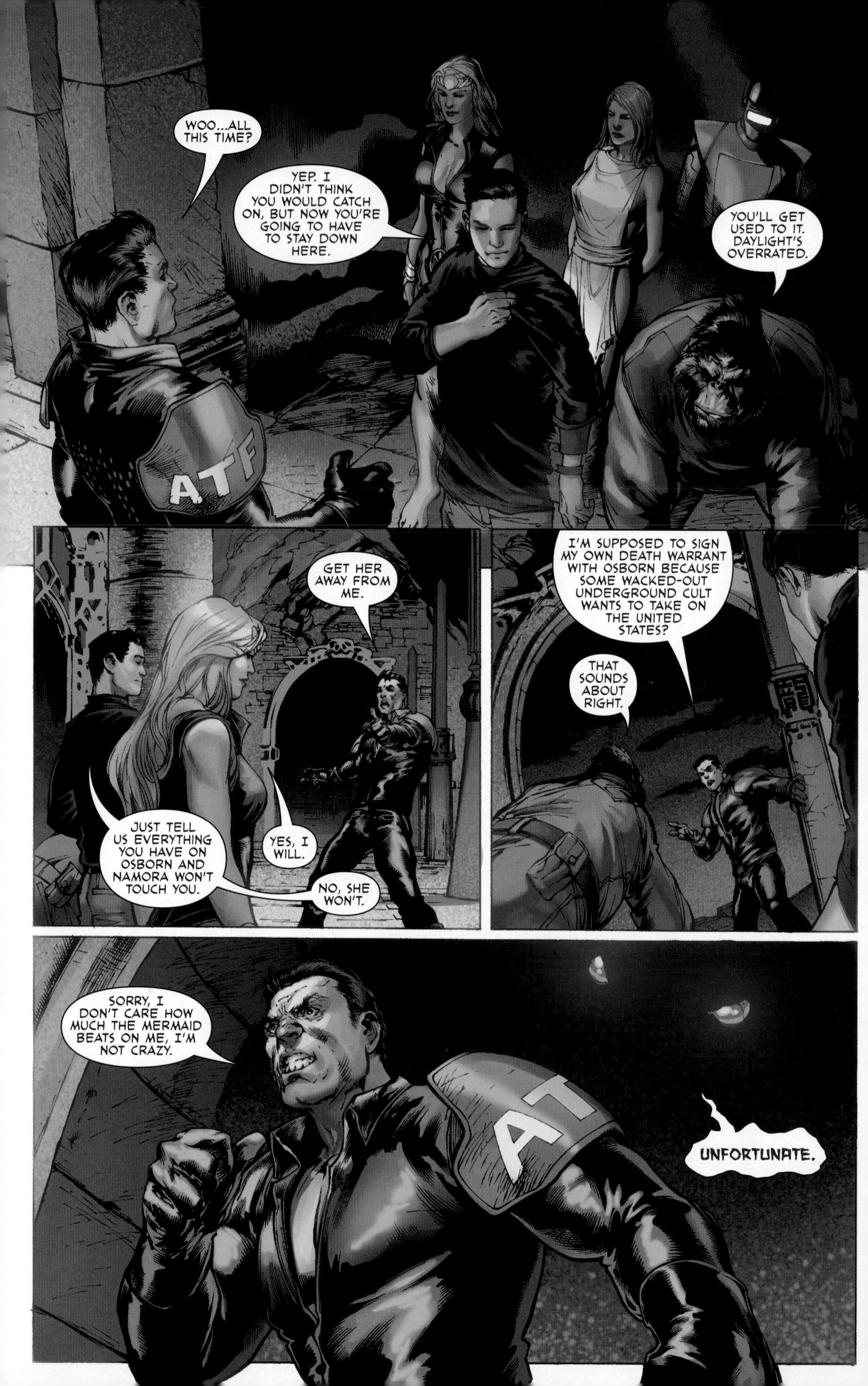
WOO...ALL THIS TIME?
YEP. I DIDN'T THINK YOU WOULD CATCH ON, BUT NOW YOU'RE GOING TO HAVE TO STAY DOWN HERE.
YOU'LL GET USED TO IT. DAYLIGHT'S OVERRATED.
ATF
GET HER AWAY FROM ME.
JUST TELL US EVERYTHING YOU HAVE ON OSBORN AND NAMORA WON'T TOUCH YOU.
YES, I WILL.
NO, SHE WON'T.
I'M SUPPOSED TO SIGN MY OWN DEATH WARRANT WITH OSBORN BECAUSE SOME WACKED-OUT UNDERGROUND CULT WANTS TO TAKE ON THE UNITED STATES?
THAT SOUNDS ABOUT RIGHT.
SORRY, I DON'T CARE HOW MUCH THE MERMAID BEATS ON ME, I'M NOT CRAZY.
UNFORTUNATE.

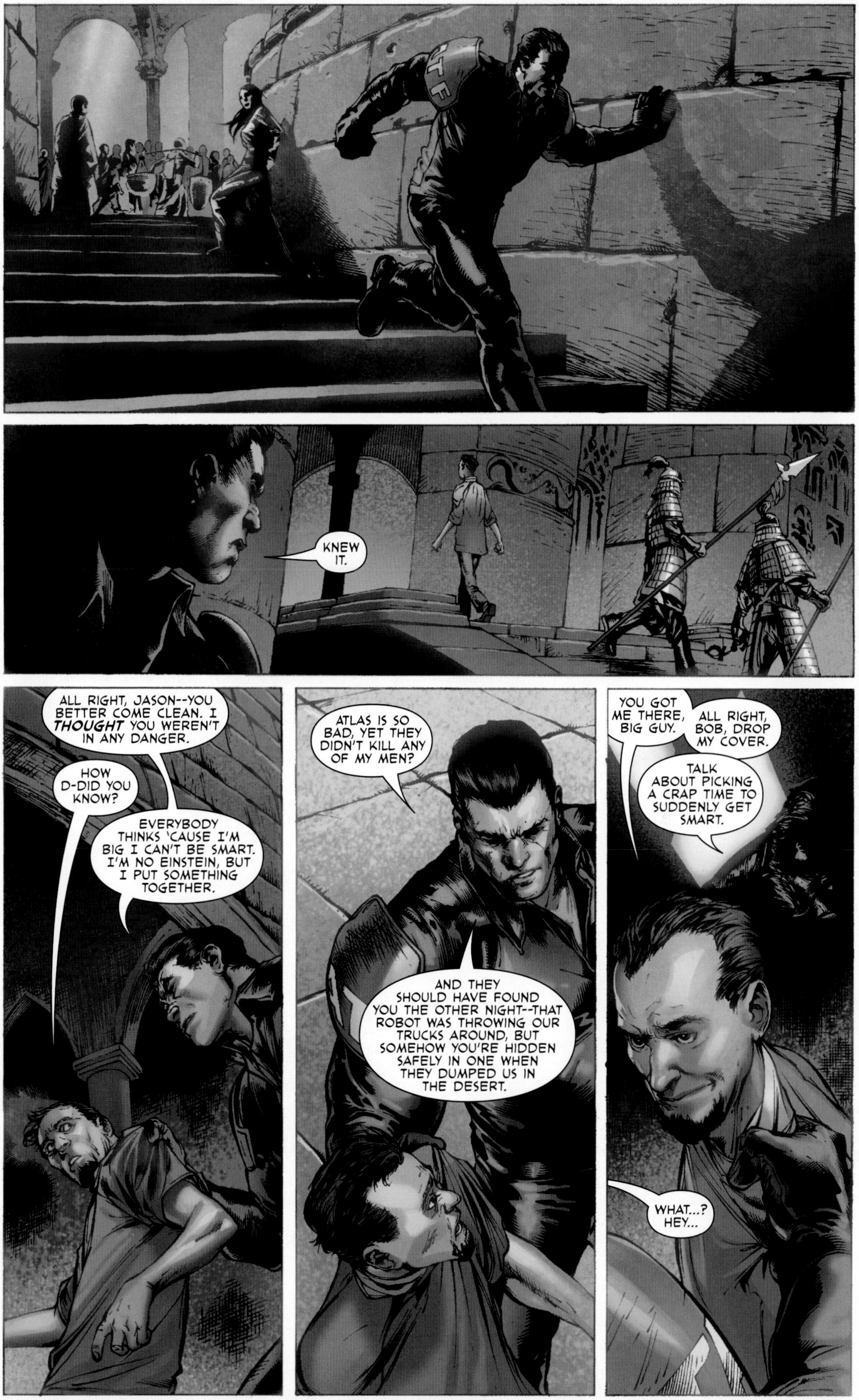

KNEW IT.
ALL RIGHT, JASON--YOU BETTER COME CLEAN. I *THOUGHT* YOU WEREN'T IN ANY DANGER.
HOW D-DID YOU KNOW?
EVERYBODY THINKS 'CAUSE I'M BIG I CAN'T BE SMART. I'M NO EINSTEIN, BUT I PUT SOMETHING TOGETHER.
ATLAS IS SO BAD, YET THEY DIDN'T KILL ANY OF MY MEN?
AND THEY SHOULD HAVE FOUND YOU THE OTHER NIGHT--THAT ROBOT WAS THROWING OUR TRUCKS AROUND, BUT SOMEHOW YOU'RE HIDDEN SAFELY IN ONE WHEN THEY DUMPED US IN THE DESERT.
YOU GOT ME THERE, BIG GUY.
ALL RIGHT, BOB, DROP MY COVER.
TALK ABOUT PICKING A CRAP TIME TO SUDDENLY GET SMART.
WHAT...? HEY...

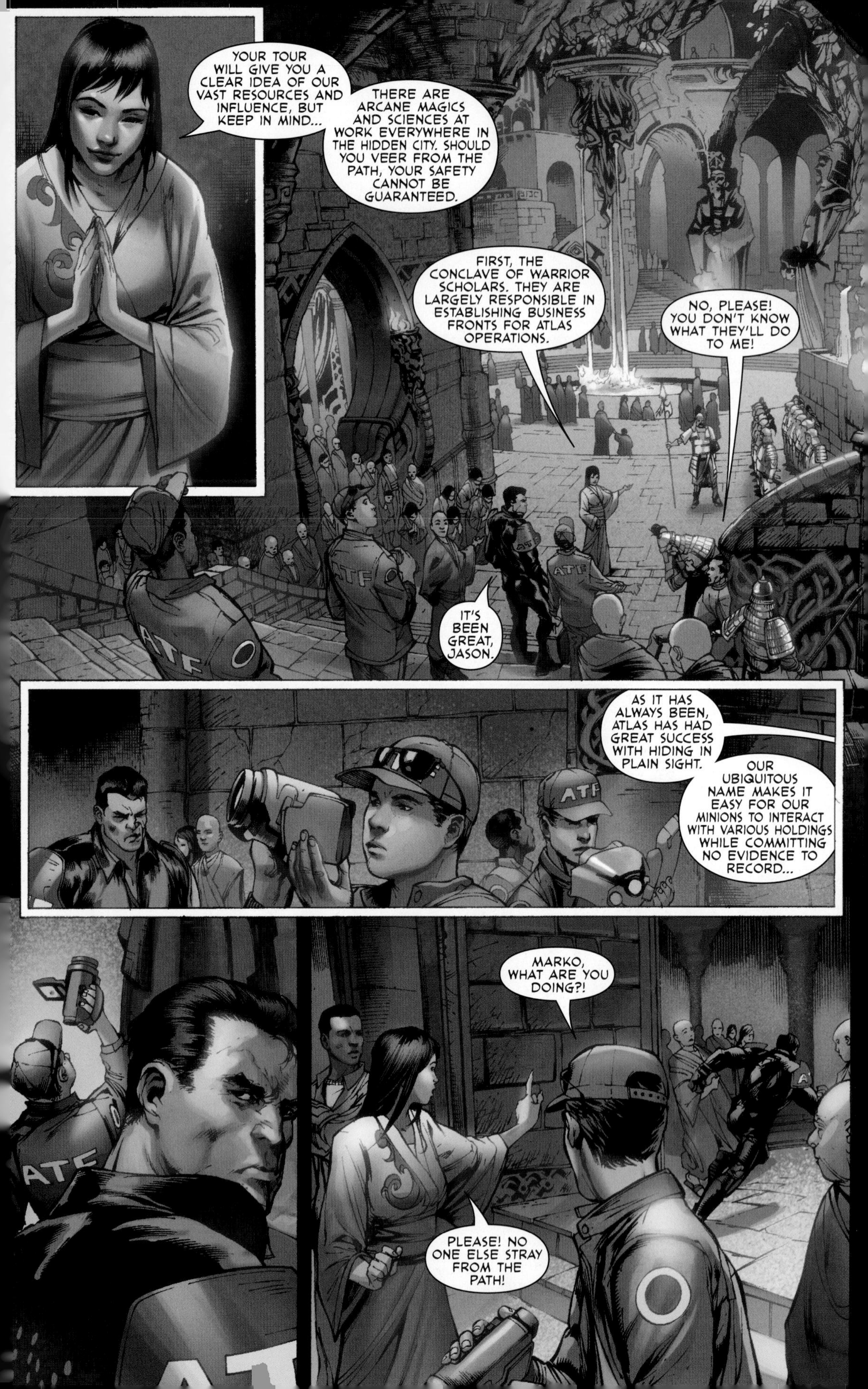
YOUR TOUR WILL GIVE YOU A CLEAR IDEA OF OUR VAST RESOURCES AND INFLUENCE, BUT KEEP IN MIND...
THERE ARE ARCANE MAGICS AND SCIENCES AT WORK EVERYWHERE IN THE HIDDEN CITY. SHOULD YOU VEER FROM THE PATH, YOUR SAFETY CANNOT BE GUARANTEED.
FIRST, THE CONCLAVE OF WARRIOR SCHOLARS. THEY ARE LARGELY RESPONSIBLE IN ESTABLISHING BUSINESS FRONTS FOR ATLAS OPERATIONS.
NO, PLEASE! YOU DON'T KNOW WHAT THEY'LL DO TO ME!
IT'S BEEN GREAT, JASON.
AS IT HAS ALWAYS BEEN, ATLAS HAS HAD GREAT SUCCESS WITH HIDING IN PLAIN SIGHT.
OUR UBIQUITOUS NAME MAKES IT EASY FOR OUR MINIONS TO INTERACT WITH VARIOUS HOLDINGS WHILE COMMITTING NO EVIDENCE TO RECORD...
MARKO, WHAT ARE YOU DOING?!
PLEASE! NO ONE ELSE STRAY FROM THE PATH!

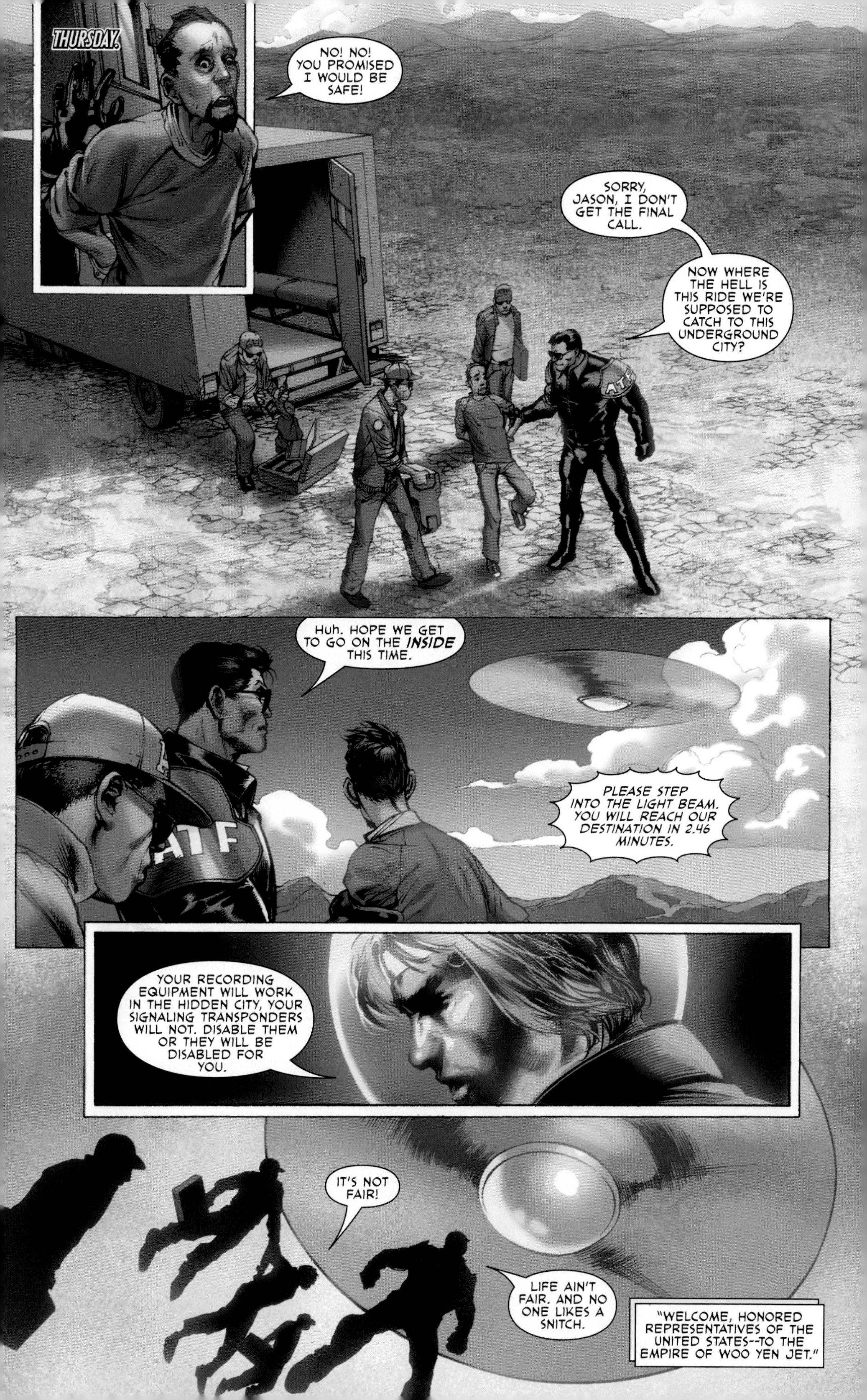
THURSDAY.
NO! NO! YOU PROMISED I WOULD BE SAFE!
SORRY, JASON, I DON'T GET THE FINAL CALL.
NOW WHERE THE HELL IS THIS RIDE WE'RE SUPPOSED TO CATCH TO THIS UNDERGROUND CITY?
Huh. HOPE WE GET TO GO ON THE *INSIDE* THIS TIME.
PLEASE STEP INTO THE LIGHT BEAM. YOU WILL REACH OUR DESTINATION IN 2.46 MINUTES.
YOUR RECORDING EQUIPMENT WILL WORK IN THE HIDDEN CITY, YOUR SIGNALING TRANSPONDERS WILL NOT. DISABLE THEM OR THEY WILL BE DISABLED FOR YOU.
IT'S NOT FAIR!
LIFE AIN'T FAIR. AND NO ONE LIKES A SNITCH.
"WELCOME, HONORED REPRESENTATIVES OF THE UNITED STATES--TO THE EMPIRE OF WOO YEN JET."

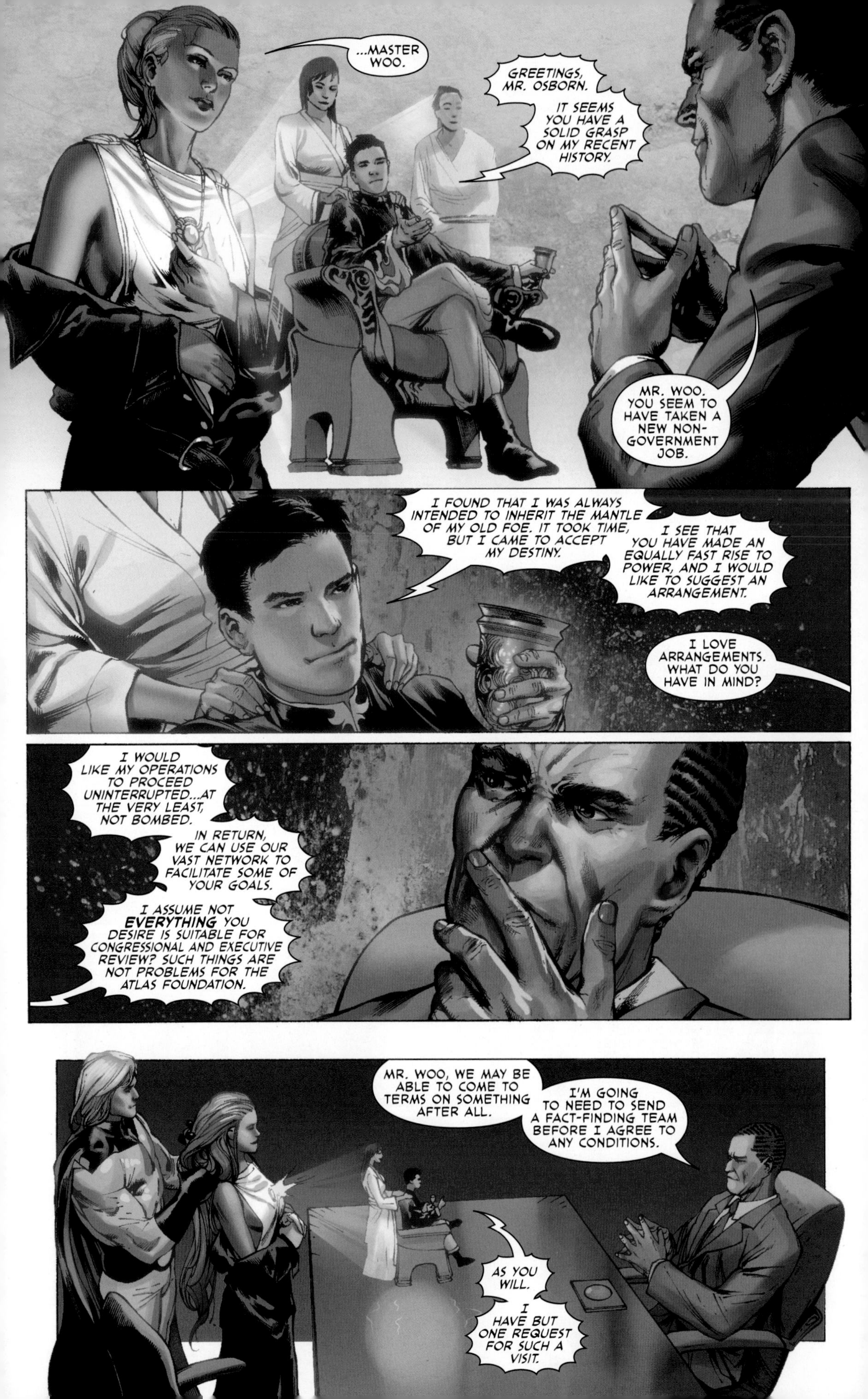
...MASTER WOO.
GREETINGS, MR. OSBORN.
IT SEEMS YOU HAVE A SOLID GRASP ON MY RECENT HISTORY.
MR. WOO. YOU SEEM TO HAVE TAKEN A NEW NON-GOVERNMENT JOB.
I FOUND THAT I WAS ALWAYS INTENDED TO INHERIT THE MANTLE OF MY OLD FOE. IT TOOK TIME, BUT I CAME TO ACCEPT MY DESTINY.
I SEE THAT YOU HAVE MADE AN EQUALLY FAST RISE TO POWER, AND I WOULD LIKE TO SUGGEST AN ARRANGEMENT.
I LOVE ARRANGEMENTS. WHAT DO YOU HAVE IN MIND?
I WOULD LIKE MY OPERATIONS TO PROCEED UNINTERRUPTED...AT THE VERY LEAST, NOT BOMBED.
IN RETURN, WE CAN USE OUR VAST NETWORK TO FACILITATE SOME OF YOUR GOALS.
I ASSUME NOT **EVERYTHING** YOU DESIRE IS SUITABLE FOR CONGRESSIONAL AND EXECUTIVE REVIEW? SUCH THINGS ARE NOT PROBLEMS FOR THE ATLAS FOUNDATION.
MR. WOO, WE MAY BE ABLE TO COME TO TERMS ON SOMETHING AFTER ALL.
I'M GOING TO NEED TO SEND A FACT-FINDING TEAM BEFORE I AGREE TO ANY CONDITIONS.
AS YOU WILL.
I HAVE BUT ONE REQUEST FOR SUCH A VISIT.

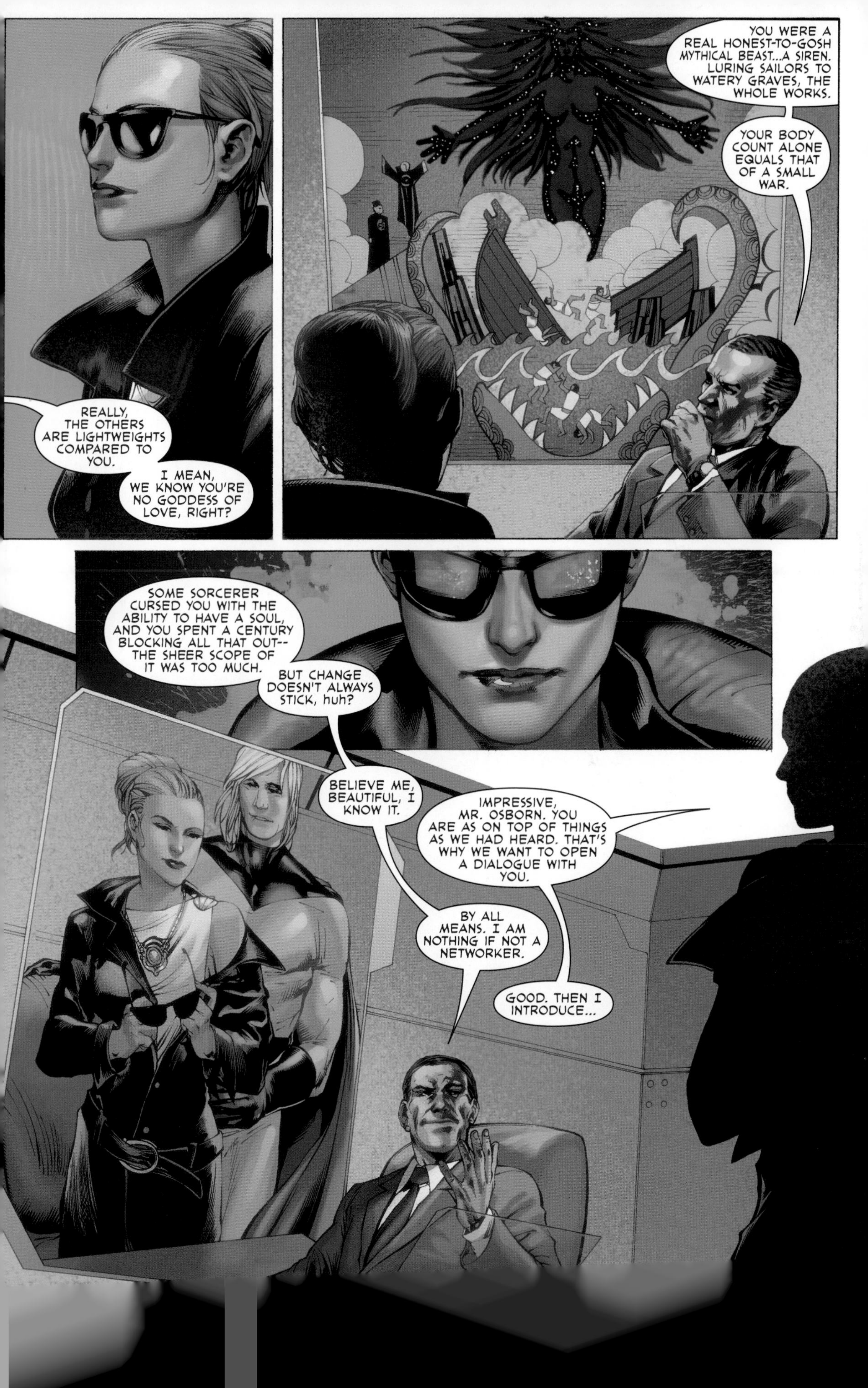
YOU WERE A REAL HONEST-TO-GOSH MYTHICAL BEAST...A SIREN. LURING SAILORS TO WATERY GRAVES, THE WHOLE WORKS.
YOUR BODY COUNT ALONE EQUALS THAT OF A SMALL WAR.
REALLY, THE OTHERS ARE LIGHTWEIGHTS COMPARED TO YOU.
I MEAN, WE KNOW YOU'RE NO GODDESS OF LOVE, RIGHT?
SOME SORCERER CURSED YOU WITH THE ABILITY TO HAVE A SOUL, AND YOU SPENT A CENTURY BLOCKING ALL THAT OUT-- THE SHEER SCOPE OF IT WAS TOO MUCH.
BUT CHANGE DOESN'T ALWAYS STICK, huh?
BELIEVE ME, BEAUTIFUL, I KNOW IT.
IMPRESSIVE, MR. OSBORN. YOU ARE AS ON TOP OF THINGS AS WE HAD HEARD. THAT'S WHY WE WANT TO OPEN A DIALOGUE WITH YOU.
BY ALL MEANS. I AM NOTHING IF NOT A NETWORKER.
GOOD. THEN I INTRODUCE...

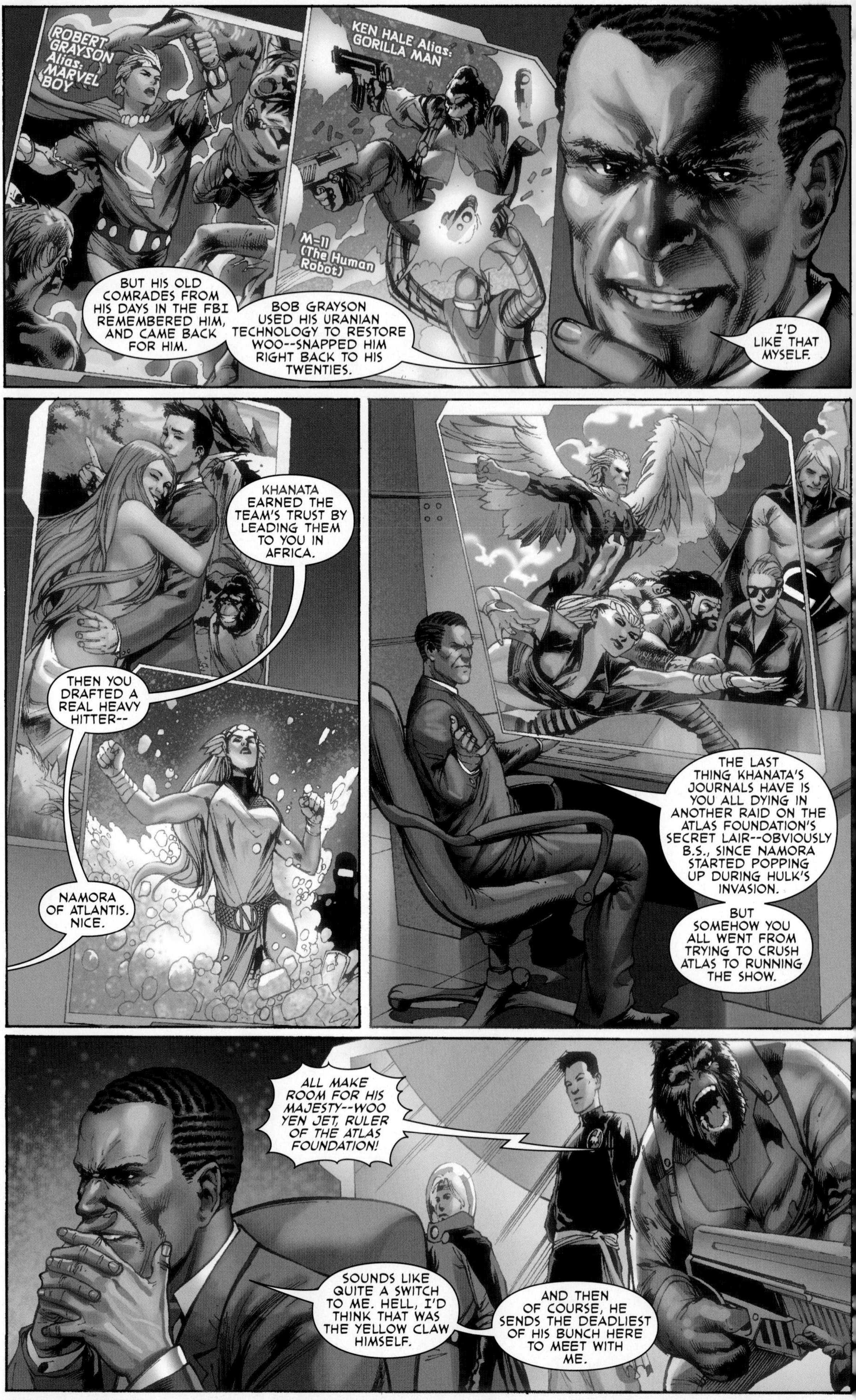
ROBERT GRAYSON Alias: MARVEL BOY
KEN HALE Alias: GORILLA MAN
M-11 (The Human Robot)
BUT HIS OLD COMRADES FROM HIS DAYS IN THE FBI REMEMBERED HIM, AND CAME BACK FOR HIM.
BOB GRAYSON USED HIS URANIAN TECHNOLOGY TO RESTORE WOO--SNAPPED HIM RIGHT BACK TO HIS TWENTIES.
I'D LIKE THAT MYSELF.
KHANATA EARNED THE TEAM'S TRUST BY LEADING THEM TO YOU IN AFRICA.
THEN YOU DRAFTED A REAL HEAVY HITTER--
NAMORA OF ATLANTIS. NICE.
THE LAST THING KHANATA'S JOURNALS HAVE IS YOU ALL DYING IN ANOTHER RAID ON THE ATLAS FOUNDATION'S SECRET LAIR--OBVIOUSLY B.S., SINCE NAMORA STARTED POPPING UP DURING HULK'S INVASION.
BUT SOMEHOW YOU ALL WENT FROM TRYING TO CRUSH ATLAS TO RUNNING THE SHOW.
ALL MAKE ROOM FOR HIS MAJESTY--WOO YEN JET, RULER OF THE ATLAS FOUNDATION!
SOUNDS LIKE QUITE A SWITCH TO ME. HELL, I'D THINK THAT WAS THE YELLOW CLAW HIMSELF.
AND THEN OF COURSE, HE SENDS THE DEADLIEST OF HIS BUNCH HERE TO MEET WITH ME.

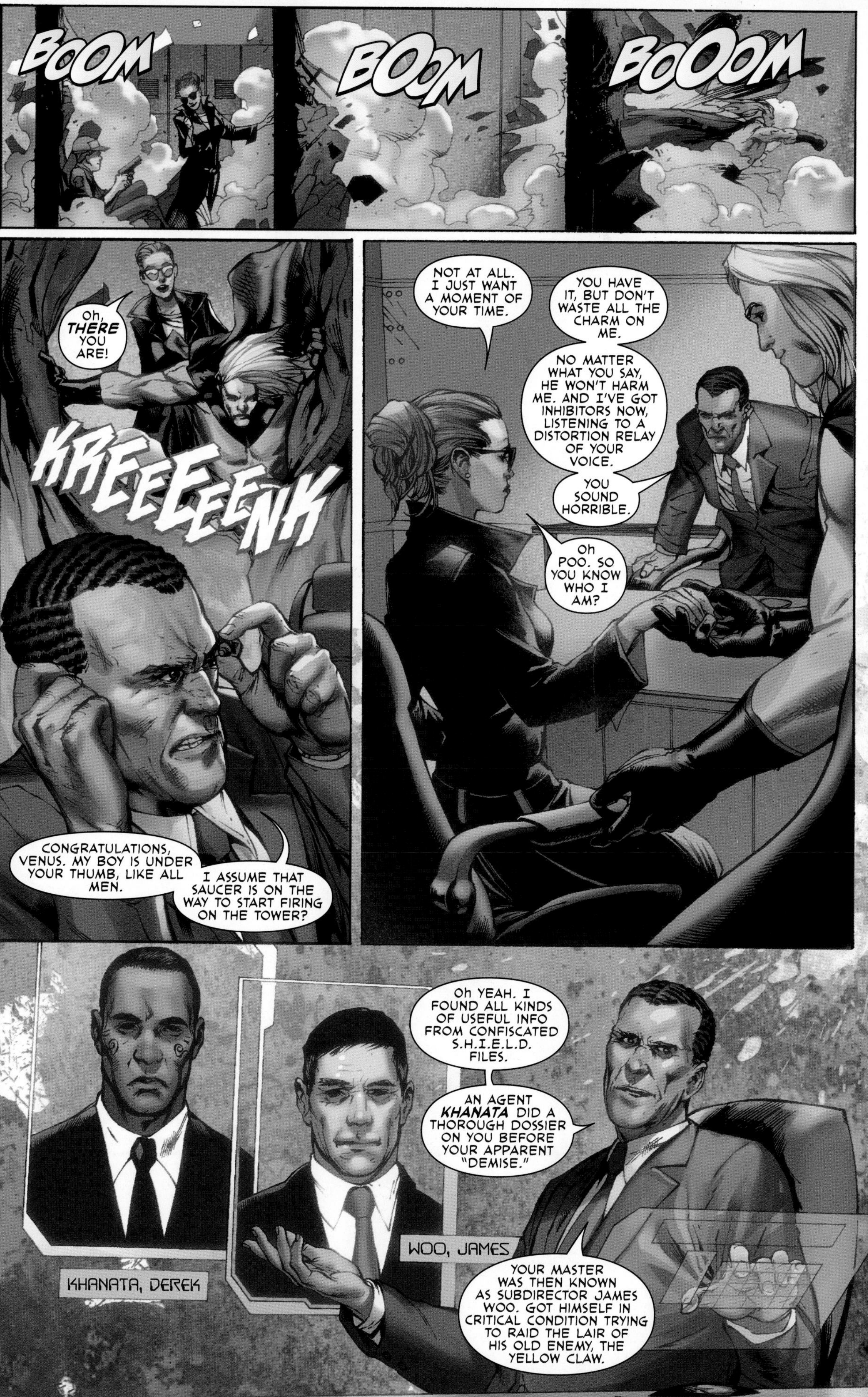

BOOM
BOOM
BOOOM
Oh, THERE YOU ARE!
KREEEEENK
CONGRATULATIONS, VENUS. MY BOY IS UNDER YOUR THUMB, LIKE ALL MEN.
I ASSUME THAT SAUCER IS ON THE WAY TO START FIRING ON THE TOWER?
NOT AT ALL. I JUST WANT A MOMENT OF YOUR TIME.
YOU HAVE IT, BUT DON'T WASTE ALL THE CHARM ON ME.
NO MATTER WHAT YOU SAY, HE WON'T HARM ME. AND I'VE GOT INHIBITORS NOW, LISTENING TO A DISTORTION RELAY OF YOUR VOICE.
YOU SOUND HORRIBLE.
Oh POO. SO YOU KNOW WHO I AM?
Oh YEAH. I FOUND ALL KINDS OF USEFUL INFO FROM CONFISCATED S.H.I.E.L.D. FILES.
AN AGENT KHANATA DID A THOROUGH DOSSIER ON YOU BEFORE YOUR APPARENT "DEMISE."
KHANATA, DEREK
WOO, JAMES
YOUR MASTER WAS THEN KNOWN AS SUBDIRECTOR JAMES WOO. GOT HIMSELF IN CRITICAL CONDITION TRYING TO RAID THE LAIR OF HIS OLD ENEMY, THE YELLOW CLAW.

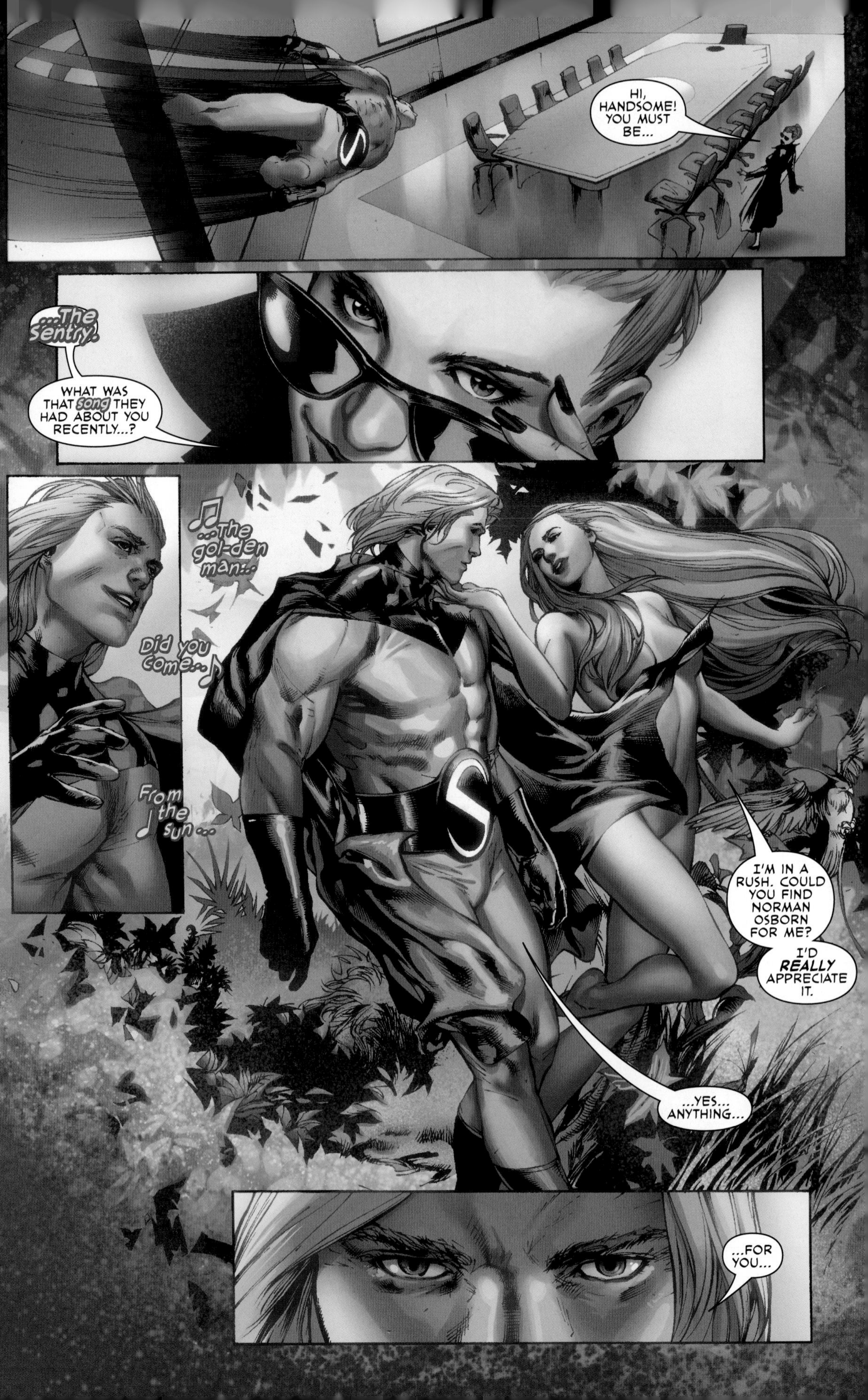
HI, HANDSOME! YOU MUST BE...
...The Sentry!
WHAT WAS THAT SONG THEY HAD ABOUT YOU RECENTLY...?
...The gol-den man...
Did you come...
From the sun...
I'M IN A RUSH. COULD YOU FIND NORMAN OSBORN FOR ME?
I'D REALLY APPRECIATE IT.
...YES... ANYTHING...
...FOR YOU...

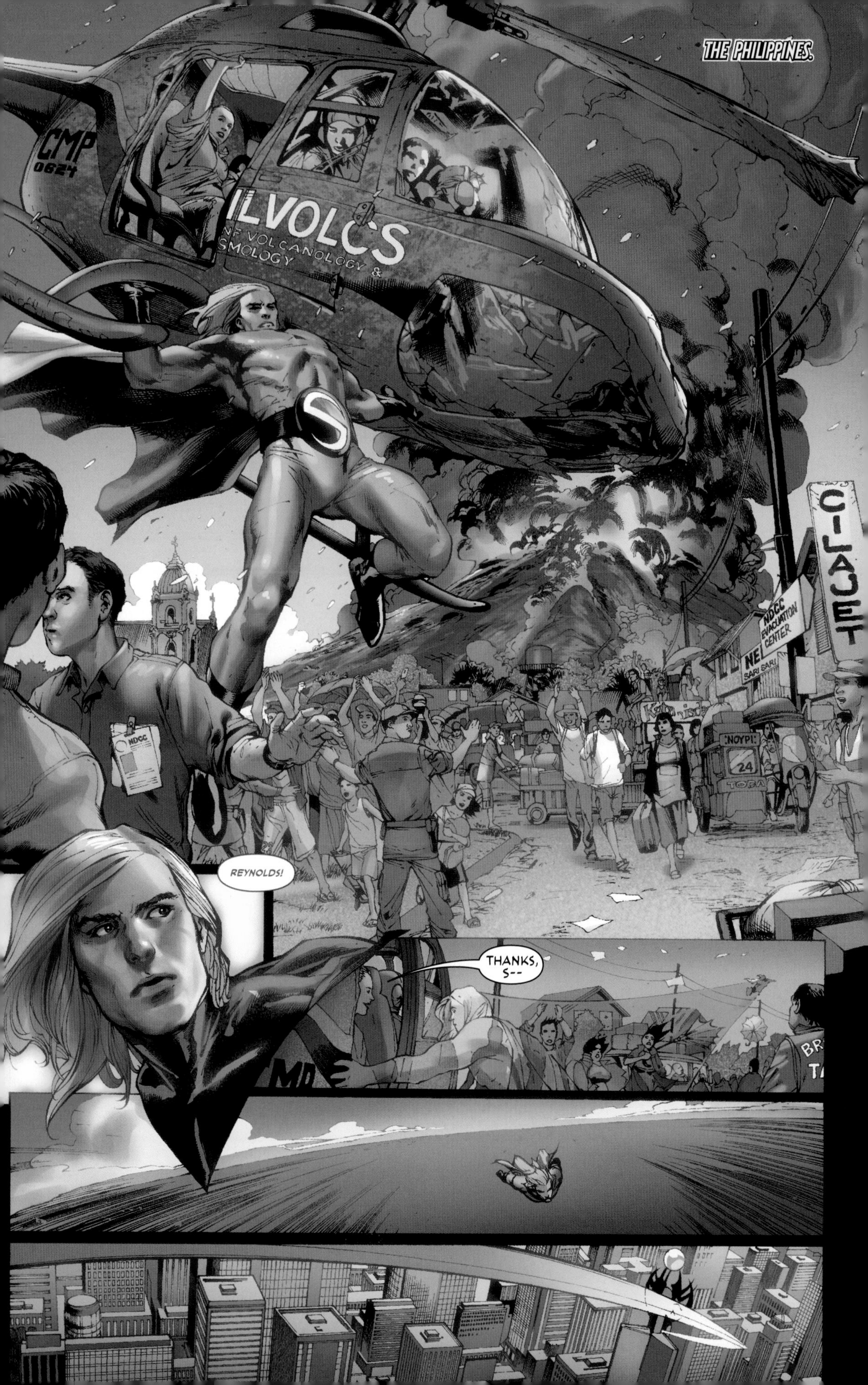
THE PHILIPPINES.
REYNOLDS!
THANKS, S--

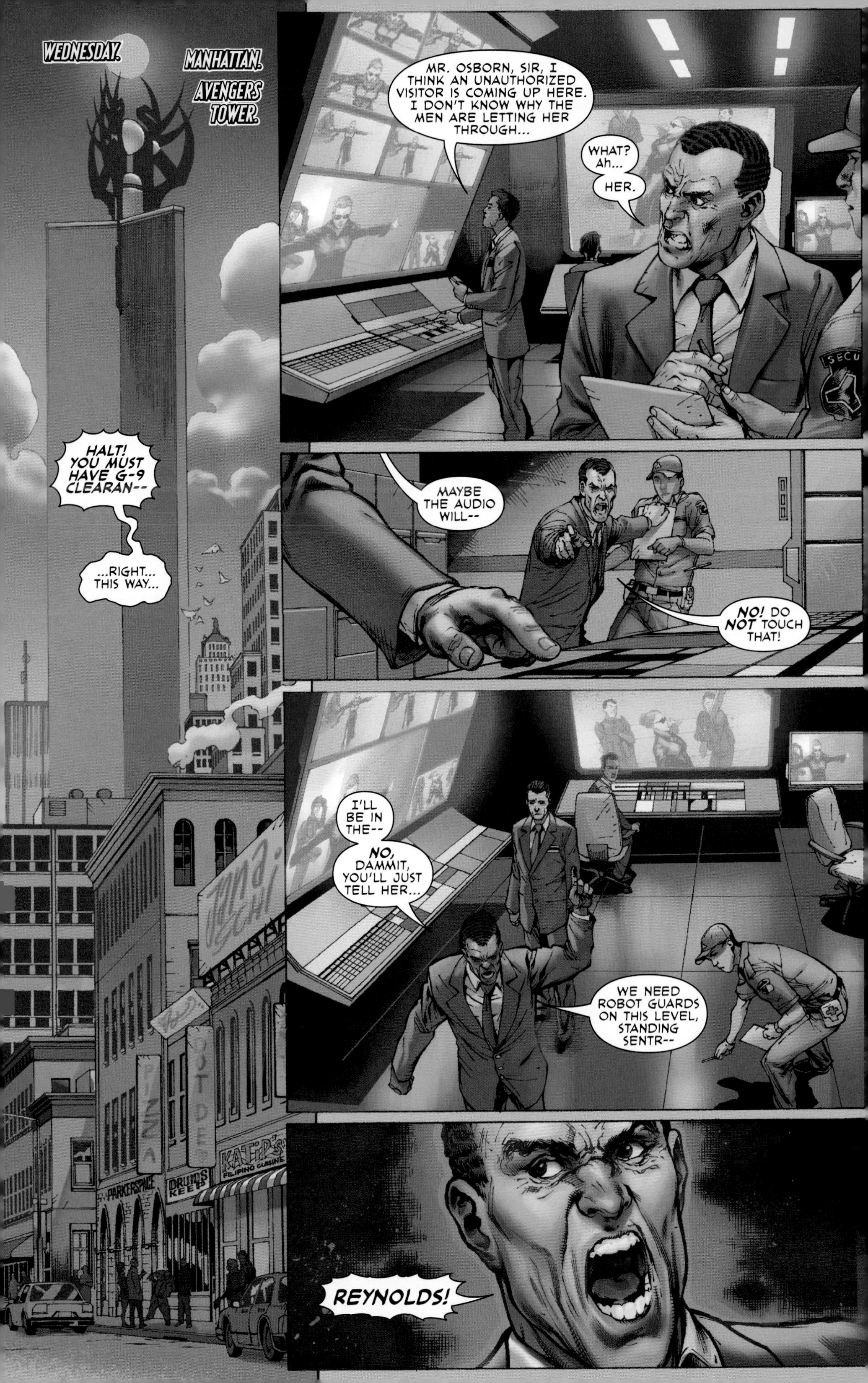
WEDNESDAY.
MANHATTAN.
AVENGERS TOWER.
HALT! YOU MUST HAVE G-9 CLEARAN--
...RIGHT... THIS WAY...
MR. OSBORN, SIR, I THINK AN UNAUTHORIZED VISITOR IS COMING UP HERE. I DON'T KNOW WHY THE MEN ARE LETTING HER THROUGH...
WHAT? Ah...
HER.
MAYBE THE AUDIO WILL--
NO! DO NOT TOUCH THAT!
I'LL BE IN THE--
NO, DAMMIT, YOU'LL JUST TELL HER...
WE NEED ROBOT GUARDS ON THIS LEVEL, STANDING SENTR--
REYNOLDS!

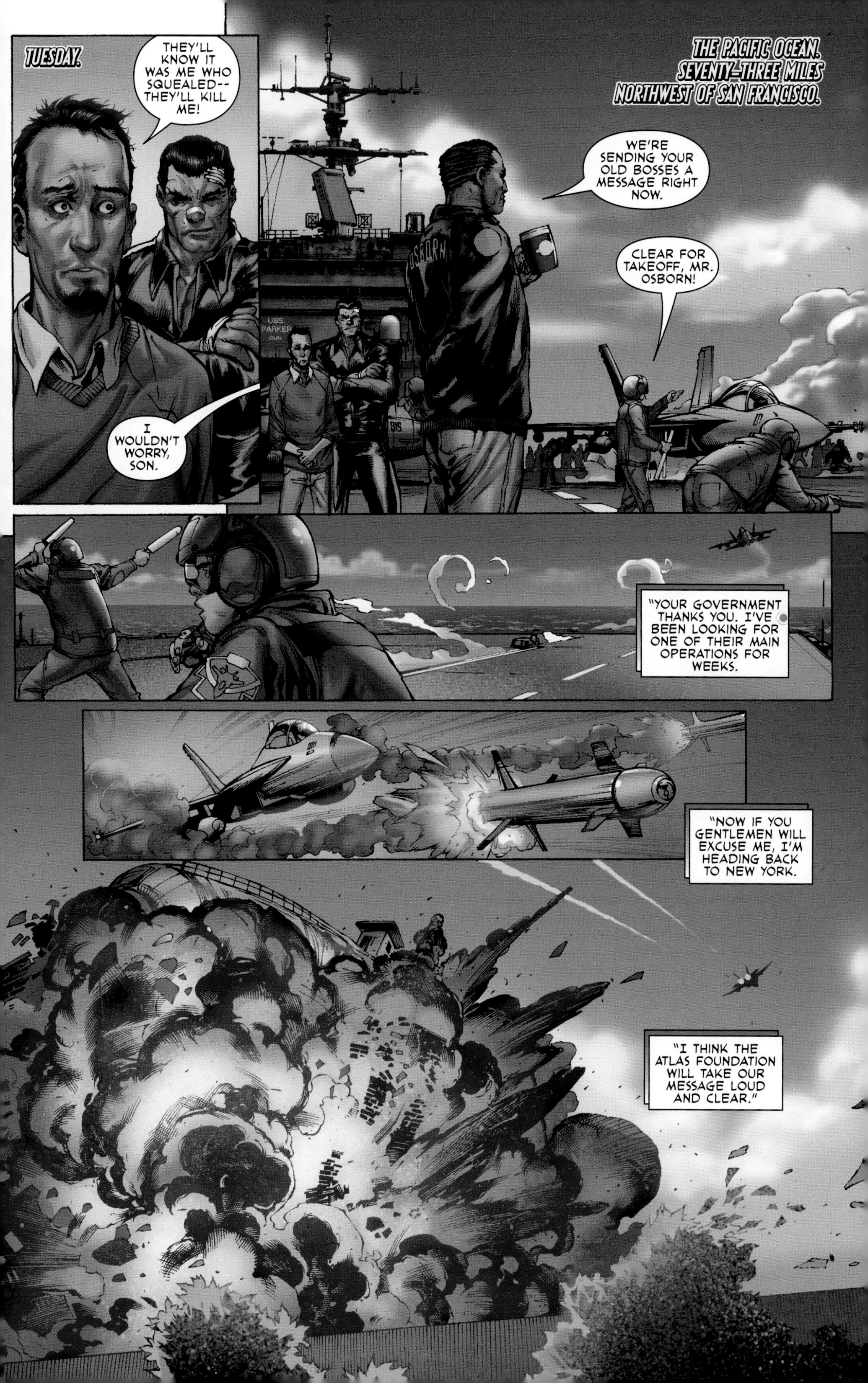
TUESDAY.
THEY'LL KNOW IT WAS ME WHO SQUEALED-- THEY'LL KILL ME!
I WOULDN'T WORRY, SON.
THE PACIFIC OCEAN. SEVENTY-THREE MILES NORTHWEST OF SAN FRANCISCO.
WE'RE SENDING YOUR OLD BOSSES A MESSAGE RIGHT NOW.
CLEAR FOR TAKEOFF, MR. OSBORN!
USS PARKER
OSBORN
"YOUR GOVERNMENT THANKS YOU. I'VE BEEN LOOKING FOR ONE OF THEIR MAIN OPERATIONS FOR WEEKS.
"NOW IF YOU GENTLEMEN WILL EXCUSE ME, I'M HEADING BACK TO NEW YORK.
"I THINK THE ATLAS FOUNDATION WILL TAKE OUR MESSAGE LOUD AND CLEAR."

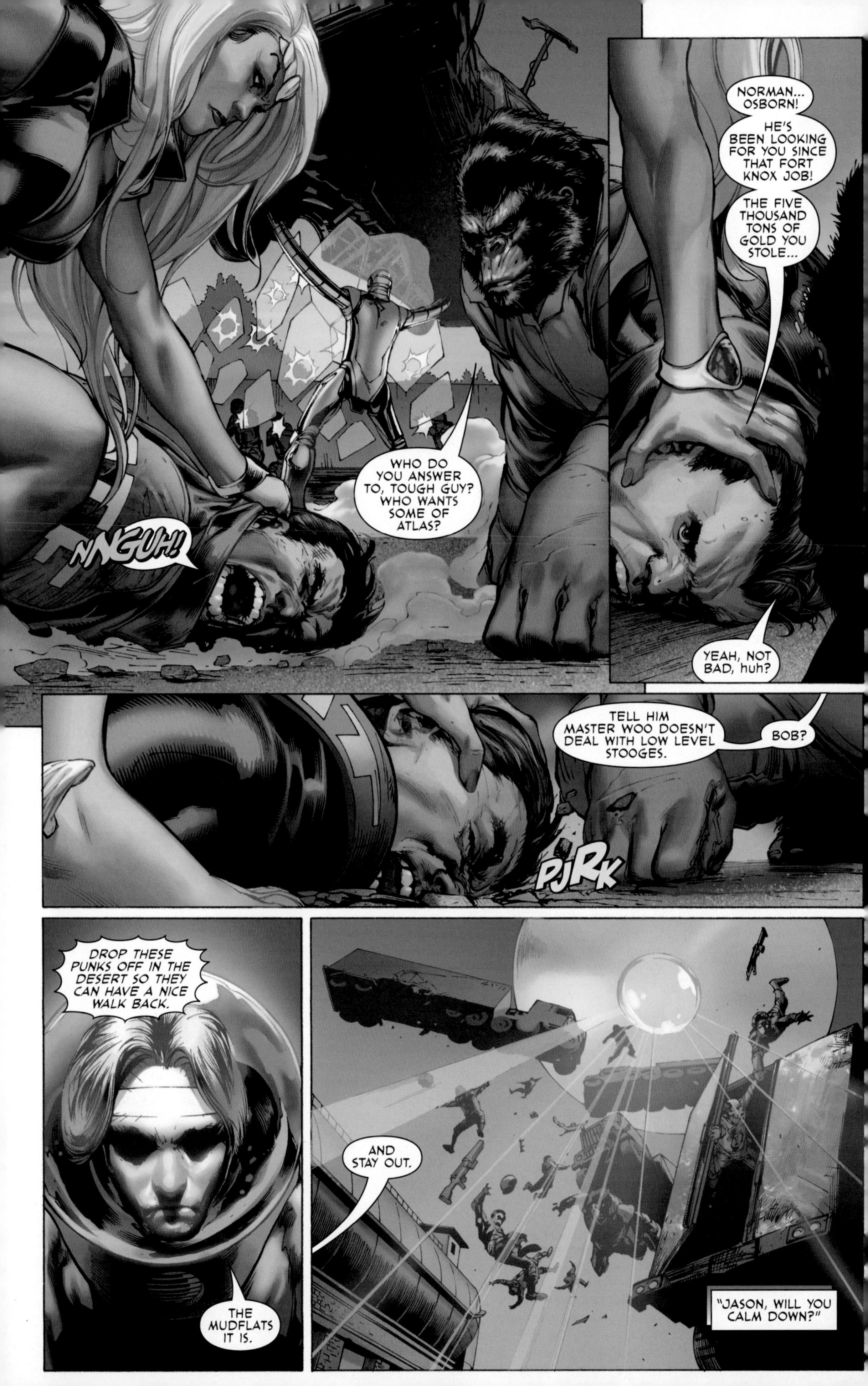
NNGUH!
WHO DO YOU ANSWER TO, TOUGH GUY? WHO WANTS SOME OF ATLAS?
NORMAN... OSBORN!
HE'S BEEN LOOKING FOR YOU SINCE THAT FORT KNOX JOB!
THE FIVE THOUSAND TONS OF GOLD YOU STOLE...
YEAH, NOT BAD, huh?
TELL HIM MASTER WOO DOESN'T DEAL WITH LOW LEVEL STOOGES.
BOB?
PJRK
DROP THESE PUNKS OFF IN THE DESERT SO THEY CAN HAVE A NICE WALK BACK.
THE MUDFLATS IT IS.
AND STAY OUT.
"JASON, WILL YOU CALM DOWN?"

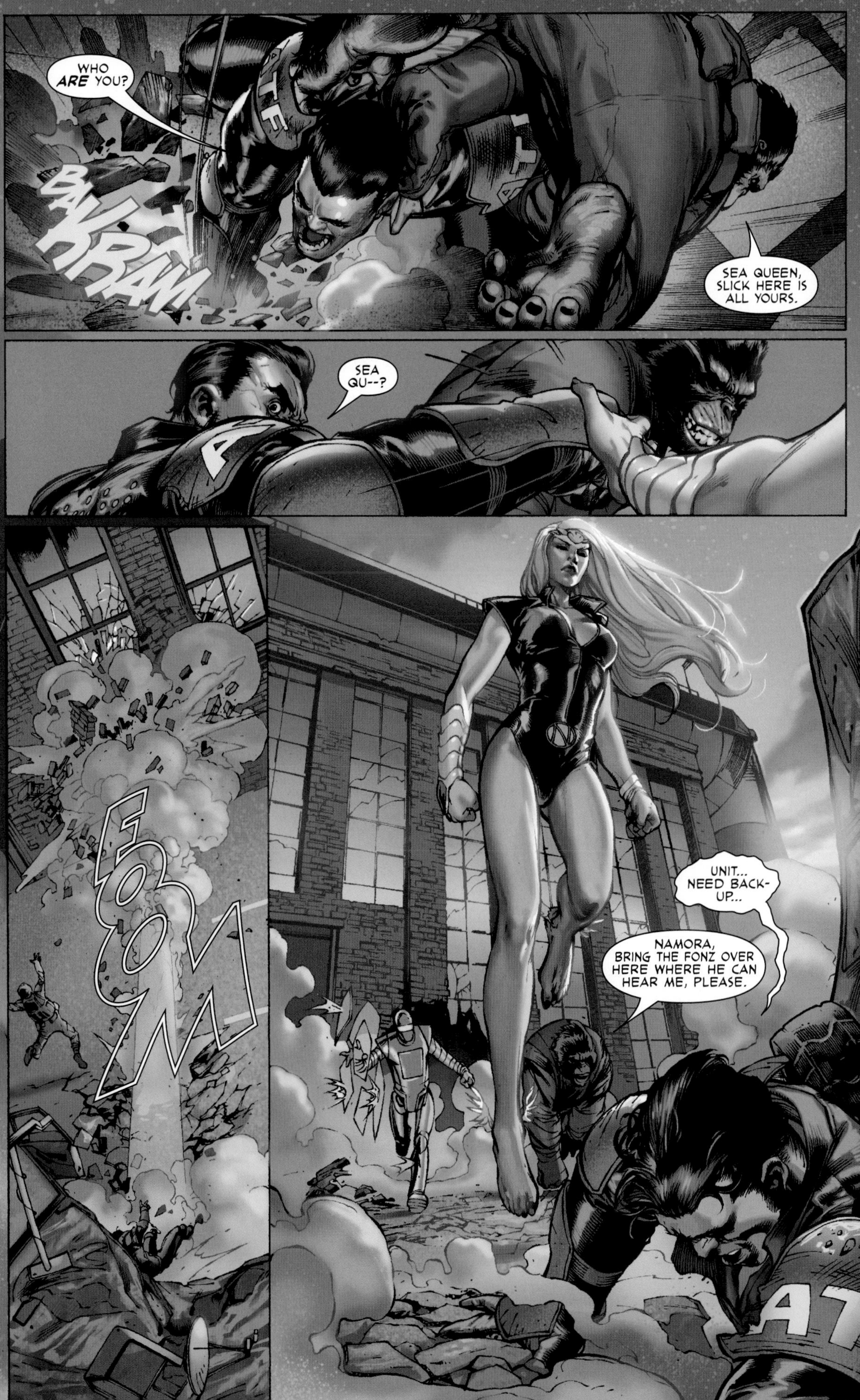
WHO ARE YOU?
BAKRAM
SEA QUEEN, SLICK HERE IS ALL YOURS.
SEA QU--?
FOOOM
UNIT... NEED BACK-UP...
NAMORA, BRING THE FONZ OVER HERE WHERE HE CAN HEAR ME, PLEASE.

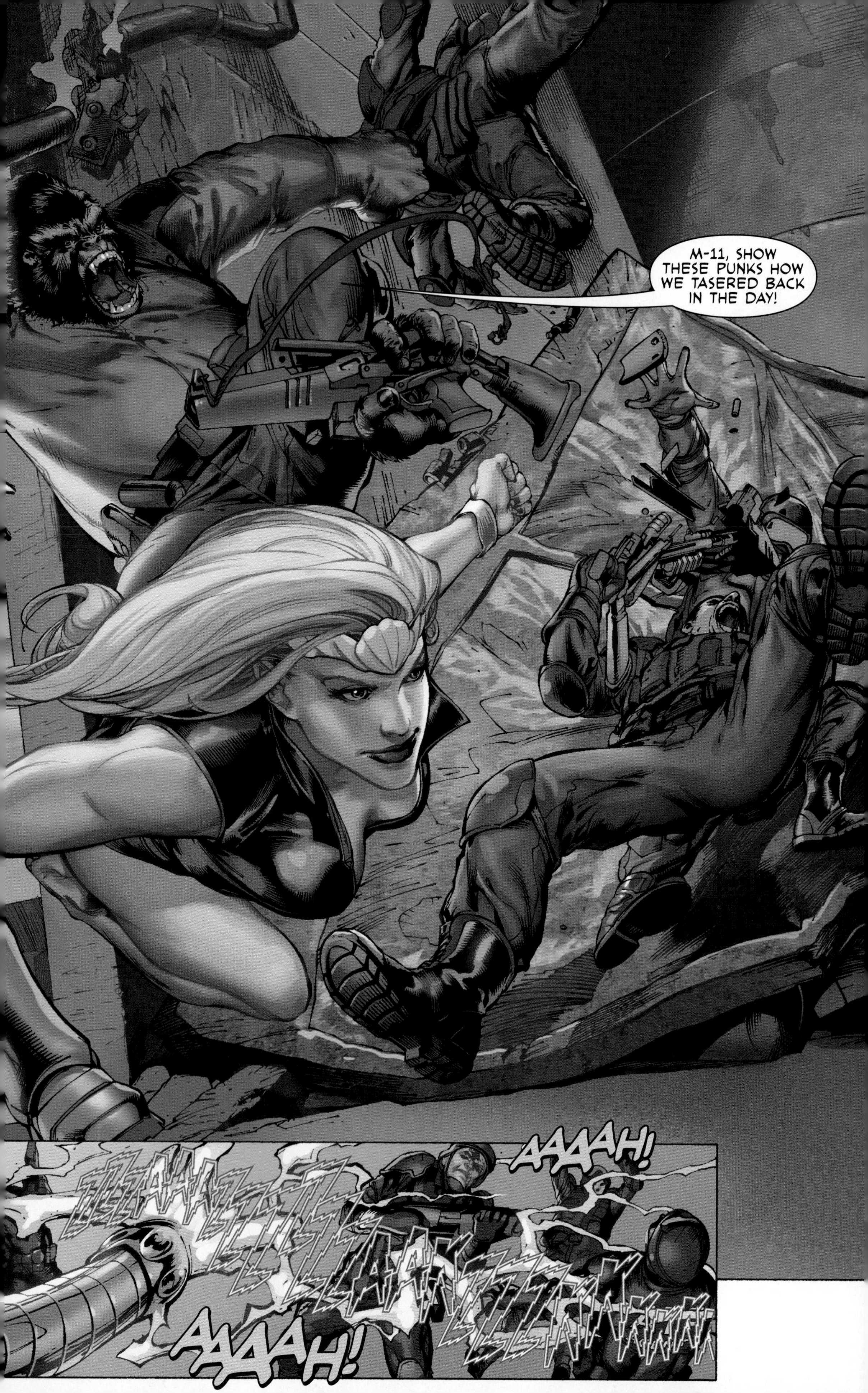
M-11, SHOW THESE PUNKS HOW WE TASERED BACK IN THE DAY!
AAAAH!
AAAAH!

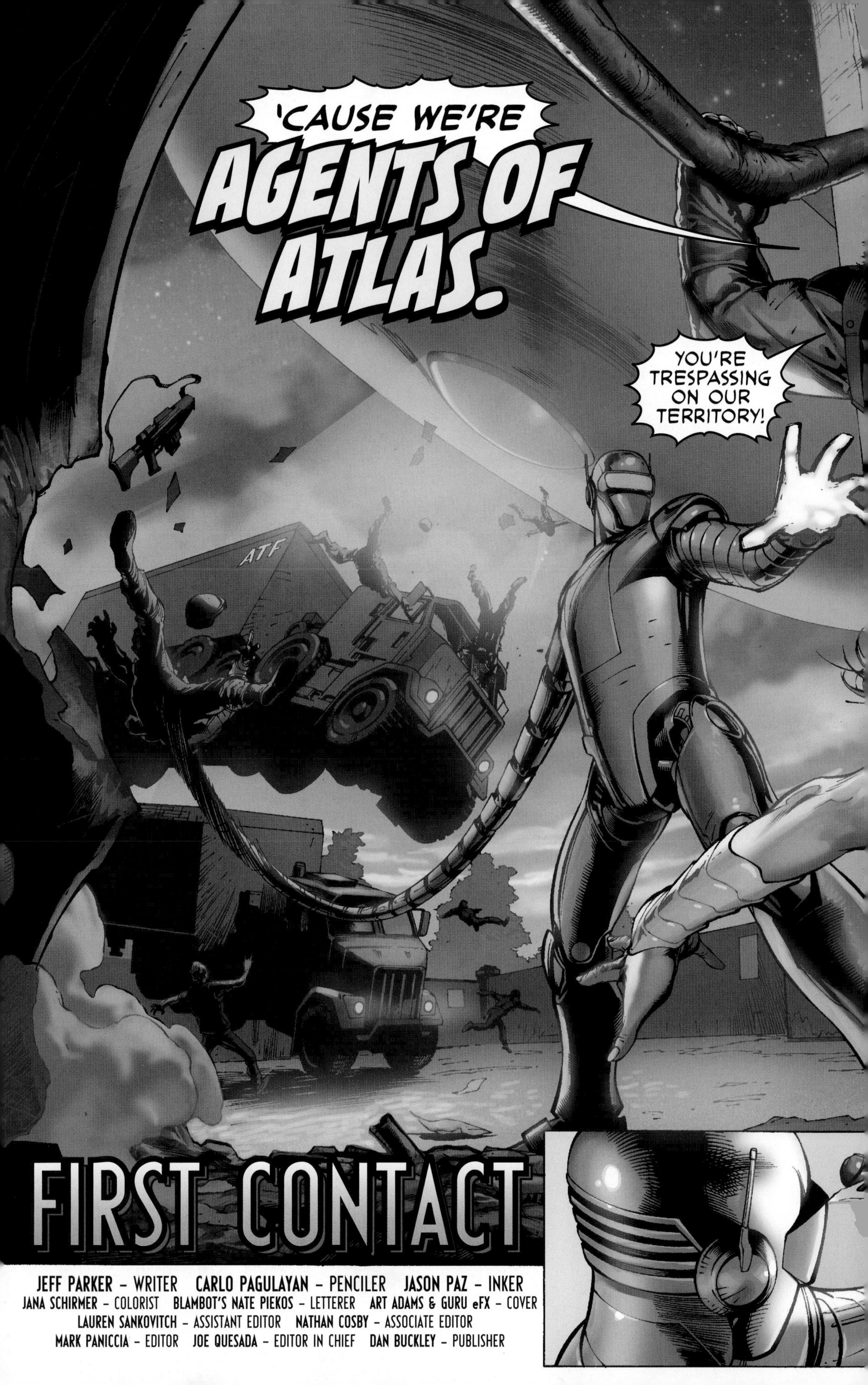
'CAUSE WE'RE AGENTS OF ATLAS.
YOU'RE TRESPASSING ON OUR TERRITORY!
ATF

FIRST CONTACT

JEFF PARKER – WRITER CARLO PAGULAYAN – PENCILER JASON PAZ – INKER
JANA SCHIRMER – COLORIST BLAMBOT'S NATE PIEKOS – LETTERER ART ADAMS & GURU eFX – COVER
LAUREN SANKOVITCH – ASSISTANT EDITOR NATHAN COSBY – ASSOCIATE EDITOR
MARK PANICCIA – EDITOR JOE QUESADA – EDITOR IN CHIEF DAN BUCKLEY – PUBLISHER

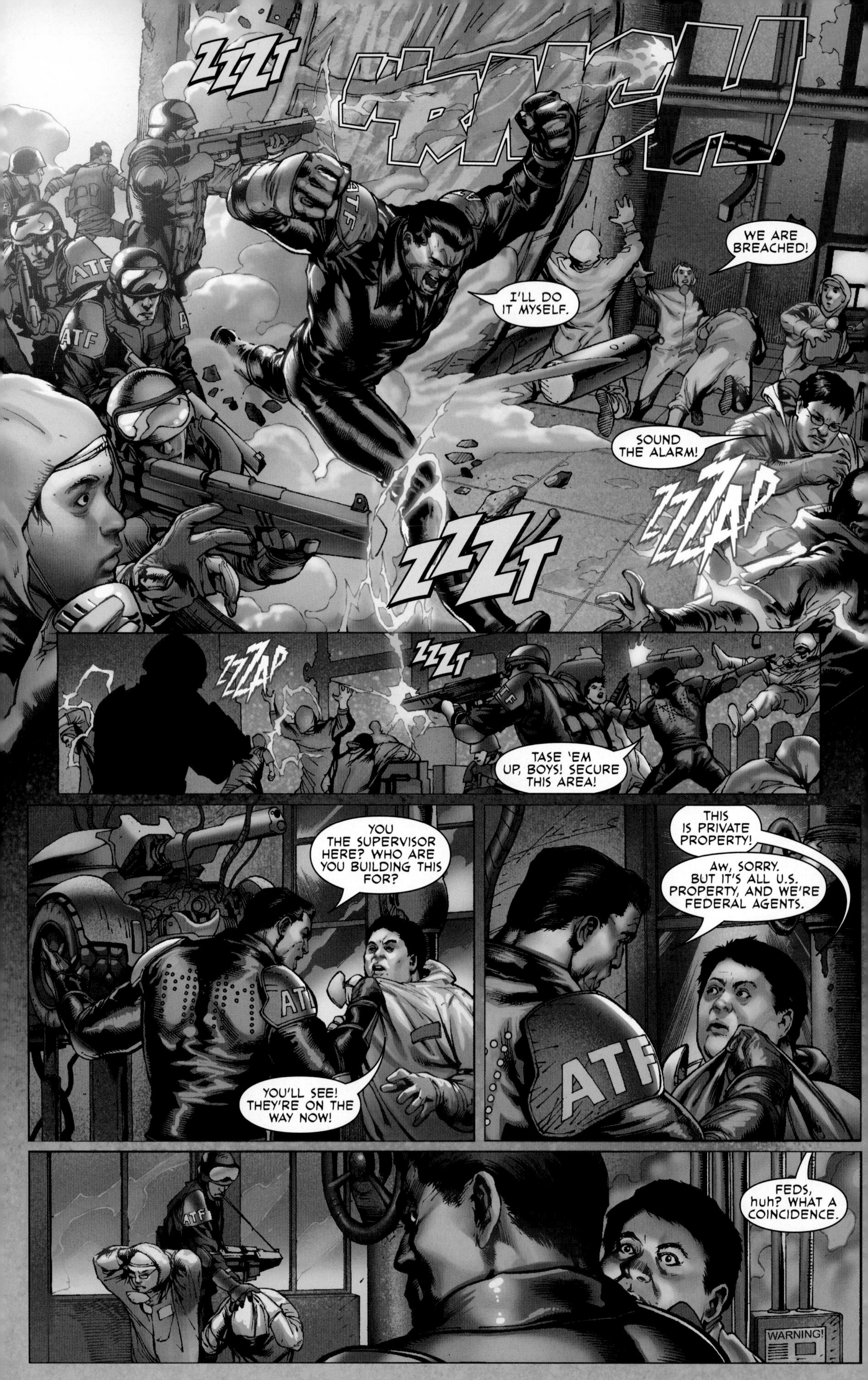
ZZZT
K'RAKKH
WE ARE BREACHED!
I'LL DO IT MYSELF.
SOUND THE ALARM!
ZZZAP
ZZZT
ZZZAP
ZZZT
TASE 'EM UP, BOYS! SECURE THIS AREA!
YOU THE SUPERVISOR HERE? WHO ARE YOU BUILDING THIS FOR?
YOU'LL SEE! THEY'RE ON THE WAY NOW!
THIS IS PRIVATE PROPERTY!
Aw, SORRY. BUT IT'S ALL U.S. PROPERTY, AND WE'RE FEDERAL AGENTS.
FEDS, huh? WHAT A COINCIDENCE.
WARNING!

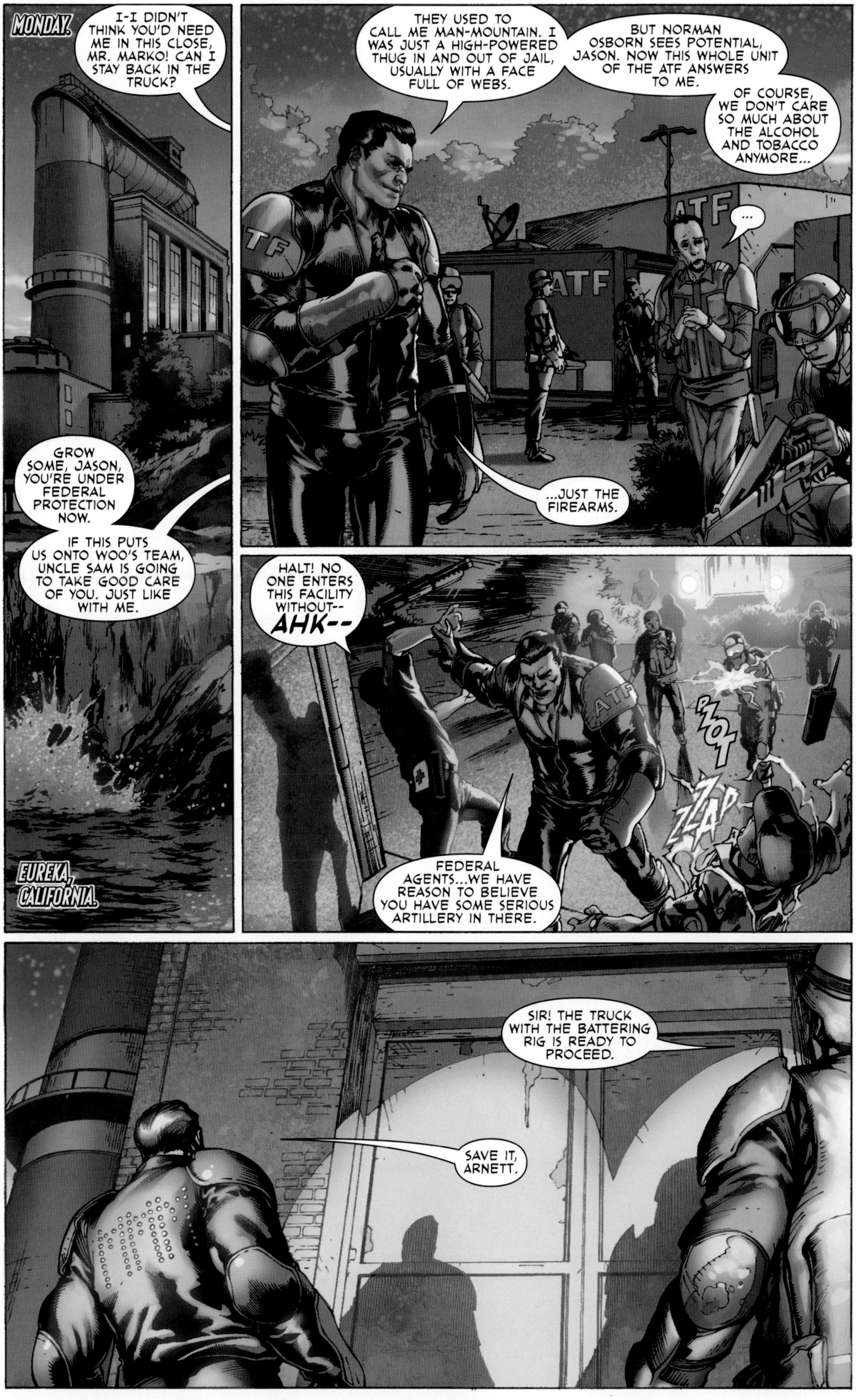
MONDAY.
I-I DIDN'T THINK YOU'D NEED ME IN THIS CLOSE, MR. MARKO! CAN I STAY BACK IN THE TRUCK?
GROW SOME, JASON, YOU'RE UNDER FEDERAL PROTECTION NOW.
IF THIS PUTS US ONTO WOO'S TEAM, UNCLE SAM IS GOING TO TAKE GOOD CARE OF YOU. JUST LIKE WITH ME.
EUREKA, CALIFORNIA.
THEY USED TO CALL ME MAN-MOUNTAIN. I WAS JUST A HIGH-POWERED THUG IN AND OUT OF JAIL, USUALLY WITH A FACE FULL OF WEBS.
BUT NORMAN OSBORN SEES POTENTIAL, JASON. NOW THIS WHOLE UNIT OF THE ATF ANSWERS TO ME.
OF COURSE, WE DON'T CARE SO MUCH ABOUT THE ALCOHOL AND TOBACCO ANYMORE...
...
...JUST THE FIREARMS.
HALT! NO ONE ENTERS THIS FACILITY WITHOUT-- AHK--
FEDERAL AGENTS...WE HAVE REASON TO BELIEVE YOU HAVE SOME SERIOUS ARTILLERY IN THERE.
PZOT
ZZAP
SIR! THE TRUCK WITH THE BATTERING RIG IS READY TO PROCEED.
SAVE IT, ARNETT.

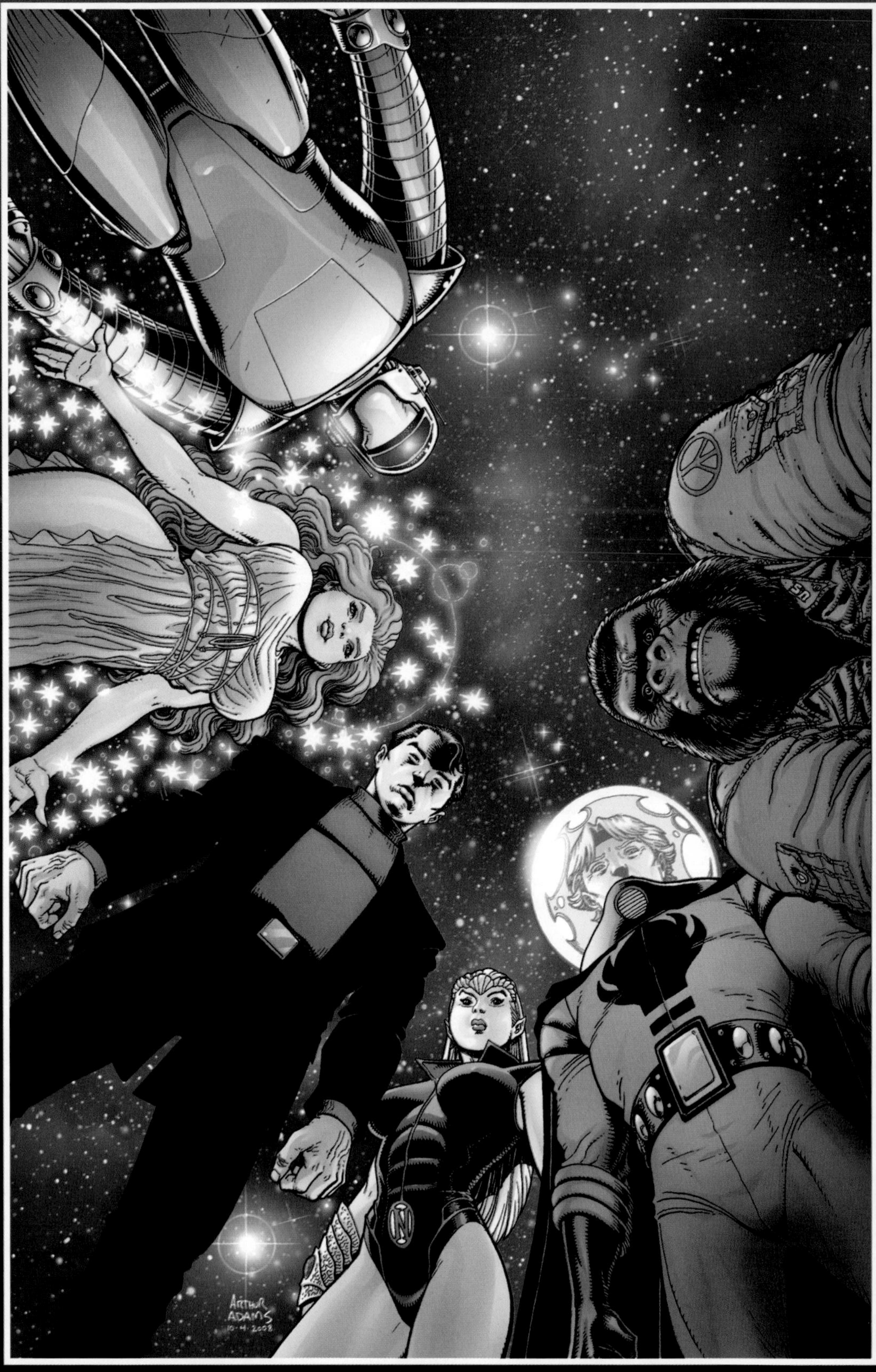
ARTHUR ADAMS
10-4-2008

#1

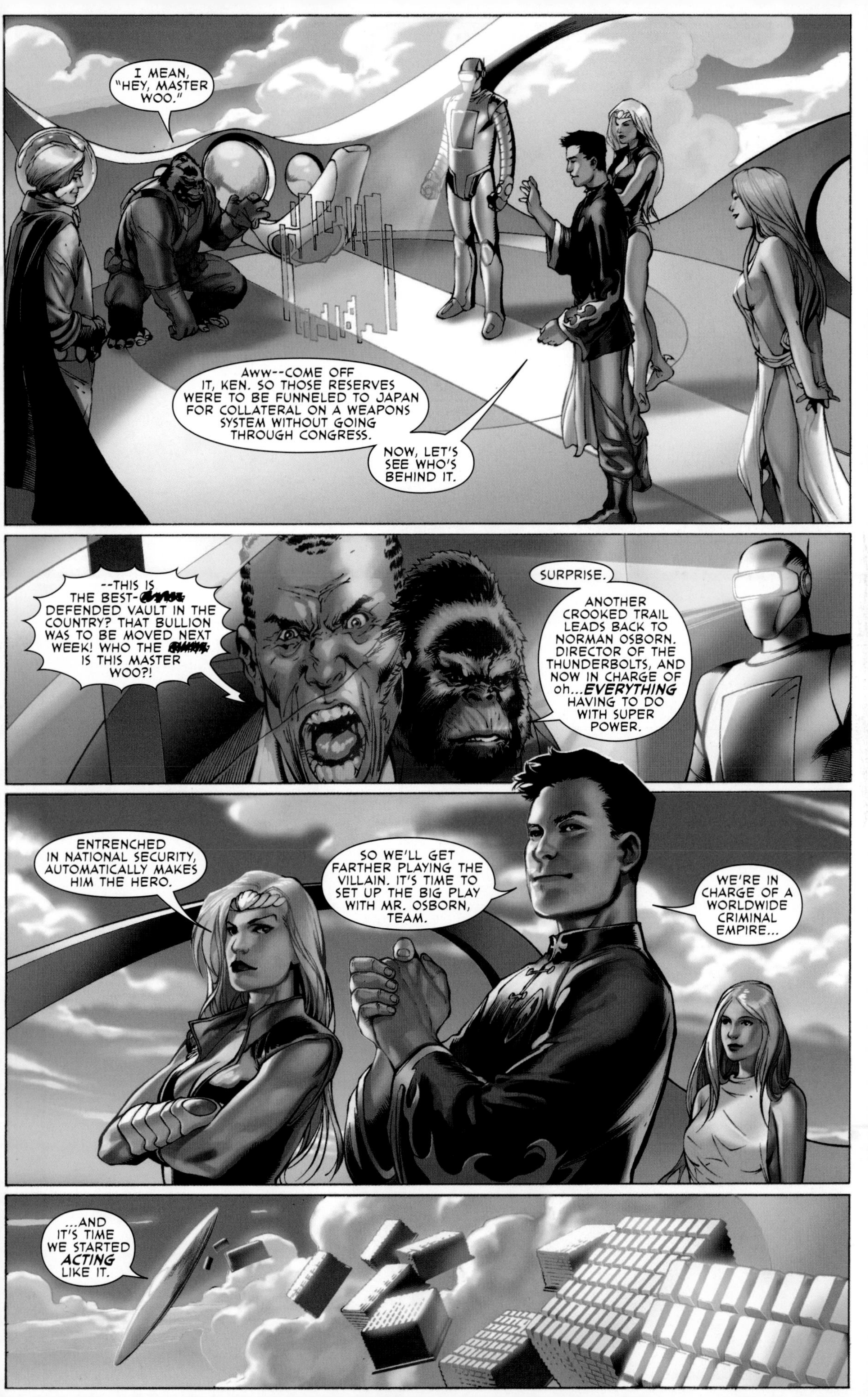
I MEAN, "HEY, MASTER WOO."
Aww--COME OFF IT, KEN. SO THOSE RESERVES WERE TO BE FUNNELED TO JAPAN FOR COLLATERAL ON A WEAPONS SYSTEM WITHOUT GOING THROUGH CONGRESS.
NOW, LET'S SEE WHO'S BEHIND IT.
--THIS IS THE BEST- DEFENDED VAULT IN THE COUNTRY? THAT BULLION WAS TO BE MOVED NEXT WEEK! WHO THE IS THIS MASTER WOO?!
SURPRISE.
ANOTHER CROOKED TRAIL LEADS BACK TO NORMAN OSBORN. DIRECTOR OF THE THUNDERBOLTS, AND NOW IN CHARGE OF oh...EVERYTHING HAVING TO DO WITH SUPER POWER.
ENTRENCHED IN NATIONAL SECURITY, AUTOMATICALLY MAKES HIM THE HERO.
SO WE'LL GET FARTHER PLAYING THE VILLAIN. IT'S TIME TO SET UP THE BIG PLAY WITH MR. OSBORN, TEAM.
WE'RE IN CHARGE OF A WORLDWIDE CRIMINAL EMPIRE...
...AND IT'S TIME WE STARTED ACTING LIKE IT.

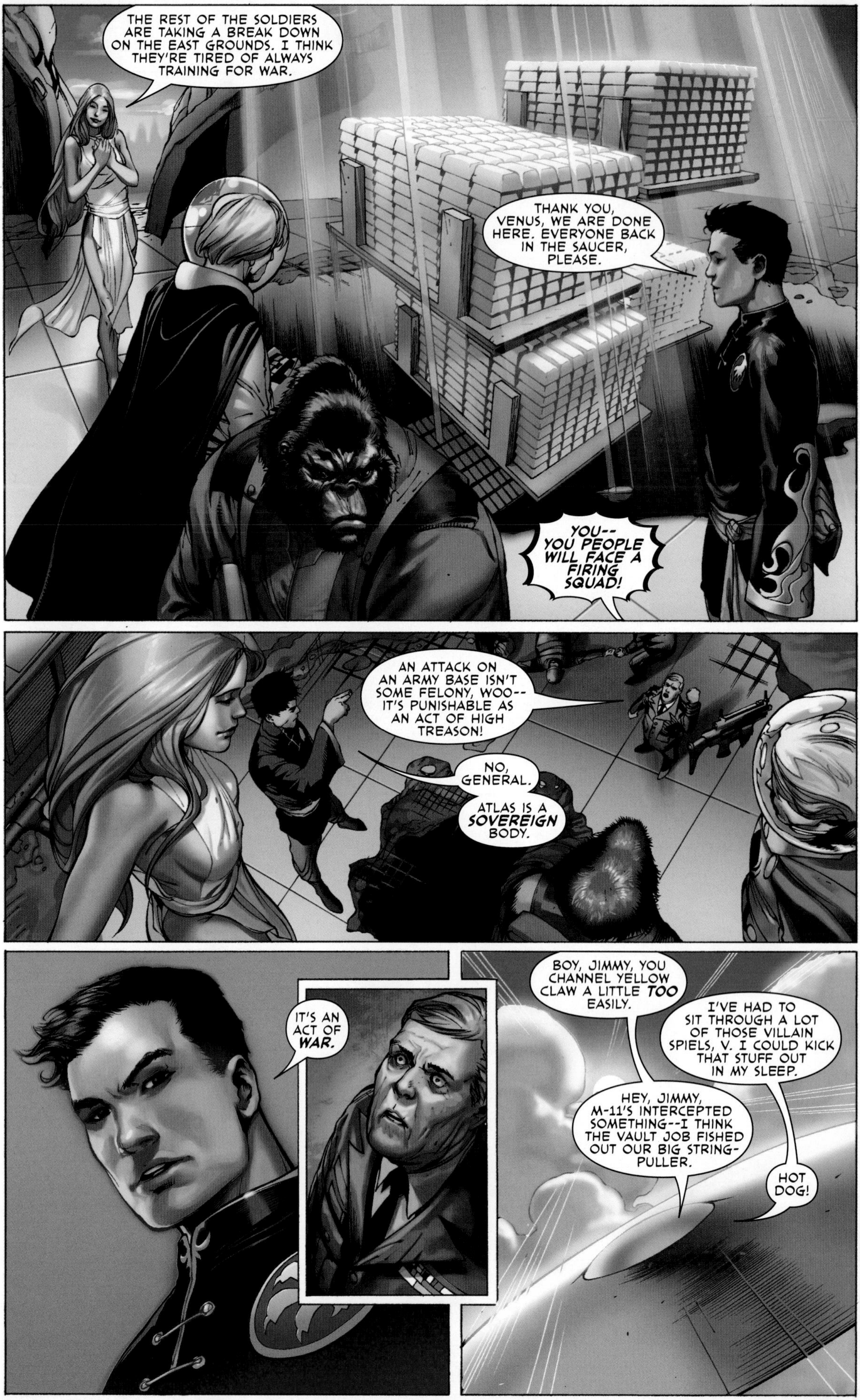
THE REST OF THE SOLDIERS ARE TAKING A BREAK DOWN ON THE EAST GROUNDS. I THINK THEY'RE TIRED OF ALWAYS TRAINING FOR WAR.
THANK YOU, VENUS, WE ARE DONE HERE. EVERYONE BACK IN THE SAUCER, PLEASE.
YOU-- YOU PEOPLE WILL FACE A FIRING SQUAD!
AN ATTACK ON AN ARMY BASE ISN'T SOME FELONY, WOO-- IT'S PUNISHABLE AS AN ACT OF HIGH TREASON!
NO, GENERAL.
ATLAS IS A SOVEREIGN BODY.
IT'S AN ACT OF WAR.
BOY, JIMMY, YOU CHANNEL YELLOW CLAW A LITTLE TOO EASILY.
I'VE HAD TO SIT THROUGH A LOT OF THOSE VILLAIN SPIELS, V. I COULD KICK THAT STUFF OUT IN MY SLEEP.
HEY, JIMMY, M-11'S INTERCEPTED SOMETHING--I THINK THE VAULT JOB FISHED OUT OUR BIG STRING-PULLER.
HOT DOG!

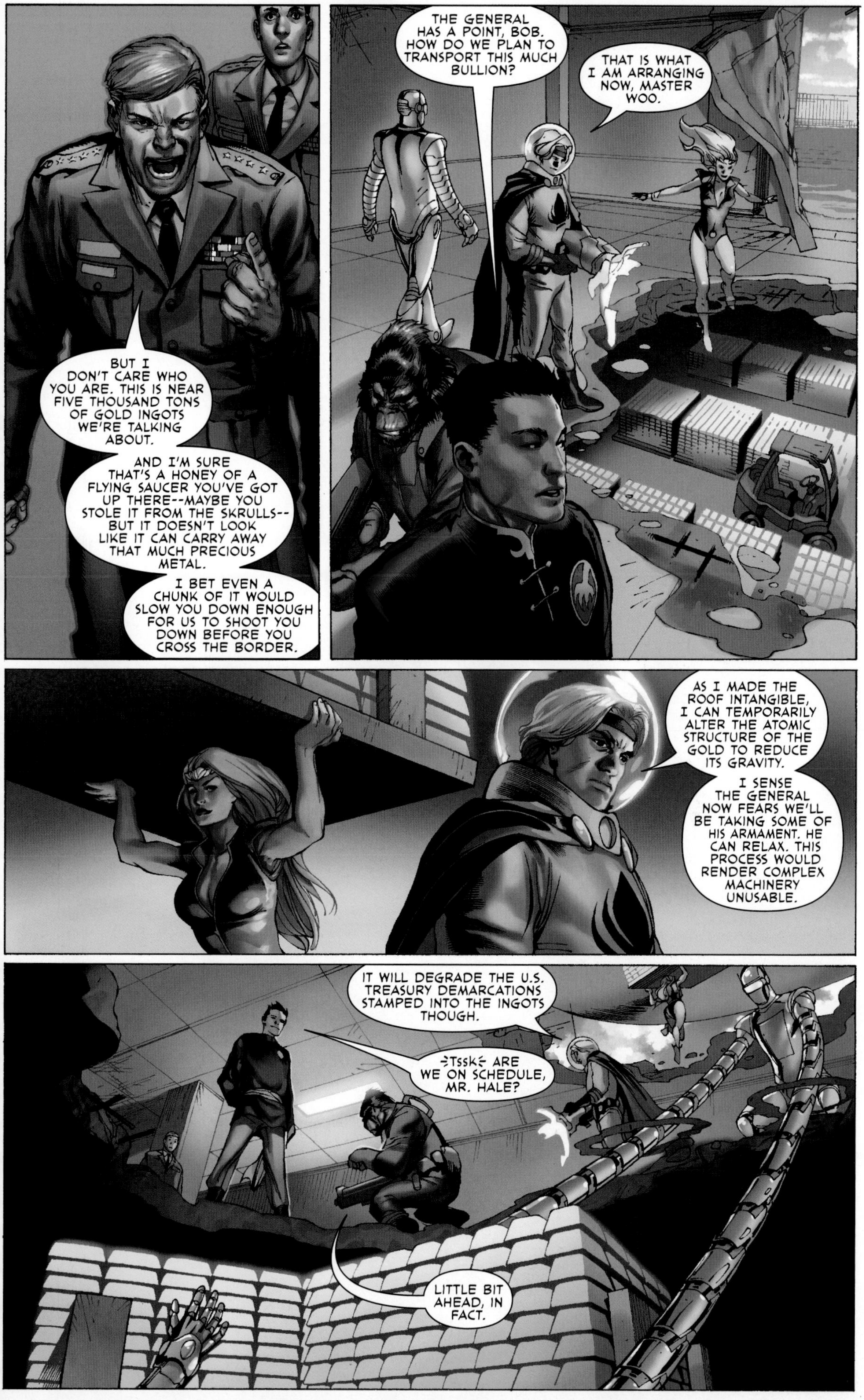
BUT I DON'T CARE WHO YOU ARE. THIS IS NEAR FIVE THOUSAND TONS OF GOLD INGOTS WE'RE TALKING ABOUT.
AND I'M SURE THAT'S A HONEY OF A FLYING SAUCER YOU'VE GOT UP THERE--MAYBE YOU STOLE IT FROM THE SKRULLS--BUT IT DOESN'T LOOK LIKE IT CAN CARRY AWAY THAT MUCH PRECIOUS METAL.
I BET EVEN A CHUNK OF IT WOULD SLOW YOU DOWN ENOUGH FOR US TO SHOOT YOU DOWN BEFORE YOU CROSS THE BORDER.
THE GENERAL HAS A POINT, BOB. HOW DO WE PLAN TO TRANSPORT THIS MUCH BULLION?
THAT IS WHAT I AM ARRANGING NOW, MASTER WOO.
AS I MADE THE ROOF INTANGIBLE, I CAN TEMPORARILY ALTER THE ATOMIC STRUCTURE OF THE GOLD TO REDUCE ITS GRAVITY.
I SENSE THE GENERAL NOW FEARS WE'LL BE TAKING SOME OF HIS ARMAMENT. HE CAN RELAX. THIS PROCESS WOULD RENDER COMPLEX MACHINERY UNUSABLE.
IT WILL DEGRADE THE U.S. TREASURY DEMARCATIONS STAMPED INTO THE INGOTS THOUGH.
=TSSK= ARE WE ON SCHEDULE, MR. HALE?
LITTLE BIT AHEAD, IN FACT.

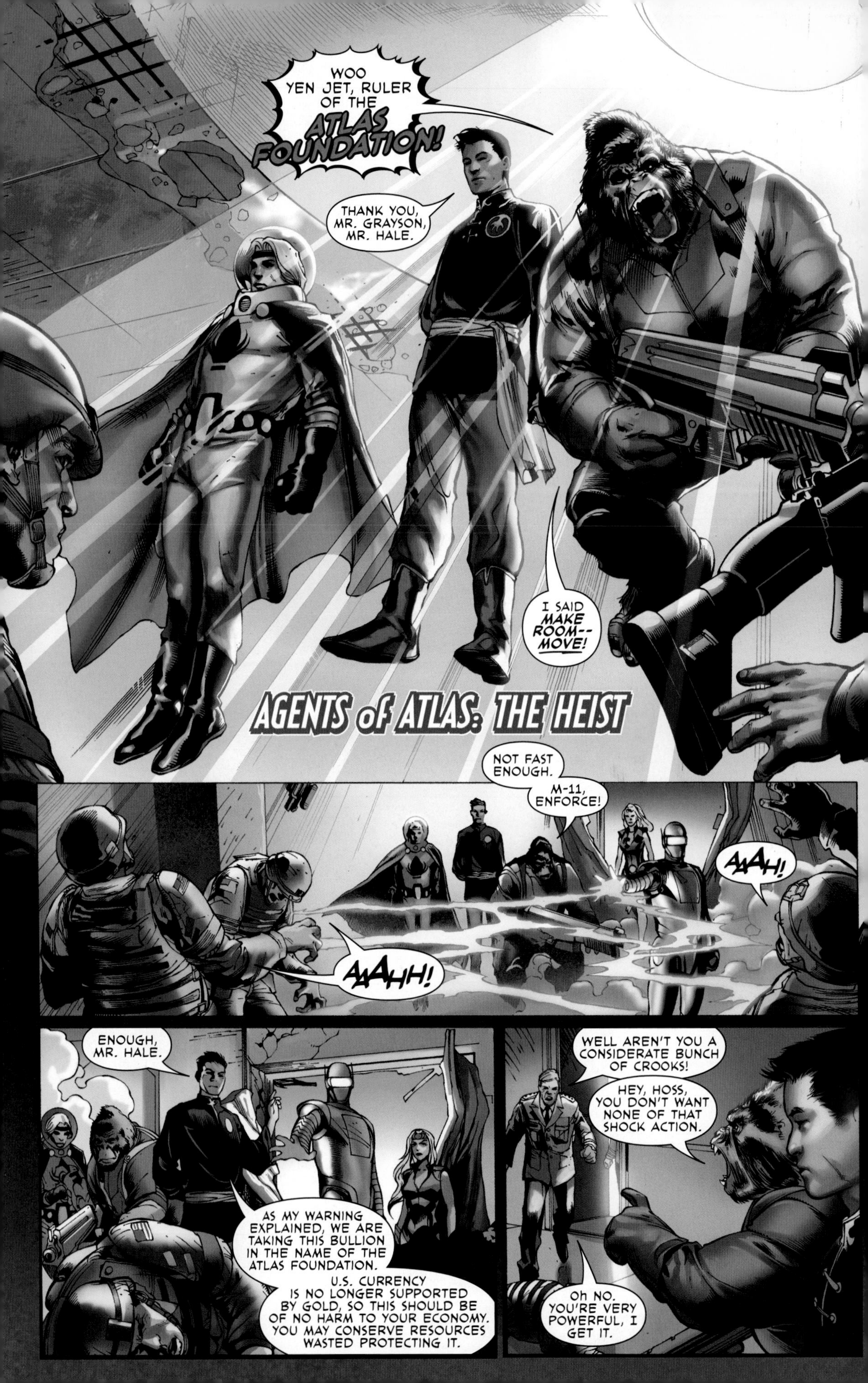
WOO YEN JET, RULER OF THE ATLAS FOUNDATION!
THANK YOU, MR. GRAYSON, MR. HALE.
I SAID MAKE ROOM-- MOVE!
AGENTS of ATLAS: THE HEIST
NOT FAST ENOUGH.
M-11, ENFORCE!
AAAH!
AAAHH!
ENOUGH, MR. HALE.
AS MY WARNING EXPLAINED, WE ARE TAKING THIS BULLION IN THE NAME OF THE ATLAS FOUNDATION.
U.S. CURRENCY IS NO LONGER SUPPORTED BY GOLD, SO THIS SHOULD BE OF NO HARM TO YOUR ECONOMY. YOU MAY CONSERVE RESOURCES WASTED PROTECTING IT.
WELL AREN'T YOU A CONSIDERATE BUNCH OF CROOKS!
HEY, HOSS, YOU DON'T WANT NONE OF THAT SHOCK ACTION.
Oh NO. YOU'RE VERY POWERFUL, I GET IT.

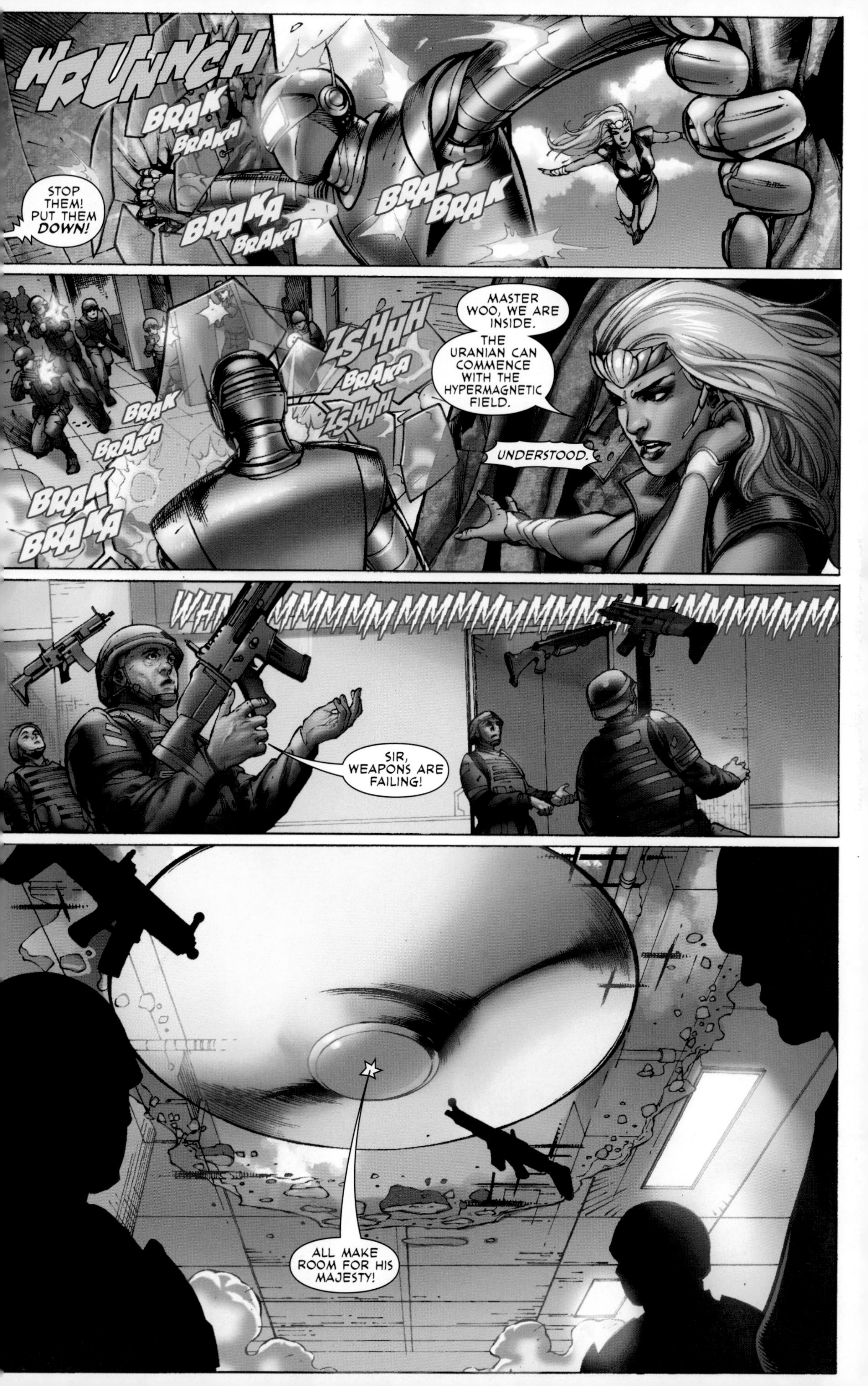
WRUNNCH
BRAK BRAKA
STOP THEM! PUT THEM DOWN!
BRAKA BRAKA
BRAK BRAK
BRAK BRAKA
BRAK BRAKA
ZSHHH BRAKA ZSHHH
MASTER WOO, WE ARE INSIDE.
THE URANIAN CAN COMMENCE WITH THE HYPERMAGNETIC FIELD.
UNDERSTOOD.
WHMMMMMMMMMMMMMMMMMMMMMMMMMMMM
SIR, WEAPONS ARE FAILING!
ALL MAKE ROOM FOR HIS MAJESTY!

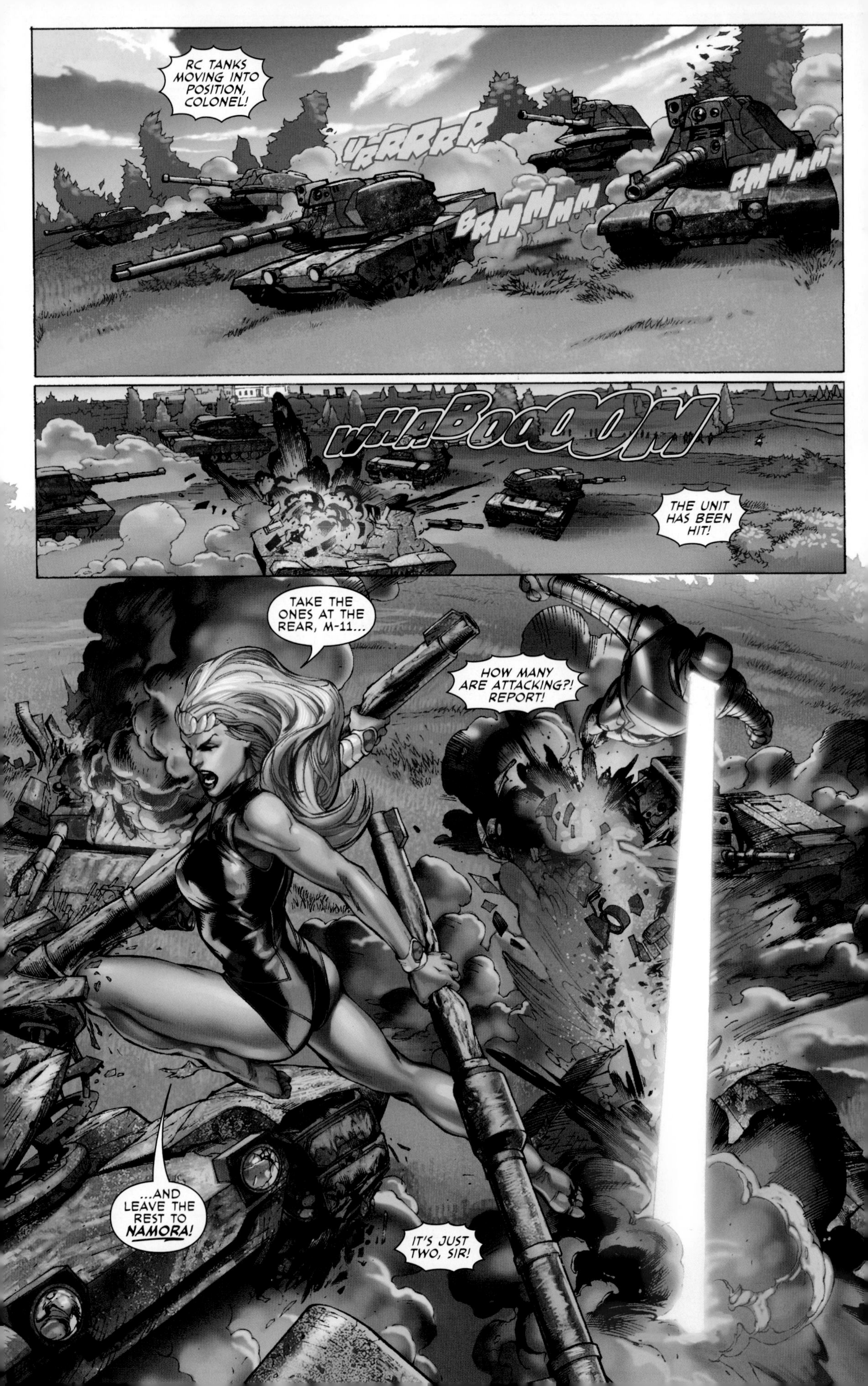
RC TANKS MOVING INTO POSITION, COLONEL!
URRRRRR
BRMMMMM
BRMMMM
WHABOOOOOM
THE UNIT HAS BEEN HIT!
TAKE THE ONES AT THE REAR, M-11...
HOW MANY ARE ATTACKING?! REPORT!
...AND LEAVE THE REST TO NAMORA!
IT'S JUST TWO, SIR!

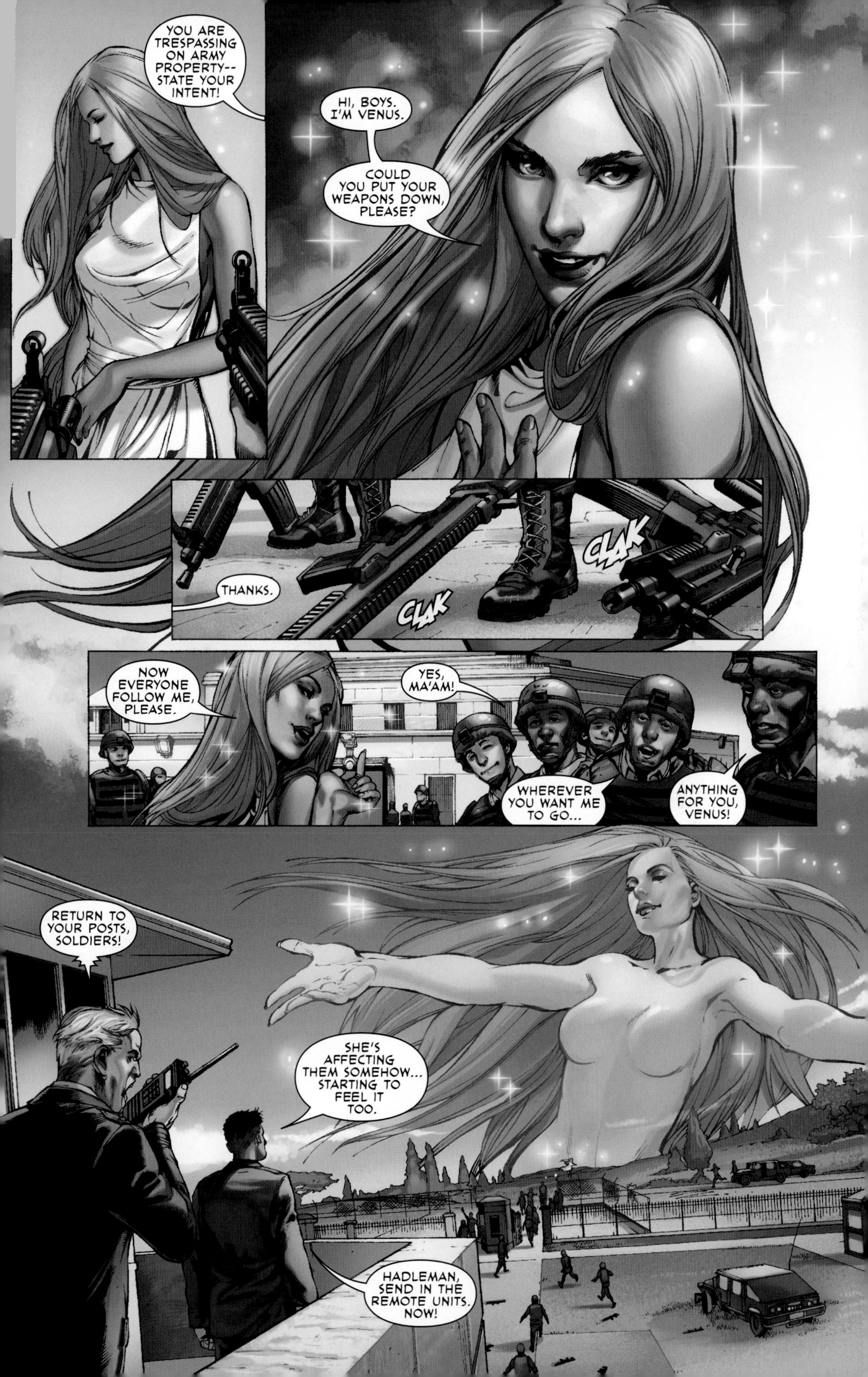
YOU ARE TRESPASSING ON ARMY PROPERTY-- STATE YOUR INTENT!
HI, BOYS. I'M VENUS.
COULD YOU PUT YOUR WEAPONS DOWN, PLEASE?
CLAK
THANKS.
CLAK
NOW EVERYONE FOLLOW ME, PLEASE.
YES, MA'AM!
WHEREVER YOU WANT ME TO GO...
ANYTHING FOR YOU, VENUS!
RETURN TO YOUR POSTS, SOLDIERS!
SHE'S AFFECTING THEM SOMEHOW... STARTING TO FEEL IT TOO.
HADLEMAN, SEND IN THE REMOTE UNITS. NOW!

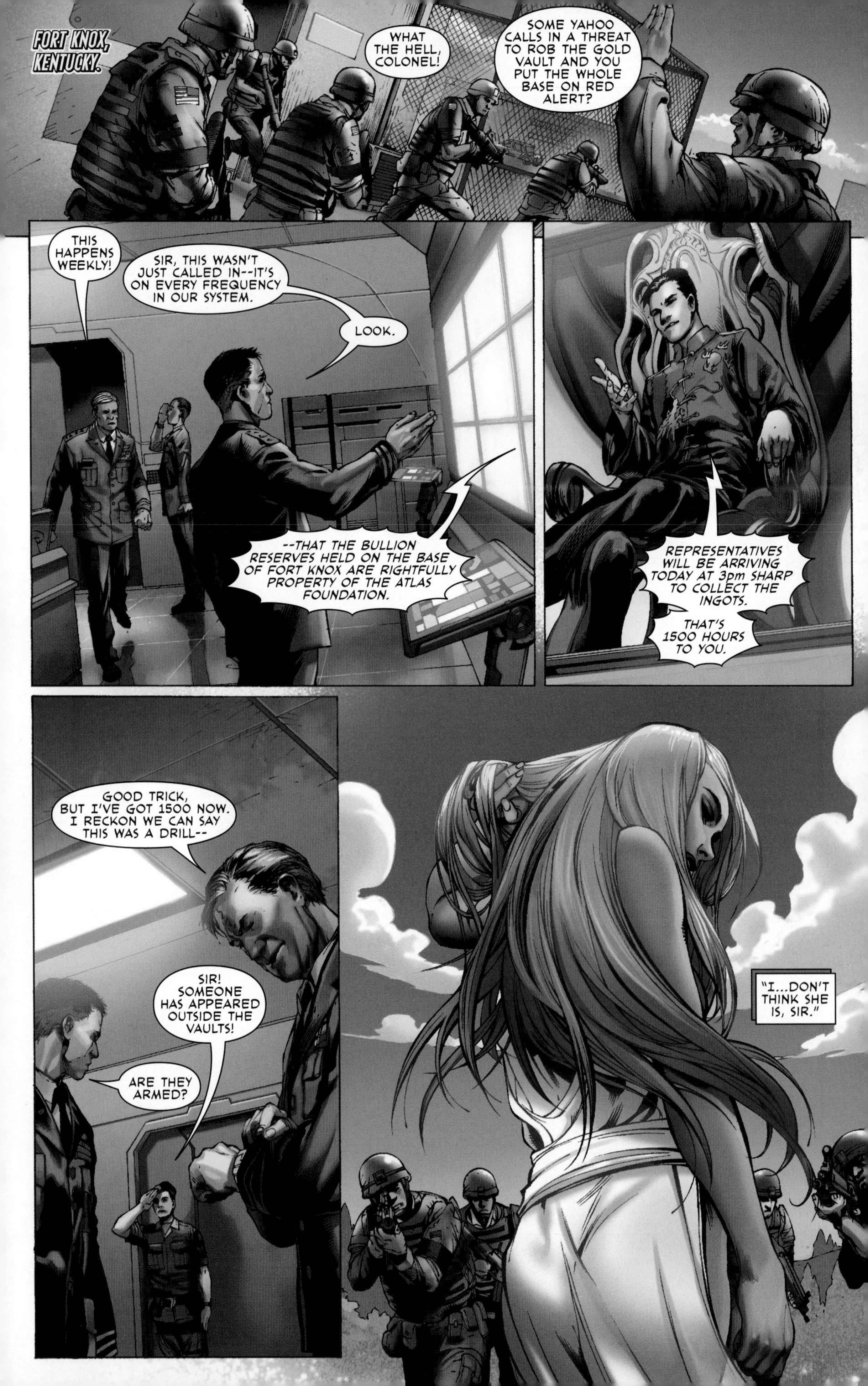
FORT KNOX, KENTUCKY.
WHAT THE HELL, COLONEL!
SOME YAHOO CALLS IN A THREAT TO ROB THE GOLD VAULT AND YOU PUT THE WHOLE BASE ON RED ALERT?
THIS HAPPENS WEEKLY!
SIR, THIS WASN'T JUST CALLED IN--IT'S ON EVERY FREQUENCY IN OUR SYSTEM.
LOOK.
--THAT THE BULLION RESERVES HELD ON THE BASE OF FORT KNOX ARE RIGHTFULLY PROPERTY OF THE ATLAS FOUNDATION.
REPRESENTATIVES WILL BE ARRIVING TODAY AT 3pm SHARP TO COLLECT THE INGOTS.
THAT'S 1500 HOURS TO YOU.
GOOD TRICK, BUT I'VE GOT 1500 NOW. I RECKON WE CAN SAY THIS WAS A DRILL--
SIR! SOMEONE HAS APPEARED OUTSIDE THE VAULTS!
ARE THEY ARMED?
"I...DON'T THINK SHE IS, SIR."

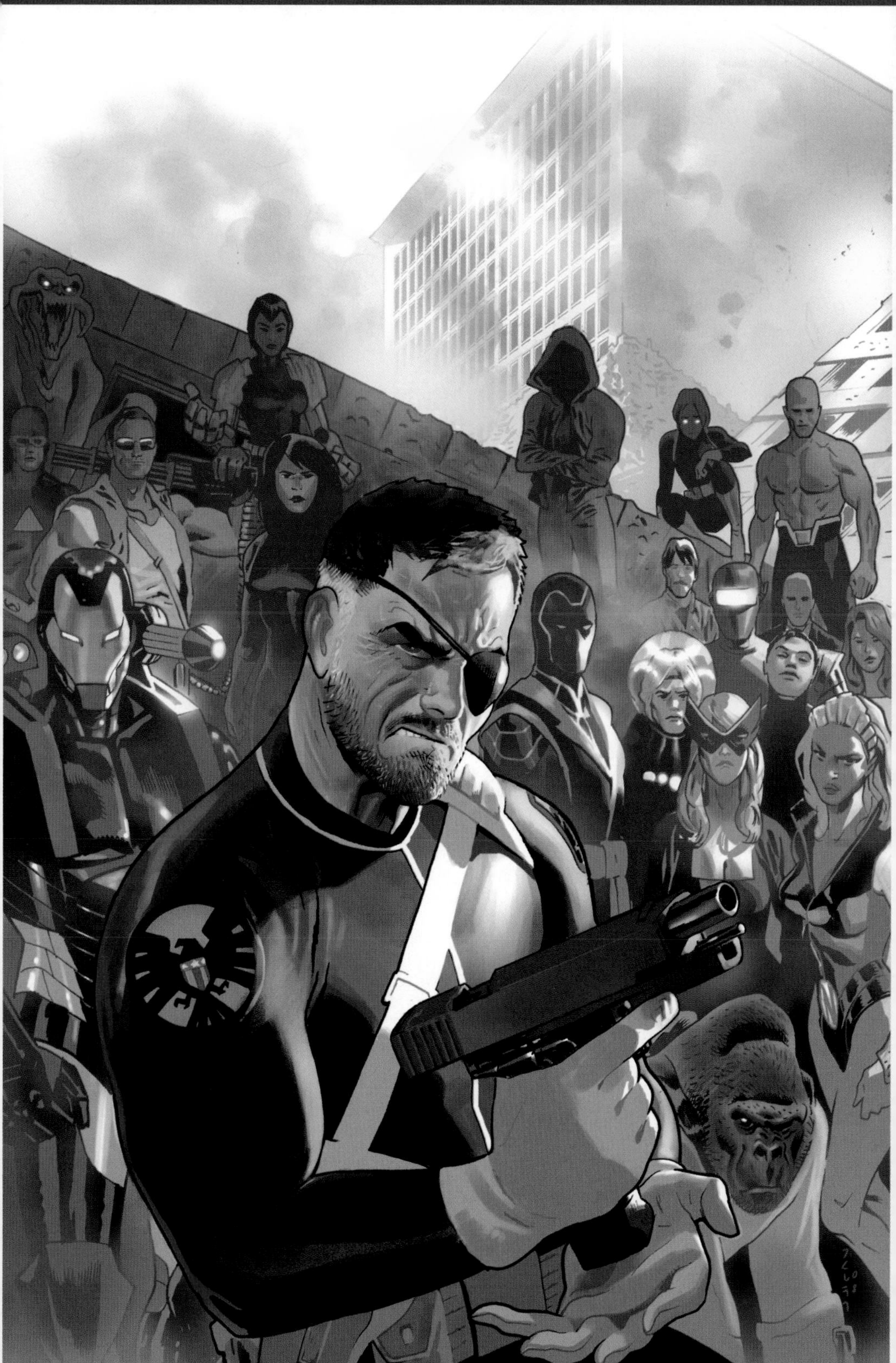

"THE HEIST"

WRITER
Jeff Parker

ARTISTS
Carlo Pagulayan, Jason Paz & Jana Schirmer

LETTERER
Blambot's Nate Piekos

"WOLVERINE: AGENT OF ATLAS"

WRITER
Jeff Parker

ARTISTS
Benton Jew & Elizabeth Dismang

LETTERER
Blambot's Nate Piekos

"THE RESISTANCE"

WRITER
Jeff Parker

ARTISTS
Leonard Kirk, Karl Kesel & Michelle Madsen

LETTERER
Blambot's Nate Piekos

GIANT SIZE MARVEL ADVENTURES THE AVENGERS #1

WRITER
Jeff Parker

ARTISTS
Leonard Kirk & Val Staples

LETTERER
Dave Sharpe

COVER ARTISTS
Art Adams & Guru eFX; Greg Land & Justin Ponsor; Adi Granov; Stuart Immonen & John Rauch;
Billy Tan & Frank D'Armata; Daniel Acuña; Phil Jimenez, Andy Lanning & Christina Strain;
and Leonard Kirk, Terry Pallot & Chris Sotomayor

ASSISTANT EDITOR
Lauren Sankovitch

ASSOCIATE EDITOR
Nathan Cosby

EDITOR
Mark Paniccia

COLLECTION EDITOR: Cory Levine • EDITORIAL ASSISTANT: Alex Starbuck
ASSISTANT EDITOR: John Denning • EDITORS, SPECIAL PROJECTS: Jennifer Grünwald & Mark D. Beazley
SENIOR EDITOR, SPECIAL PROJECTS: Jeff Youngquist • SENIOR VICE PRESIDENT OF SALES: David Gabriel
PRODUCTION: Jerry Kalinowski • BOOK DESIGN: Spring Hoteling

EDITOR IN CHIEF: Joe Quesada • PUBLISHER: Dan Buckley
EXECUTIVE PRODUCER: Alan Fine

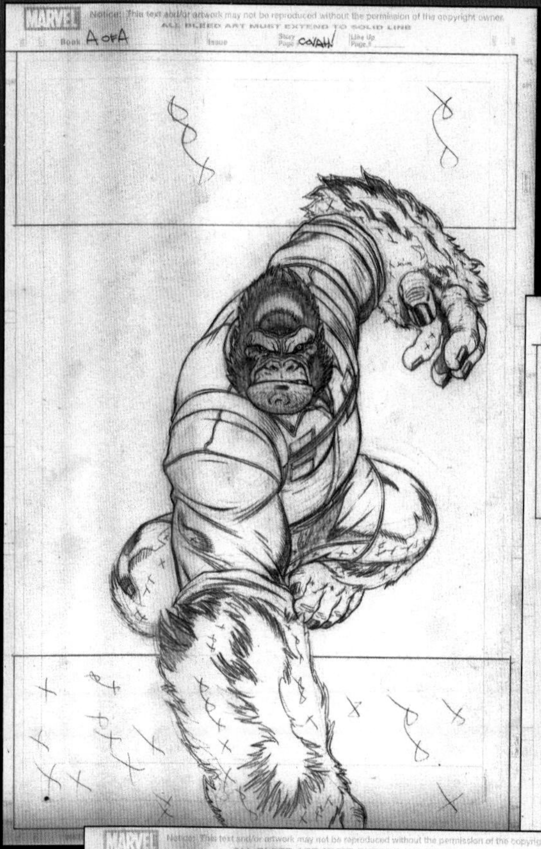
MARVEL
Notice: This text and/or artwork may not be reproduced without the permission of the copyright owner.
ALL BLEED ART MUST EXTEND TO SOLID LINE
Book A of A
Issue
Story Page # COVAH!
Line Up Page #

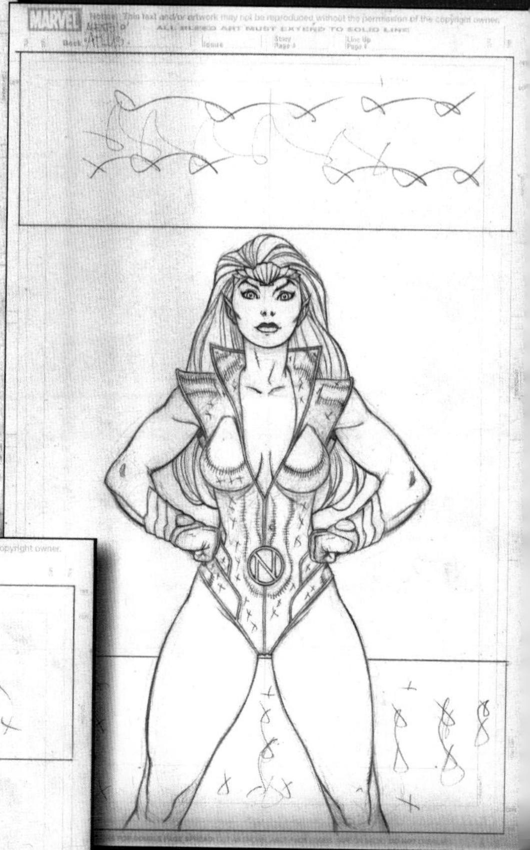
MARVEL
Notice: This text and/or artwork may not be reproduced without the permission of the copyright owner.
ALL BLEED ART MUST EXTEND TO SOLID LINE
Book
Issue
Story Page #
Line Up Page #

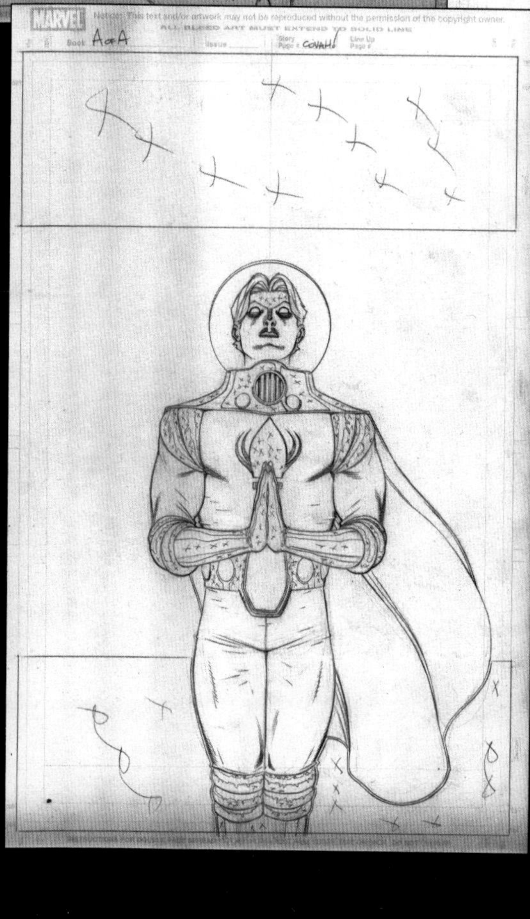
MARVEL
Notice: This text and/or artwork may not be reproduced without the permission of the copyright owner.
ALL BLEED ART MUST EXTEND TO SOLID LINE
Book A of A
Issue
Story Page # COVAH!
Line Up Page #

VARIANT COVER PENCILS AND SKETCHES BY ED MCGUINNESS

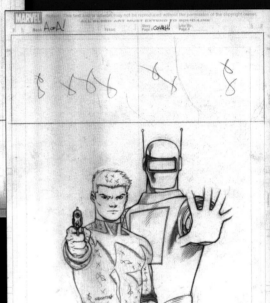

FRONT FIGURES
IN FULL COLOR

ENTIRE BACKGROUND MONOCHROME
IN A COLOR THAT
BEST SUITS THE
CHARACTER

STATS OF THE OTHER
TEAM MEMBERS IN
BACKGROUND

EX. VENUS — PINK

VENUS